泰戈尔在中国

Rabindranath Tagore in China

（第三辑）

孙宜学 编

同济大学出版社·上海
TONGJI UNIVERSITY PRESS

图书在版编目（CIP）数据

泰戈尔在中国. 第三辑 / 孙宜学编. — 上海：同济大学出版社, 2022.10

ISBN 978-7-5765-0443-9

Ⅰ. ①泰… Ⅱ. ①孙… Ⅲ. ①泰戈尔 (Tagore, Rabindranath 1861-1941)—思想评论 Ⅳ. ①K833.515.6

中国版本图书馆CIP数据核字（2022）第213181号

泰戈尔在中国（第三辑）

孙宜学　编

责任编辑　尚来彬　　**责任校对**　徐春莲　　**封面设计**　张　微

出版发行　同济大学出版社 www.tongjipress.com.cn

（地址：上海市四平路 1239 号　邮编：200092　电话：021-65985622）

经　　销　全国各地新华书店

排　　版　南京文脉图文设计制作有限公司

印　　刷　上海安枫印务有限公司

开　　本　710mm × 1000 mm　1 /16

印　　张　22.5

字　　数　450 000

版　　次　2022 年 10 月第 1 版

印　　次　2022 年 10 月第 1 次印刷

书　　号　ISBN 978-7-5765-0443-9

定　　价　108.00 元

序[1]

进入20世纪以来，先前闭关锁国的中国被迫慢慢敞开了自己的大门，中外文化、文学的交流也在这个过程中慢慢丰富起来，拜伦、雨果、托尔斯泰、屠格涅夫……中国人面前出现了一个五彩缤纷的文学世界。印度诗人、哲学家、社会活动家泰戈尔也是在这股潮流中对中国文学和文化产生过很大影响的外国作家之一，中国的许多现代作家，如徐志摩、冰心、郑振铎都受过他的影响，徐志摩甚至称他为“老戈爹”，赞美他像泰山日出般辉耀中国大地。迄今为止，他对中国作家最集中产生影响的事件，是他1924年受梁启超、徐志摩等人的邀请对中国的第一次访问，他的这次访问实际上成了中国思想文化界的一大盛事。中印两国本就是邻邦，又同是受到西方列强侵略、压迫的国家，两国人民当时都在试图找到一条救国于危亡之中的道路。泰戈尔在获得诺贝尔文学奖后，曾在欧洲各国巡回演讲，宣传以印度《奥义书》为代表的印度泛神论思想及东方文明优胜于以物质主义为特征的西方文明，主张以东方主“静”的哲学治疗西方主“动”的思想带来的社会弊病，这当然也令自鸦片战争以来深受西方文明侵略的中国人深受鼓舞。但对于他的来华，许多中国知识分子，如陈独秀、茅盾等左翼知识分子表示激烈反对，认为泰戈尔来访尽管主观愿望是好的，但客观上却会不利于中国革命；他所宣传的哲学思想是“奴才哲学”，是要让中国人继续受西方列强的压迫而不思反抗。这种看法在当时的环境下也确实是有道理的。结果，欢迎者和反对者都从自己的主观愿望出发对泰戈尔作了不恰当的吹捧和驳斥，从而造成中印现代思想、文学的这次交流以不欢而散告终，弄得泰戈尔这位满怀爱心而来的白胡子诗哲最后伤心而返，

[1] 此为贾植芳先生为孙宜学所编《诗人的精神——泰戈尔在中国》（江西高校出版社，2009年）、《泰戈尔在中国》（第二辑，上海三联书店，2016年）所作的“序”，为了纪念贾先生，本书仍用此“序”。

至今让人引以为憾。但泰戈尔并没因这次伤心而对中国抱有成见，而是始终以博大的胸怀关心着中国的命运，特别是1937年日本发动侵华战争后，他屡次发表公开信、谈话和诗，支持和同情中国人民的正义战争；逝世前，他在病榻上还念念不忘中国人民正在经受的这场残酷的战争，表现出对中国人民的崇高友谊。这些都是中印两国人民文化交流史上的宝贵财富，时间愈久愈能显出其可贵。

作为文学家的泰戈尔无疑是世界文学的一座丰碑，也是亚洲文学的骄傲。他的诗，如《吉檀迦利》《飞鸟集》《园丁集》《新月集》等已经影响了一代又一代的中国读者。这些诗都是源于作者内心的“生命之歌”。在这些诗中，他歌唱着生命的荣枯和现实世界的欢乐与悲哀，歌唱光明和自由，寻找一个人与自然和谐统一的澄净世界。读这样的诗，使人如在一幅风景如画的田园美景中信步漫游。诗人要求自己人格的完善，要从自己的思想中摒除虚伪，要从“心中驱除一切丑恶”，使爱开花。这种泛爱论，用于个人道德的自我完善还可以，但若用于救国救民方面，则只能是幻想。泰戈尔并非没有意识到这种理想的虚幻，如在20世纪30年代他就认识到：“那些毒污了你空气的，那些扑灭了你光明的，你能饶恕他们？你能爱他们？”

诗人若一味只唱个人的歌，那这个诗人可能很优秀，但绝对称不上伟大。而泰戈尔的伟大在于他的歌都是为印度、为世界祈求和平的人所唱的。他毫不留情地揭露了封建制度下人的不幸，他还积极参加政治活动，以实际行动反封建、反法西斯，甚至向每个人发出了战斗的号召：“准备战斗吧，反抗那披着人皮的野兽！”

总之，泰戈尔给现代中国的思想家们留下了不可磨灭的影响。这种影响首先来自他的精神、人格，在于他一心为了印度的民族独立与自由而呼吁、斗争。借用柳无忌的话：“在印度的作家中，与我们关系最密切的要推泰戈尔了。这位新近逝世的德高望重的诗人，曾与中国的文坛结下了美满的因缘，受到我们的尊敬与赞美；而且，他曾经是我们一派新诗人的灵感的泉源，东方文化的伟大的支持者，在他的身上，实现了中印文化的交流。”

中国对泰戈尔作品的翻译介绍已经为数不少，研究文章也很多，但至今却还没有出现一部系统的研究资料总结泰戈尔在中国的传播和被接受的过程。孙宜学君搜集整理的这部泰戈尔研究资料非常详细地梳理了泰戈尔与中国思想、文化、文学的交流过程，对中国的泰戈尔研究无疑是一件十分有益的工作。故乐为之序。

贾植芳

2008 年 1 月 8 日写于复旦

目录

[1] 因文章写作时代和作者的不同，“泰戈尔”英文在本书的形式有：“Tagore”“Rabindranath Tagore”“RABINDRANATH TAGORE”及“R. Tagore”等；而泰戈尔的中文译名也有多种写法：“泰谷尔”“太戈尔”“太谷儿”“泰莪尔”“泰歌尔”“太戈儿”“泰果尔”“塔果尔”等，本书为了体现资料的真实性，力图保持文字原貌，因此不做统一处理——编者注。

第一章

行 | 踪 | 追 | 寻

Tagore Arrived Singapore

A Singapore despatch to the *Asahi* reports that Sir Rabindranath Tagore, with Mr. W. W. Pearson and the Rev. C. F. Andrews, a well-known Indian missionary and scholar, and Mr. Mukhul Chandra, an Indian art connoisseur, arrived at Singapore on the 15th instant and left for Japan via Hongkong the following morning. The Indian poet is expected to arrive in Kube on the 27th inst. and he will land at the port to see his friends and pay a visit to Kyoto and Nara. He is expected to stay in Japan for several months.

— *Peking Gazette*, May. 25, 1916

Tagore Decided to Visit America

SIR Rabindranath Tagore, the Indian poet and holder of the Nobel prize[1], who has been visiting in Japan since early in June where he has been received with great enthusiasm by the people, has decided to visit American and has booked passage from Yokohama on the Canada Maru sailing at the end of August.

— *The North-China Daily News*, Jul. 3, 1916

Plot to Slay Tagore

San Francisco, October. 7.

Word of a plot to assassinate Sir Rabindranath Tagore, Hindu poet and Nobel prize winner, reached the police yesterday and led to extraordinary

[1] 原文即 Nobel prize，此处保留 prize 的首字母小写形式，后文亦同样处理——编者注。

precautions to guard him in his apartments at the Palace Hotel and at the Columbia Theatre, where he lectured in the afternoon.

The plot led to a change in the plans of Tagore, who canceled one of his engagements in San Francisco and left last night for Santa Barbara, detectives remaining with him as bodyguards until he boarded the Lark train.

The Hindu poet was a storm centre throughout his stay in San Francisco yesterday. Professor Bishen Singh Mattu, a venerable Hindu, who came from Stockton to induce Tagore to lecture in that city, was assaulted and had his white turban torn from his head in front of the Palace Hotel.

Two Under Arrest

Umrao Singh, savant and companion of Bishen Singh, helped to beat off the attack on the old man, and two Hindus who took part in the riot were placed under arrest.

The prisoners gave the names of Singh Hates-hi and Jewar Singh, and said they were employees of Ram Chandra, editor of the local Hindustan *Gadar*.

The *Gadar* party represents the radical Hindu revolutionists in San Francisco, and the assault on Bishen Singh Mattu, who is a leader of the more conservative Khalsa Diwan Mattu, was prompted by the fact that the professor was to invite Tagore to lecture in Stockton.

The police upon receipt of word that an attempt to assassinate Tagore was to be made, Detectives William Proll and Frank Black to the Palace Hotel to guard him. They accompanied him to the Columbia Theatre when he went to lecture, Black remaining in the wings on the stage and Proll seating himself in the body of the house with the audience.

William A. Mundell, head of the Mundell International Detective Agency, was active with the police, and his men were seen circulating among the audience, alert to everything that was going on during the lecture.

Theatre Bars Hindus

The management of the Columbia had been told about the plot on Tagore, and admittance to the theatre was denied to several hundred Hindus who tried to buy tickets for the lecture.

Tagore was escorted out of the theatre by Mundell men and police detectives through the stage door, and was taken back to his apartments in the Palace through the side entrance usually used for baggage. The detectives also used this entrance last night when they left the hotel with him for the Lark train for Santa Barbara.

Umrao Singh, who was with Professor Bishen Singh Mattu when the latter was attacked in front of the Palace yesterday, said that when they were journeying from Fresno to Stockton on Wednesday they were joined by another Hindu.

"This emissary learned of our plans to ask Tagore to lecture in Stockton before the Rhalsa Diwan Society," said Umrao Singh, "and he then hurried to San Francisco and hold the members of the Gadar party. We were told on arriving here that we must not deliver the invitation to Tagore, as the Gadar party did not want him lecturing in the United States. We properly ignored this injunction and the attack on Professor Bishen Singh Mattu followed. We did, however, succeed in delivering the invitation to Tagore to lecture through his secretary, but we did not get to see the poet himself. We were told he was being guarded, and that fear of assassins would prevent one from seeing him."

— *The Shanghai Times*, Nov. 4, 1916

Indian Public Opinion on Present-Day Japan

Shastri H. P.

In 1916 Sir Rabindranath Tagore, one of the noblest sons of India, visited Japan and the people gave him a cordial reception. Young and old came from far and near to see the Indian poet and the vernacular press wrote a lot about the distinguished visitor. His utterances were taken up and published broadcast throughout the whole of the Island Empire. This fact created an impression favorable to Japan in India, and people were gratified to learn that Japan was doing honor to a great Indian which he fully deserved.

When Sir Tagore left for America he was given a hearty send-off. But Tagore did not prove a flatterer, and while in America he made some remarks about Japan which the Japanese, who are so open to flattery, did not like and all at once the journals of Tokyo turned hostile to Tagore because he had dared to speak what he truly thought about Japan. When Sir Tagore returned to Japan in 1917, on route to India, no notice was taken of his presence and no reception of any kind was given to him.

Emperor Meji.

— *Millard's Review of the Far East*, Jun. 8, 1918

Popularity of Tagore the Indian Novelist

"Macmillans have sold 45,000 copies of Sir Rabindranath Tagore's first book done in English, 'Gitanjali.' of the 'Gardener' they have sold 16,000 copies, of the 'Crescent Moon' 17,000 copies, and of 'Sadhana' 15,000 copies. Those figures do not actually come up to the present date, so to make them complete you must make some mental additions to them," says the "Book Monthly."

"Now there is available a full novel by Tagore. 'The Home and the World,' and it is doing very well at the libraries and elsewhere. This is the first long story we have had from him, but he has written several in the Bengali language, and so we may get others. For one reason or another he is taking a definite hold on the English people and on the America people. He is also penetrating to the British Colonies."

— *The Shanghai Gazette*, Nov. 20, 1919

A Hearty Welcome
— His Joy that He Has Won True Friends

Those who know Rabindranath Tagore only through his translated works had an opportunity of seeing the Indian poet in the flesh at Caxton Hall, Westminster, recently, when the Union of East and West presented him with an address of welcome.

Like a Biblical prophet out of the wilderness, with flowing beard and curling locks, and wrapped in a long mantle that added to his commanding height, Tagore presented a singular contrast to the gathering of his Western admirers.

Mr. Charles H. Roberts in introducing him, spoke of the wide appeal of his ideas, although they were fundamentally and characteristically Indian. There were new forces at work throughout the East. Mr. Roberts said, which it was well for us in the West to understand. The external manifestation of them was the almost universal desire throughout the East to experiment in our principles of self-government.

A Poetic Greeting

As a result of the war there had come a real reaction of feeling against the callousness of militarism, and we looked to our statesman to repudiate the idea that the justification of the Empire was founded on force.

Miss Sybil Thorndike declaimed a poetic address of welcome written by Mr. Laurence Binyon, the concluding stanza of which ran as follows:

Rivers of India, populous wide plains,
From lips of boatmen and of villagers.
Singing amid their labors, hear these strains
Of lovely solace: India knows them hers.

Thames, too, has heard and welcomes him that sings
Our Silver Thames, of poets loved not least;
And listening to that music, England brings
Her laurel to the singer of the East.

The Poet's Reply

Rabindranath Tagore, in replying, said that for the first 50 years of his life he had enjoyed the intimate seclusion of his obscurity. He spent his youth like a solitary shepherd of the desert, watching the silent stars which never judge nor discuss our merits nor distribute praise and rewards. This had made him unfit for accepting public applause with the grace that comes of habitual assurance. But, after all, honour, like the tombstone, was for the dead, and love, like the sunshine, was for the living, and what gave him abiding joy was the grateful feeling in this land, where he came as a traveller and where he hoped to retain his seat as a guest — not for any literary skill of his, but for some service of the heart, some harmony of the spirit. (Applause)

Tagore and Mary Pickford

Through a dense crowd waiting outside Kensington Palace-gardens in the hope of seeing Mary Pickford, passed an Indian gentleman, tall and dignified, wearing a brown velvet turban and enveloped in a grey frieze cloak. He paused to scan the gathering through his gold-rimmed glasses and stroked his long iron-grey beard, as if wondering what the gathering could signify. Then he proceeded on his way unnoticed by the crowd, who were unaware that they had in their midst the Indian poet and mystic.

He was overtaken at the entrance to his flat by a "Daily News" representative who, in the course of conversation, explained to him the meaning of the crowd. In answer to a question as to his opinion of the significance of such enthusiasm for a cinema actress, the poet replied: "I do not wish to say anything which may seem in the least disparaging to an individual about whom I know nothing whatever and whom exercises such an immense power over the minds of the people. I could not have imagined the purpose of the meeting of such a crowd as I have just witnessed if it had not been explained to me. I always believed that the unsophisticated mind of the people had an instinctive wisdom which unconsciously attracted it towards the deeper needs and enjoyments of life.

Surprised at the Crowd

"In India crowds collect to have the sight of a man who, they believe, has the sanctity of spiritual life. In Japan the whole population comes out in spring to see the cherry trees in blossom; I have watched in Yokohama ordinary laborers gathering during short intervals of work in the wooded hills near the seaside, not in a rowdy exuberance of animal spirits but in quiet enjoyment of Nature's beauty. I felt I had, as it were, a glimpse of the human soul in its spontaneous movement towards the eternal.

"In ancient Greece the performance of great dramas attracted not merely the men of some exclusive coteries of culture, but the common people who had the sensitiveness of mind to be able to enjoy immortal works of art. But the sight of a great concourse of crowds come to express their adoration for a power that satisfies some momentary craving for sensation is disconcerting to my mind. For such large gatherings of people are their acts of unconscious worship — the kind of popular worship — which in olden days created mythology."

"But all worship should be for that which has some element of permanence in it, for it is the true instinct of hero-worship which expressed and creates the greatness of a people. However, it is not for me to judge but to try to understand being a mere special to — who finds it difficult to enter into the heart of things that are unfamiliar to him."

— *The North-China Daily News*, Aug. 26, 1920

What Germany is Reading

Rabindranath Tagore, whose gentle philosophy has superseded the fiery creed of Nietzsche which nurtured the young German mind before the war. Tagore's success is astounding — he is the bestseller of the year. No German novelist, dramatist, or poet is in it with the Indian gentle dreamer. A row of Tagore's works in many prices and styles appears in every bookseller's window. The cheapest edition I saw was fifteen marks the volume. But I saw many complete editions of Tagore at 250 marks to 300 marks the set. Altogether the house of Wolff has sold 800,000 copies of the books of Rabindranath Tagore.

— *The North-China Herald and Supreme Court & Consular Gazette*, Nov. 18, 1922

印度哲学家太戈尔准定来华

印度大哲学家（Tagore）太戈尔氏昨致其留沪印友杰斯菲尔函，称彼决应中国之聘，于秋初来华讲演。昨有人往访杰氏，叩以太戈尔之略历。据杰氏云：太戈尔是印度当代大诗家，亦大哲学家，氏生于一千八百六十一年印度彭加尔，其父有天才的人，曾到过法国当过梵语教授，故其思想，更有西洋色彩，东西思想混合后，便成为一宗教改革家。其丧母甚早，有兄弟七，姊妹三，后入学校，感学校生活专制，连入数校，均未竟业，故其家人，都轻视之，惟其父不然，后携之往喜马拉雅山，去享受那真美的自然，发展爱自然的天才，但不久又回家。此短期间，为太戈尔思想萌芽之一段，后来又在英国学法律，不一年即回国。三十岁时，伊父命在沙求挞地方管理田产，住在帕拉马江边，此地风景极好，足以供太戈尔视察，研究赏玩，促长思想，又日时与平民接触，于是除自然大师外，又添许多农人作伴侣，后又办一山铁奈克当学校，其教育除智育德育体育之外，还加上灵育，根据他那返“真”的原理，去求

"美"的意志，成绩很好，社会皆称许，一九一五年到日本，人皆欢迎，一九二十年到美国，美国朝野迎接，一九二一年到德国，德国更表敬意，今年预备来中国，中国人亦必欢迎云。

——《申报》，1923 年 6 月 19 日

Rabindranath Tagore Telegraphed to Mr. Liang Chi-Chao

Rabindranath Tagore, the Indian poet, has telegraphed to Mr. Liang Chi-chao, a famous Chinese scholar and reformer (who was formerly Minister of Education and Justice), stating that he expects to reach Shanghai on October 1 next, reports that "Shanghai Journal of Commerce".

— *The North-China Daily News*, Jul. 20, 1923

泰戈尔今日到沪

印度诗人泰戈尔，由新嘉坡启程，乘日本邮船热田领来华，将于今日午前抵沪。本埠预备欢迎泰氏之各文学团体，于昨日集商欢迎方法，并派员在汇山码头欢迎。氏平生所作诗歌甚富，其经我国翻译者，有园丁集[1]、飞鸟集二书，小说月报曾出泰戈尔专号，刊载泰氏历史及其著作甚多。此次泰氏来沪消息传布后，此种出版品销路亦为骤增。

——《民国日报》，1924 年 4 月 12 日

[1]《园丁集》在《民国日报》中即没有书名号，下文《飞鸟集》《小说月报》书名号亦无，此处保留原始资料格式。后文亦有不加书名号的情况，不再一一标注——编者注。

Arrival of Famous Indian Philosopher and Poet in Shanghai

Sir Rabindranath Tagore, the noted Indian philosopher and poet, arrived in Shanghai from Hongkong on Saturday afternoon on the Str. Atsuta, and remained here a few days before continuing his journey to Peking where is to deliver a series of lectures on philosophy.

Sir Rabindranath was met in Shanghai by Mr. Tse Mou-hsu[1], of the Peking Lecture Bureau, who came to the Settlement to greet China's noted guest and to conduct him to Peking. It is to be hoped that he will be induced to deliver a lecture here either before or after his trip to the capital, where he is to appear in public on six occasions. Foreigners and educate Chinese there are proposing to portray his play "Chitra" in the Peking Union Medical Auditorium if that hall may be obtained.

The poet, who is now 63 years old, refused to see any but special callers at his quarters in the Burlington Hotel, as the voyage proved quite a strain. He is a prolific writer and has published not less than 30 poetical works including novels, short stories, essays, sermons and dramas. He was awarded the Nobel Prize for Literature in 1913. Not only has he written in the Bengali dialect but he has also himself translated many of his works into English, in addition to which scholars have further translated them into other languages, several into Chinese, which have been greatly appreciated by scholars in this country.

— *The North-China Daily News*, Apr. 14, 1924

[1] 疑似徐志摩（Tse-mou Hsu），但原始资料即如此，此处保留原文形式——编者注。

泰谷尔莅杭续闻

印度诗人泰谷尔，昨由沪到杭后，当与徐志摩等乘舟往谒岳陵，游观西湖风景，随处足增诗兴。曾对徐君云，何不三十年前，邀余来游，足证其心志愉快。泰氏现年六十四，游兴甚豪，惟来华期间局促，不能遍历名胜。张教育厅长，十五日上午九时，至西湖饭店往访，坚邀叙餐，泰氏婉辞。定十六日讲演后，十七日早车离杭，拟由沪赴宁一行，往游山东泰山云。

——《新闻报》，1924 年 4 月 16 日

泰戈尔莅杭续志

印度诗人泰戈尔，十六日中午，而教育厅长张宗祥，在西湖饭店欢宴，并邀格纳葛玲瞿菊农[1]等八人作陪。下午四时冒雨乘车，赴省教育会讲演会。时男女各校学生均先到会，楼上下一律满座，不下二千余人，李副会长暨各评议干事，并各学校代表，亦俱莅止。先由李副会长致介绍词，并请在座诸君，万勿喧哗，因声浪过高，泰戈尔心为震荡，于讲演殊不便利，于是众皆翕然。继由泰氏登台讲演，题为到中国底[2]感想，由徐志摩译作华语，讲词容俟续志。讲毕引导至楼上开欢迎会，茶叙而散。杭州教育工艺厂代表姜敬庐，新制就西湖模型，美丽可观，藉赠泰戈尔氏，为游杭之纪念，即定十七日清晨，各教育界，赴城站欢送泰氏上车云。

——《新闻报》，1924 年 4 月 17 日

[1] 这些人名在《新闻报》中没有顿号，此处存其原样，其他文献亦有此类现象，文中不再一一注明——编者注。

[2] 现用“的”，当时写作“底”，其他文献也有此类现象，后文不再标注——编者注。

日侨欢迎泰戈尔

泰戈尔氏前日赴杭游览，定于今日返沪，本埠日侨方面，由野田副领事岗村武官及东方通信社之池田氏等发起，于今晚七时在蓬路日人俱乐部举行欢迎晚餐会，欢迎泰氏，并闻泰氏允于今晚八时，在北四川路日本小学校用英语演讲，各界均可自由往听。

——《民国日报》，1924 年 4 月 17 日

欢迎泰戈尔今日开会

泰戈尔欢迎会，今日下午三时半在宝山路商务印书馆对面图书馆会议厅开会，主席郭秉文博士，将于今晨偕殷芝龄，沈信卿，黄任之搭快车抵沪。入场券共印发一千二百张，至昨日正午，券已送罄。昨日五时，筹备委员会全体在全国青年协会接洽筹备情形，众以泰氏演讲至有价值，请郑振铎君担任记录，俾便汇印，以留纪念。

——《民国日报》，1924 年 4 月 18 日

今日各团体欢迎泰戈尔之集会

印度诗人泰戈尔，于日前赴杭州游历，已于昨日正午乘沪杭车，由徐志摩君伴同抵沪，仍寓沧州旅馆。各国团体欢迎会，将于今日下午三时半，假座宝山路商务印书馆之图书馆会议厅开会，太[1]氏将即席演讲，预料今日本埠各界人士之前往听讲者，必甚拥挤，故参与欢迎会之各团体，将各派出招待员一人，于二时前到会，支配招待事宜。至加入欢迎之各团体，至昨晚止，已增至二十七个，计为文学研究会，中华学艺社，省教育

[1] 因泰戈尔亦写作“太戈尔”等，因此当时文章常常“泰氏”“太氏”混用，书中均保留原始资料形式——编者注。

会，青年协会，青年会，基督教育会，实验剧社，商务书馆，中华书局，讲学社，徐州同乡会，大同，约翰，商大，中国公学及商科，南大，自治学院，美术学校，广肇公学，广东中学，时报，申报，时事新报，中华新报。公平通信社，及本报等诸团体云。

——《新闻报》，1924 年 4 月 18 日

Tagore at Hangchow: Lecture on Unity of Nations as Swaraj Might See It

Hangchow, Apr. 16.

The Indian of reputation whom I mentioned in my last communication is Rabindranath Tagore. He addressed a meeting of several thousands of students in the Educational Association Auditorium this afternoon, in beautiful English.

He emphasized the unity of nations, and brotherhood of man. We are path-makers, not for profit or power, but for brotherhood. Improved communications made it easy to get together, but tourists only saw the surface of life, and had no time for mentality to come close to humanity.

Many come near to each other by geographical excursions, but do not establish spiritual relationships. A crowd is not a community. He said the channel of communication between the Indians and the Chinese was overgrown with weeds, but the line could still be seen. If there was the real love for man all the mischief in the world would be removed. Natural bias and prejudice must be overcome. We are blind to the realities of life, and good in others, because we see them through the mists and do not really know man.

Let us come together as brothers, joining hands, guests and friends doing it naturally and simply, and the race problem will be solved. Not uniformity, which is dead and external, but unity, which is living and profound, is what is needed.

In closing, he said that we are all the children of the immortal, and we dwell in the Kingdom of Heaven and when we realize this through some illumination of the soul we shall work for the elevation of humanity

He told the audience that he hoped to tell them of the object of his mission to another occasion.

— *The North-China Daily News*, Apr. 22, 1924

泰戈尔来华之目的

文汇报云，关于印度诗人泰戈尔氏之来华，据新到沪之印度报纸载称，泰氏于由印启程之前，声明其此行之目的，为以印度之音信送至远东，彼国恢复文化上精神上与印度之联络，彼拟复活对于佛教文字及梵文之研究，因此等文字乃从前曾经联络印度与中国、日本、安南、柬埔寨、暹罗、爪哇为时甚久者，在此等国中，从梵文翻出之书籍，及佛教美术品，有不少之存在，大可作研究资料，以期于古印度之历史及文化上得可实之发现云。

——《民国日报》，1924 年 4 月 22 日

中美公司新到泰戈尔名著

中美图书公司（南京路二十五号）最近运到印度诗哲泰戈尔名著多种，若国家主义 Nationalism[1]、家庭与世界 The Home and the World、创造唯一 Creative Unity、飘流 The Fugitive、开壁之歌 Songs of Kabir、沉船 The Wreck、姨母及其他 Mashi And Other Stories、迷路之鸟 The Stray Birds、春之循环 The Cycle Spring、园丁集 The Gardener、撷果集 Fruit Gathering 等，均有价值。其中《开壁之歌》，系由泰氏译自开壁，开壁亦为一大诗家，有名于古。另如《园丁集》《迷路之鸟》系泰氏得意之诗歌，读之荡气回肠，如置身幽谷中。至《国家主义》一书，专鼓吹大同主义，

[1] 书中英文书名均保留资料中的原始格式，不斜体，全书同——编者注。

凡人应以四海为家，《飘流》系一剧本，有歌有剧，流利动人。《沉船》系一婚姻问题之小说，备局之奇，令人叫绝。《春之循环》系泰氏新近著成之剧本，描摹自然的美，亦不同凡响。以上诸书，国人已有译本者，约三四种，然文情之流利生动，自当求之原书，凡欲研究泰氏文学者，可向中美询问各书价目，前往购置云。

——《申报》，1924 年 4 月 22 日

Sir Rabindranath Tagore on the True Spirit of Eastern Civilization

Peking, Apr. 25.

Sir Francis Aglen presided at a luncheon of the Anglo-American Association today, when Sir Rabindranath Tagore was the guest of honour. Dr. Schurman, who is personally acquainted with Sir Rabindranath, delivered a speech welcoming the poet, after which he said that the Association was a sort of unofficial organ of the English-speaking family of Peking.

"While we cherish just pride in the civilization which our peoples have developed in their homes in the four continents," Dr. Schurman declared, "we are aware that, measured by the standard of the perfect ideal, it abounds in imperfections and superficialities and even in injustices and inhumanities. Practional are, but the depths of their nature are a hidden fountain of idealism. This is the ultimate source of their highest achievements. No one could convince us in the English language that we are wholly given up to materialism and things of sense, which perish in using, for the speech he used would return him. Yet, the West had much to learn from the East.

Dr. Schurman compared Chinese civilization with that of Ancient Greece. Different peoples, he said, develop their own characteristic civilizations and all nations contribute their quota. Above all nations is humanity.

Sir Rabindranath Tagore, who was warmly greeted, selected as a topic the Bengal educational institute bearing the Sanscrit name "*Visva Bharati*". His eloquent discourse was really a plea for idealism instead of nationalism which meant materialism. He referred to his early education and yearnings to see and understand the civilizations which had developed abroad. He spoke of his visit to England, Japan and America, where he had studied national and domestic life. He said that in England he found the chivalrous spirit of humanity almost more than in any other country. He was dismayed at the nationalism among the younger Japanese, which almost amounted to barbarism. He condemand Japanese inhospitable exclusivism, but among older Japanese he had found the true spirit of Eastern civilization. Sir Rabindranath spoke of the materialism of America and their disregard of the views of others, which, he thought, must have ill effects. After the war he again visited Europe where he was reviewed with the utmost cordiality. His experiences there created the belief that Europe was not satisfied with its former materialism and wanted something better, which might come from India.

The attendance at the Luncheon was very large and many were unable to obtain seats. — Reuter's Pacific Service.

— *The North-China Daily News*, Apr. 26, 1924

Sir R. Tagore at Nanking

Sir Rabindranath Tagore, the celebrated Indian poet and philosopher, called on the Governor General this morning and had a long conversation with him, urging him to promote peace in order that the old civilization of the East might be preserved. Marshal Chi explained to the famous poet that, although he was a soldier, he was one who moved peace and order which he meant to maintain to the best of his ability. He thanked Sir Rabindranath Tagore for his kind advice and assured him that he would always observe his words.

— *The North-China Herald and Supreme Court & Consular Gazette*, Apr. 26, 1924

Visit of Tagore to Tsinan

Tsinanfu, Sung., April. 22.

Sir Rabindranath Tagore's visit to Tsinan today has greatly stirred educational circles. He has broken his journey to Peking and stayed off a day to speak in the Provincial Assembly. Such a large crowd assembled that the visitor had to leave the hall of the Assembly and give his address in the open air. Some three thousand students and others assembled for this meeting when the distinguished guest spoke on "Materialism and the Spiritual Life."

Sir Rabindranath Tagore and his party, in spite of the shortage of time, kindly accepted an invitation to visit the Shantung Christian University, and at five o'clock the staff and students listened to a delightful address by the poet on his school and the ideals that animated him in founding it and developing it in simple, dignified and beautifully phrased English he painted an inspiring and attractive picture of the institution, where he has put into practice his ideals of freedom and beauty and the spiritual life. He made his audience wish to see his school in working, and convinced all that he is thereby making a much needed contribution to the cause of education. It is greatly to be hoped that Sir Rabindranath Tagore can pay a further visit to Tsinan before he returns to Indian. Peking is very happy in the prospect of listening to such a teacher.

— *The North-China Daily News*, Apr. 26, 1924

泰戈尔见宣统

独　鹤

泰戈尔到了我国，除备受我国教育家文学家的热烈欢迎而外，并没有和什么达官贵人相交接，却偏偏去见宣统。我不知这位印度老诗翁，见了这个小朝廷的皇帝[1]，心中作何感想。

有人说泰戈尔的思想，是偏于守旧的，是竭力反对西洋物质文明，而保持东方文化的，所以他去见宣统，不免怀着几分复古的观念。我道不然。文化自文化，专制自专制。东方旧文化，诚哉自有价值，却断非专制时代种种不自然的制度和仪式所能代表的。若说因保持旧文化的缘故，便当爱慕着专制的旧观，我想他老先生，断不至于如此误会。不过他此番到中国来，随处都有演说，究竟对于宣统，说些什么话，却是我们所亟欲闻知的了。

泰戈尔见宣统，由郑苏戡陪着。中印两诗人，藉此携手，倒也是桩妙事。不过这印度诗人，遨游寰球，早已博得诗圣的尊号。这中国诗人，却依恋宫闱，仍守着遗老的生涯。比较起来，未免减色了。

——《新闻报》，1924 年 5 月 1 日

Tagore in Peking: The Devout and Irreverent

Rodney Gilbert

Peking, Apr. 24.

It is probably no very humiliating matter to confess that most of us have not read more than casual sparks from Sir Rabindranath Tagore's forge. It would mean eternal immersion in the everlasting slough to confess any such thing in Peking at the moment, however. Apart from all else the various pronunciations of the holy name which are in vulgar use here even among the devotees, would probably make the most superficial Anglo-Indian squirm in horror.

To be very thoroughly condemned while he is about it the writer must admit that he has never read Tagore at all and has only the vaguest possible conception of his importance; but no one who has glanced over the following description of the Indian savant, which appeared in our local "Far Eastern Times," can fail to be moved by what Harvard used to describe as intellectual curiosity. Life is

[1] 此时清廷已亡，宣统于 1912 年 2 月退位——编者注。

so dull to most of the hard cases in this case-hardened community that when a man comes along with sparking eyebrows, straight aquiline noses and the beloved patriarchal manner, we smash our "w and s" glasses together with our equanimity on the alleged mahogany barrier and rush out to get a new thrill. By way of showing what really moves Peking to action, the following quotation from the "Far Eastern Times" (front page, 2nd column) is attached:

An enthusiastic reception was accorded Sir Rabindranath Tagore, the world famous Indian writer, poet and philosopher, at the Chien Man station, yesterday evening by more than two hundred students of Nankai and Tsing Hwa, as well as by a larger gathering of his own countrymen, upon his arrival from Tsinan, to deliver a series of lectures here.

Dressed in flowing brown robes or his native land and wearing the his tonic turban. Sir Rabindranath greeted his admirers with the same quiet reserve and warm hand clasp which have won him so many friends. He stated that he had had a most interesting trip from Shanghai stopping at Nanking and proceeding from thence to Tsinan and on to Chufu, to visit the birthplace of Confucius. He is neither short nor tall with the face of an aesthete, deep set eyes beneath bushy white eyebrows that sparkle continually, a rather straight aquiline nose" and a flowing white beard that reaches nearly to his waist, giving him quite the appearance of a beloved patriarch.

— *The North-China Daily News*, May. 1, 1924

泰戈尔来校讲演之消息

印度诗哲泰戈尔氏现已在京讲演。本校师生固有一部分结队前往听讲，但大多数咸以特约泰氏来校讲演一次为快。日前凌主任亲自赴京与泰氏面商一切已蒙允诺。闻订于本月二十日前后当可来校云。

中华民国十三年五月二日

——《南开周刊》，1924 年 5 月 2 日，第 92 期

Tagore's "Chitra" Enthusiastically Received by Peking

Thursday, May 8, will be very memorable in the annals of the Crescent Moon Society as their Tagore night, says the "Far Eastern Times." The packed auditorium of the P.U.M.C. bore witness to the nature of the celebration which was a birthday offering to Dr. Rabindranath Tagore, a salute on his 64th Indian birthday, and a mark of his Indian birthday, and a mark of his christening with a Chinese name.

Dr. Hu Shi, who acted as master of ceremonies, explained from the stage how it all happened and translated for Mr. Liang Chi-chao who carried out the naming ceremony. He declared that Dr. Tagore's name meant sunlight and thunder and that by research he found that the original Indian name for China could be transliterated "Thundering Morning" "*Chen-tan.*" If to this was added a part of the old Chinese name for India, "*Chu*" then Dr. Tagore's name and surname became "*Chu Chen-tan.*" "The Thundering Morning of India." Which made a deep and perpetual union between the two cultures, Indian and Chinese.

Long applause greeted this clever linguistic *tour-de force.* The audience was then entertained by two Indian disciples of Dr. Tagore's. Dr. Sen, who recited an ode in Sanscrit to the amazement of some of the audience who thought that "you couldn't speak a dead language", and by Dr. Nag, who gave one of Dr. Tagore's poems in Bengalee.

Dr. Tagore, wearing Bengalee dress, now took the stage to the sound of immense applause, and explained how he came to write "Chitra" and the motive behind it. His phrasing and his exquisite command of poetic English were delightful to listen to, his powerful thought penetrating his prose as light pours through a gauze net.

Miss Phyllis Liu followed with the tableau vivant "the crescent moon," which revealed her as a charming and very pretty young lady.

"Chitra" followed, — adapted for the occasion. While the Crescent Moon troupe was composed chiefly of very young amateurs, with little or no experience, the natural Chinese artistic temperament was revealed in the very remarkable colouring of the scenery, and the correctness of the dressing and posing. Miss Lin's perfect English phrasing was noteworthy in so young a girl, and Dr. Chang, as the warrior Arjuna, and Dr. Hsu as Madana, the God of Love, were likewise very good. Sitting highly interested, beside Dr. Tagore was Mei Lanfang, dressed in a dinner jacket; and it was plain that the colour scheme of this Indian night was giving him ideas.

The Crescent Moon Society is to be highly congratulated on this Song offering to Dr. Tagore which was one of those graceful courtesies in which the Chinese excel all other peoples, and which brought together in one hall all the art and literature there is in Peking, and included all nationalities. But if we may be allowed to address, this moon of our delight, we would declare that a clock must be brought with an alarm which will ring loudly to prevent a performance from dragging. It was over and that was too late. The cast was as follow:

CHITRA

A One-act Play

By Dr. RANATH TAGORE.

Dramatis Personae

Chitra...Miss Phyllis W. Y. Lin

Arjuna...Chang Hsin–hai

Madana – God of Love...Hsu Tse-mou

Vasanta – God of the Seasons...Lin Chang-min

Villagers...Miss Monica Y. Wang

Mrs C. Yang

Chiang Fang-cheng

Ting Sih-lin

— *The North-China Daily New*, May. 15, 1924

A Reception in Honour of Dr. Rabindranath Tagore

A reception in honour of Dr. Rabindranath Tagore was held yesterday afternoon at Messrs. Currimbhoy's. The Indian Moslem community of Shanghai were the hosts. Mr. A Hirji welcomed the eminent Indian philosopher, who, in replying, dwelt feelingly on his mission for the unity of the peoples of the world. The ceremony was brief owing to the many engagements of Dr. Tagore. Dr. Rabindranath Tagore will leave for Japan today on a lecturing tour.

— *The North-China Daily News*, May. 30, 1924

Model Province Has Something of Interest for All Inquiries into China's State

Taiku, Shan., May. 27.

It is becoming the fashion nowadays for distinguished visitors to China to include this province, or at least Taiyuanfu, in their itinerary. The latest person of note to come up here was Dr. Rabindranath Tagore. He and his party arrived in Taiyuanfu on May 21. They were escorted all the way from Peking by representatives of the educational institutions in Taiyuanfu, and received a great ovation upon reaching Taiyuanfu. On the afternoon of the 22nd. Dr. Tagore addressed a great audience in the "Hall of Self-examination." The number present was reported to be about 5,000. Twenty-three different organizations cooperated in arranging for this meeting. The theme of Dr. Tagore on this occasion was village as contrasted with city life. He pleaded for the conservation of village habits, customs and standards of living, opposing the rush of population to the cities. The main speaker was followed by his English secretary, who has been spending some time in the study of village conditions in Indian. The party departed from Taiyuanfu on the morning of the 23rd.

A number of schools from outside this province have sent deputations of teachers and students to visit the capital of the province, paying particular attention to the schools and other institutions established there. One such party considered of pupils from a normal school for girls in Japan, accompanied by two or three of their instructors. Recently over 30 members of the Agricultural College of Shantung Province have come up here on a similar visit.

— *The North-China Herald and Supreme Court & Consular Gazette*, Jun. 7, 1924

Rabindranath Tagore's Mission

During his visit to Shanghai, Dr. Rabindranath Tagore visited the Parsee Social Hall as the guest of the Parsee community and delivered a most striking address. He was welcomed with the reading of an address drafted on behalf of the local Parsee community in which appreciative reference was made to him as "one of the most illustrious sons of Asia of the Twentieth Century" and he was hailed as one who followed the teaching of Zoroaster. Dr. Tagore, addressing his audience as Sisters and Brothers, said in part:

I am expected to make a formal speech on a subject which in itself is so deep, the theme so intense, that I very often feel it is an act of impiety to be talking about it in a meeting of a formal character. My speech shall needs be with limitations. The Ultimate Truth, I feel too many, sounds so small, trivial and insignificant, but in reality what sounds like children's work has a deep significance requiring profound thought to unravel it. In modern parlance it goes unheeded regardless, and is considered something superficial. The idea is very great; it is all along with them but is too difficult to comprehend for those of us who are thickly surrounded by and move about in fashionable circles. Unfortunately for our age, we do not heed people who fearlessly strive to stand before us with some message to deliver, but we turn our backs to the message which arises from the heart of humanity. We live in this age, the age of Journalism, of cheap ideas and cheap glory and we forget the immense seriousness of life and lose sight of the great purpose of human history.

All the great countries had the basis of their greatness on the sound value of men. These were the great individuals upon whom has been built the great civilization and culture of the world. Now the time has come when our age, which has been a good deal dimmed and shrouded in externals, should strive to clip some of these externals. We cannot afford any longer to remain within our enclosures of national abnegation. All the great teachers of the world strove hard to bring to light the supreme truth which till then remained dormant in unexplored regions. One of the greatest and the earliest of these masters was Zoroaster. They appealed to men, aroused them form their deep slumber of ages to come out from their self-centred egoistic lives and exert their breath for the realization of Truth. Men have not lived up to the ideals and standards set by them. They raised their voices in vain and the world goes on in its boundless revolutions and disasters. And who am I? I have not the strength to utter. My voice is too feeble to arouse humanity from its stupor of slumber and its intemperance. We have not attained our goal. Materialistic ideals pervade the present atmosphere, but they are of no account. The success of the powerful, the rich, the vain-glorious cannot enter the higher field. The rich, the powerful, self-centred souls are rejected. They leave nothing behind them. They have not that illumination which may lighten and shed its lustrous beams on their onward path. Riches, which they strive hard to master, die with them without any trace.

Realizing the Ideal

Humanity has been struggling for centuries for the realization of the ideal and I feel the inadequacy of my strength and my voice. I am not able to convince men of the great truth of this mission — the realization of Spiritual Unity. For those who have a natural kindling of faith, who follow dictates of their nature, it is quite easy to love their own people. This is not of much moment, but the time has come when the links of the chain of fellowship and brotherhood of humanity should be strengthened and further cemented. We are in the open, and we have met together, and what path is there which can make us one, which can unite us together? That is the obligation resting upon us and which has tended to flow during the whole course of history. One after another great masters arose, taught people and vanished. The world still goes on its course, throbbing. Still it is on its way towards Spiritual Unity. Miseries and sufferings there are without number and the present age is aching with pain. Why is that the case? Because we have not attained the Truth. We are all suffering from the lack of that essential potent element — Truth. We are out of touch with reality. We are like shadows not in touch with light and grapple with common leaves which fall off and are of no account. We attach importance to every-changing passing clouds which change their line and colour. But we have been gifted with souls, and that has its own illumination, but its horizon is all obscured by our selfish passion and indifference. A cloud of dust obstructs the vision. We lose our birth-right in this world — the edification of our soul. Only it has to be tuned, it has to be revealed. It pines for that and that must happen. The inherent voice is every urging us to bring out the lamp which is vanishing, unnourished.

Due to such convulsions, the whole of nature suffered and is suffering. The Great War and the rivalry amongst the class divisions are producing conflagration and a spirit of hostility all over the world, which is but the sign of the failure of humanity to attain the supreme essential Truth. Are we going to languish in this state of affairs? Are we going to make bliss? We have not come in touch with supreme Truth and have no faith to approach it. We are doomed and rejected and swept off like drooping shadows and passing clouds. I do not know how to make it clear to you; how to call you out in the joint meeting when all depends upon individuals.

Never think that we as individual are insignificant. The great history of men from times eternal has been founded on individuals. The Western culture also rests upon one individual. You have mentioned in your address the name of that great master and leader men, Zoroaster; he was the one ardent soul who, with his dauntless efforts and teachings, has saved millions of men from utter futility and ruin. Truth is wailing for individuals. You may be ignored by the fashionable, spurned by the powerful and clever, but any individual, although he has no name or fame, may find his soul higher and brighter by the touch of Truth and he is our leader without knowing it. We are waiting for such a leader who has all the ideals. My friends, do not ask me to make formal speeches about the subject, about people of weak faith and vacillating minds. I think that it does rot rest upon me to claim any result, if I hear the call of truth. I am responsible for the work (the University at Shantiniketan) for giving expression and shape to it and the rest is in the hands of the Almighty.

Parsee Enthusiasm

My friends, before I sit down, I must express my deep-felt gratitude to the Parsee community. From the beginning, when my ideal was cherished by me, they have come out and have offered me their valuable help with real enthusiasm. I must say I am deeply grateful to them. Two or three years ago, I had no experience of Paresees, or of what they were like. It was because I was far away from that part of India, Bombay, where they live. I had no opportunity to meet you before and I am glad that this mission of mine has brought me in contact with you, and let me tell you are very near my heart. I feel at home with them, not because they are my friends, but some time before, when they failed to realize the ideal, they have helped me in its realization and for this I am deeply gratified and I take this opportunity to express my gratitude to you, thought far away from India.

— *The North-China Daily News*, Jun.18, 1924

Tagore's Failure with Young China

Wuchang, June. 8.

"Young China" is filled with the passion for material progress and force and is continually comparing herself in speeches, in print and in diverse manners (one of which is the student preaching of hate for Japan) with the nations that possess these things. It is a "complex" which takes strange forms — some laudable, some of "self-humiliation" and attempts to stir oneself up by the internal combustion of excited verbiage — not always realized by those affected by it.

Tagore has found already rampant in China the danger he warns the world, swift undigested material progress and mere masses of abstract scientific facts overwhelming the spirit, and such abstractions being accepted as a substitute for real creative truth and concrete moral personality. To such an extent has this gone that those with some knowledge of natural science in China, often very imperfect, usually profess the philosophic theory of materialism, in a way that is 50 years out of date even in the materialistic West.

Rejected of Young China

This Chinese situation explains the unfavourable reception given to Rabindranath Tagore in Peking, ever after he had been officially and nationally invited, and his coming to Wuhan on May 25 suddenly, unannounced, and leaving the same night for Shanghai en route for Japan.

Disappointed of a newspaper record himself, the writer is supplying, by request, from his rough notes, for the benefit of those who were disappointed even of hearing the speaker, an outline report of Rabindranath's one utterance in this centre, given in the Wuchang public athletic ground to a hastily gathered and miscellaneous audience of some 700.

The speaker, tall, with a flowing beard, wore a plain and dignified robe and spoke in a clear and beautiful natural voice with great carrying power, almost without any gesture. His English was exquisite; simple and quite without repetition. The Chinese translation that followed the whole speech was very brief and imperfect, and so the address must have had very little effect.

"When invited to come among you," he said, "I did not know if you wanted a man from India. I heard some were opposed to my coming because it might check your special modern enthusiasm for western progress and force. And if you want a man who will help you in these things you have been mistaken in asking me. I have no help to give you here: you already have 10,000 able teachers; go to them. My warning is, that those who would have you reply on material force to make a strong nation do not know history, or understand civilization. Reliance on power is the characteristic of barbarism, nation that trusted to it have already been destroyed, or have remained barbarous."

Greatness Not Material

"But other nations added intellect to teach how to use power and we can no more despise the science and material progress that has resulted than we can despise our own bodies; but still it is not that that makes or has made nations great; nations that have so relied have either been destroyed or are even now reverting to barbarism. It is cooperation and love, mutual trust and mutual aid which make for strength and real progress in civilization. New spiritual and moral power must continually be developed to enable men to assimilate their new weapons and machines or these will dominate, enslave and slay them. Men have been losing their freedom, their humanity and their lives to fit themselves for vast mechanical organizations, scientific, political, economic, and military. We see today civilizations of vast power and great intellect veiling in a decent way mere cannibalism. It is the nemesis of Science dominant rather than subserving the spirit of man, for the world of mere science is not a world of reality but an abstract impersonal world of force."

"But many will point to the weakness of China and India and tell you that among these strong and progressive world people it is necessary to emphasize power and progress in order to avoid destruction. And I would not have you deceived by the Sunday-School talk that no advantage is won by unrighteousness. In the words of one of the great ones of my nation:

'With the help of unrighteousness men do prosper,

With the help of unrighteousness men again victories over their enemies,

With the help of unrighteousness men do attain what they desire,

But they perish at the root.'

We have seen victories won by diplomacy and lies and material force, but there are signs in the civilizations founded on diplomatic lies and blind force that even now their doom is on them. Lies do prosper for a while, but the true life dies at the root."

The World Defied

"You must accept this prosperity and power today, but there is tomorrow. This today is burdened with lies and oppression, it is overburdened, it is sinking. I defy today and refuse to let it dominate my purposes. I rely on tomorrow with peace and faith. How do I prove it? I have no proof outside myself, in the depth of my soul. Even at the cost of martyrdom and insult and suffering we must continue to believe in peace and love and kindness and idealism. What is the value of success if it be at the cost of humanity and if it makes a desert at of God's world? I speak at you as a member of a nation that has gone under in the race for progress and I tell you that I am ready to accept defeat and insult and oppression and weakness in the body, but I will never accept the defeat, the last insult, the utter ruin of my spirit being conquered so that I lose my faith and purpose. My enemies may conquer and slay my body, but they cannot make me adopt their methods or hate them. The devil helps in the sphere in which he is master, but we must reject such aid to save our life from utter destruction. Seek righteousness even though success be lost. I believe this not through the evidence of facts! Facts mislead and oppress you with mere numbers and quantity: the world of personality surpasses facts on every side. Truth comes from above, is conscious of infirmity and is creative. We have accepted and followed and venerate men who gave us such truth and lost success. We need to hear this again and again and never more than in this modern world of slavery and cannibalism in decent guise."

"By the help of righteousness men do prosper, men do gain victories over their enemies, men do attain what they desire: but they perish at the root."

— *The North-China Herald and Supreme Court & Consular Gazette*, Jun. 21, 1924

印度诗哲太戈尔

印度诗哲太戈尔（R.Tagore）先生到华后的游踪，在本报四月号里已叙述过了。他从北京到太原开封，再由汉口经长江到上海，在上海住了三天，即乘上海飞到日本，徐志摩仍旧伴送他同去。他动身的那一天是五月二十日；前此一天，张君劢君曾在他自己的住宅，慕尔鸣路三十七号开一个欢送会，这个地方，就是他到中国时第一次向我们谈话的地方。第二天的清晨，我们送他上船，而他离开中国的地方，也就是他第一次登上中国陆地的汇山码头。然而这一次欢送他的感情与那时欢迎他的感情却不相同，当我们看他立在甲板上，银白色的鬓发飘拂着，向我们，向中国的土地，向中国的人民，点头道别时，我们都觉得一种惘然的别意，尤其使我们抱愧的是，他匆匆而来，匆匆而去，（在中国只有三十七八天）；当他前次到日本时，他把一本《国家主义》（Nationalism）给了日本，（太戈尔在日本的演讲集），同时，从日本那里得到了一本《飞鸟集》（Stray Birds）（受日本俳句的影响而作的），但现在的中国呢，他已给了我们许多次极恳切的谈话了，而我们究竟还给了他什么呢？这真是使我们想起来便觉得难堪！

——《小说月报》，第 15 卷第 6 期，1924 年 6 月 10 日

泰戈尔在东南大学之讲演

△ 过扬子江而觉自然之可爱

△ 哀人类之幸福受物欲之害

△ 智的动物而不善用智可叹

南京快讯。初到中国之世界大诗人泰戈尔氏，四月二十日乘扬子江招商轮船，由上海安然到宁，宁人士渴慕泰戈尔先生之风采道貌。闻先生抵宁，群往江头欢迎，抵埠时咸鼓掌祝诵，先生合十称谢。记者时亦在人业中，见先生危立船首，着印度淡色古装，银髯白发，形容高古，于静穆庄严之中带温美和蔼之气，令人肃然起敬，尘念都消。惟先生应北京讲学社之聘，不能在此间小作勾留，流览白下之山光水色，宁人士至为失望乃群恳作一次演讲，藉慰半生期待之忱，先生颔之，即兴从行者并汽车至东南大学体育馆公开讲演，时已下午二时矣。在事前大多数之宁人，并不知先生将欲过宁，更不知先生能在此演讲，然不到几分钟内，而此可容七八千人之东大体育馆几无容膝地。诗人，心灵感应力之伟大，诚非伊所思矣。先由东大校长郭秉文先生致欢迎，略谓泰戈尔先生为世界之大诗翁大哲学者，此次应北京讲学社之聘，道出白下，吾辈能蒙先生在此锡以教言殊属欣幸万分。先生足迹遍欧美，欧美人亦莫不表示热烈之欢迎，即在日本及吾国亦然。良以先生为孩提之天使，大爱主义之歌唱者。在先生之诗的灵魂中，实有无限大的生的魄力给予吾侪，惟望诸君尽心领受云云。致辞毕，同行诸君如徐志摩王统照及一印度学者，二英国研究印度哲学之教授，一一介绍于听众者之前。遂即由泰戈尔先生起立合十，而后演讲。

先生曰，吾乃东方之讴歌诗圣者，讴歌宇宙之大爱者，我年虽老迈，然自信亦仍为青年之精神，极喜与青年人把晤一堂，坐谈学理。青年为人生之始期，朝晨阳光，园囿之花苞，我实有无穷之希望，在青年身上。诸君青年对于我之主张，不论有无信仰而均能如此热心之欢迎感激，奚似吾知诸君近日所日日费心血，校脑汁。在研究室内之工作。科学也工艺也，所时时竞相夸效，而不忍释口者。电灯也，汽车也，西方之物质文明也。

然君等亦知道此类之文明，实为黑暗时期之文明，足以汩没人类之天真，毁灭人类之性灵，使吾人竭志尽虑，疲劳于物质之性望，而不自解脱随处只感、觉无边之苦痛，不可言喻之烦闷，初无一毫之真光，可以照彻吾人之心灵。初无细微之和风，可以吹散吾人之尘虑，而一方适足以使野蛮无心肝之强暴者利用此种虚伪之文明，为没灭同胞之利器。宇宙之美，本极可爱者也，然今科学的业障所遮掩，侵假而变成灰色矣。人类之心灵，本活泼而有生气者也。然今为物质的妖魔所欺弄，已沉沉欲死矣。我对此景象，除寄之以诗歌，托以无穷之哀伤外，更有何说。昔有一童话，中述一公主为妖魔所夺去，后由某太子用智慧的设计，从妖魔之手中复奋力救出。诸君，吾侪真真所需要之文明，犹比玲珑可爱之公主也，今亦为妖魔封销于黑暗危险之地矣。然则孰能具彼太子之智力，抱彼太子之毅勇救出我可爱之文明乎，则吾诚不能不希望于富有生机之青年。我亦当奋力前进，和诸君与此妖魔宣战，一举而扑杀此獠也。吾昨晚由上海乘轮而来，领略扬子江上之风景。时则暮暮三月风吹不寒，余独坐甲板之上，俄而新嫩可玩之月光，从乱云之罅隙间穿出几点星光。倦眼欲睡矣，柳树上之音乐，亦停止唱奏矣。夹岸之茅舍，荒江之渔舟，宇宙之一切均已卸装睡去矣。吾在此际默坐遐想，实有无限之感觉，油然而生。嗟彼众生，夜梦正深，殊不知可爱之文明，均被岸然可怕之妖魔，乘机盗去矣。大多之醒，不知尚在何时，遂使妖魔猖獗真和全消，可痛也已。余初到中国，随处觉着富有历史成绩之文明古国，非常可爱。在船板上，兴至流览，不图东方已鱼肚白矣。少选一缕，温柔之曙光，在水波上荡漾，时则穿越林隙，时则涂染舟之布帆上，幻成紫红深绿之色，诸君此即吾人所需要之光明也。吾人真真的文明，亦当如曙光之温柔可爱耳。然则如之何而可以实现乎，但当反求诸君而已耳。只有将吾侪固有之东方文化，从城垣壤壁中复活过来，使科学的物质的西方文化，一扫而空，谆化于自然之世界，诸君设能生活于此世界中，吾知必能觉到美感觉到爱感觉到无上之愉快也。在洪水冲积期，人类未光顾地球之前，世界为蛇龙怪兽之所居。此类顽豸，有大庞之身体，坚硬之皮甲，锋锐之爪牙，然人类一至，全体消灭。此则智力之猛，尤超过于蛇龙怪兽之皮甲爪牙也。人类为灵智之动物，故造世界文明者人类，毁灭世界文明者亦人类也。人类苟不善用其智力，则其可畏，实在蛇龙怪兽之上耳。今之人不图发扬内知，徒慕外铄，不急于追求纯粹天员的信仰，而徒事物质科学之工作，世界实预伏着绝大之毁灭，虽有大力，莫之能挽。然我决不因此而失望，我仍歌唱我之光明。我仍如春朝之鸟，在杨柳树上欢迎曙光一般的歌唱，希望我理想的光明之到来。

说毕，众大鼓掌，由郭校长报告休息半小时，再由徐志摩君用中语将泰戈尔先生讲演词重述一次。泰戈尔先生之英语抑扬悠远，声声如鸾歌之悦耳，为通译者徐志摩君富有文艺天才，态度亦甚温文可亲，将来中国之泰戈尔也。当泰戈尔先生讲演之开始，体育馆之侧楼，因人多重压，几欲倾倒，全场为之震动，喧声大起。而先生仍怡然不动，神志如初，足见诗人神秘之心灵，自有独特之处。演说既毕，先生与徐君，危坐汽车上。男女青年皆争睹风采，群围汽车，不忍使之忽然开去，爱慕之情，几如孩提之与其慈母。此亦颇可记者也。

（南京 K）

——《台湾民报》，1924 年 7 月 21 日，第 2 卷第 13 期

Rabindranath Tagore Preaches Union of Asiatics and Disparages Western Materialism

Dr. Rabindranath Tagore accompanied by Nandial Bose, the famous Indian painter, Kshitimohan Sen Shastri, and Dr. Nag, D. Litt, reached Shanghai on April 12. The party was given a hearty welcome at the wharf by the local Indian community headed by Professor H. P. Shastri. The poet was garlanded by Seth Lalehand on behalf of the Indians and Professor Shastri introduced the prominent Indians and the Japanese pressmen to the poet, on the deck. In all his utterances in Shanghai, Dr. Tagore pointed out the great need of the revival of the spiritual civilization of Asia as the Western civilization founded on materialism and competition was falling to pieces and the world needed something higher for the salvation of humanity. He also remarked on the need of greater cooperation among the Asiatic nations for their cultural and spiritual benefit.

The day after arrival the poet, on the invitation of the local Sikh brothers, visited their Gurudware where several hundred Sikhs received him most cordially. After a song by two Indian sisters, an address of welcome was read by Professor Shastri, following which Dr. Tagore spoke, reminding those present of the sacrifices which the Indian monks had made and urging them to be faithful to their teachings. That evening a tea was given by more than a hundred representative Chinese and the delegates from Peking welcomed Dr. Tagore in a most cordial way. On his return from a brief trip to Hangchow, the poet was guest of honor at a dinner party given by the local Japanese residents which was attended by Japanese firms and banks in Shanghai. After the dinner a meeting was held in the hall of the Japanese school which was filled to the utmost capacity, the audience being cosmopolitan. Dr. Tagore was given a rousing welcome. He delivered an inspiring address in which he states that if the Japanese welcomed him because of his European fame or the Nobel Prize, he was not pleased, but if they welcomed him for the idealism he preached he was very glad to accept their welcome.

On April 18, a great meeting was held in the new auditorium of the Commercial Press, which was attended by representatives of several well-known Chinese organizations; Tagore and his party arrived at 3:30 P.M. A cinematographic film photo was taken as Dr. Tagore and the party entered the big hall where an address of welcome was read by Mr. Sun, president of the Educational Association of the province of Kiangsu. The audience numbered more than twelve thousand. Dr. Tagore commenced his address by thanking the Chinese for the cordial welcome they had given him and remarked that the connections between India and China were so old and were founded on such a spiritual basis, that he did not feel that he was among strangers. Then he quoted from the poet Kalidasa, showing how China was respected by the great poets and paid a glowing homage of ancient Chinese pilgrims to the land of Buddha and after referring to the cultural greatness of China, remarked that he had come to China not as a critic but as a pilgrim to pay homage. He eloquently appealed to the Chinese not to copy the commercial spirit of the West and destroy the natural beauty of the land and the simple hearts of the people. He said with his characteristic force that love for abundance, for quantity alone, was a sign of vulgarity and that China was facing a great danger in going too much into the spirit of profit-making at the sacrifice of art, beauty and the people. He warned them against the dangers of over-production and the spirit of competition which could never bring peace and beauty to the people.

Dr. Tagore concluded his long and inspiring address by sounding a grave note of warning to the Chinese against the adoption of the philosopher of materialism and made an eloquent appeal in favor of lofty idealism. After the meeting a vegetarian dinner was held in a Buddhist restaurant.

There is even more in the personality of Rabindranath Tagore than his works reflect and those who come in close touch with him realise his spiritual peace. He has given everything he possesses to the Viswa Bharti University founded by him, including his Nobel Prize and the copyright of his books, more than a hundred and fifty in number.

— *The China Weekly Review*, May. 3, 1924

泰戈尔在燕大演说

反对现代教育制

六日下午，北京英文教员联合会，假座燕京大学女子部开茶话会，欢迎泰戈尔，由国立北京师范大学英语系主任鲍明钤介绍毕，泰氏即起致谢词，并发表其对于“近代教育制度”之意见。略谓今日获兹机会得与贵大学诸女士相见于一堂，实为平生快乐之事，余尝谓苟有人焉，漫游一国，画得其山川草木之秀，名流哲士之交，而未尝一领略其国妇女界之接待者，不得谓为已能了解其国风，今日乃身享中国女界之盛意接待，实为吾身最美的一种经验云云。至泰氏对于近代教育之制，非常反对。盖以现代教育为极专暴极强制的一种教育，因即以各人童年在学时代之经验，证明其理由。泰氏曾于十三岁入学，谓教室中四面灰白之壁，讲台上辞严色厉之师，皆呈可怕之景象，于每晚九时，迫学英文之法，其呆板无生气之教法，较慈母胸前之可爱故事的美，真有天国地渊之别。嗣后遂抛弃此种强迫的教育，从事自习，遂阅英国著名小说家狄堪氏所著《古老玩铺》一书，此卷系由乃兄书斋中觅得者，对于书中之词句，极为喜悦。泰氏所得之名誉，大半系由青年时用武力取得之自由中得来，旋由恒河流域外出，从事援助其他儿童脱离此种不合宜之教育制度。遂即设立学校，投考学生五名，一面教育学生，一面与彼等共同游戏，成绩卓越，以致投靠学生异常踊跃，致使该校无容纳之余地，学额虽已增加，但校规毫无改变。泰氏聘请技术专家与文学家入校讲演，学生听讲与否，均由自择，并不加以强迫。泰氏最末演说，注重现在时代之观念，各代均有一种大规模化生的观念。泰氏所抱之观念，即设立人类之真实关系，方能弘扬现在时代之和平与真理，各国有各国精神的关系之结合物，此种结合物如不存在，则该国必致发生战端，不至灭亡不止，甚至人类相食，故一国之要素，在弘扬人民道德上与精神上之关系。泰氏以为人类如能相互联合，则将来世界各国总有结成一家之一日，则战祸可免，故吾人教育目的，应使儿童实行现在时代精神的观念，质言之，即人类间之同情谅解，与博爱是也云云。

——《民国日报》，1924 年 5 月 10 日

泰戈尔在京时之临别赠言

△精神与物质之调剂希望中国学者到印度考查

廿一日各教会团体在真光剧场欢迎泰戈尔氏，此为泰氏将离京之前一日，亦可谓之欢送泰氏。泰氏略谓此次来华，颇受各界人士热烈之欢迎，实深感谢，今日又承各教会各团体欢迎，尤深荣幸。余以为在二十世纪之宗教而能存在，必各有其精神，不然已淘汰无余，已无立足之余地。既各

有其精髓处，尝各互相推重，互相吸引，不可互相排挤，互相仇视。鄙人此次来华演讲，自然引起不少之同情心，一方面又不免惹起少数人之反对，其反对余者，以为太趋重精神文明，而鄙薄物质文明。余未常鄙薄物质文明，不过物质文明太偏重，而不加以精神文明之调剂，其结果不能免除苦痛。吾相信精神文明，印度与中国不能否认，而佛学亦果有调剂世界之可能，吾甚愿世界之兄弟姊妹得精神物质二者之享乐，由痛苦而达到愉快，是余所最切盼。最后吾以为学者研究学术之态度，第一当先观察，观察后再分析比较，然后再批评判断，乃能得最后之结论，否则隔靴搔痒囫囵吞枣，毫不中肯。吾望欲了解吾之学说者，当先了解吾之著作，且吾之学问，得力于佛学者颇多，此显而易见者。吾深望吾离华后，深望中国学者，到印度作实际之考察，将来对于中国当有莫大之帮助。吾归国后之事业，当奋力发展余自创之国际大学，以传播吾之思想，以直到吾之死时，不稍懈怠，余将来不幸而死，吾之弟子等能尽余未了之志，以期达到真理上之胜利。

是日西人到者甚多，莫不首肯，而中国各界顿生感动。前夜梅兰芳又为洛神之剧以贺泰氏，闻泰氏昨晨拟出京，后又改为夜十一时出京，中外人士到车站欢送者，亦如来时，临别均有依依不舍之意云。

——《新闻报》，1924 年 5 月 24 日

Over 1000 Heard Tagore's Last Address In Peking

For three hours on the afternoon of May 19, Rabindranath Tagore, Indian philosopher and author, was the leading spirit of an assemblage of over 1,000 foreigners and Chinese, representing sixteen religious organizations of Peking. Dr. Gilbert Reid, Professor Sen, Dr. George Wilder and Professor Nag made brief addresses following that of Dr. Tagore, who summarized his philosophy as follows: "You may analyse the rose like the scientist — analyse its perfume, and color and shape, but this does not explain how it is that the rose makes an appeal to your soul and makes you love it. Today we are always analyzing, and we allow material things, the fret of life, to crowd out the appeal of the beauty hid away beneath all forms visible to the eye."

— *The China Weekly Review*, Jun. 7, 1924

Tagore in Wuchang

Wuchang, May. 30.

Dr. Rabindranath Tagore paid a brief visit during the weekend. He stayed in Hankow, where he addressed a large audience on Sunday morning; but in the afternoon he crossed the river in order to speak to the students of Wuchang.

There was on sign of the opposition which has manifested itself in some other places, and the expectation which Tagore's visit had aroused was shown by the large audience of between three and four-thousand students who, on a very hot afternoon, cheerfully waited in the open arena of the athletics ground to hear his address.

As in other places, the appearance and personality of Tagore made a great impression. With his flowing Indian robes, his erect spare figure and earnest, dignified bearing, he might have, been some Hebrew prophet of old. His message, too, was worthy of a prophet. Even so might Amos have stood before the evil Jeroboam by the altar at Bethe, or Jeremiah upbraided the people for their sins in the streets of Jerusalem. In flowing, even English, he addressed us, and the vibrant tones of his clear voice reached even the outskirts of the audience, so that for those who understood very little was lost. When the English address was finished, it was very ably interpreted by Mr. Hsu Chi-meng, a Chinese scholar educated at Cambridge. Unfortunately, the interpretation was a mere summary, which lost much of the force and expression of the original. Nevertheless, it was the man who spoke, and the circumstances of the time that made his address impressive. It was the Indian mystic speaking to the modern Chinese student. It was the old Oriental sage speaking to the Oriental of a transition period. Even so might Confucius, or still more Mencius, have stood and spoken to his countrymen.

Dr. Rabindranath Tagore warned his hearers that the new desire for the fruits of Western science and progress in material riches will not give lasting satisfaction. Rather, if it is divorced from moral aims and spiritual development, it will end in ruin. He did not condemn scientific inquiry, or the desire for physical well-being — here his sanity is above the mere fakir or devotee. But moral values are the only lasting wealth, and if these are neglected, all that is worth seeking will be lost in the end. The West, as well as the East, may well take heed and learn.

— *The North-China Herald and Supreme Court & Consular Gazette*, Jun. 7, 1924

武汉佛化新青年会欢迎印度大诗哲太戈尔先生词

粤维太翁，诗哲称雄。誉腾欧美，迹遍西东。
我邦新士，云集风从。翻译名作，艺林钦崇。
今来鄂渚，榴火正红。曰有佛音，天竺之钟。
一经讲演，寰宇咸通。欢喜无量，逖听下风。

——《海潮音》，第 5 卷第 5 期，1924 年 6 月 21 日

Tagore's Message

The visit of Dr. Rabindranath Tagore to China during the month of May called forth such a welcome as has been given to few visitors in recent years. The honored guest made the usual "swing around" from Shanghai to Tientsin and Peking and back by way of Hankow, stopping for addresses in several cities. He was the guest of various student, civic and social groups. Everywhere his message centered about the appeal to the spiritual values of life. Speaking to the Japanese students in Tungwen College, Shanghai, Dr. Tagore urged them to abandon that oriental false pride which kept them from accepting that best which other races might offer. Then he exclaimed, "I hope there are dreamers here. The dreamer and the worker mush go hand in hand." Material values were contrasted with the eternal spiritual values of life, and the students were urged to rise above the materialism of the life about them.

A most unusual meeting took place in Peking on May 19th. Dr. Tagore as his farewell message gave and address on religion, for a full hour, in which he claimed that what he knew of religion and the reason he believed in a Supreme Spirit of love was not derived from argument but from personal experience. He was followed by two other Indian scholars who dwelt on other phases of spiritual truth. The audience of one thousand persons of many nationalities and creeds listened with deep respect and interest. They filled the auditorium of the largest theatre in Peking, cheerfully lent for the occasion by the management. The Committee of arrangements, under whose auspices Dr. Tagore spoke, was composed of some thirty persons from nine religions and six Associations of moral and spiritual ideals. This Committee is of one department of the International Institute of China, and Dr. Gilbert Reid was chosen as chairman and presided at the meeting. By this unique gathering the spiritual training of the soul was placed first.

The poet-philosopher summarized his philosophy as follows: "You may analyse the rose like the scientist — analyse its perfume, and color and shape, but this does not explain how it is that the rose makes an appeal to you soul and makes you love it. Today we are always analyzing, and we allow material things, the fret of life, to crowd out the appeal of the beauty hid away beneath all forms visible to the eye."

— *The Chinese Recorder*, Jul. 1, 1924

What China Greatly Needs

Writes a young poet and teacher, a worker among and a friend of the Chinese: "...the misunderstandings between East and West are due to a failure to appreciate the guiding spirit in each other's civilization. I don't believe, however, that the West will ever understand China until the latter develops a new literature and a new art expressing her present day self. I contend, quite vainly, with my students that one great poet or novelist would be a greater asset — even commercially — than ten thousand miles of railway; but of course they don't believe me!" The recent visit to China of India's great teacher and literature, Dr. Rabindranath Tagore, and the message brought to China by him from his native land show with unmistakable clarity the true meaning of the statement quoted in the preceding paragraph. Tagore has done more than any other man in this generation, or in many generations, to interpret the sound of his country and its civilization to the world at large, East and West. Tagore has done for his country what Tolstoy and half a dozen other literary masters have done for Russia. Without interpretation there can be no understanding, and lacking understanding physical reapprochement can but lead to clash instead of tranquility. China's Tagore or Tolstoy has not yet appeared. Modern China is known to the Western world chiefly for its politicians, militarist, diplomats, brigands, and pirates: Republican China is to most Westerners a living Gilbert and Sullivan opera with Howard Pyle illustrations. China points proudly to its past: Confucius and Mencius and Mo-ti; Ku K'ai-chih, Wu Tao-tzu, and Wang Wei; Li Tai po and Tu Fu; and the classical Ssu-ma Chien — all these are names to be juggled with, but they are names of dead geniuses and a dead genius cannot interpret modern life whether it be in the East or in the West.

— *The China Weekly Review*, Jul. 19, 1924

泰戈尔先生

田 埜

泰戈尔先生（Dr. R. Tagore）之行述，各报登载之綦详，无庸赘述。先生于四月二十三日抵济，受各界之欢迎于省议会，并有演讲。本校趁此时机，请其来校一游。先生为吾人述其躬自创立之孟加拉国际大学，关于自由教育之种种方法言之极详，其所举启发人类天赋本能之教授法尤令人钦佩无已，故先生之得享盛名，洵无愧也。

——《齐鲁医刊》，第 4 卷第 3 期，1924 年 7 月

北京中外各教联合会讲演词

印度泰戈尔（稿） 中国王治和（译）

予行将离去北京，且不久亦拟离去中国。今日得与诸君会面，诚为荣幸之至。予当趁此时机，将予心中以为至宝者，向诸君声述。且予自到中国以来，尚未遇过如此之机会也，今得与诸君晤谈一堂，更觉欣幸。

据予所闻，中国对于宗教，似无亟需之必要。此不过所云如是，予亦未感深信。普通人士常以本人狭义之见解，评论他教之优劣。倘予能在中国，多作几日之勾留，则对于中国人心之所嗜好，即由精神上所发之乐趣，必当有所领悟。但因多处地方之预约，未便久留，致不能与多数中国人士接近，亦一憾事。然中国人对于相沿之习俗，尚能保存之，此亦予所乐闻者。

诸君既欲乐闻予本人对于宗教上之意见，予亦深愿有所贡献。予对于此事，常不乐为人道者。盖予本非宗教中人，即对于本国之宗教，亦无若何之趋向。不过因身生斯邦，在被动地位，遂领悟一种特别之信仰。予家中人根据印度先哲之学说，为提倡宗教奋兴会之先驱。但予个人特别性成，未尝因左右之人，信以为然者，遂容纳之。又不能因素所信任之人崇拜何教，而已亦盲从之。盖予本人似处于自由地位，予之理想，不受任何

宗教之束缚，亦未尝因何宗教之学说，致受影响。是以遇有关于宗教问难之事，予既未投身在任何教派，故亦无答复此项问题之经验也。

予自到中国以来，不过一次有人请予对于宗教之信仰，表示意见。某大学之学生，曾问予关于予之信仰上帝一事，究有何说，予亦略述理由，勉为答复。然予所述说之理由，与实情迥乎不同。犹如光学之视觉力，与光学之学理不同者。然倘予所说之理由，即或不确，然予灵性上之信仰，亦不至因此失去效力。盖予所论之真理，其实据系由于幻想，非由于学说也。是以凡有问于予者，对于幻想之说，非特不必信以为然。即对于所举之证据否认之，亦无不可。故关于宗教问题，凡为大多数人士视为至宝之书籍，则较诸个人演说教理，其效力实不啻天渊矣。予个人非特未敢以演讲宗教自任，更未尝自命为宣教师也。

予之宗教，即诗家之宗教。此宗教之能与予相接触者，乃借一不可见且不易测之曲径，犹一种音乐之感觉于我心也。予之宗教生活，又与予之诗歌生活相同。盖同在一玄妙之境界也，此两种生活萃于一身，盖早已结成一体，而予仍未之知也。及至后日，予始恍然大悟亦云奇矣。

兹将当日之情形，为诸君略述及之，彼时予寄居乡村，诸事如常，似无甚奇特。予每日于晨工完毕之后，必沐浴一次。惟当时于未沐浴之先，予站立窗前，作顷刻之眺望，目观恒河两岸之市尘，予忽觉魂魄震荡，举世亦似大放光明，真理显然，朦胧间似含带无限意味。予当时之情形，犹如人行于云雾间，虽趋向亦莫能分辨，而倏然间站立于自己之门前。此情此景，想诸君必当瞭然也。予记忆幼时，尝学印度字母。一日读字母连缀法，至“下雨及树叶颤动”之字时，予心目中恰似有一幅幻想之画，饶有兴趣。各字母在其单独地位时，本无意味之可寻，俟连缀成字，遂有此幻想之画毕露于前。上述予对于平生之真理，恍然大悟一节。其中之情形，即与此时相同，予当时视万物如汪洋之浮浪。自此以后，始有一种信仰，知人与万物，莫不有灵性中之真理基础也。

予当日所受之感觉如何，谅在诸君洞鉴中。但有一事，尚祈诸君原谅。倘予自谓能诗，诸君勿以予为夸张之辞。予以为诗者，为最能传情者也。自幼时脑力即易受环境之感觉。予有一小园，与宿舍相毗连，予视此园为一仙境。内多奇景，气象万千，每晨必趋赴此地远眺，但见日光斜穿椰树。盖此园之四周，皆以椰树环绕，青草带露，为晓风飘荡。予此时视诸物，显有一番天然之景色。故每晨必来此园游玩。各物自予视之，皆为至宝，较守财奴视金尤为宝贵。予以为赏此佳景，诚为一生之幸福。故对于读书一事，常忽略之，盖读书则使予不得与一切天然物接近也。且学校之课本，最能限人。予十三岁时，即脱去此种束缚矣。

以上各事，即予所谓予之宗教者。予生于斯世，故不得不与诸物相接近。予尚记忆有一次有一医学学生，持一人造之气管，令予视之，欲使知其构造之精巧，并向予解释，此气管即为人声音之发动机，予当时甚不以为然。予所注意者，非制造人之灵巧也，予以为制工之灵巧，在隐而不在显，须由现约中表示其构造之功用，方为适宜。观地面上历代物质之痕迹，此固能表彰上帝之大能，然上帝以为美者，并不在此。其所以为美者，乃天然物不言而有之表示，如花草争妍，云雾变态，及河水之流声是也。

予心中似常受外物之感觉，而亦不知其感觉之由来。譬如婴儿，不知其母亲为何人者。予之感觉，显系与环境接近而发生，且予对于环境诸物，最易受感触。予深觉云者为云，花者为花，且均似与予觌面相谈者，故从未淡漠视之。回忆幼时，一日自学校归家，甫下车，即见浓云密布，起于舍后，与空气相接触，予睹之，似发生一种欣喜之感觉，有如与朋友相晤谈，至极乐时，遂不觉放浪于形骸之外也。

关于人与物之接触，予尝设一比例，今请为诸君述之。譬如有人，自他行星来至地球参观，见有留声机，自行旋转，闻其发声，而不见一人。只知机盘之旋转，系赖科学之作用，摸之亦实有物在，而不知其发音之由来，必此机器之能言为甚奇。倘将此发音之理，予以解释，则彼将与发音人亦可稍适接近，藉悉此机不过为吾人之传达器而已。吾人知识之由来，本系由浅而深，此理尚易解释。惟吾人与外物之接触，而发生一种欢乐之感觉，其究系何故，此非吾人所易知也。查世界万物之安排，与吾人生之欢乐，亦有绝大之关系。吾人与万物接触，遂发生感觉，此非专由于物力，乃由于一种不可解之幻术使之然也。此种情形，觉之则易，言之则难。吾人对此，似无法解释。犹如他行星之人，只知留声机之发音，而不能证明发声音人于其同人也。

吾人所重视者金也，盖有金则诸物皆不难购备。予独爱玫瑰花较胜于金，岂以其形圆而色红，遂较胜于金乎。倘谓玫瑰花能供吾人之乐较胜于金，则诸君必不以为然。虽然，予所论之价值，非人定之价值，乃天然之价值也。盖天然之价值，则较诸金价不啻之倍蓰矣。譬如人行沙漠间，倘所见之沙，皆为金粒，则其返照之光，必令吾人头目晕眩深感痛苦。于此时，其环境尽为玫瑰花。则吾人所在之地，实无异于一极乐世界，其愉快可胜言哉。故吾所谓玫瑰花能供吾人之乐者，非由其形圆而色红也，犹诸留声机之发音娱耳动听者，亦非由于机盘之旋转也。有时吾人藉玫瑰花传达吾人之爱情，即如以玫瑰花赠与所爱之人，此亦时有之事。盖其传达爱情之效力，有非人言之所能及也。吾人之所以赠玫瑰花于故人者，系欲藉此表示吾人之欢爱者也。

印度有一最有仪式之宗教，名瓦斯拉哇者 Aaishuava，其教主善吹笛，能按韵拍之高低，奏各种乐曲，以普渡世人。其所奏之乐曲，显有欢迎世人之表示。吾人深知上帝亦常以慈爱之声，呼唤世人，俾出离幽暗而得入光明。所惜者吾人或因嗜欲熏心，或以己之计巧而欺诈他人，或以己之势力而夺取他人之财物，虽有上帝之呼唤，亦不暇顾，致使吾人所居之大地几成为一种苦海矣。

予今日所欲论之宗教乃一真实之宗教，然法门不一，结果亦因之而异，约言之可分为二。一曰俗务门，一曰正果门。其俗务门内，有如一大工厂，纷华靡丽之事，无一不有，吾人可任意择取，然终无厌足之日。但无论获得若何世俗之利益，其结局仍归虚空。吾人倘能入其正果门，得见大慈大悲之神，与之同处一堂，则所有真实永生及欢乐，吾人皆得享受。且无尽期欢乐者，即真理之表证也。吾人倘能与真理相接触，则自有一番真实之欢乐。苟仅赖物力之讲求，则终难达此真实无伪之境地。倘能达此真实无伪之境地，则吾人之真欢乐亦必勃然而生，此为宗教真实之基础，非片面教条之所可同日语也。吾人达此境地，原无所假藉，非似藉以脱之波浪，得见日光者之可比。且以脱之传光，亦不待科学家为之介绍也。故欲入此真实之境地，吾人心中须先有一种真实仁爱之感觉，非仅赖人言之解释，及教理之讨论所可达到也。

予之宗教，系诗家之宗教，前已言之。予对于宗教之感觉系由于幻想，非由于知识之关系，故对于死后之果报，予不能作一满意之答复。然予之心，每与无极之灵接近，则不觉异常欢乐，此为予所深知者。据Upanishad宗教家云，吾人因心思言语之阻碍至不得与上帝之真理接近。倘能因欢乐之感觉，得与真理接近，则一切疑虑，必皆化为乌有。

至解释上述之真理，亦诚非易事，此与解释地理科学不同。盖地理学，尚有图画及经纬之疆界可凭。此真理与早晨日光相似，不得以图画限制之，惟有赖其光力得睹诸物也。譬如吾人行于夜间，虽知各物之所在，而难免倾跌。俟晨光发现，吾人始能辨别诸物也。吾人倘能心地光明，则必能洞悉世界各族，显为一种完全之精神所联络，对于诸物，亦无隔阂，必知和平。由于心地真实之和谐所生，非外势使之然也，故吾人欲知晓各事，必须先讲求真理。俟与真理接近，则万事自当瞭然矣。

——《昌明孔教经世报》，第2卷第11期，1924年8月

Dr. Tagore on the Materialism of the West

In striking contrast to the aggressive note in Mr. Panikkar's eulogy of the Princes as the custodians of the military spirit was a speech recently delivered by that venerable poet, Dr. Rabindranath Tagore, on "The Rule of the Giant." Obviously referring to his obsession, the materialism of the west, which he exploited to the utmost during his visit to China he said, "A society which produces hugeness of organization in its politics, commerce, religion, education and amusement, fetters its living limbs, smothers the movements of its spiritual expression, continually builds round itself its own tomb, though for the time being this appears like a tower of victory. In the temple of a living principle has been enshrined an iron monster, productive of things and destructive of life. There was a time when the profession of fighting and the business of profit-gathering were restricted to specially trained groups of men, while the rest of the people had full freedom to cultivate their human personality. But because the scientific facility of communication today has spread its conquest in every realm of the elements, the field of fighting and profit-making has also become boundless in dimension. I preach the freedom of man from the servitude of the fetish of hugeness, the non-human, who defies the big, the gross, and wins victory at the end."

— *The North-China Herald and Supreme Court & Consular Gazette*, Apr. 3, 1926

泰戈尔病耗

履　冰

印度诗人泰戈尔，前曾一度游历我国，极受政学界之欢迎。泰氏返印后，颇事休养，惟应各处演讲甚多。近忽因劳顿，胃病陡发，其势颇剧，闻已入医院治疗，一时戚友问询者殊繁。印度报纸，亦记载病状，并希望此著名诗家得以康复云。

——《新闻报》，1926 年 4 月 3 日

Dr. Tagore's European Tour

Dr. Tagore was greatly pleased with his tour in Europe, judging from some of the remarks he made on his return. During his travels he visited Italy, Switzerland, England, Norway, Sweden, Denmark, Germany, Czech-Slovakia, Austria and Hungary, delivering lectures in all those places. His experiences seemed to have made a great impression on the poet and one wonders rather at the new nots of admiration, in view of the fact that but short time ago he had little good to say of western civilization which he described as materialistic and not be compared with the spiritual civilization of the East or so one inferred. Now he speaks of the "mighty intellectual mind of Europe" and the "tremendous collaboration" European countries have made towards the advancement of common culture. He was also not without a word of criticism of his own people.

Thus, he said he had to speak to European people about what he felt to be wrong in their present condition. "They listened to me patiently and enthusiastically appreciated my criticism," he said: "I know what such criticism would produce in my own country. It is produced in my own country. It is a weak mind which cannot appreciate truth if it is unpleasant and has to be fed with flattery."

— *The North-China Herald and Supreme Court & Consular Gazette*, Jan. 29, 1927

What Price Poetry

In these days when American bricklayers receive sixteen and eighteen dollars gold a day, it seems rather an outrage that some of the more intellectual pursuits do not receive greater recognition and reward. What brings this to mid is the offer of the University of the Philippines to pay Dr. Rabindranath Tagore one thousand pesos for ten lectures. That he declined the offer is not remarkable since he is an aged man and perhaps does not care for the hardships entailed in such a lecture course. But it is even more remarkable that such an offer should have been made since Dr. Tagore is one of the outstanding poets of this century, and on his world lecturing tour received more for one single lecture — yes, twice as much — as the Philippines offer for ten.

One of the curious angles of this invitation is that the University authorities, accused of being miserly, justify their action on the ground that to offer more basis, which might hurt his feelings. Why is it that literary men, all down through he ages, have been treated as a sort of children incapable of earning money? The world always has been willing to accept their work and delight in it, but when it comes to payment — the most the poet gets out of it is posthumous honors after being compelled to spend his life in struggles that might well have been devoted to the exercises of his art.

Dr. Tagore is a sensible man and one of many charities. His lecture tours are not made with the idea of personal profit at all, but to secure funds for his schools and other benefactions. The highest compliment the Philippines could have paid him would have been to suggest a hire that was more worthy of the eminence of the man, for how could he be offended it he was able to add some considerable sum to the endowment of his various works of charity?

— *The China Press*, Nov. 15, 1927

Indian Philosopher is Due Here Today

Dr. Rabindranath Tagore, philosopher and poet, and hailed by his fellow-countrymen and millions of other people throughout the world as the greatest living Hindu will reach Shanghai aboard the P. and O. liner Naldera this morning, coming from Bombay. There were many who went to the Shanghai and Hongkew wharf last night, believing that the ship was due then, but they were later informed that she would not be here until 8 a.m. today.

A reception committee will welcome Dr. Tagore this morning, and he will probably be the guest of Mr. W. Assoomall, No. 6 Quinsan Gardens during this, his second visit, here. It is reported Dr. Tagore is on his way to Canada.

— *The China Press*, Mar. 19, 1929

Tagore's Arrival in Shanghai

Sir Rabindranath Tagore, famed Indian writer and philosopher and the foremost intellectual in the Hindu world today arrived in Shanghai yesterday on the str. Naldera en route to Canada, where he will be the guest of the Canadian Government at the meeting of the National Council of Education to be held in Vancouver and Victoria in April.

Later he is going to Los Angeles at the invitation of the University of Southern California where he will lecture on Indian literature, philosophy and art. A later invitation that he may or may not accept, depending on the state of his health, includes a tour of the British Isles and a series of lectures at Oxford University.

The eminent visitor though reputed to be in ill health looked hale and hearty yesterday on arrival, but would not talk for publication and went immediately to the home of Mr. Tsemou Hsu at 613 Avenue Foch where he will stay until the Naldera leaves for Japan. There he transfers to the Empress of Asia on which the Pacific will be crossed. He was accompanied by his two secretaries, Mr. A. K. Chanda and Mr. B. W. Tucker. Also in the party was the Bengal poet, Mr. S. Dutta.

Sir Rabindranath was knighted in 1915 and is a D. Litt. of Calcutta University. In 1913 he won the Nobel prize for Literature and in addition to his many poems and philosophical works has set to music over 3,000 songs.

— *The North-China Daily News*, Mar. 20, 1929

Rabindranath Tagore Comes to Shanghai

Dr. Rabindranath Tagore, of India, who arrived on the P. & O. 6. S. Naldera yesterday morning at 6:30, was met by many Chinese Indians and Europeans at the Hongkew wharf. He looked to be in good health but it is learned that he is making his voyage to Canada and the United States contrary to the advice of his physicians. On this account he was enable to receive visitors but attended a reception at the Hindu Merchants Club, 19 North Szechuen Road, at 4 p.m. where he spoke of his life work as an effort to bring East and West to better mutual understanding, since each has much to give to the other, and what is most needed is closer contact.

In reply to a question by a representative of one of the American press agencies concerning Dr. Tagore's opinion of the political situation in India, he stated that he disliked to say anything about polities since his work was educational and not political.

One of the donations yesterday for education was $500 given by an Indian to Santiniketan Institute at Bolepore under the direction of Dr. Tagore. He is the guest of Mr. Tsemou Hsu, 613 Avenue Foch, and stays in Shanghai two days. This afternoon at 4 p.m. he will visit the Sikh temple at 300 Paoshing Road Paoshan district, Chapei.

The poet-philosopher will take the s. s. Empress of Asia to Canada and will speak at an educational council convened at Vancouver and will lecture later at various places in the United States, staying some weeks at the University of Southern California in Los Angeles where his subjects will be art and philosophy.

— *The China Press*, Mar. 20, 1929

泰戈尔昨晨抵沪

文汇报云：印大诗家及大哲学家泰戈尔氏，今（十九）晨乘莱尔特拉号邮船抵沪，本埠印侨特派代表在公和祥码头迎迓。氏迩来体气不甚健全，但丰采愉然，携有秘书两人，一为强达氏，一为德克氏，而孟加剌[1]少年名诗家杜达氏亦同行焉。氏在沪，仅少住两日，现税驾福煦路六百十三号徐志摩君宅，将乘原船赴日，然后于四月六日改乘亚洲皇后号，由横滨赴加拿大。盖应加政府之聘，于下月中旬，莅维多利亚及温哥武举行之教育协会演讲也。其演讲题，一为安适的哲学，一为美术的意义。加游既毕，将应美国南加州大学之聘，赴该州都会演讲印度哲学文学美术，为时约六星期。英伦及欧洲数处，近曾函聘前往讲学，尚未允诺，须视体健若何，再定行止。如赴英伦，则将参与牛津大学之希白特演讲会。氏以舟行劳顿，且体不健康，故拒见宾客，此次远征，未得其医士完全许可，故谢绝一切酬应。惟今午徐宅曾有私宴，为其洗尘。午后四时，

[1] 现一般写为“孟加拉”，书中亦有诸多当时地名的不同写法，因篇幅所限，不一一加注——编者注。

北四川路十九号印商总会且举行茶会欢迎之，以示尊崇云。

本市三区党部，昨呈市执委会文云，呈为呈请事，窃读本日报载，以诗哲自命之太戈尔，将于明日抵沪，查太戈尔系印人，印度民族，苦帝国主义者之蹂躏久矣，民族思想已见发轫，乃太戈尔独高唱玄学，鼓吹出世，以山林生活为标榜，对科学文明作攻击，肆为邪说，麻醉人心，使青年受其催眠，趋于消极颓废之途径，直接为帝国主义者作消灭民族自觉观念之工作，使弱小民族，沦于万劫不复之地位，其思想之悖谬，流毒世界。前次来华，一般失意政客无赖文人及研究系余孽，奉为偶像，到处招摇，曾经本党先进严加申斥，乃阅时未久，故态复萌。传闻此辈，又将藉此机会，筹备欢迎，希图私人在社会方面，有所活动。窃思党国奠定之日，正我民族，共同奉行三民主义及努力物质建设之期，而此等丧心病狂之徒，竟敢假亡国之妖孽，广事招摇，传播邪说，淆惑人心，实为青天白日下所不容，为此恳请钧会，迅予明文制止各学校各团体之欢迎，并禁其演说，庶反动份子无由乖张，邪说诐词不致猖獗，实为党便，谨呈云云。

——《申报》，1929 年 3 月 20 日

Tagore Given Contribution for University

Dr. Rabindranath Tagore was the guest of honor Tuesday night at a reception held by the Indian merchants in Shanghai. He had so many engagements and interviews that day that he appeared to be physically exhausted. Because of his genial disposition he appeared at all the functions in spite of his doctor's advise to the contrary. Today he sails for Japan, with his secretaries, by the P. & O. boat "Naldera."

At a reception given him last evening at the Gurudwara by the Sikh community, when he was presented with a purse representing their contribution towards the maintenance of the Santiniketan University near Calcutta, an international institution of education and goodwill fathered by Dr. Tagore, he said:

"My Brothers,

"Your welcome has deeply touched my heart. When I came last time to his place you gave me a seat in the Gurudwara; it is quite unique. In other places to which I go I have to be in the center of commercial life. But this here has the old Indian spirit. We met in the name of God and that is the deepest bond of unity between man and man and I fully appreciate the honor which you have done to me by bringing me to this holy place where you offer your services to God."

"When I was very young I was once taken by my father to Amritsar (India). I spent there a month and every evening I used to visit that holy place — Gurudwara — with my father. He himself was a great admirer of Kuru Nanakjee and he used to recite the "arthi" every morning with other devotees and worshipers who used to come to that place. I was very young then and I also joined in the worship. That memory is revived now when I am in your midst and I must express my gratitude to you for the sympathy that you have shown my cause and respect for my labors. I hope I have done something to help you — to bring you before the notice of the larger world and if I have been fortunate in doing it. I feel grateful not because it has conferred upon me individual honor but because I have the opportunity to share my honor with my countrymen.

"I am now going to Canada and other parts of the world where I have my duty to perform. It is a solace to me to know wherever I go in those distant parts of the world, that I represent you, every one of you, and when I travel I feel a great pride, the pride that I am fortunately an Indian in this world who belongs to every one of you and not to a particular family or part of the country."

— *The China Press*, Mar. 21, 1929

Criticism Aimed at Dr. Tagore by Kuoming Members

Deprecate Doctrines of Poet in Petition to Headquarters

While Dr. Rabindranath Tagore, the famous Indian poet-philosopher, who arrived in Shanghai day before yesterday on board s. s. Naldera on his way to Canada and the United States, is welcomed in Shanghai by many Chinese, Indians and Europeans, he has however become the target of attack by the local Kuomintang district headquarters.

The Third District Kuomintang Headquarters in Shanghai yesterday sent in a petition to higher Kuomintang Headquarters to the officer that inasmuch as Dr. Tagore is an Indian and in as much as Indian has been under impenetrate rule for a long time and the Indian people now no longer permit any imperialistic retro in their own country, Tagore should not in the course of lectures and writing attack the material and recommend civilization of the West. Dr. Tagore has been charged with having been responsible for discouraging the peoples of a small and week nation to keep themselves awakened towards emancipating their own nation from being controlled and suppressed by imperialistic interests.

The local Kuomintang men pointed out that the doctrines and principles hold by Dr. Tagore were just as dangerous and poisonous as those of Karl Marx. The above petition says that Dr. Tagore has been welcomed in China simply by a group of retired politicians and unemployed scholars, and that at this juncture whence every one in the country should strictly observe the San Min Principles or the late Dr. Sun Yat-sen in order to develop China in a more material way for the welfare of the Chinese people.

Hence, it is requested that the Kuomintang authorities stop and prevent and school or any public body to extend welcome to the Indian poet-philosopher.

— *The China Press*, Mar. 21, 1929

Orientals Should Be Drawn Closer, Tagore Declares

Indian Philosopher Sees Need of Common Thinking Ground

Undoubtedly greatly fatigued and unquestionably in urgent need of a good deal of undisturbed rest, but still exerting himself unnecessarily in his desire not to disappoint his Japanese admirers who seem to be legion, the aged Indian philosopher, Dr. Rabindranath Tagore is receiving a stream of visitors daily at the residence of Mr. K. Okura at Moguro where he is recuperating from his recent illness.

"I have just received three cables asking me to write on the philosophy of leisure," he said. "Just think of it, here I am occupied every moment of my waking hours. I have so much to do and I am busy every minute with visitors and other matters, and they ask me to write on the philosophy of leisure!" Dr. Tagore remarked ironically in speaking with a representative of The Japan Times Thursday.

At that very moment several visitors had just departed after having spent several minutes with the sage, as had a score of other callers before them; in the parlor below a dozen scholars were waiting for an interview, and in fifteen minutes he was to receive 3,000 students. Even his conversation with the representative of The Japan Times was interrupted by the entrance of two girls with books to be autographed. This the Indian visitor did ever so graciously.

AT EAST

And strangely, Dr. Tagore seemed not in the least disturbed or agitated. He was completely at ease. He seemed, in fact, to be perfectly at leisure! What matter that the continuous appointments engagements and interviews which he had gone through during past weeks, or was in the act of giving or which were just ahead of him were such as would keep a dozen ordinary humans excitable for hours, hustling about and on the verge of collapsing from a nervous stroke.

Well might Dr. Tagore write on the philosophy of leisure!

But perhaps, one felt, it was because the Indian sage no longer had the strength to be excitable or to decline to receive callers. Sitting restfully in his loosely flowing garment, and occasionally waving his hand wearisomely in a gesture, he appeared to be greatly fatigued, but never irritated, and it was he, moreover, who carried on the greater part of the conversation.

"I think the peoples of the East should have some common ground by which their feelings can be drawn closer. The peoples of the West have this feeling developed in them, they have what might be called a Continental mind. But we peoples of the East are so different from each other. We do not seem to understand each other. The things we do are dissimilar. We are deviating from the course we should take."

NOT SERIOUS

"There was a time when Buddhism spread through the East and showed signs of drawing us together, but the people of the present day do not take religion seriously. We must therefore find something else, and it is this which I am trying to teach in my school."

Questioned regarding his views on the Pan-Asiatic movement, Dr. Tagore declared that he had not even heard that there was such a thing as a Pan-Asiatic Conference much less that such a conference had met at Nagasaki.

"No, I did not know there was such a gathering," the sage explained. "Besides," he went on, "I don't think much of these 'pan' movements. I received an invitation from the Pan-Pacific Union but did not accept. I don't think they do any real good."

Dr. Tagore will leave Tokyo for his homeland early next week.

— *The China Press*, Jun. 19, 1929

太戈尔表同情于中国

△谓不久将打破一切难关

（中央社）印度诗圣兼哲学家太戈尔氏，近受德国大学联合会聘往柏林讲学，颇受德国人士热烈之欢迎。太氏近在柏林接见路透社记者，曾谈及中国不安定之情形。太氏对中国人民遭受军阀不断的蹂躏，深为惋惜，并表示十二分的同情。太氏之言曰：中国人民对目前所受之耻辱与不满，与印度人民感到往昔之自由而劣力奋斗以求未来之光明大道，大致相同。此种努力，必能得良好之结果，一旦获得一种坚强的生机之后，即可打破一切难关，超过一切阻碍，而进于非目前所受之恶劣环境的新境地。请君（指路透社记者）藉传达之便，将余对彼等目前的困厄的深挚的同情，代为传达，并为余致意。余前在中国短时间内所认识之朋友，更为余祝中国前途之光明与幸福。

——《新闻报》，1930 年 8 月 11 日

太戈尔的近状

杨昌溪

太戈尔到俄国游历后，因为政府想藉他作政治的宣传，待遇他甚为优渥。在莫斯科对访问者宣称他关于俄国的感想时，认为俄国已经演出了一种神迹，而在戏院展览室，以及一切文化中心里都可以看出他们已经在过去十年内表演了怎样的神迹。虽然他底思想同俄国是不相融洽，他因为他是在哲学上代表东方的文化，他有他底人生哲学，他有一个惊人的国际大事，更兼着六十九岁高龄的老人有着明净的皮肤，深陷的樱色眼睛，有力而柔软的手，雪白的长须，俄国的儿童们也还爱他。

离开俄国后，他去到美国几个教育中心区域讲演，同时展览他底绘画。因为在最近几年间他对于文学创作等于废置，全部工夫都专心在绘画上。不过，在刚作公开讲演时，心病忽发了，现在已尽可能的力量游历，

想早回到印度修养。

——《青年界》，第1卷第1期，1931年3月10日

慕索林尼[1]拉拢泰歌尔失败

海 波

意大利的法西斯蒂[2]为着宣传自己的教义起见，一切手段，均无所不用其极。过去拼命拉拢罗马的诗人，尤其是抱“神曲”的作者但丁底大腿，硬要捏个黑帽子戴在他底头上。反正这些死人是不都开口抗议的，所以我们地黑首相倒不会被告发而遭反坐的罪。

黑首相底把戏愈闹愈奇，现在不但要裁污死尸，而且想收买现代的文学者；近来对印度诗圣泰歌尔大送秋波，说他亦是法西斯蒂的同志；不幸泰歌尔虽老而糊涂，但他终竟还不能像但丁已埋在土里，不能自己反身。所以最近泰氏写信把他底朋友说：

“我始终爱自由，我始终爱自由！对于无慈悲的压抑运动，那与我底良心是不能相容的。那暴力的罪恶虚伪的血的路啊，我如何敢走?!”

这样，泰歌尔底态度，当然算是表明了。

慕索林尼在意大利虽然杀人不展眼，但是对这位拉拢不上的印度老诗人又有什么办法呢?!

——《读书杂志》，第1卷第3期，1931年6月1日

An Essay on Tagore

G. B. S.

Rabindranath Tagore, His Religious, Social and Political Ideals, by Dr. Taraknath Das, M.A., Ph. D. Saraswaty Library, Calcutta, 1933. 55 Pages.

---

[1] 今译为“墨索里尼”——编者注。

[2] 今译为“法西斯”——编者注。

This essay on Tagore was delivered in November, 1923 as a lecture in Munich under the auspices of the India Institute of Die Deutsche Akademic. The author, an Indian Scholar, has revised his material for publication. The book has an appreciative preface by Mr. Winternitz of the German University at Prague.

Dr. Das has written an appreciation of Tagore, not a critical study of his ideals. In such an essay it is quire permissible to omit facts which might detract from the praise poured upon the subject of discussion. We, ourselves, enjoy a more penetrating analysis of character than this study furnished, but Dr. Das gives us one side of the picture. One can scarcely do more than this during the life-time of one great man.

We remember that when Tagore visited Shanghai some years ago and spoke at the Hall of the Commercial Press Library, students picketed the gates to the building enclosure, pressing into our hands radical literature denouncing Tagore for his inconsistencies. When the Indian poet and idealist was in America recently he had misunderstanding there, which, we heard, caused him to cut short his tour. But Tagore in his books and by his presence, as we saw him in Shanghai, has an attraction and a power that accompany really great men. We can feel this in his writings and when we see him before us. Nothing Dr. Das says really increases our interest or admiration for Tagore.

Dr. Das cannot forgo various pin-pricks and a few sword-thrusts at the British in his essay, but he throws out a sop of appreciation to Americans and thinks Japan will have a hard time if she attempts alone to unite and lead Asia. The author quotes extensively so as to give the poet's ideals in his own words.

Although those who have read the Indian poet and heard him lecture will gain little from this small volume, those who have not had such opportunities to know the mystic, and as Dr. Das calls him, the "radical political thinker" will find two of these well chosen quotations very illuminating. We give two of these showing Tagore's thoughts on man and his privilege. "Man is now in his career of creative life; he is to give from his abundance. By his incessant movement of renunciation he is to grow. Whatever checks the freedom of growth is sin, which is the evil that works against man's eternity." "Our society exists to remind us, through its various voices, that the ultimate truth in man is not his intellect or his possession; it is in his illumination of mind, in his recognition of the world, not merely as a storehouse of power, but as a habitation of man's spirit with its eternal music of beauty and its inner light of divine presence."

December 20, 1933.

— *The China Weekly Review*, Jan. 13, 1934

Tagore Gets Backing for China-Indian Society

Nanking, June 4. — It is learnt that Mr. Tai Chi-tao, president of the Examination Yuan, is sponsoring a scheme for the organization of a Sino-Indian Cultural Society. The plan was proposed by Mr. Rabindranath Tagore, the famous Indian philosopher and poet, who communicated with President Tai and other cultural leaders regarding the feasibility of the project. President Tai has asked Mr. Tagore to proceed with his plans.

— *The China Press*, Jun.5, 1934

Indian Philosopher Appeals for Support of Indo-Chinese Culture

An appeal to scholars in China to cooperate in the promotion of Sino-Indian culture is voiced by Mr. Rabindranath Tagore, famous Indian philosopher, who in a letter to Chinese friends here, offers Shantinakatan as the center for the activities of a Sino-Indian Cultural Society to ensure a continual interflow of cultures between the two peoples. The text of the letter follows:

"I will not send you empty greetings from across the barrier of space and indifference that have divided us for centuries. Let me fill my greetings with hope that they but herald the time when our two people will once more understand each other and add to each other's achievements."

"There was a time when India and China stood very near, when they joined their hands and their hearts in one common homage to the Spirit of Love and Renunciation. Today when the world is being divided into hostile camps, each ready to strangle the other, let us recall that spirit, which still lives among us and permeates our being, and prove in our relations that the forces of love and understanding are greater than those of hatred and aggrandizement."

"It gives me great pleasure to have you as co-workers for the cause with which I have identified myself all my life, and I am proud to offer our Shantinakatan as the center for the activities of a Sino-Indian Cultural Society which with embody the cause for which we are striving."

"It will take some time to build up this great society which should ensure a continual interflow of cultures, but we would be wise to make a beginning immediately in the form of erecting here a Hall called the Chinese Hall, where students and scholars from China could stay and cooperate with us. That Hall will serve as a foundation on which to build our higher hope."

"I appeal to my friends in China to help in the working out of this plan both with their sympathy and their funds."

"Yours in common fellowship, (sd,) Rabindranath Tagore."

— *The China Press*, Jun. 14, 1934

泰戈尔将来华

印度诗人泰戈尔，他是个极端菲薄欧西文化而推崇东方精神文明的人。这种“反科学”“反现代”的书，在他的诗集中《新月集》和《飞鸟集》表现得很为显明。最近泰氏为沟通中印文化，及组织“中印文化协会”事宜，以便光大东方文化，征服欧美的科学文化，特电致中委戴季陶，请求赞同，言将来华云。

——《摄影画报》，第10卷第21期，1934年7月21日

Sino-Indian Association is Being Pushed

Nanking, Nov. 21 — (Central) — Cultural relation between China and India will be greatly strengthened with the establishment of the Sino-Indian Cultural Association in India recently and also a center association in China.

The idea of forming scholarly co-operative cultural organizations was first formulated by a number of Chinese officials and scholars, including Mr. Yen Chu-tsang, Mr. Tai Chi-tao, Mr. Chen Li-fu and others, who in view of the close relations, between the civilizations of the two countries, felt that some part of organization for promotion cultural co-operation was necessary.

The suggestion was made to the world-renowned contemporary Indian poet Dr. R. Tagore, founder of the International University, through Mr. Tan Jen-Shan, a professor of the same university. With the hearty support of the Indian poet, the Sino-Indian Cultural Association was inaugurated some time ago with its office at the International University.

Mr. Tan arrived here yesterday from India to make s report on the association to the original promoters and other parties concerned, preparations for the establishment of the sister association in China are understood to be under way.

According to Mr. Tan, as soon as the sister association is formally instituted in China, cooperative cultural activities will be started, such as the establishment of research institutes, exchange of professors and students, and dispatching of cultural missions from one country to another.

— *The China Press*, Nov. 23, 1934

印度泰戈尔大学中国馆落成典礼

印度通讯：中国馆乃中国要人蒋介石将军及其他之中国闻人捐助而成，为谋中印文化之沟通起见，故组织中印文化学会，该会乃中印两国佛教徒及学者研究之所，内有规模宏大之图书馆，藏书十万，所有关于艺术，宗教，文学，哲学，历史，各类，无不搜罗其中。四月十四日为中国馆成立纪念日，泰戈尔博士于此宾朋毕集而充满东方文化庄严气象之中举行纪念典礼，先歌唱“利未达，”赞美中印团结及合作之精神，嗣即举行印度古时之“曼陀罗”礼佛仪式。继由泰戈尔博士演说。继由中国总领事当众宣读蒋介石先生及中国各名人贺电，嗣后由泰戈尔博士读甘地，雷洛及莫克基（印度大菩提会会长）等颂辞。

蒋介石将军贺电：（衔略）今日中国馆落成，余深觉快乐，余深望诸同仁能为中印文化而联络一致，以达到和平仁爱之幸福，并祝大学中诸同学进步及馆中诸同仁健康。

中央研究院院长蔡元培，中央考试院院长戴季陶，国府考试委员会主席及中印文化协会秘书长陈大齐等联名贺电：（衔略）中国馆落成，未得恭逢盛典，谨电申贺，敬祝中印文化前途胜利，并颂与会同仁康健。继后由中国谭云山先生演讲，（讲词另录）演讲毕，即由泰戈尔博士行揭幕礼，礼毕如仪。

——《海潮音》，第 18 卷第 7 期，1937 年 7 月 15 日

第二章

思 | 想 | 研 | 究

Lives of Great Writers: Sir Rabindranath Tagore

周越然

"Give me the strength lighting to bear my joys and sorrows."

It is an honor to be a great poet. It is a greater honor to be a great poet in a land where poetry is a commonplace thing, a part of daily life. And it is the greatest honor for a poet, who not only has no equal among his fellows but is admired by scholars of all nations.

Such is Rabindranath Tagore, the Nobel prize winner for literature of 1913, the greatest living Hindu poet.

Sir Tagore was born on the 6th of May,1861. His father was one of India's greatest spiritual leaders, and so devoted himself to the cause of social and religious reform that the people called him "Great Sage." His grandfather was a landlord, a founder of Landholders' Society, a philanthropist, and a social reformer. His granduncle was a political leader and writer. Among other ancestors of our poet's may be mentioned a distinguished painter, an authority on music, a writer on legal and educational subjects, and many other useful and prominent men. The family of Tagores, in short, has rendered great service to India in political and industrial nationalism, in the revival of art and music, and in social and religious reform.

Tagore was the youngest in a family of eight sons and three daughters. At exactly what age our poet's education began we do not know. But we are sure it began very early; it was before he was six years old that he was placed under a tutor. For when he was about six years of age he begged to be sent to school, after he had seen his elder brother and his sister's son Satya go to school and had heard from Satya unduly accounts of the adventures on the way. The privilege was refused. He cried and cried. His tutor lost his temper and snapped him on the check, saying: "You are crying to go to school now, you will have to cry a lot more to be let off later on." (see pp.5,6,

"My Reminiscences" by Rabindranath Tagore, and pp.37,38. "Rabindranath Tagore" by Basanta Koomar Roy).

This prophecy was fulfilled. He was soon sent to the Oriental Seminary, where he found nothing interesting or enjoyable. He was transferred to the Normal School to see if that suited him better. There things were worse. Most of the students were unpleasant to him, nasty in their manners and habits; and he hated one of the teachers, whose language was foul that he steadily refused to answer any of his questions and that he sat silent for a whole year in the class, meditating and attempting the solution of his own intricate problems of life. After the Normal School he was sent by his guardians to Bengai Academy. He did not like that school either. In his work, "My Reminiscences", he says, "The boys here were annoying but not disgusting..." And again: "The rooms were cruelly dismal with walls on guard like policemen. The house was more like a pigeonholed box than a human habitation. No decoration, no pictures, not a touch of colors, not an attempt to attract the boyish heart."

Young Tagore was not to blame for his dislike of schools. He was born a great poet and was being trained in wrong places and under wrong men. His father saw this and decided to take him go to Nature's school. One day he was asked if he would like to go to the Himalayas for a trip. He shouted out the loudest "Yes." He was glad to get out of school and to see the mountain world. At the Himalayas he found what he like and enjoyed. "The terraced hillsides...were all aflame with the beauty of the flowering spring crops." He roamed about from mountain to mountain, finding company in the rocks, trees, springs, and the broad expanse of sky overhead.

The next year, when he was twelve, he was back at home. School became more unbearable after that trip, and he was allowed to stay at home to pursue his artistic studies. He had finished reading the most important books in Bengali. He was writing poem and began to publish them. However, this kind of effort was unsatisfactory to the guardians who decided to send him to England to study for the bar. He went and within a year returned to his beloved country.

In England Tagore began a poem entitled "The Broken Heart," which gained many readers and was liked at that time by the writer himself. That was when he was eighteen. Between the age of fifteen or sixteen and that of twenty-two or twenty-three, he wrote many poems on love. His early poems of a sensuous nature and in a new style at first received attacks from moralists and stylists of the old school. But there is really nothing immoral in his thought and vulgar in his expression. The so-called moralists and stylists could not understand the preliminary works of a future great poet who introduces to the world a new kind of poetry and a new kind of style.

Sir Tagore was early initiated into poetry by Jyoti, a son of a niece of his father's. One afternoon, when he was about eight years old, Jyoti sent for him and asked him to try and make up a verse. He tried and succeeded. Some of his juvenile poems were praised, and others were published. Since then he has been writing novels, plays, and poems on love and on philosophical and religious subjects. His works in Bengali are read wherever Bengali is spoken and are translated into English and many other languages.

His principal works in English are: "Gitanjali" (Song Offerings), "Fruit Gathering" (A Sequel to "Gitanjali"), "The Crescent Moon" (Child Poems), "The Gardener"(Poems), "Stray Birds" (Poems), "Chitra" (A Play), "The King of the Dark Chamber" (A Play), "The Post Office" (A Play), "The Cycle of Spring" (A Play), "Sacrifice and Other Plays", "Hungry Stones and Other Stories", " Personality: Lectures Delivered in America", " My Reminiscences", "Sadhana: The Realization of Life" (Lecture), "Nationalism".

"Gitanjali" won for him the Nobel prize in 1913. "Chitra" is a study of man in his enjoyment of life in the flesh, which many of my friends and I enjoy best. "My Reminiscences" pictures vividly the various stages of our poet's mental and spiritual development, which every lover of Tagore wishes to possess.

In conclusion, let me quot Mr. Roy's words on Tagore's philosophy: "To him (Tagore) the world is full of joy and love, and an undying bliss dances throughout the universe. Sorrows there are in this world, but they are like the flitting clouds of Indian autumn — clouds that intensify the glory of the moon."

——*The English Student*, Mar. 1, 1920, 第 6 卷第 3 号

印度泰莪尔之物质文明与精神文明论

枕江（译）

物质文明者，与吾以活动力，独立思想者也；精神文明者，与吾以和平，平等思想者也。吾人言活动时，非竞争不可，非决胜负不可。然由人类之宝地观之，世界云者，不外一梵之实现物耳，爱情之结合物耳。故世无纯粹之平等思想不可；而物质主义非根本于精神主义不可。若仅偏重于物质主义，则人类必倾向于个人主义。抱个人主义者，必有排外，憎他，鄙视非我族类之恶念。彼妒人之功，视人如敝如盗者，皆由此个人主义而生者也。

谓予不信，诚以今次之欧战观之，德意志国民费多年心血，力图工商业发达，因以致富，而其结果不外实行其排他主义而已。岂独德意志为然哉？英法等方面亦未尝不然。此种惨剧，皆生于精神主义之缺乏，即由于物质主义而生者也。

若世界对于排外，憎他，鄙视，非我族类之恶念，终世不灭，则所谓世界者，荆棘已尔；所谓人类者，蛇蝎已尔。幸而人类天性喜爱和平，父爱其子，夫爱其妻，此种爱情，到处流露。而人与人相接，国与国相交，亦无不以此爱情为媒介。是则古圣贤常言之矣。由此可信爱情为人类之本能，益信吾人与其言人类有排外天性，无宁谓其有爱他之天性。总之，排他之罪恶，皆由个人主义而生者，无待言矣。

——《解放与改造》，第 2 卷第 10 期，1920 年 5 月 15 日

太谷儿主义

王 靖

印度《大经典》Upanishad的思想歇绝后，印度的哲学亦随之同时衰落。但是现在已由瞑想的幻梦，觉醒过来，急起直追所谓生命的力，以入于复兴的时代。太谷儿就是此时东方精神运动的前驱，所以称为东方主义第一人。太氏以生命派哲学做基础，对于久绝印度的精神，加以进化学说的新解释。因此所谓印度的新精神，始有根据。太氏由二十五岁至三十五,十年之中，著述甚富。他是崇拜自然，得着精神解放的人，并且能彻底了解人的价值是超过于世间一切物质的效能，生活于充满的爱力中；他所做的诗都是慕“真”的意趣，与爱“美”的情思的表现。他的诗集最佳最脍炙人口的有五种[1]。

《偈檀伽俐》Gitanjali。这部诗都是说宗教的，其实就是他哲学思想的显示；不但可以代表他的诗意，并且可以代表他的人生观。我读了这部诗美感踊跃于中，不觉神游于物外。原第二十七首云：

“光，咳！光在什么地方？他用欲愿熊熊不息的火点着！

这里是灯终不见一星闪动的火——你的命运是这样，我的心吓！咳！不如死好！

痛苦叩你的门，他的使命便说：你的主已醒，他叫你经过夜的黑暗，来到你的爱之地方。

天为云所遮，两脚下如轴。我不晓得这在我心里骚扰的东西究竟是什么——我不晓得他的意义。

电光忽然一闪，在我视线里出现更甚的悲惨，我的心就摸索路径，以赴‘夜的音乐’之招。

光，咳！光在什么地方！他用欲愿熊熊不息的火点着！雷啊，风啊，突然空中不住的轰轰呼呼的响。夜间也黑如墨色。不要令时间在黑暗中过

[1] 文中标点符号等大多遵循原始文献格式，略有改动——编者注。

去，且用你的生命把爱的灯点亮。”

又原诗三十五首云：

“那里心是不恐惧的，头是昂然高举的；

那里知识是自由的；

那里世界是不被狭窄的局部的墙，隔成断片的；

那里言语文字是由真理的深处说出来的；

那里不疲倦的努力，伸其长臂向于‘完全’；

那里澄清真理的泉流，是不会迷途而直流入‘死的习惯’之寂寞沙漠上。

那里心灵是被你引而向前于‘永久广大’的思想与行为里的——入于这个自由的天中，我的上帝，使我的国家由酣睡醒来。”

原诗第九十一首云：

“咳，死，你是生命最后的完成，我的死，你来和我耳语！

我每日想见你；因为你使我受生命的快乐与痛苦。

一切我的人格，我的财产，我的希望，及一切我的爱情都永远在秘密之中向你而流。从你眼里出来最末的一瞥，我的生命便是你了。

花已织好，新郎用的花园也预备了。举行婚礼之后，新婚将离伊的家庭，在夜的寂寞里，很单独的遇见伊的丈夫。”

原诗第九十二首云：

“我知道这时候快要到了，在这时候，我将不见此世，生命也将沉默的离别而去，引上最后的幕幔在我的眼帘上。

星光在夜里还是照着，早晨也仍旧的现出来，时间如沧海波涛一样的流去，抛弃了快乐与痛苦。

当我想到我的瞬间的这个结果，瞬间的围棚破了，我由死的光里看见你的世界与他不注意的宝物。我的最低坐位是尊贵的，最卑的生活是尊贵的。

我所求之不得的物，与我所已得的物——让他们一齐逝去。使我所认为最真实的只有我一向所轻蔑所不注意的东西。”

读了以上数首诗，便可以推知太谷儿是极端信仰宗教的人，但是他的宗教，不是形式的宗教，是“自然宗教”。他也可称为泛神论者，因为他相信万有即神，神即万有。

《新月集》Crescent Moon。这部诗是儿歌，描写天然的美感，活现纸上。其余《园丁集》“The Gardener”、《拾果集》“Fruit-Gathering”、《迷途之鸟》“ Stray Birds” 也都包含有许多哲理。因太氏心灵与自然诉合无间，所以发而为诗，无不幻渺神奇，似自然界的音乐，赤裸裸的将人生的真际表现出来。其余太氏所著的剧本如：《邮便局》“The Post Office”、《暗室之王》“The King of Dark Chamber” 和《惜特拉》“Chitra” 等：都是风行全球的名著。伦敦 Pall Mall Gazette 报评《惜特拉》说：——“Over and over again we find that perfume of phrase which has always marked Mr. Tagore’s work at its best... He has given the soul of the East disembodied of its sensuality, and within it shines the most perfect tribute to true womanhood and its claims.” 这就可见他的剧本的价值了。全印度的人，没有一个不读太氏的著作，即全世界也没有一国不转译他的著作。太氏的诗风，震动全球，所以没有读他的诗不受天然美的感觉的传染。印度有一医士曾说：“我每天都读太谷儿的诗，只读了一行，一切世界的烦恼都消灭了。”岂但某医士如此，即全印度的人，也都有这感觉。因太谷儿能把深深的哲理无形之中，尽量寄托于诗；所以感人格外觉得容易些。太氏现在已做全印度人信仰的中心；一说起印度，没有人不联想到太谷儿。于此可见现在的印度正是太谷儿的时代了。

太谷儿叙述他的哲学最有系统的莫过于《人生的实现》Sadhana 一书。书中多祖述《大经典》的思想，词意甚强，且多含诗趣。太谷儿的思想与法国柏格森 Bergson 颇有相似，就是表现哲理的文词，其巧妙练达处，也不亚于柏氏的《创化论》。太氏的哲学，以爱为归宿；一言以蔽之，“爱的哲学”。他看“爱”是全体的知识的理解是部分的；因爱是全体，所以经过“爱”才能达到真理。再看柏格生的哲学，是直觉的哲学，或称人的哲学。他把直觉放在理知上面，以为知慧，只能见到时常不变时事物表征，永远不能贯彻一个单独与不可分割的生命活动。在柏氏哲学里，直觉算是我们对于生命实际的一种心灵的心赏，并且是与生命同体的，因为直觉能了解生命的真谛。由直觉才可以懂得生命的意义——就是达到真理。由此看来，太谷儿的哲学思想也有与柏格森“不谋而合”的地方了。

《人生的实现》，共分八章：

（一）个人与宇宙的关系 The Relation of Individual and Universe.

（二）灵魂意识 Soul Consciousness.

（三）恶的问题 The Problem of Evil.

（四）自我的问题 The Problem of Self.

（五）在爱里的实现 Realization in Love.

（六）在行为里的实现 Realization in Action.

（七）美的实现 The Realization of Beauty.

（八）无限的实现 Realization of Infinite.

读了这本书，便可以明白太谷儿全部哲学的思想和他所抱的主义。我现在把这部书“提纲挈领”介绍过来，使研究太谷儿哲学的人，先明了他的大概，而后去读他的著作，便能“迎刃而解”。

（一）个人与宇宙的关系

此章首述欧洲文明与印度文明的不同：欧洲的文明发源于希腊。古希腊的文明是孕育于城市墙壁之间；所以近代所称文明各国都带有瓦灰泥土的色彩。因此人人心中都有一种分界，以区别与支配为原理，故欧洲的文明可称为区别与支配“Divide and rule”的文明。太谷儿说：“……故我们以国与国相区别，知识与知识相区别，甚至人与自然也区别起来。这就使我们对于我们创造的环境以外的各物生出强固的猜疑 Strong suspicion 且各物入我们认识 Recognition 的缘故，必经很利害的奋斗。”印度的文明，就不是这样。当第一次亚利安 Aryan 人，初入印度时，印度是一个森林的旷地，新来者即借森林获得许多的利益；因为森林可庇日光的炎灼，避风雨的飘零，草场可以牧蓄，木料宜于建筑。凡此种种都是自然所赏赐。所以印度的文明，完全是孕育于森林，其来源与环境带有极显明的色彩，与欧洲的文明居相反的地位。当时印度人的生活是被广大无垠自然生命 Vast life of nature 所环绕，得自然界好处既多，由是与自然有极亲密的关系；故人与自然互相调和，互相交通，而人我之间，也没有城府，也没有支配他人的欲望。太谷儿说："古印度森林生活的状况，并不征服个人的心意 Mind，也不孱弱个人能力的活动 Current of energies，只是给个人一种特殊的趋向 Particular direction。因为时常同自然的生长相接触，个人的心意便没有设立界墙扩张领地的欲望。其目的不在获得，而在实现，并要与环境 Surrounding 相和合，去扩张其自觉 Consciousness（或译意识）且觉得真理是包罗万有的，没有绝对的单独 Absolute isolation 的东西能够存在的，至获得真理的唯一方法是由我们与万物相合而来。"换言之，太氏就是承认人类的灵与宇宙的灵其间有大调和的可能。这大调和的实现，就是我们的志向。太谷儿说："我们与自然和谐，是一件大的事业；人与事物和谐，所以才能思虑；人能为自己目的运用自然力，也无非他的能力与宇宙的能力相和谐罢了。因此人的目的才永远不至与宇宙目的相冲突。"这一段就可证明个人与宇宙的关系的重要了。所谓人类的灵与宇宙的灵，其间大调和，就是个体与宇宙，人类与大自然间的调和。印度前哲都努力于此，认为信仰的目标。欧洲的人以为人与自然之间有极分明的界。"自然是专属于无生之物与兽类的，人类天性起始的地方，有一种突然不可思议的破裂。照这样说，不论何物在公秤上，低的是纯粹的自然 Mere nature 有圆满的表现——聪慧的或者道德的——是为人类天性。这好像分花与蕊出于各别的原理。"（P.7.）印度人的思想，却没有此种的谬误。印度人不以"创造的根本统一 Fundamental unity of creation 看做只是哲学上的企图 Philosophical speculation，只看做是生命的目的，必须在情感与行为里去实现这大和谐。"（P.7.）印度人以为个人孤立，不与宇宙联合，必至灭亡，所以奉"人与自然和谐"之给条至深。"地球不是单容人的身体，且愉快其心灵；因为人与自然相接触，不只是物质的接触——这是一种活泼的态度。当一个人不能使同世界的亲谊实现时，这人简直像被拘在牢狱里，被四围牢狱的高墙所隔绝。当人遇着万物里的永久精神时，于是他便解放了，因那时他发现他所生存的世界的完全意味；他觉得自身是在完满真理之中，同万物的和谐也成立了。”（P.8.）所以我们必实现自己，于自然之中。我们不能于城壁之间，得到生命的粮食，好像蜜蜂不能于自己蜂房中间酿蜜，求于无限的自然。人若使自拘于人类，夸张他的富有，这不是真富有；因只求物质上的富有，把生命——精神方面——抹煞，必至物质愈富有生命愈饥荒，倘物质一消灭，生命也随之而亡。好像“对于生命放火，在火的惨白光焰里弹琴，这快乐是可暂不可久的。”（P.11.）

“近代西方的文明，以其所有组织能力，正在极力使人民智，德，体三育的效能完全发达。用国家极大的能力 Vast energies of nations 去扩张人的权力，使超越于环境，而联络人民所有每种能力，去占有他们所能染指的东西，克服他们战胜路上的各种障碍物。他们永远训练自身与自然抗抵，并征略别的种族；他们的军备日新月异；他们的机械，器具，组织增加到可惊诧的度率。”（P.13.）印度所谓文明，就与此大相径庭。印度于军事上政治上，虽是劣败，不足与西方并驾齐驱，然印度参与真实的神秘 Mysteries of reality 里为人类所求的大道，经历万世都是常新的。这大道就是人类热望的极大表现 A supreme manifestation of human aspiration，换一句说：就是宇宙的灵在个人中之实现，个人的生命在宇宙中的实现。简单说：就是人类与自然的大和谐。

印度人所最崇拜的，唯有“感灵者”Rishis。“感灵者”是什么呢？“有些人已经在知识里面得到最高的灵魂，一身就被智慧所充满，并觉得自己是与宇宙灵魂相联合，而内部的自我也完全和谐；他们实现这神于心中，就解放了一切的欲念，若以神是在于世界的活动中，就可以得静寂的境地。所谓‘感灵者’就是这些人由各方面达于最高之神，找见本有的平和，与万物合为一体，入于宇宙的生命。”（P.14.）这“感灵者”就是印度人的理想，奉为人类最后目的与满足。太谷儿具实现这理想的一个“感灵者，”这理想可说是太谷儿哲学的真髓。西方的哲学家往往以印度的梵是抽象的，看做不容易实现。只看印度的祈告：“我再三祈祷那在水火中的，透过全世界的，在每年收获中，同时也在多年树林中的上帝。”由此看来，可知印度人所谓神，决非抽象的。印度人以为一切事物，在在有神，神虽居于万有之中，然我们心中也有神存在的。《大经典》说：“凡人在他本质 Essence 里是万物的光明与生命的，又是世界的意识的，就是波罗门——

梵——了。”这梵是居于万有之中，也居于我们的灵魂里。我们所有的完全意识，与世界所有的完全意识，其实都是一样的东西。所以欲达世界意识的梵，必须我们的感情，与此普遍无限的感情，互相联络；因此我们应该解脱自我的束缚，《大经典》说：“你要得必先弃，你不可强求。”就是这个意思。所以“真实的联合知识与情爱，并和众生服役，这样去实现一个人的自身于万有的神中，就是善的精义，而且就是大经教训的本旨：‘生命是伟大的。’”

（二）灵魂意识

我们已晓得古印度的热望是要推广意识的范围于全世界，希望得到婆罗门的快乐而生存游泳于其间。有人说还是不可能的，但太谷儿的意却不这样，他以为“每个人天天必须解决那广大他界限与调整他的负担的问题。一个人负担太多，竟至不能胜任，但他晓得采取一种方法，就可以他负担的重量。若使他们觉得太混杂笨重，他就知道是因为不能依照那安置高物于适当位置和均衡一切重量的方法。这种方法，实在是用来探求和一Unity与会通Synthesis；我们的企图是以内部的调停Inner adjnstment使外部物质的各种繁杂能够相和谐。在探求时，我们渐渐的明白只要寻出一个One，就可以得到全All；这实在是我们最后的而又最高的特权。这是根据于和合的定律，这定律倘我们一晓得，就是我们内存的力。其永久的原理是在真理里的权力；包函多数的那种和合的真理。”事实虽杂多，真理只是一个。动物的知识知道事实，人的心灵有权力了解真理。譬如苹果从树上落下，雨降于地——你只能记得这事实，永远不能得结果。倘你一经获得摄力的定律，就不必去收集事实了。因为你已得到一种管理无数事的真理。”（P.26.）我们晓得世界万物罗列，所呈现的事都是茫无涯涘，若一一去记忆，必至神劳而疲，且还不知道万物的秩序究竟是怎样。然我们一寻出统一万物的定律，无论事实如何繁杂，都可能加以归纳，而尽有一切。“因为单纯的事实，好像一条绝路，只能引导自身——没有前途。但真理能开展全体的地平线引我们到无限。”（同上）故真理含有一切事实，并非单纯事实的集合。真理于任何方面都超越于事实之上，到无限的真实。譬如“达尔文发见关于生物学普通真理时，真理决不停止那里。却像一盏灯所发光线射过于所照的目的物，照耀到人生和思想的总体，使原来目的成为卓越。”（P.26.）

“知识界这样，意识界也是这样。我们必须求统一一切意识界事实之意识界真理。就是求包函一切意识，而超越意识达到无限实在之中心真理。Central truth《大经典》说：‘认识你自己的灵魂。’就指这个目的。或者换一句话说，实现人人所有的一个联合大原理 One great principal of unit.”（P.27.）

我们必先自知我们的灵魂，而后才能解脱自我的束缚，与神合而为一。“我们所有一切自私的冲动与私欲，都能蒙蔽我们灵魂的真视觉。当我们自觉我们的灵魂时，我们就明白那越超我们的自私而且有同万有较深类缘的内部物如 Inner being.”（P.27.）

我们灵魂深闭于自我中间，好像分开的字母，没有什么意义，如果字母连成字，成文，用以传达思想，这原始无意味的字母，就包含有广大的意义了。我们灵魂也是这样。倘把灵魂禁锢于自身的狭隘界限里，便失去重要的意义。惟有把灵魂自身同别的相联——与相合——才能找出灵魂的真理与快乐。

我们欲抛弃自我，又当以爱表现灵魂的真意义。所以我明白人是灵的存在者，虽然肉体消灭，物质损失，都不足影响于灵魂的本体，我们既是灵的存在者，我们必先除去意识的蒙昧，复返于灵。这蒙昧能使灵魂沉睡不醒，不能洞察四周的最高实在。譬如小鸡啄破蛋壳，才知道深闭不许他外出的硬壳，实在不是他生命的一部分。这硬壳不过是一种死的东西，不能生长，不能透视在壳外面广大前途的任何景物。我们物质的蒙昧，也像蛋壳一样，无论眼前怎样快活圆满，都必须打破，才可以取得外界的日光与空气。我们人类的历史，无非求解脱这蒙昧罢了。因此我必抑制物的种种欲望，求其合一。譬如地球，起始不过是星云，其中碎片，因热力膨涨，四处飞去。这时地还未成固定的形体，无所谓美，也无所谓目的，只有热与运动而已。以后渐渐将这纠纷争乱的物质，都一一支配于惟一的中心，结做一个圆满的形体时，就在太阳系中占一个适宜的位置。像绿翡翠悬在金钢钻颈环中一像。人类的灵魂也是如此。当灵魂困惑于肉情的热与盲目冲动时，我们不能有所予，也不能有所受。以后藉自制的力，发见灵魂的中心；就把各相争夺的要素，成为调和，一切孤立的意见也成为智慧；那时我们心的暂时冲动在爱里找得完满了，并且人生的种种用意都启示无限的目的，即一切的思想与行为，在内部和谐里成为难解难分。

《大经典》说："你们认识唯一，就是灵魂。这是引入不灭生类的津梁。"（P.35.）

"找得在人里的唯一，是人的最后目的；——人的真理人的灵魂，也是精神生活的钥匙。人的欲望是很多的，而且这欲望狂追世界的各种物件，因为在那里这欲望有生命与成就。但是在人里面的唯一是永过去找寻，和合——和合知识，情爱与志愿；其最高快乐是在永久和合里达无限的一致时候。"所以经典说："除了那些心志沉静的人，并没有他人能够以在灵魂中实现一种显示于众生相里的要义去获得常在的快乐。"

总而言之，自我近于物质，常常被物质所诱惑。经典说："在宇宙活动里显示他自身的神是常住在人的心中，常做至高灵魂。那些由心的直接知觉去实现这灵魂的人可以得到不灭。"由此可知我们探求自然的真理，是由分析和科学的方法得来的，而我们理会灵魂的真理是由直觉来的。太谷儿所谓直觉就是爱的力，与柏格森直觉哲学相差不远。太谷儿以知识为部分的，不能由之达到最高的灵魂；惟意识的爱算是全体的，可以藉做求真理的渡船。此说与柏格森直觉于理知之上，可称若合符节。

印度祈祷之词说："啊，你自身是一个显示者 Self revealing one，显示你自身于我。"其意谓：神的意志可以由于人的意志中，求其表现，使人的意志服从神的意志，且同时我们的爱也与无穷的爱相联合。虽然神是不强人服从的。只等我们开门，他如宾客一样，从容入内。所以我们惟藉爱发挥自我的真意义，以后才能物我两忘，与梵合一，达到人生最高目的。

（三）恶的问题

恶是什么？何以有恶的存在？太谷儿解释得很明白。太氏以为何以有恶存在的问题是与何以宇宙有缺点是一样的。换句话说：何以在宇宙里有创造。创造有缺点，是不能不这样的，那么，恶的存在也是不可免的。恶好像一条河的两岸。岸能障流，也可以激水有前进的行动。恶又像一条缚船的索，同时也可以使船顺流前驶。由此可知人世有恶的存在，无非趣人于为善。恶是假相，善是真相。死为假相，生为真相。必然是假相，而自由是真相。以此类推，就晓得自我也是假相而与宇宙生命相融合之我才是真相。假相是有限的，真相是无限的。所以我们应该努力抛弃假相求真相的实现，舍有限要达无限的完满。世界里有障碍与痛苦都不足以为异，所可异的在那里有规律与秩序，美与快乐，善与爱。人类有神的观念 Idea of God 是尤可异的。因此在人类生活的深处，已觉得凡现露出来似有缺点的，都是完满的显示。犹之倾听音乐，虽仅听一节，立即领悟其完全的曲调。其实，缺点不是完满的负面，有限不是反对无限的；因为缺点只是显现于一部分的完全，显现于有限中的无限。明白这道理，那所谓生与死，必然与自由的关系，都可以由此而知。

太谷儿意谓，死是生活的负面景象，譬如我们眼睛，虽每秒钟都要关闭眼帘，终算眼睛是睁开的。倘若我们使观察的探海灯不住的照到死的事实上，那么世界就要像藏尸所了。但是在生活世界里，死的观念是不能占据于我们心中的。因为生活的全体不以死为意。虽死是刻刻不可免的，当生活时，仍是死的表面上笑，跳舞，游戏，建造，积蓄，并爱人。设我们只看到一个死的单独事实时，那时就垂头丧气，以为死是最可怕了。那晓得的生活的全体中，死不过是一部分的。譬如从显微镜中看一块布。这布就好像一只网；我只注视着布的大孔，不见布的全体，自然由想像[1]中生出恐怕来了。但无论如何，死不是最后的真实。死看起来似黑的像天空似青的一样。死并不玷污生存，也像天空不使其污点染着鸟翼一据。这是证明死是生活全体的一部分，恶也是善全体的一部分。

所以我们应取较宽的眼界，看到生活全体与善的全体。于是才能从抛弃假相而就真相，从思到善，以善当做人类积极的要素。

但我们要问善是什么？我们道德的性质什么意思？太谷儿以为当人晓得有更大于现在的自我时他才自知道德的性质。人既自觉有较大于现在的自我，就必定希望实现其较大之我；要实现较大之我，必须抑制供媚于现在小我的种种物质欲望，并要对于未来的生活，较现在的生活尤为倾心；更要牺牲现在的种种不良嗜好，以求尚未实现之未来，有实现之日。于是才能实现真理，成伟大之物。这种真理，就是作恶的人，也不能不承认，不服从；因为不稍顾真理是不会强的。譬如一队盗贼必须赖有道德才能结

[1] 书文“想象”均沿用原始资料的写法，故仍写为“想像”，下文与此同，不再一一标注——编者注。

合团体。他们可以劫夺全世界，但不能彼此相劫夺。所以世间所称为不道德都不是绝对的。恶也是这样，因恶之中有不恶的。不过我们不可限于狭小的范围罢了。所以我们于时间既晓得为未来而牺牲，于空间更当明白我们常为自己所限制，难得真的自己，必须把自我以外的较大自己——现在以外尚有未来的自己，刻刻求其实现。总之所谓善的生活，必破除时间与空间的范围，而生活于全体。因为过善的生活，就是过普通的生活——道德的生活。快乐是为一个人自我的，但善是关系于全人类的幸福而始终的。从善的观察点看，快乐与痛苦有不同的意义；因有一般为要使他们生命得较高的价值，常避乐寻苦以达其目的。这样，苦乐就不成为绝对了。这好像我们从海里汲了一桶水，便觉得水的重量，若我们置身海中时，虽有千万倍之水，由头上流过，也并不觉得。由此就晓得在自私平面上，快乐与痛苦都有全重量，若在道德平面上，就没有了。所以释迦的教训是要培养这道德的势力到最高度，并使我们知道我们的生活的范围是不限于浅狭自我的平面上。果能如此，我们便解脱了快乐与痛苦的束缚，自我所空虚的地方，也充满着从无量爱里跳出来的一种不能言状的愉快。

还有一层：我们的个性要强，因愈强就愈普遍。因为个性不是我们最高的真理。在个性里有所谓普遍，应实现这普遍才是。倘我们只注意自我的范围里，不啻把我们关闭在牢狱里面；因为人类最深的快乐，是在渐渐的同万物愈联合愈长大。否则，我们单独的欲望必与普遍定律——宇宙法则——相冲突，我们就要受苦了。太谷儿以为到处所惹起冲突与纷扰，倾覆社会的均衡和各种的不幸，无非我们自我生活——单独欲望——在那里作祟。遂至我们为维持秩序起见，必须创造阻压，组织专制的形式与暴戾的制度，因此人道就被遏服了。所以我们要能力，必须顺应宇宙普遍的法则，使这法则实现于我们自身。我们要幸福，必须使单独的意志顺从普遍意志的主权，而且在真理中我们觉得这是我们自己的意志。当我们达到的地步，我们里面的有限与无限的调和是圆满的。佛说“皆大欢喜”就是这个意思。

（四）自我问题

太谷儿极尊重个性 Individual。他说：“我是绝对的单一。我是我，我是不能比较的。这宇宙的重量也不能压碎我的这个性。在外像方面，个性是藐小的，在实际上面，个性都是伟大的。因为他能坚持他所固有的去抵抗外力的引诱和侵掠。”由此看来，可知印度的思想，并不是以自己寂灭，自己否定，认为人类的最高目的。印度所否定之自己是非真的自己，自由的自己。印度所以尊重个性，因个性是根据于宇宙之生命。“若是这个性毁坏了，就是形体上的物质没有丧失一点儿，一个元子也没有散乱，那种结晶在形体里的创造乐 The creative joy which was crystallised the rein 是已轻消灭无余了。如其我们抛弃这特性——个性——便是绝对的真破产。因为只有这一点东西，我以可称为是固有的，倘再失落了，就如丢弃了全世界一般！个性是最有价值的，因为这是不普遍的 Universal，所以只有经过这个性，我们方能明白这宇宙，比较着昏昏沉沉睡在那愚昧的境遇里要真确得多了。”（P.70.）

“去保存自我的离相 Separateness of this self 是我们一种恒久的竞争与痛苦。在事实上看来，就是这种痛苦，能度自我的价值。价值的这方面，是牺牲；牺牲所以表示已经耗费的多少。价值的那一方面，是获得 Attainment；获得所以表示已经收入的多少。若是自我对于我们毫无意义，不过是痛苦与牺牲，那么，自我那有什么价值。我们也用不着，也不情愿，去从事于这种牺牲。在这种状况里到最后时候，人类最高的目的便是自我的消灭，那是无可疑了。”（P.71.）

观此可知太谷儿所谓自我就是无我；因人要自我有价值，应尝痛苦与牺牲，形体消灭，而真自我才可显露。这无我的思想，不但佛教，就是基督教也是这样。基督教以死为脱离于不真的生活与佛所谓涅槃 Nirvana 是无差异的。印度以为人类真的解放在人自脱于愚昧 Avidya，愚昧能遮断人的真观，使人类以自我为真实，以为自我中存有许多意义。这便是把自我看错了。太谷儿说：“自我譬如线，生命譬如织机，线必定要在机里穿过，方能成布。若是黏住这根线不肯放，那里有做成衣裳的布呢？如其一个人苦心孤诣专为安排自我的娱乐，他好像在罏里生了很大的火，却又不预备面，去烤面包；火烧着，喷出许多火星来，一会儿又慢慢自熄了。又好像那种无情的兽吃了他自己的子孙，以后自己也死了。”（P.73.）

所以我们惟有揭去愚昧的幕，才能认识真自我。所谓真自我，就是超乎自我界限的理想，使我们不至桎梏在自我的狭小范围里，认自我本身做最后的目的。自我譬如油灯，若以火燃之，就有光辉显出来，没有光辉，便失灯的真正意义了。太谷儿说："灯里盛满着油，高高放在灯台上，却不去燃烧，还是很鄙吝的，并且这灯与周围的事物也隔离了。"（P.76.）灯牺牲他的油，放出光辉，以全灯之目的，犹之佛陀之舍抛假自我，以求真自我。灯之牺牲非徒然的，要放光才去牺牲。光好比我们的真自我，非备尝痛苦是求之不得的。这牺牲叫做"爱。""我们的历史里找着从前佛陀在 Nirivana 地方用'爱'来讲经的故事，我们便晓得这地方现在还是爱的最高累积地。无论什么事物常在我们心里提一个'为什么'的问题，我们便应该举出一种理由去答覆这个问题。如我们说'我爱'那么便没有地位可以容得这个'为什么'的问题；因为'我爱'便是很满足的最后答复。"（P.77.）故为爱而牺牲假相的自我，非以死而终的牺牲，是要求无限之生。并且这种牺性，必快然自足。因为生于真自我，是无异生于广大的爱。爱是我们真正的使命，太谷儿说："我们在完满的爱里，就找着了自我的真自由。天下只有为爱而做的事，才是愿意很自由的去做，虽引起了许多的痛苦，也不为意。"（P.78.）我们之生，由于神的爱；抛弃小我不过将此爱还于神罢了。我们既知为神所创，那么我们的不死也与神的不死一样。死是假相，不过是无限的生一个界线。佛以死教人，所谓死并非寂灭，乃是永生。所以我们欲得真自由，应脱种种物质的束缚，以广大的爱做我们的引线。所以太谷儿说："自由只能在爱的工作里可以得着。"又说："创造是从真快乐的充满量里推演出来的，创造是他的爱；爱便创造了宇宙万象。"

（五）在爱里与行为里的实现

我们都晓得太谷儿的哲学，完全以爱为归宿。所以他以知识为部分的，爱为全体的。惟有爱可以使我们参透一切，藉之以达于梵。知识与理解是假相，立于宇宙因果律支配之下，住在有限必然的世界。爱就不是这样，因爱是究极的物能融合万物。爱又称做乐。乐有自由之意；所以爱就是自由，也就是乐。大经典说："凡一切生物都是由乐而生，被乐所维持，向乐前进，而加人于乐。"可知世界一切都由神的爱神的乐而生；神乐充满，由是赋万物以一切形态，犹如诗人兴趣充满，发为诗词。形态就是限制的，也就是法则。一切事物都有法则，不过这种种法则是假相罢了。法则为我们所应顺从的，所应晓得的；但我们徒知道法则，终没益处，我们应该超越这种种的法则；因为法则不是究极的东西也像文字不算是文学，韵典不算是音乐一样。自然界外面的活动世界，在在都受法则所支配；然而我们心中都贮满自由与快乐。譬如一朵花在自然界里，因受因果律支配，所以旦夕以开花结果尽其职务，他的忙碌非我们所能详细晓得的。虽然这样，如果这花映入我们心里，就变为美与和平的表现，生出自由与快乐。由此可知自然界里一切都有反正两面——二元性——一方面拘于自然法则，做自然的奴隶，一方面乃生于快乐与自由之中。我们若观察自然的表面，只见事物一概是受束缚的，一到内部去观察就明白原来里面尚有自由与快乐。在此二元相中间，法则与必然是假相的，自由与快乐是真相的。真相生出假相是由爱的分离。我们的自我都是由神的爱而生；因神的爱情洋溢，乃取别一形式，而生我们的自我——此即所谓神的别一个自我。神以爱造人，好像诗人以兴趣作诗。诗人以别一自我所作的诗，必须以法则表现出来；神以别一自我，所造我们的自我也不能没有法则。宇宙万物都以神的爱，而与神分离；所以我们以这爱的分离，返之于神，就是以我们的自我返于神的自我之中。换句话说，就是返于梵，这就是人生的目的。太谷儿说："缺乏爱便是无情的一个阶级；因爱是意识的完全 Perfection of consciousness。我们不爱，因为我们不了解，或者可以说，不了解是因为我们不爱。爱是环绕我们事物的最后意义 Ultimate meaning of everything around us，爱不是一种纯粹感情；爱是真理；爱是在创造的根株上的欢乐。爱是从波罗门所发射的纯粹意识的白光。"太谷儿以为由法则返于爱，由道德世界返于灵魂世界——就是人生目的。我们所谓超越法则并不是抛弃法则；法则我们固然应当承受，但承受之后，应脱于法则之外。太谷儿是极端主张爱的，他以为没有爱，就没有同情，因此做人的根本消失了。所以他说："我们忙得似发狂的，用宇宙的势力去得更多的权力；我们从宇宙的贮藏室得到衣食，又去掠夺其财富，由是宇宙就变为我们极剧烈的竞争场了。试问我们只为这物质而生活吗？我们只扩张我们的所有权，使世界成为一件容易流通的商品吗？若我们完全的心灵专注于利用世界物质时，世界就失去对于我们的真价值了。我们以鄙陋的欲望，使世界变低贱；到了末日，我们不过鼷鼠似的，在世界上果了腹，失去世界的真理，这好像贪心的小孩从珍贵的书籍撕下数页吞下。”（P.109.）又说：“在吃人风俗盛行的地方，把人看做食品似的。在这种国里，文明永远不能发达，因在那里人失去较高的价值，只看做像平常的事物。但还有别种吃人的风俗，或者没有这样坏，然也是极可痛恨的。纵是称为文明较高的国里，我们有时也可以找得把人看做纯粹似肉体的东西之举动；且按照人的肉价在市面销售。有时人也有一些价值，不是看做像一部机器的价值，资本家可以用钱来买，替他赚得更多的金钱。这样，待到结果人类的真价值就消灭了。这就是我们的自欺。我们的欲望能使盲目，看不见真理是什么，这就是我们对于自己的灵所做的一个最大错误。因此我们的意识就减少了，无异精神上一和逐渐自杀的方法。所以虽称为文明国，也一样的生出许多残虐暴戾的事情：如复仇刑法，不合理最忍心的牢狱制度，并侵犯别民族的自由，使别民族万劫不复，没有自治的希望。”太谷儿意谓人有最高的灵魂，不可只看人是机械。这灵魂只有爱能够真实知道的。所以我们应由爱里实现人生。没有爱无论什么文明都是假的。

太谷儿又说：“有一天我坐一只船，容易于恒河中流。这时正是秋天美丽的晚景，太阳刚刚下山去；天空的静寂中装满了不可描写的和平与美丽。广阔的河流，微波不兴，反映着天空斜照刻刻变化的红光，格外好看。数里荒旷的沙滩，被光射着像大洪水前两棲[1]爬虫类的鳞甲在那闪闪发光。当我的船静寂的撑过那险阻的河岸，忽然有一条大鱼跳出水面上，立刻不见。秋晓的颜色衬着，愈觉动人。这好像暂时拉开许多色彩的屏风，在屏风后面显出一个充满生命快乐的静寂世界。这鱼似由神秘的深处走出来做了一个跳舞的举动，并且使他自己的音乐加入于垂尽日子的静寂和音中。我觉得这无异由别一世界来的一个友谊的礼意，使我心中触着一闪的快乐。那时把舵的人用一种清晰带叹惜的口吻喊道：‘呵，好大的一条鱼！’他立刻现出幻想的图片，以为这条鱼已捉得预备做下酒物。他只能从欲望里看这条鱼，所以失去这鱼生存的全部真理了。”（P.110.）太谷儿这段话，说得很明白，我们就可以从此领悟爱的重要与人生的真价值了。

我们由此可以晓得爱能够融和一切，所谓自由与必然，快乐与法则，

[1]“栖”的异体字——编者注。

有限与无限，凡此种种矛盾，都可以在爱消灭，受与与之间，因爱也可以得到平衡。譬如：情人要得自己于爱之中，乃时时投身于爱之中而不顾。所以爱虽算自己的，也可以说非为自己的。我们一方面主张自我的存在，一方面又主张无我。无自我固无所谓爱，然仅仅有自我也不足以行爱。这是太谷儿最深奥的思想，也是他哲学的精义。

太谷儿又以爱与行为相结合，意谓人生的真义，非从行为上无从实现。观此印度所谓涅槃的思想，并非不活动的。《大经典》说："你唯有在动作中，可以生活一百岁。"动作活动，实为快乐的表示，快乐与自由，必藉行为而始显。神之快乐，乃生万象，可见神是为生而动作；宇宙万象就是神动作的结果。所以经典上称做婆罗门信徒中领袖的人，是"一个活动的人 Active one，他的快乐是在婆罗门里，他的运用 Play 也在婆罗门里。没有快乐运用的快乐，全然不是快乐——没有活动运用算不是运用。活动是快乐的运用。'Joy without the play of joy is no joy at all — play without activity is no play. Activity is the play of joy'……所以凡深信婆罗门的人，他的快乐在婆罗门里的人，必定是婆罗门里也有他的完全活动——他的饮食，与生活及他善行，正像诗人的快乐在诗里，艺术家的快乐在艺术里，勇者的快乐在运动里，智者的快乐在真理的认识里，永久的用活动来表现。可见婆罗门信徒的快乐，是在每天小工作里，在真理里，在美里，在秩序里，在善行里，对于无限求有所表现。"（P.131.）

我们已明白人必自知有较大于现在的，才能够自知道德的性质。要求这较大于现在者的实现，除行为外，没有别的方法。人必须藉行为才够明白较高较大的自我，才能够发挥真性，而脱于无识的蒙昧。倘若我们的心灵，严闭于灵性之中，那么将至窒息到死。所以心灵唯有自破范围，在行为上尽量发挥，才能得着自由。于此可知行为是破除无识与发挥真性的唯一好方法。

（六）美的实现

太谷儿说："凡我们对于事物不能取得乐趣，这事物在我们心里，是一个负累，无论如何应除去的；或者对于我们有利益，不过是暂时或一部分的关系，等到效用一失，又变成为烦恼了；抑或这事物是玄深飘忽的，我们尚未加考察工夫就为过去了。所以天下事物真算是属于我们的，便是我们认为可由之得到愉快而把持不释的。"（P.137.）

这样看来，使我们能够生出愉快的事物，必定是美的。美就是调和，若是我们强为区别，什么是美，什么是丑无异滥用美识 Sense of beauty 去寻烦恼，也许在各种不齐不平的事物融洽点上横加障碍。

但是当我们实现 Our realization 未完满之前，我们必定有所区别于其间。所以太谷儿说："……古时人生科学 His science of life 便在有生命与无生命之间创出一种严厉的区别。等到科学渐有进步，这种有生与无生的界限，又渐呈出混合的状态。在我们觉悟开始的时候，这种界限对于我们未尝没有帮助，但是等到了解渐深的时候，那些痕迹，自然会慢慢消灭无余的。"（P.138.）由此可知"我们与美第一次认识的时候，总是光怪陆离，看不出他本来面目；但是到了因缘成熟时，彼此又都是相化于无形。譬如：不和的音调都被那合拍的节奏所纠正了。我们认识美的手续，可分为三期：起始将美离开他的四周；接看便仅仅得到其全部里的一部分；最后，我们才在各方面实现其'和谐'Its harmony。"（P.139.）到了这时期，我们的审美识已扩充到无限了。我们也有力量脱解自乐与那欲念固执要求。无论考察什么事物，都存着一种"无所不在"的美观；所以那不能使我们生出愉快的事物，也可以看出美来，因这美是在真理里头。太谷儿说："我们能够多了解一分这物世界里的和谐，我们的生活便可多享一分创造的愉快；那么，我们美的表示在艺术方面又愈加普遍。若使我们的灵性方面，有了和谐的觉悟，世界精神幸福的了解，也成了公同或普遍的。那美的表示在我们生活里，便直向'善'与'爱'而趋，直达无穷——这就是我们人类生存最后的目的！"（P.141.）太谷儿又说："我们既晓得'美即是真，真即是美''Truth is beauty, beauty truth'。我们便应在'爱'里实现这世界来，因为爱产生世界，维持世界，并且呵护这世界。所以我应备有心意上的完全超脱，因这种超脱，能给我们一种力量，去深入地狱，饱尝苦里的乐，这乐是属于波罗门的。"（P.141.）

按太谷儿的意，以为人惟有藉爱，才可以找出万物的美，能在爱里实现人生，那美也能到我们眼前来。我们心灵若被私欲蒙蔽，就很难得到真理，美也是就与我们远离了。因为万物都是和谐的，惟有达到真理的人，才懂得这和谐的乐趣。太谷儿："美即是真，真即是美"就是这个意思。

我们感着美的愉快，是不可言状的。且看太谷儿说："昨天晚上，万籁俱寂，黑云漫天，我独自一个人站在空地里；听见一种令人意远的歌声。我回去睡觉的时候，便静静的闭上眼睛，那最后的想象，忽然涌上心来。我想就是我酣睡的时候，生命的蹈舞，仍旧还要在我睡身的安稳战斗场里和那一闪一闪的星光合着拍跳动。我的心还要在腔子里拨动；我的血还要在筋脉里愤张；我身体上无量数的活元子，也还要和着真宰所拨动的弦声微颤咧！"（P.144.）

（七）无限的实现

我们人生的目的，是求与梵——波罗门——合为一体。所谓梵就是神，神是无限的而且为万物之母。我们必先弃自我，投身于爱，爱可说是走入梵所必经的路途。爱必牺牲，必受痛苦，没有牺牲与痛苦，不足以显爱之深浅，也不足以言爱之普遍。故欲达到梵，非先牺牲无由获得。梵是普遍于宇宙之间犹之普天之下没有一处不被日光照耀。可见梵是无限的普遍的。能达到梵就是无限的实现。

人不是完全的生物，必力求进步。"将成""To be"实开我们无限的前程。所谓"将成"，是要求与梵合一之意，我们不可以现在"所成""Is"而自足。倘永远拘于现在的状态，那么，人生的真意义就消灭了。所以我们有"将成"的希望，才有无限与自由的希望。但"将成"必由爱方可达到，否则，人生也无从实现。太谷儿说：科学都说世界是历史进化而不息的，不肯以神为"Is"，而以神为"渐成""Becoming"，故他们不知道无限这东西，是较大于假定的界线，换言之，即不晓得所谓梵，一方面是进化，一方面是完全，一面为显现，一面就是本质。所以我们一面为创造与进化，一方面就是无限的实现。太谷儿说："神有两方面的关系，是像歌词与歌的行为。他的轻视作歌人的意思，唯注意于唱歌，以为是无歌。我们仅仅知道歌的行为，固然不能明白歌全体的意义。但必有完至的歌，存于作歌人的心中，这是我所能知道的。"

所谓"渐成"，也有不变的本在意义。这本在与渐成虽一齐出显，却先渐成而存在。犹之唱歌人未唱以前，其歌早已存在一样。可知这歌并非作歌人心中的歌，也不是唱歌人所唱的歌，是由两者相合，歌乃成立。所以仅有本在不能成为宇宙，仅有渐成也不能成为宇宙，两者合一，宇宙乃成。太谷儿说："有一日早晨我的心中深念昨天夜祭时所闻的歌，至今犹不能忘。歌词说：'渡人呵！你渡我到彼岸罢！'我们于事物纷扰之中，往往听见这歌声。御夫驱车时，商人售货时，没有不唱这句的歌。还歌真意的所在，是谓我们这样勤勉尚未达到我们的目的。"

我们的心，像小孩子一样，每到不满所欲时，都有"非此"的感想；但是"非此"必"有彼"。所谓"彼"是什么呢？所谓彼岸又在什么地方呢？在我们"Is"之外么？在我们所居之外么？两者都不对。这就是在我们活动的真理中间，就是在快乐的海中间；并没有此岸彼岸之差别。太谷儿以为由我们的劳功，委身于神，我们才可以无限的实现。一方面虽在创造渐成的途径，一方面已达于完全无限之地。这好像川流将成为海，其存在的一端就是海。又如歌的一字一句，都合有歌的全体之活气。所以我们将走入于梵，就是在梵之中；因此我们于梵中间得"Is"的信念，应存着"将成""To be"的想像。换句话说：就是常住于神之中，求无限的新生命。人惟有藉"To be"的志，才有"Becoming"，才可入于梵的路，而后才能得无限的实现；而美与真的泉源也在此。

以上所述，都是太谷儿哲学的中心思想。他的哲学已受进化论的影响，所以处处都有进化论的色彩，且多宗教的与诗的意味寄寓其间。读者欲明白其全部哲学思想，请阅《人生之实现》一书。

一九二〇，十二月二十日夜十时脱稿，王靖

——《新人》，1921 年第 1 卷第 7～8 号

太谷儿传

青　青

拉宾德拉奈司太谷儿 Rabindravath Tagore（以下简称太谷儿）生于一千八百六十一年五月六日，现在已五十九岁。[1]他的出生地，在印度朋伽尔。Bangal 父亲达宾德拉奈司太谷儿 Debeudranath Tagore 是个著名的

[1] 太谷儿，现全名译为"拉宾德拉纳特·泰戈尔"，出生日期现在一般认为是 1861 年 5 月 7 日，出生地一般认为是印度西孟加拉邦加尔各答，此处保留原始资料的表述，后文亦同——编者注。

哲学家，虽笃信上帝，但不是信无知妇孺所共信的上帝，是信像老年的托尔斯泰所信的上帝。他以为人要生活，就必须有信仰，人须在信仰中间求人生，不能在信仰以外求人生。他觉得上帝是“钻之弥坚，仰之弥高，瞻之在前，忽然在后”的上帝，并不是有迹象可寻的上帝。他看着日光，月光或星光，就想像上帝或者也是一个光明的结晶体。他本应承袭王爵，但他却鄙屣王爵，不肯承袭爵号。他乐为平民，深表同情于平民式的劳动生活。拉宾德拉奈司太谷儿是他的少子。

祖父德华拉伽奈司太谷儿 Dwarakanath Tagore 虽袭德华拉伽 Maharaja 的王号，但不像平常的印度贵族；平常的印度贵族，都是骄纵，奢侈，残暴，淫佚的代表者，他却是温恭，简朴，慈祥，精勤的一个人。他看见印度国民阶级里最低一级的生活状态，几乎都不是人的生活，他很不以为然，时时主张改造制度，将那些坠于惨酷生活中间的人，拯救出来。他对于地方慈善的事业，极力提倡，并捐助许多金钱。他又曾极力攻击妇人殉夫的恶习，说活的妇人，决不应殉那已死的男子。当时为他这话所感动的人，实在不少，就是眼前的印度空气里，也弥满了“活的妇人决不应殉已死的男子”这一种声浪。

太谷儿稚年的时候，好像是一艘满载着快乐的船。他常常从事于不期高尚而自然高尚的游戏。他所著的《新月集》大抵都从他儿时所得的经验而成。他稚年游戏最勤的一种，是将纸船放在水里。当纸船流到他眼睛看不见的那个地方的时候，他极希望那纸船能够被别个小孩子得着。他每次放出纸船，还附着鲜花或树叶。夜中做梦，就梦见这载着所爱的鲜花的船，在有新月的地球上，河道中很自在的航行不息。

太谷儿生来便有神秘的甜味，在他心里；他没有不愉快的时候；他的保母虽然时时置他于寂寞的处所，但他并不觉得寂寞。他以为最好的境界，常常在静寂里呈露出来。——无论河流的声音，树木的声音，歌鸟的声音，这都是寂寞中很奇妙的音乐，也就是他以寂寞为最好境界的一个理由。他的感觉也和普通儿童不同：遇着无论什么东西，他都觉得这东西是为他而有的。比较上容易动感情的东西，系花，鸟这一类，一过他的眼前，他就将这东西的影子，印在心里，留着这影印的痕迹，做长期的甜蜜记忆；每一记忆，好像都带一点蜜汁。

他稚年的时候，有一件东西，最能启发他的神秘的思想；这东西就是他屋里的窗子。这窗子外面，有太阳，有月，有星，有云，有花，有木，有飞鸟；他对于这太阳，月，星，云，花，木，飞鸟，都引为最良的伴侣。他一生所有的神秘思想，大抵都是这窗子赐给他的。

太谷儿六岁的时候，极羡慕学校的生活，很想跟他的哥哥同到校里，但他的家庭教师，却不许他进校。

到太谷儿应该入学的年龄到了，太谷儿便欣然入学抛弃其“家庭约束的生活。”

但太谷儿是自幼就渴望得着“个人自由的生活”的：当未进学校以前，他极厌恶“家庭的拘束生活，”到了学校，又厌那“学校的拘束生活。”他最初进了东方学堂，以后又改了师范学堂，在师范学堂里极不满意于那里的教员，因为那里的教员惯将无礼的语调，侮辱学生。

不久太谷儿又由师范学校，转到英印合办的朋伽尔学院。这学院就是太谷儿所目为“监狱”“病院”的学校；他十一岁从这学校出去，随他父亲去游世界第一高山——喜玛拉耶山，第二年死了母亲，又进学校，但他却用旷课的方法，迫学校将他斥退，由是他十四岁的时候，又重出学校了。

太谷儿在学校里如此不肯用功，真的么？这就不然了。原来太谷儿在学校里并不是不求学，只是不求“无用的学问”，并不是不求“有用的学问。”他在校里，往往在静默中求最高深的学问，常常提出极重要的问题，自问自答，好像老僧参禅。他晓得无尽藏的宇宙里，包含着许多猜不透的哑谜而又天天迫他来猜这个谜，所以他对于各种重大问题，都异常烦闷，大有虽不能猜，也要勉强去猜的神气。当他稚年的时候所以常用竹竿挖土，也是为着挖土或许能发见地里一二神秘的东西。他曾说过：“我回顾我儿时的生活，……那时我心里总觉得世上有好些事情是不能了彻的，也决没有一个确定的时期，实在的机缘能与真宰相见。我想他必惯握着拳问我道：‘你猜我的手里是什么？’我因为没有一个东西不能从那里寻觅而出，所以总不敢答应。”这也可见他对于一切重大问题的烦闷。

十五岁太谷儿到英国学法律，仍不惯于“学校的拘束生活，”当年又回到印度。

那时太谷儿已经有极富的著作了。他已著了诗，小说，剧本一百余

卷，他并且善于演戏，朋伽尔地方的人，那时都称他为诗童，名剧家，

太谷儿十八岁以至二十二岁，被累人的性欲本能，拖到荒淫的境界。他自己对于这事很是痛心，曾在回顾自己的时候，说：“那时候的我，已经成了废物。”

太谷儿从人欲最险的地方勒马回头以后，便从事于诗。太谷儿原有做诗的天才，加以得着许多别人所得不到的诗料，来帮助他的天才，做诗自然容易深入人心；所以太谷儿一经专心一志来做诗，不久就得着“东方诗人”的美誉。

太谷儿到了三十岁他父亲就命他来管理沙来打 Silaidah 的农业。他到了沙来打，便在帕德玛江边一个船屋住下。他一生与“自然”的接近，没有再比那时候更多的，他所住的地方，除了他的家，和“生铁那克当学校”Shaouti Niketan 以外，也没有一处是比这里更长的。他在那地方，除了和农民共同操作以外，并天天领略帕德玛江的风景。

太谷儿四十岁，创办生铁那克当学校，这是太谷儿大彻大悟以后的计划。他觉得印度人大半都是死的，躯壳里没有精神的，如果不从教育着手补救这个极普遍的死症，印度人是没有生命而生活的，所以创办这个学校，极力提倡“灵育。”他办这学校，和俄国托尔斯泰办学校的理想，有一大部分相同，像提倡“自由”“互助”“博爱”“平等”等等，无一不和托尔斯泰的理想相合。所不同的地方，就是托尔斯泰不注重诗教，太谷儿极注重诗教。

太谷儿五十四岁到日本，大受日本朝野的欢迎。当太谷儿没有到日本的时候，日本没有太谷儿的著作，他这一次到了日本，那著名戏剧《邮便局》在日本就有了译本；不久《邮政长》那篇短篇小说，也在日本报上发见，渐渐的那有名的《暗室之王》《园丁集》《新月集》也就出现了。

太谷儿到日本大有影响于中国，先时中国人是完全不知道有这太谷儿一个人的，以后因为看见日本人个个发了崇拜诗人太谷儿的狂热，由是也晓得有这么一个太谷儿了。太谷儿的名字，既被中国人晓得，就有一个日本老留学生陈仲子将日本人所译的《邮政长》那篇小说转译出来。到了今年，大家都有点知道太谷儿是个东方的诗圣了，由是各报各杂志，就也可以不时看着太谷儿的著作，并且有《撒那士》这篇戏剧的单行本。

太谷儿五十七岁又到英国一次，这一次到英国，英国全国的人，没有贵贱贫富，都深致其景仰的意思。英皇并且待以殊礼。从前英人对太谷儿是敬畏的，其待遇太谷儿是取监视态度的，那一年英人就由畏敬改为爱敬，由监视的态度改为联络的态度。他曾上书英政府，要英政府准印度自治，虽然没有达到目的，但感动了好些的英人。

以上是太谷儿的略传：这略传的结语，是祝创造的诗人太谷儿万岁！

以下是略传以外的闲谈，这闲谈也是和略传有关系的。本来我所读的太谷儿著作并不多，太谷儿的历史，我也不认楚，要说替太谷儿作传，我就只好说一声“岂敢！”不过新人社托我做篇传略已经四个月了，催稿的信也来了八九封了。我托人去买《太谷儿传》的原本，既还没有寄到，而参考资料，又只有一点点，所以只得将这些参考材料，凑拢起来，作了这么一篇《太谷儿略传》。但做了以后，自己看着实在对不起《新人》，对不起大诗人太谷儿，由是便又拉杂介绍一点有关太谷儿的事，做这略传的尾声：

（1）太谷儿最初的诗缘

太谷儿最初的诗缘，大概是结于五岁以前。那时候他就有要和自然结婚的意思。他住的地方，有一个很光明的窗，当保护他的人离他左右的时候，他的眼神，就从这窗内跳出窗外，在空中大游泳。他《新月集》里头题为“希望”的那一首诗，中间有“我的视线穿过未闭的窗子……”等语，题为“天文家”的那首诗，所说“当我们游戏窗外，母亲俯首和我们接吻……”等语，大抵都和太谷儿幼时的诗缘有关。又《迷途的鸟》那本书上，第一段就说小鸟飞集窗上，中间每间十来段，也有一些窗景布在那里，我们由此可以想见太谷儿的诗，和太谷儿幼时所对的一个窗子是有极大关系。窗子所以和太谷儿的诗有这极大的关系，自然因为窗子是屋外宇宙的介绍人，我们中国土语开一扇窗，就名为开一扇天，也有以开窗为别辟一天地的意思；不过中国人开窗虽晓得是别辟天地，但都不晓得神游这个天地，太谷儿就晓得游泳于这窗外的大宇宙，因游泳的结果，就结了未来的诗缘。

（2）太谷儿第一次和诗的接触

太谷儿五岁的时候，就和诗作第一次的接触，有一天早晨他读了“水溅”Jal Pawray 叶颤 Pata nawray 两短句，他对于这无声的水溅，幻想的叶颤，都有极深刻的感想。他曾说：“这是诗集感动我心的第一首诗，当我回忆到那不可言喻的愉快的时候，我同时就想着那些字句。我因此才发见音韵在诗的里面，确是重要的元素。因为声韵虽有尽，那字意却是长的。他的声响，引长他的意味。本来音韵的声响是在耳里延长，在心里颤动，我的心里那一天简直是整日的欣跃……”

（3）太谷儿开始学诗的时期

太谷儿七岁开始学诗的第一次，是他侄儿教的。所学的是十四缀音的诗。

（4）太谷儿与喜马拉耶山

太谷儿十一岁的时候，他父亲带他去喜马拉耶山，就从山中得了许多宇宙的秘蕴，好像我们中国的杜少陵一入四川，便将剑阁巫山的秘蕴抉发无遗，以充他自己的诗料。现在太谷儿所有意境奇突的诗，就像那世界第一高山喜马拉耶。

（5）太谷儿与帕德玛河

太谷儿三十岁以至四十岁，差不多天天和帕德玛河接吻，河的真美，几乎被他吸收了一大半。太谷儿生平著作，十篇中间总有八篇写河，就为着与这河近的缘故。他生平说河的话最多：——像“河水流过黑暗的夜，好像是一部天然的音乐。”“河在生命之晨，且歌且逝，入于大静寂之中。”“河对儿童歌舞，”“河对岸说：你守我是无用的，我是守不住的。”……等等，都以河为著作的重要材料。

（6）太谷儿与“静寂”

太谷儿极喜欢“静寂”，他以为“静寂”中有美丽，和平，音乐等等。他常常于静寂中和“自然”握手，说“静寂”中的意境是愉快到不可思议的意境；但他虽极端喜欢“静寂，”却也不反对“喧闹，”因为“喧闹”是能替“静寂”加冕的人。如果没有“喧闹，”便显不出“静寂”的佳处，没有“大喧闹，”便显不出“大静寂”的佳处。——好像飘风，骤雨的反衬晴和。

（7）太谷儿与音乐

太谷儿对于音乐的观念，是很精确的。他说，“谐和”是从两不平中间发生的。音乐的声调所以有最高音和最低音，就是预备产出“谐和。”他对于诗的音韵，也抱这种观念。

（8）太戈尔的“权利”“爱情”比较观

太谷儿对于“权力”非常憎厌，对于“爱情”非常赞美。他在《迷途之鸟》那本书上曾说：“权力对世界说，‘你是我的。’世界便坐伊的王位，将权力当奴隶。爱情对世界说‘我是你的。’世界便将自由给爱情。”

（9）太谷儿的教育理想

太谷儿的教育理想，是将儿童训练使他成人，而又将成人训练使他成为儿童。肉体求其老成，精神求其幼稚。他所办的生铁那克当学校里，现在已能够实现他的理想了：那里走出来的学生，体魄都强健异常，神情却都像一个小孩子。

（10）太谷儿与“东方文化”

太谷儿在《人生的实现》那本书上，曾证明印度的文化，是从树林发生，这生于树林的文化，是自然的，完全的。他同时反对欧洲的城市文化，以为是反乎自然，而又不完全的。所以日本有些人，就将太谷儿名为“东方文化主张者。”

青青一九二零年，十二月，三日，草于杭州。

——《新人》，1921 年第 1 卷第 7～8 期

读太戈尔《生命之实现》的笔记

柳钟文

太戈尔的诗文，都富有生命的意味，“真”与“美”都赤裸裸的流露出来，使读者自然的能得一度的美感，受一次的灵洗，鼓舞自己生命的弦，与他相和谐而奏那自然的爱歌，更使小己拥怀着大我，在里面成了永生的泉源，直涌到欢乐。所以人都称为“诗圣”“诗哲”。印度有一医生说：“我每日都读太戈尔的诗，只读了一行，一切世界烦恼就都消灭了”。我也常感受这种的愉快，每读他的《生命之实现》，或报纸上刊的他的译诗，便不知不觉的由私欲里解放出来。

《生命之实现》一书，是太氏精神的结晶，他本着《大经典》的思想，以“进化论”的新解释，发挥印度的新精神，而建立“生命哲学”“爱的福音”。太氏曾以这部书得过诺贝尔的奖金，号称东方主义之第一人；其书有研究的价值，无须赘言了。全书共八章：（一）个人与宇宙的关系；（二）灵魂意识；（三）恶的问题；（四）自我的问题；（五）爱里的实现；（六）活动里的实现；（七）美的实现；（八）无限的实现。[1]其词意甚为妙达，——多述他对于生命的了解及爱的真谛。——且富有诗趣，如《爱里的实现》一段说：

花似一个由我们伟大情人那里来的使者。

我们被……外界繁华傲慢的精神，用蛊惑的手段来……逼我们做他的新妇。

正在危急的时刻，这花由对岸衔着消息而来，对着我们的耳边低声说道：“我来了。他遣我来了。我是美的使者，他的灵魂就是爱情的天福。

那孤立的岛他已经架通了桥梁，他没忘记你，现在还要救你。

他将要偕你们到他那里，做他自己的新妇。

这个幻像永不在束缚里牵制你们了。”

这正是一首美的诗；这样的文字，里面很多。但是太氏的学说，不是他自己的创见；不过是发挥《大经典》的思想而光大之，以中兴沉沦已久的印度精神，所以要研究太氏的哲学，必须先研究印度的经典，才能摸着首尾。但是我不但没读过佛经，没研究过印度的哲学；就是任何哲学我亦没研究过；就是“哲学”二字的意义（Definition）我也不懂，何敢谈太戈尔的哲学呢！不过我读太氏的书，不以哲学的解释去研究他，更不以文学的方式去治理他；乃是依他对于我的心理，我的思想的关切，去读他。所以我的笔记，也是随读随录的。

（一）个人与宇宙的关系

生命是什么？怎样的活生命？人生的目的是什么？这几个问题从早

[1] 本文只介绍了《生命之实现》第一部分，即“个人与宇宙的关系”。

就在我脑海里盘旋，经过好多的酝酿，总没得着彻底的解决。虽然有时观察他人活的生命，也是莫名其妙，只能见出他们的结果，不明白他们的根原就有的略知道一点，但是不十分满意于他们的，于是也就不发生什么效力了。既至察考《圣经》(Bible)，从耶稣基督活他的生命中的，得了一种特殊的感想就是：耶稣基督整天的忙，时时的奋斗，并不愿环境的支配，潮流的魔力，前途的困难，自身的危险，总是往前顶，勇进的去活他的生命，并且也觉得他活很有意义，很有兴趣。回到自身，自己爱慕的了不得；但是再一想人的精力有限，若是整天的忙，时时的奋斗，最易疲倦；将来，感受的苦痛，更较深重，于是自己就自馁不能勇进的去活了。虽然，切心爱慕这种勇进去活的生命，但因为误解生命不明白生命的真意义，所以，也就不敢去实现了。对基督的生命，虽觉得生命的美妙，然不知他的所以然，就“特殊”二字把他放下了。

但是我所以如此的麻木，就是因为不了解生命是什么，人生的目的是什么呀！并且，我想世界的罪恶日深，生命的沉沦日多，就是不能了解生命的结果！实在在这物欲魔力之下，物质范围之中，有谁能真了解生命？又有谁了解了生命，肯背着环境，逆着潮流去活呢？

我现在所记的是个人与宇宙的关系：

个人与宇宙的关系，是了解人生第一步要了解的；但是从物质的文明——城垣的文化侵入于人类的心灵中，对于这种关系，就生出强固的积疑。人与宇宙中间竖立屏障的高墙，造成一种绝高的隔离，把美妙的生命只缩限于物质的范围里。生活也就脱离了有最亲切最亲近，赖之得丰富衣食的自然；而趋于征服自然，去劫夺我们所需要的。但是有人以为自然的生活，能降低生存的程度，或至蒙蔽人类的智能，并减少进步的阻力，在天演的淘汰中，势难实现的。但是太氏说：

我们晓得森林生活的境况，并不是要征服人的心灵，也不是孱弱他内心之流动，只是给一种特殊的趋向。因为时常同自然的长相接触，人的心意，便由要建立疆界于他所占得的地之周围，而扩张领土的欲望，释放出来。

诚然，人当处于城垣之中，整天惟与红尘相接触，所见的不过是井天，所闻的不过人赖而所知的形形色色，更是以遏阻意识的扩张，设使至一山清水秀的所在，或充满自然的，林野与自然相接触，即得着一种美的炙感，前有的欲望，全行消灭了，觉得万物都充满了生命，而对于自己的生命，又是一种观念。因为人与自然的和谐呀！

太戈尔的主义以个人与宇宙的和谐，是一最大的真理；也是一件可能的事实。他说：

我们和自然和谐是一件大事实，因人和万物相和谐，他才能思想；人能为他自己的目的去运用自然能力，也不过他自己的能力与宇宙的能力相和谐罢了，因此他的目的永不至与宇宙的和谐相冲突。

但是人总是闭着他的精神的眼睛，不能领会宇宙无尽的意识，用广大欢乐与和平的情感，去实现这大和谐。人之所以这样的盲目，就是因他不了解人生的意义，只是被科学的知识，物质的利益所逼迫；不能超越牢狱的墙堵，去解放自己，获得完满的真。

太氏说人同世界的认识若不有比科学所引导的更深切，终不会明白有精神视力的人，在这些自然的现象所导出的东西是什么。水不只是清洁人的四肢，且澄清人的心；因水能接触到他的灵魂。地不过是载人的身体，且舒快人的心灵；因地和人相接触是远过于物质的接触——这是一种活动的态度。当一个人不能使他同世界的亲谊实现时，他简直是住在牢狱里，牢狱的墙，隔绝着他。当他过着万物里的永久精神时，于是他就解放了，因为那时他发现他所生存的世界之完全意味；那时他于完满的真之中，［按太氏所说之，真是包罗万有的，没有绝对的隔离（Absolute Isolation）的东西可以存在的。］寻着他自身了，而且他同万物的和谐也就成立了。在印度的人是像有所命的完全觉悟到这种事实，就是他们和周围的万物，无论物质和灵魂方面，都有亲密的关系，他们祝贺早晨之太阳，流动之水，结果之地，好像是同样活动的真的表现，这真拥抱他们在怀抱里。

由这一段也足证明出耶稣基督的生命所以活的那样的有力了。所以人不联合外来无限的能力，总难解脱。

太氏说：

离开自然的无穷生活时；当我们变为纯粹的个人，而非宇宙中人时，我们就造成了困惑的问题，连这些问题解决的源头也断绝了，我们只能试用人工各种的方法，结果便生出了无限的困难。

人类必须在无限里，实现它生存的全部和他的地位；他必须知道他无论如何勤勉。终不能在蜂房里，造出蜜来，因为他生活的食物的供给是从墙外来的。他必须知道当他与无限之活动的纯洁的接触隔离，退而求他自己的维持和调解时，他必至激刺自身而至于疯狂，将自身裂为碎片而且吃他自己的物质。所以我们必须实现自我于自然之中求得生命之粮于无限之库藏。倘若人自限人类，自拘于物质能力去维持和调解，势必至于永不能达到无限，他的生命永在饥渴的岸边，因为，人的生命是要活于无限的灵海里，不在乎体外的浸润，而在乎内部的溶融。人若只求体外的浸润而不愿其内部之枯，他的生命必随之消亡。耶稣说过："人若赚得全世界，失掉自己的生命，有什么益处呢？"由此可见人的生命决不在乎物质的世界内。然现代的文明仍不能解脱出这种圈套，但是，以他所有的组织能力，正正试使人民的体育，智育，德育三种尽量发达。用国家最大的力去扩张人的权力，使超越他的环境，而且人们也都是联合，引申各种的效能，去占他们所能染指的东西，并克服在战胜路上的各种障碍物。他们是永远训练自身去战胜自然和非同种；他们的军备日新月异，使人惊吓；他们的机械，器具，和他们的组织加增到可怕的速率。

但是这决不是人类最后的目的与成功，人类最后的目的与成功是要做到人类的代表——感灵者（利希 Rishis）。

感灵者为何？他们在知识里得到最高的灵魂，一身充满了智慧，在宇的大灵的联合里，内部的自我是完全和谐的；他们实现这最高的灵魂于心中，由一切自私的欲望解放出来，又晓得这大灵是常在于世界各种活动之中，故能得静寂的境地。感灵者是由各方面而达于最高之神，获得常在的和平，与万物和合为一体，走入宇宙生命之中。

因为人之所以伟大，是在乎他的灵魂了解万物；不在乎能破坏，劫夺，赚钱，储蓄，创造发明呀。

倘若他的灵魂封在恶习的死壳里，工作的盲目怒潮旋转于他们的四周，像狂风挟沙土弥漫于地平线，他就有可怕的毁灭了。这样就很能够残杀他的真精神——了解的精神。要之，人不是他自己的奴隶，也不是世界的奴隶，但他是一个情人。他的自由与成功都在情爱之中，这爱就是完全了解的别名。以这了解的能力，生存的透彻，他便同普遍的精神相联合，这精神也是他灵魂的呼吸。

感灵者是要实现人类同万物的关系，并由与神联合后而加入于万物的情形；所以《经典》说：达到人生目的人是“和平”“与神合为一体”意谓他们是在人和自然的完全和谐里，所以便能同神联合为一。

不论何物如果我们为自己储蓄的，便使我们同他人隔离了；我们的占有就是我们的限制。凡是只知积蓄，自私之念达于极点的人，必不能穿过精神世界的了解门户；他被关闭在他的有限所得物的狭窄围墙里。

因为

孳孳为利，实在是抛弃万物，只获得些微的东西，这不是达到完全的方法。

由此观之，太氏哲学之神髓，人生最终之目的，就是与神合一。但是这神决不是抽象的，如彼言：

我们似有所指示而知道世界中所有的东西，都是被上帝包封的。
我再三向水中火中，乃至收获中，古林中的神祈祷。

可知。神是无所不在的了，神是不与世界分开的了，神居于我们的灵魂上，神居于我们的生命中，我们在神的精神里是充满了乐，正如释迦说："不论动静隐愿，在波罗门——梵——神——的精神，都有你们欢乐。"

那精神是什么?《经典》上说："凡人在他的本质内是光明，和万物的生命又是世界觉悟的，就是波罗门——梵——神"觉悟万物就是他的精神。我们是沉浸在他的意识——精神里。太阳吸引地球是由于他的意识；光波在这行星到那行星转动，也是由于他的意识。

但是

要获得世界的悟，必须以我们的情感，和浩瀚万物无限的情感相联合。其实，人类真正唯一的进步。就是和广浩的情感范围相一致。……虽然，我们必须付那得到意识自由的代价。代价是什么？就是把个人的自身撇开。我们的灵魂，只有由于否认他自身，才能够使自身真实。《经典》上说："你要得，必先弃，你不可贪。"耶稣也说："爱惜自己生命的，就是失丧生命，凡为我丧掉生命的必保持生命到永生。"所以人要完全了解万物的真实，必须跳出私欲的圈子，渐渐地去扩充个同万物相一致的意识去实现。

《经典》上说："至高的神是浩瀚一切的，所以在万物里他是天生的善良。"真实地在知识里，情爱里，服务里，和万物相联合，实现个人自身于浩瀚一切的神中，就是善良的精义，而且《经典》教训的本旨是：

"生命是至大的。"

总之，太氏之意思以个人与宇宙不容顷刻相隔离的，个人如与宇宙相隔离，必不至于穷困；所以我们必须由自我的有限里，解放出来与万物相和谐，与神合一，以实现真实意识……精神的生命。

——《南开周刊》，第 29 期，30 期，31 期，1922 年 2 月 28 日，3 月 10 日，3 月 15 日

对于太戈尔来华的感言

柳钟文

太戈尔来华的声浪，吹到我们的耳里已经好久。我们素日敬爱他的人，都已竖着耳朵，瞪着眼睛，站在东海的岸上，候着听他的足音，望他的来影，预备欢迎这位“不速之客”。近来国内的出版界也都争先恐后的出了几本刊物介绍他；至于他们所介绍的是否真纯，不是我在这里所要讨论的；我现在要说的只是我对于他来华的几句感言。

现在国内的学者对于太戈尔来华多半是持着欢迎的态度；独树一帜的只有《创造周报》发表的郭沫若君的《太戈尔来华的我见》一文。郭君说：“太戈尔如以私人的意志而来华游历，我们由衷欢迎；但他是被邀请来华，我们对招致者便不免要多所饶舌。”由此可知，郭君对于太戈尔这次以公的意义来华，他是不赞成的。但是郭君的意见很可以给欢迎太氏的人们一个提醒，就是我们请太戈尔来，是否“是因为他是东方的诗人?”是否“是出于一种爱地方的私情?”更是否“是他是得过诺贝尔赏金，是英国的爵士，是世界的诗人，是近时欧西所欢迎的说教者，我们是出于一种慕名冲动?”若是为这种缘故——慕名的冲动，那最好是我们快关上门，或是另换换方向，去欢迎那位轰动全球的英国的乔治首相，勿须站在东海岸上候这位乔治首相治下的亡国奴；因为他，也是不来受你亵渎的！如果是为介绍学术，进展文化，所以才要太戈尔来华，那末，我们是否仍袭着以前的“杜威去了罗素来，罗素去了杜里舒来，来的时候哄动一时，就好像乡下人办神会，抬起神像走街的一样热闹。但是神像回宫去了，他们留给我们的是些什么呢?”——杜威罗素杜里舒等留给我们的是些什么，或是他们对于我们近来文化上的影响，我不能说定，不过我总不信“可怜只有几张诳鬼的符箓，抬神像的人倒因而得了不少的利益。”——如果仍是要这样，最好我们也回到新世界大罗天去看“一二三四五，金木水火土”的戏法，听那“乾隆爷下江南”的大鼓书。这位穿宽袍的印度人是不会凑热闹的。果真想抬起来他去赛会可以哄动一时，那是定会失败的。我们倒不若把我们先人的“天仙圣母”抬出来马路上走走，或者还可以哄动这沉睡的社会，跑出来看看。

所以郭君的话，很足以提醒我们欢迎太戈尔来华，好好持着这次的机会，别凑着热闹过去，为我们只留下几张诳鬼的符箓！

但是这里新发生了一较大较根本的问题："在我们凡百事情都是羊头狗肉的中国"，是否有请太戈尔来讲演的急需。在经济问题没解决的中国，是否有要这种唯心主义（注一）[1]来助我们解决国家世局的必需。

对于解决中国世局的问题，恐各人有各人的主张。陈独秀鼓吹热血的革命，吴佩孚迷信武力，胡适和梁任公努力文化的宣传，吴稚晖提倡科学救国：这是不可强而同之的。本来一个国家，或是一个社会所包括的极复杂，所需要的亦决不能只是一桩；而且现在我们国家社会问题的解决，更不是独一的供给——无论是科学，文学，物质的，精神的，——所能够奏效的。因为中国现在的病症，不特是外感，还有内伤；他的病因也自然不是一个——面包的缺少。——至于私产制度的束缚，固是死灭我们东洋的病症之一；但是我们中国致死的重要病症，还不在此，乃在乎精神上的饥荒，生命力的微弱呀！

中国是有精神文化的国家，我不信；我更不敢狂大自夸的说中国是世界最精神文化的国家！如果我们硬要靦然无耻的坐世界上精神文化国家中的一把交椅，那末我就要自不讳忌的作一个叛徒，问一问这位自认为是有精神文化国家的中国："你老，你的精神文化在那里，搁藏在什么地方？你有什么东西可以拿出来蒙蔽我这小孩子说'这是我的精神文化'呢？"我恐怕他老人家要羞红了脸儿，没有什么回答。或者他的孝子佳孙要出来代答说："我们有诸子百家。"但是诸子百家是些什么东西？诸子百家在历史上影响于中国的社会，又有多大？或者也有把我们的"至圣先师"请出来的。但是我们的"至圣先师"留给我们的精神文化又是些什么？——啊！可怜！可怜我们所谓的精神文化，只是些玄之又玄的空谈，出恭入敬的礼式！二千年来的大成功，只是制造了亿万数的狱囚牢徒似的病夫，机械盲动似的奴隶！这尚有什么精神文化之可言？实在如果我们有一点精神文化的活力蕴藏在我们的社会里，我们的社会也不至于这般的失了生

[1] 本文中保留原始资料的注释格式——编者注。

机！——没有活力的文化，算得什么精神文化？

我们这个没脑筋，没灵魂，没生命力的国家社会，是否只要唯物史观的见解所能解决了他的世局？固然我们信吃饱了才能干活，但是我们这失魂丧魄的民族，吃饱了不过是一群“身广体胖”的蠢物，盲动的机械！或是一般争霸称雄的强者！然而“文化的估定，不在乎势力扩张的量，乃在乎人类爱的表现的多少。所必须解答的第一问题和最后问题是视人类以灵性的多呢，还是以机械的多呢？古代文化的颓微而至于灭亡，都是由人心之酷刻，而卑视人类之价值。所以无论是国家或有权力的团体，以人为其权力的工具时，他的伟大的基础，自由平等的爱，即受了打击。文化他不能存在任何形式的残忍上（Cannibalism)，因为文化只能生育于人类的爱和正义里。”（注二）

所以在我们现在的中国的国家社会，决不能说我们只要得面包的方法，对于“为着不死的青春，不断的放弃其年龄，几次埋没，几次死亡，其人格不绝的近接宇宙，刻刻前进，时时更新其个性的生命，一步一步的触于宇宙之根本的统一。”（注三）这种求生命活力的教训，便拒绝了不要太戈尔所宣传的不特是爱的福音，是要人“起来活动”，“继续生活”，“生命对生命的呼声！”（注四）我们可以信太氏的来华能赈济些我们精神上的饥荒，至少也能给我们注意内部生命的一个提醒，决不至于“在大体上，给中国不过是更死沉一点。”（注五）

（注一）谟克吉（Dhan Mukokji）在《太戈尔的印度》一文中称太氏的思想是唯心主义。

（注二）参看太戈尔的《生之实现》的《爱里实现》一章。

（注三）《生之实现》的《自我问题》一章（冯译）。

（注四）参看太戈尔的《春之循环》。

（注五）夏来騣君给徐培德君的通信内说的，见《十日文报》第三期。

一九二三，十一，八。

——《南中半月刊》，第1卷第1期，1923年11月

太戈尔对于运命的拒绝

柳钟文

世界的民族中，较古的民族——指历史上的进化而言，大概都有“运命”的这种势力，存在他们中间巡游。这种势力，可以说是这民族活他们生命的凭山，也是他们处置生命的不二法门，我们试看世界较古的民族的历史上生命的表现——藉文字记载的，再亲自来调查他们承袭下来的遗产——风俗习惯，便可以明了运命的威力，在世界的民族中，成全了他的伟大。

虽然，运命成全了这样的伟大；运命她并不信她的自身有这股大的威力；因为我们察出她坐在世界民族的头上，很局促不安，显出她是意想不到的侥幸了成功。但是她胯下的人类倒为她大大的吹嘘，把他看得特别的着实了。于是世界较古的民族，他们背弃了他们自由生命，活动生命，发展生命的真神，去事奉他们手造的金牛犊——运命——（旧约出伊及第三十二章载以色列人见摩西迟延不下西乃山，他们要亚伦为他们作神像，铸了一只金牛犊。）他们遂污辱了上帝选民的资格。

但是在“运命之女神”治下领域的太戈尔，他实在有些胆大的揭竿了，他叛逆这位女神的宣言说：

“运命，如同莲花似的无常，
时候一到她便闭了厚情。
噫，愚人呀，你如何能信她，
她忽然而来又慌张而去的？”

“运命永远拒绝我们，我们也永远拒绝运命。我们到处走去，整天的导引青年于拒绝运命的神圣崇拜中。”（《春之循环》）

太氏以运命不过是无常的虚伪，刹那间的幻影，无可信仰的。但是生命是真实的，自由的，活动不息的，发展无限的；这样伟大的，如何要遏抑他的贵重，降低他的价值，俯伏于虚伪幻影的支配下，而陷入灭亡之门呢?

实在，运命不过是人类退缩的别门，自造的束缚镣铐罢了，啊，人类呀，运命治下的民族呀，快站起自己来，脱离那虚伪巫妇——运命——的胯下，揭开生命之幕，跑出到这生命运动、永久活动的游戏场来，跳舞着吹着笛儿走着高唱“拒绝运命”之歌。

“谁如运命似的推着我向前走呢?”

错了

“那是我自己在身背后大跨步走着。”(《迷途鸟》一七三)

——《南中半月刊》，第1卷第1期，1923年11月

太戈尔研究

刘寿祺

祷歌

我的生命底流失，
我未尝见其所终，
我知道，我的上帝，我很知道，
这并不是徒然无用。
刚开的花，
落于道中，
我知道我的上帝，我很知道，
花死并非无用。
江河乱流，
在无边的沙漠中，
我知道，我的上帝，我很知道。
水涸并非无用。
为这一切，在我底生命里，

迟延而且较远，
我知道，我的上帝，我很知道。
我等待着并非无用。
一切总不到来，
其声而无闻，
我知道，我的上帝，我很知道，
这都不是徒然无用。
因为一切无声的音正颤动着，
在一切神明的诗才底心中，
我知道，我的上帝，我很知道
他们并非突然的颤动。

——《新月集》

（一）太戈尔传略

太戈尔是印度当代一位大诗家——是世界一位极优美极玄妙的大诗家，是一个探窥宇宙之秘密的大哲学家，是一个厌恶侵掠，战争，极力鼓吹人道和平的健将，是“自然”的儿子，是人类救主，人类啊——静候救主，解脱一切苦难——太戈尔生于一千八百六十一年印度彭加尔地方，他的家庭是一个望族，世代出了许多哲学家和艺术家，就是他的父亲也是一个有大天才的人，曾到过法国当过梵语教授，时与法国的思想家接触，因此他的思想更添上西洋色彩，东西思想混合，后来便成为一个宗教改革大家。他的母亲丧得很早，他有七个兄弟，三个姊妹，他是他们中最小的一个。他很活泼敏捷，温和愉快，并赋有细腻的风光，自幼好诗，人都称为诗童。他母亲死后，他就受仆人的虐待，这也是养成他忧愁深思一个原因。他小时候未入学校以前，见他人入学校，他便要求他家里送他入学校，后来他既入了学校，又感觉学校生活专制，愈增苦闷，所以连入了几个学校，竟没有一个学校成功。有一次学校里的先生们以为他不可教育，竟使他休了学，因此家里的人都很轻视他，惟他的父亲还识得他的个性，不轻易去责他，也不使他再入学校，从此就跟他父亲到喜马拉雅山，去享受那真美的自然，发展他爱自然的天才；但不久又回到家里。这短短的期间，也可算是太戈尔思想萌芽之一段。

后来家里的人又使他到英国去学法律，这我们当然知道是不能的了，不到一年他就回到本国。他是喜欢自然生活，而憎恶机械生活的。他三十岁的时候，奉他父亲的命在沙来挞地方管理家产，住在帕德马江边。这个地方，风景极好，足以供太戈尔观察，探究，赏玩，促长他的思想。他又时与平民接触，于是除了自然大师以外，又添了许多农人作伴侣。他了解农人的痛苦，而与农人同过甘苦的生活，减轻农人的负担，于是众心所归，这个地方，只知太戈尔，而不知有政府。后他又办了一个山铁奈克当学校，他的教育，除了智育德育体育以外，还加上灵育，根据他那返“真”的原理，去求“美”的意志，成绩很好，社会都皆称许。后又加入在“光明团”，鼓吹印度独立，英政府竟允许印度自治。

一九一五年他到了日本，日本人皆欢迎，一九二十年又到美国，美国朝野迎接，一九二一又到德国，德国更表敬意。听说今年预备来中国，中国人谅必除欢迎之外，更有十二分尊敬啊。

（二）印度思想与太戈尔哲学

我们研究太戈尔哲学，必先要知道印度思想，因为太戈尔的哲学，很受了印度思想的影响，所以这里必须把印度思想说明一下，但古代印度思想，非常复杂，这里不能详细说明，只阐述其大干罢了。当纪元两千年前亚里安人（即今兴多族）由中央亚细亚侵入印度，赶去印度的土民，占领其地，那时亚里安人就奉了一种“美”和“自然”的原始宗教，这种宗教以天地万物为神的表现，尊奉自然，以欢喜去与自然接洽，他们在自己四周，及人和自然中都认发出无限的实在，并力求实在的表现，于是生一种纯美的情热的敬虔，诵爱一切，是为吠陀文学。由是则有婆罗门，再进而为佛教，婆罗门教的哲学就是从陀罗尼沙发生出来的。而乌婆尼婆度所说就是梵——神——宇宙人生之秘义，就是实现梵，求解脱，与自我之实现。

自乌婆尼婆度印度哲学日日勃兴，学派也就分歧成百余种，但其共同哲理，不外吠陀，以梵包围世界一切，个人之中为梵之存在，就是说大我与小我合一。太戈尔受了这种影响，亦以这种哲理去观察自然，可说太戈尔的哲学就是印度古代哲学，然而太戈尔与印度思想不同的地方，就是印度思想往往偏于消极，施为厌世悲观主义，否定人生，否定生活。太戈尔去玩味自然，一切生命，都活跃充满于宇宙，一切都表现一切喜爱，由喜爱而生出无限美妙与一切谐和而合一，就是实现梵——神——宇宙人生之秘义。总之太戈尔的哲学，不是否定人生的，并且爱人生而爱一切的，更力求实现人生实现一切的。

（三）太戈尔思想之产生

上面说太戈尔的哲学是受了印度思想的影响，但是千万的印度人，为什么独太戈尔能在印度思想上树一帜呢？这里我们不须明白太戈尔所以如此者，是他的环境关系。我们已知道他的家庭是一个望族，世代有许多哲学家和艺术家。他的父亲又是大思想家和宗教改革家，在这一点，我们可以看出他所处的优美环境，能造成他伟大的思想。这是他思想产生一个原因。最要紧的，就是他的父亲德氏他自己是一个思想家，而培养太戈尔思想的地方很多。现在可以把他的思想说一下。他的思想也受了印度古代的思想影响，他的哲理还是脱不了乌婆尼娑度哲学，抛弃小我，脱离小我，将属于神的东西一切忘却，去掉一切物质的欲贪，去求梵——神。即是抛弃小我以实现无限生命，所以他舍去自己一生的富贵，抛弃一生的荣达，去实现神人合一的真实境界。而德氏底思想中不同于印度思想的，就是不崇拜偶像，他以为人类的心灵和自然——神直接合一，在一种不可思议的神秘的现象里。完成我们“新生”之人，这就是德氏思想的特点，德氏因为要求“新生”，所以就带他的儿子太戈尔到喜马拉雅山去过观照生活，他们父子一到喜马拉雅山，那些无尽的“美”和“真”都凝集在他们的心里，他们心内藏着无限的欢喜，神的“意志”与他们的“意志”互相调和，实现他们的“新生”。太戈尔承继他父亲德氏的思想的哲理，在这“新生”的意义中，力求这个“新生”的实现，发掘求“新生”的路，指示人类求“新生”方向，这就是太戈尔哲学所以的产生一个大标点。

（四）太戈尔的人生观与宇宙观

宇宙间充满的是生命，而创造生命，实现生命的就是“爱”。换转来说：“爱”就是造化宇宙者——就是神——就是宇宙之实现。人类不能脱离宇宙——自然——而孤立，人类与宇宙之间就是必须有一大调和，即人类之灵与宇宙之灵必须合一。宇宙之灵在自己生命中实现，自己生命在宇宙中实现。两者互相抱拥相互交通，以求统一。人类若不知道自己和宇宙之关系，那就断不能实现自己，得唯一存在的一个东西。或如西洋人仇视自然，以人类底力去征服自然，那就是自造牢狱，灭亡无日了。因为宇宙万物莫不有永远的意志，如此，人和宇宙——自然——开了无大的战争，无论怎样，人类终归失败。人类逃不脱宇宙，这就是一个证据。我们人类的目的是从灿烂光华路上，步进庄严境界，去实现无限。在灵魂上能悟出一切之一点，在这一点上能认出神的姿态来，去求万有合一，就是宇宙根本统一。我们知道宇宙有根本统一，宇宙是不断的创新，而宇宙间的生命也不断的创新，人类的生死也是创新的路径，生死就是人类出没的表现，我们只要与梵天接触了解神，我觉得人类一切死都不可怖，并且无怖之必要。因为死即是生之一段，而生是伟大的，无限的，无穷的，永远的，如海中波浪一样，现又灭，灭又现，然而永久生命无增无减。又如木一样，春发而冬枯，发即生，枯即死，生死皆是完成生命，又如枯木变为炭变为灰变为泥，我们可说是死，但在此种变之经过，又何尝不是生呢。由此可见一方面生一方面死，“生即死，死即生”，不断的死，不断的生，生生死死，就是无限之实现。

（五）太戈尔善恶之评判

我们知道太戈尔对善恶的评判，必须知道他所取的几点：上面说过，宇宙一切不断地创新，时时是老，又时时是新，善恶的问题，就在此“老新”之间上产出，怎样产生在这中间？因为善恶不是绝对的，换一句话说：就是恶没有永远存在的根据，不过在“老新”之间一种经过影子罢了。善恶之成为问题；就是完全与不完全之分，完全为善，不完全为恶。恶为假相，善为真相，如小我为假象，而与宇宙生命融合之大为真相，小我表现不完全，大我表现完全，即小我为恶，大我为善，善恶不过是一物之两面罢了。我们平常在世界上感觉无数恶的存在，这是我们没有看到恶的成因，把恶看做一个绝对固定停滞的东西。我们知道恶是产生于“老新”之间，那末恶也要跟着进化，在不完全的时候，向着完全路上走，就是未走到善的时候，就是恶。恶是指示人向善一个符号。如船，其首有缆为引，不绝的前进，而缆决不是船的究竟，只是使向究竟地方走。又如小孩，在没有成人的时候，他仿效走路，必经多次跌倒，但终能行走如意，可知失败就是成功的基础，恶就是善的路径了，由此可以看出恶绝不能防止善之前进，而助善之成功，所以我们不必对着世界罪恶抱什么悲观。善恶之分不过一件物之两面罢了，世界上没有绝对的恶，恶之中所含的也许是善。关于恶我们说明白了，善到底怎样的呢？善就是全体的生，就是宇宙的大生命，就是梵，就是神，就是包含人类善恶一切究竟和绝对的东西。就是灵魂上之至微一点，我们能认出这一点：这就是善。

（六）太戈尔爱之实现

太戈尔的哲学可以用“爱”字来概括，人类的自我，皆由神之爱而生。佛陀以超越小我，返于神之爱，即宇宙万物都是神之爱，与神分离，把这爱的分离返于神返于神之爱，这就是我们的自我返于神之自我中，这就是人生的实现。人类理解悟出一切完成自由，就必离不却爱。宇宙间由爱而创造，被爱所维持，向爱而转动，以入于无限之爱之实现。如缺乏爱，与爱互相倾轧的人，就失了人类存在的价值，因为人类的灵魂——最终的目的，——要与宇宙相接，宇宙被爱所抱拥，我们当然在爱里找我们的永远的真见解了。

我们四围和上下都含有无量数的爱。在一切生物中都能用着我们的爱以求他的爱互相合一以求实现，更推广之无限。那时我们在爱里的，有限和无限都皆合一，大我与小我都皆调和，而缚束与自由亦不矛盾。我的灵魂与宇宙接合为一，而宇宙的灵魂与无上之爱合而为一,一切合一，以实现无限之爱。

（七）太戈尔的艺术论

太戈尔把艺术的解释，说得很明白，他以艺术就是人格的表现，而艺术又为人类所独有的，人与禽兽不同的地方，就在人类除了适于生存之外，有过胜的能力和知识，可以自由享用，而禽兽的一生就尽消磨于生存竞争里面，所以人类是有余胜知识的动物，就是有创造艺术的能力，而艺术的表现就是一种情感的流露，所以艺术的发生，就是从人类情感和人格里濡浸出来的。换一句话说：艺术就是人格和感情的表现。

人类既产生艺术，到底艺术有何做用？这句话很难说明；因为我们要问艺术的作用，而艺术的作用就失掉了。我们在创造艺术的时候，并不问艺术的效用，到成功之后自然有他的真价值存在，这价值建筑在我们的精神上，使感觉到无限的愉快，这就是艺术的效用，就是艺术的最后的目的。所以人类欲求高尚的精神，建筑真美的生活和真实的世界，就不能不藉着艺术的功用了。但这说来：我们不是被艺术指导，受艺术的熏陶？这我们要知道：艺术并不是指导的教训的，又如宗教样的劝告的命令的，艺术是使人类快乐，从无意识界里达到至尊的境界，解脱一切，得到精神的自由和快乐。在这里千万不要误会，艺术就是供通常人的娱乐的，那就不是真正艺术了。所谓艺术者，必超乎时间空间，在无限里与心灵接合的一点。

（八）太戈尔之著作

太戈尔的作品，被世界各国翻译的很多。世界人无论那一个读他的作品，总要得着许多安慰，无论怎样烦闷忧愁的青年或老人一读他的著作，烦闷忧愁立刻可以消去，而忘物我一切，这可见太戈尔的作品艺术的功夫了。但我既不读梵语，英文程度也不好不得读他的原著，所读的不过已译为中文的。现在只好暂把他已译为中文的分三种说一下。

1. 诗

太戈尔的诗有飞鸟集，新月集等，其散见各杂志者甚多，现在我们把新月集中提一首出来说一说：

在无穷世界底海滨，孩子们集会着。

无穷的天空是在顶上不动的，不宁静的水却狂动着。在无穷世界底海滨上，孩子们叫跳着相会。

他们用砂来造他们房子，他们用空蚌壳儿玩耍，用枯叶儿编他们的船，还笑嘻嘻的把来放在广大的海上。孩子们有他们的玩耍在世界底海滨。

他们不知道怎样游泳，他们不知道怎么投网。取真珠的都为着真珠下水，商人都在他们船里航行，那时候孩子们把些小圆石儿堆集，再把来拆散。他们不搜寻隐藏着的宝物，他们不知道怎么投网。

海笑着起了大浪，海边底微笑发青白色的光。致死的波浪唱着没有意思的小曲儿向着孩子们，恰好像一个母亲在摇着她宝宝底摇篮一样。海同孩子们玩耍着，海边底微笑青白色的光。

在无穷世界底海滨，孩子们集会着。暴风雨回走在没有道儿的天空，船都破在没有轨路的水上，死在泛滥，孩子们却玩耍着。在无穷世界底海滨上，是孩子们底大集会。

——《在海滨上》

我们读了这首诗，大概可以看出太戈尔的宇宙观和人生观来，无穷的世界，我们人类——孩子们，都是集会在这无限的海滨上，使我觉着无限的慨感和愉快，在第三段里写及人类的罪恶，在第五段又写及人类的恐怖，只有孩子们天真烂漫，无所谓罪恶，无所谓恐怖，安妥地在这无限的海滨上玩耍，跳舞。他用小孩儿玩耍的故事，写出宇宙的神秘，这是何等的伟大的艺术啊！

2. 小说

小说译成中文的有邮政长，喜兆，芳邻，尊严之夜，黄云，命运，河阶，归家等篇，现在就把归家这篇提出来说：这篇是描写一个失爱的孩子，在将成人未成人的时候的悲哀，又写到母子天然的爱。他取材就是两个小孩为着游戏而生问，后来就引到无限的失爱与爱上去了。我们读这篇小说，知道巴的克却克拉华谛是候美罕的兄，他们在河旁为着游戏相打，引起他母亲的评判，她母亲因为巴的却克平素顽皮，有点袒护美罕。美罕因为要顾自己的面子，就不得不说谎，而巴的克听着忍耐不住，冲到美罕身边拖打美罕。这一节里我们可看出太戈尔描写个性，竟不亚于中国的水浒。正在这件相争的事发生，而巴的克的舅父恰好来到，谈及巴的克的教育，后来巴的克同他舅父到加儿答受教育，当去的时候，巴的克将他的游戏器具都赠给美罕，并表示无限的慷慨。在这一节里我们看了生出莫可言说的感情，觉得小孩天真烂漫，那纯洁的心丝毫没有成人的习气。描写的动人，正像中国红楼梦。最后描写巴的克受舅母的虐待，及巴的克离家的痛苦，在病里逃离回家去，仿佛中犹忆起故乡，后来病势更重，舅父接他母亲来，巴的克还问，假期到了，可以归了。这一节里我们看了是怎样的一件可怜的事。失爱的小孩子太戈尔，是你们永远不能忘却的爱人啊！总之太戈尔的小说，我读了非常感动，不但艺术完全，而指示我们宇宙神秘的处所也不少，我希望大家去研究研究，以认识宇宙一切真美。

3. 戏剧

戏剧有春之循环，暗室之王等。暗室之王这篇戏剧，就是他求神的道理和方法，他以王喻神，稣马卡玛和老父是知神的人。王妃维答霞娜等，用尽许多方法和精力去求见神，终归失败，竟至生出无限危险和痛苦。后来他们知道前一切办法不能，非抱着牺牲决心和虔诚意志不可，于是坚决志愿，忘却一切危险，结果终到神之所在。这篇剧可算太戈尔的哲学剧，完全是表现他的哲学的，我们读了觉得人类应当抛弃小我，去求无限向上的大我之实现，即实现我们的真生命。

我们对于太戈尔的著作，大概已经知道一点了，我们要注意的就是著作中处处含有他的哲学，我们要读他的作品，必从他的哲学着眼，才能领悟到深奥的处所。不然恐怕读了乏味咧！

（九）结论

前面关于太戈尔的各方面都说了一个大概，自己看浅近得狠，算不得什么“有所得”，加至功课甚忙，不能多备参考，错误之处在所不免，望诸位读者原谅，我做这篇的原意，只是把太戈尔介绍于诸位，将来太戈尔来华，再做进一层的研究罢了。

——《大公报》，1923 年 6 月 11 日，8 日，25 日，7 月 2 日

Tagore as Novelist

The Wreck by Rabindranath Tagore

Macmillan. 8s.6d.net.

The ordinary English reader must put himself into a certain mood if he is to enjoy this novel. By the ordinary English reader we mean one who knows India only by hearsay and who has not even been well broken in by a course of Tagore the poet to submit to Tagore the novelist. But probably that ordinary person does not put himself into the mood: it is the book that does that, or fails with him utterly. The present reviewer confesses to being no worshipper of Tagore, though interested afar off. But the queer, slow distant charm of this story in not to be resisted. There are moments when the distance becomes too great; and the whole thing is blurred our fault; not Tagore's, do we ever know this people of such different race? Not really, but we recognize here and there the common root of them and ourselves, or, unrecognizing, are glad of the difference. It is a restful book to drift through, though we felt it too long. It has a queer plot. Two bridegrooms neither of whom had seen his bride, were wrecked as they sailed down the river on the bridal night. Afterwards Ramesh, the English-taught lawyer, imagined pretty Kamala to be his wife, whereas — but "whereas" is the story, which is so slowly unfolded, with glimpses of quiet poetic beauty, and charming touches of tenderness and gentle human affections. Strange and remote it all is, but curiously healing in its remoteness if one happens to be tired by fiction that is too near and actual.

— *The North-China Daily News*, Jun. 18, 1921.

Rabindranath Tagore: His Tour on the Continent: the East's Message to the West

I have had a most interesting chat with Mr. S.R. Bomanji, an accomplished Parsee gentleman well known in London, who has just returned from a two months' tour among the chief capitals of the Continent as the companion and coadjutor of Sir Rabindranath Tagore, Indian philosopher and poet, and Nobel Prizeman (an "Observer" correspondent writes). The object of this tour was to enlist the sympathy and cooperation of the intellectuals of Europe — a crusade supplementary to a previous one by the same Bengali "Peter the Hermit" in America — for the establishment of an "International University" at Bolpur, in India, where Dr. Tagore, for the last twenty years, has conducted an open-air school on the Platonic or "groves of Academe" model — a University intended, in brief, to act as a sort of "clearing house" for the intellectual treasures of East and West.

The philosopher-poet and his Parsee companion visited in turn France, Switzerland, Germany, Denmark, Sweden, Austria, and Czech-Slovakia and everywhere received a most enthusiastic welcome.

But it was in Germany that the pilgrimage achieved its most striking triumph. Wherever Dr. Tagore stayed people flocked to his hotel with gifts of flowers. When his train stopped at stations the people gathered round his carriage. His public meetings were attended by many thousands, and almost as many more had to be turned away. He was asked for this autograph so often that he was sometimes unable to continue writing from sheer exhaustion of hand.

Dr. Tagore's Message

The message delivered by Dr. Tagore in his lectures (said Mr. Bomanji) was one of harmony and peace. He strove to show that the Indian way of life, thought, and religion was not one of war. The materialistic civilization of the West had found its fruition in militarism and imperialism — both radically the same; but what the war-worn world now needed was the spirituality and mysticism of the East, which could alone give lasting peace. The peace of the West was no real peace. As expressed in the Treaty of Versailles it was not worth the paper written on.

To rise superior to the nationalism of the West, which was barbarism and cannibalism, the peoples must find spiritual unity with Nature and with the life of God in all humanity. Hitherto the West had gone to the East merely to exploit its material resources; whereas Dr. Tagore now invited minds to the East to acquire all that was best there of Eastern culture, and in return to offer all the intellectual fruits of the West.

No Hatred of England

"It was touching to observe," remarked Mr. Bomanji, "how the people of Europe, intellectuals and popular masses alike, responded this appeal. The Germans, in particular, drank it in as though it were the great new gospel for which they had been thirsting," "We found," he continued, "that there was now no bitterness against or hatred of England, such as found original expression in Lisauer's notorious 'Hymn,' but the German people cannot forgive the policy pursued by the Allies since the Armistice — a policy, however, for which they believe France to be mainly responsible. We came into contact with and were entertained by all sorts and conditions of Germans — federal Princes and Professors, and industrial magnates like Hugo Stinnes, and the Principal of the Berlin University, who treated us to a banquet in the Aula, or Senate Hall.

"At Darmstadt we were most kindly entertained for a whole week by the Grand Duke and Duchess of Hesse, grandson of Queen Victoria, and first cousin of the ex-Kaiser, whose guests included Prince August William, one of the ex-Kaiser's sons, as well as his youngest sister Margaret and her husband. Prince Frederick Charles of Hesse-Cassel (that was), and they all spoke to us about the causes and consequences of the war with frankness which it would be unbecoming and indiscreet of me to speak in detail."

Princess Bismarck

"One of our most memorable experience was a day spent at Freidrichsruhe near Hamburg, with the Dowager Princess Bismarck half-English by origin, and a most intellectual type of woman, beloved, not to say adored, by her three sons, the eldest of whom, Bismarck Ⅲ — maned Archibald after Lord Rosebery, a great friend of her father — while the second seems to have inherited much of the character of his grandfather. Pointing to the chair in which Bismark I used to sit, the Princess repeated much of the pessimist prophecy indulged in by the Iron Chancellor when speaking of William Ⅱ, and as repeated in the lately published third volume of his memories."

"We came into contact with no Germans, high or low, who did not admit that in plunging Europe into war the ex-Kaiser committed a fearful blunder due to his vanity, his megalomania, his instability and his sentimentality. Believed by Europe to be an autocrat they said he really was a ruler without any real will of his own. At the last moment he allowed his will, as so often before, to be over-ruled by the military caste, the General Staff, and in fact he never knew what it was to have a will of his own."

— *The North-China Daily New*, Aug. 23, 1921

The Teaching of Sir Rabindranath Tagore

胡哲谋

Tagore is coming to visit us! By the time this issue of our magazine is in our readers' hands, the greatest living poet of the East — nay, of the whole world — will have safely landed in one of the busiest intellectual centers in China, and will be eagerly welcomed by many thousands of enthusiastic admirers of his works. Many magazines will be putting out their special Tagore numbers, telling about the story of his life, reviewing his works, or otherwise featuring him for the benefit of their readers. It would seem strange if we should be silent about him, for the English-speaking public in China has naturally a greater claim to know him and to talk about his writings. But before we proceed to give some account of his life and works, we must ask ourselves these questions — How far do we understand his teaching, and how are we worthy of his visit?

No poet is a great poet if he is not a great moral teacher. World worth, Browning, and many other poets have each a great message for us, through which they have attained their ever-lasting fame. So has Tagore. But the teaching of Tagore cannot be summarized in a few sentences. Like other great poets, too, he does not wish to give us the bare truth, but prefers to clothe it in the many-colored robe of his poetry. It is with the language of his soul that he generally addresses his message to us, and it must be with our souls, also, that we understand him. “Gitanjali”, “Fruit Gathering”, “The Gardener”, “Sacrifice and Other Plays”, “Chitra”, “The Crescent Moon” — these and other volumes of his plays and poems must be thoroughly chewed and digested, experienced and assimilated by our inner consciousness, before we can form some correct idea of his central ethical teaching. In these books, we are sometimes inspired by his high ideal of culture, sometimes by the strength and purity of his faith, sometimes by his appreciation of natural beauty, and sometimes by his understanding of the feminine soul and the soul of the child; but his central message is the sum total of all these inspirations. To extract any individual poem or play from the body of his works, and hole it up as representing his teaching in general, would be pitiably inappropriate as it is ridiculous. Our readers must go to those works themselves, if they wish to have a real understanding of the poet, and not merely to have a shallow acquaintance with him.

Happily, however, Tagore is not only a great poet, but also a great prose writer. His central ethical teaching, to be gathered with some difficulty from the great body of his poetical works, is clearly revealed in his prose writings, in his essays and lectures, collected under such titles as “Nationalism”, “Personality, “Creative Unity” and “Sadhana: The Realization of Life”. And this central teaching is: In spite of all bewildering facts, in spite of the many artificial and unhealthy influences that induce us to forget and ignore what is by nature plain as daylight to us, the one thing most important and most worthy of our achievement in our brief span of fifty or sixty years is to live a beautiful life. To live a beautiful life is not the same as to live a successful life; for material success, and even intellectual success, is regarded by Tagore as one of the many illusions that have so often misguided the course of our life career. In order that a man's life may be beautiful, he must first of all preserve his inner light in its original brightness, he must develop his individual personality according to the dictates of this inner light, keep it pure from corruptions of every kind, and then with this broadened and purified personality to extend his sympathy to such a degree as to identify himself with the entire world, animate and inanimate. "The ultimate truth in man is not in his intellect or his possessions; it is in his illumination of mind, in his extension of sympathy across all barriers of caste and color; in his recognition of the world, not merely as a storehouse of power, but as a habitation of man's spirit, with its eternal music of beauty and its inner light of the divine presence." Such a life will be a constant source of pleasure to others as well as to the man himself. Such a life is truly successful, and truly worthy of realization.

This doctrine of the paramount importance of developing a man's personality spiritually, with its necessary corollary of the expansion of sympathy, is the key to all Tagore's writings. He is quite insistent upon it in its application to all practical relations. His attacks upon modern nationalism, upon the capitalistic tyranny, and upon the pursuit of science for materialistic purposes, are provoked by their ruthless disregard of human beings as human beings and their tendency to still more widen the gaps between man and man. Here Tagore is different from other great individualists of modern times, such as Hinrik Ibsen. Ibsen, perhaps, would never have condemned science as being an obstacle to the expansion of individual nature and the establishment of harmonious relations between men. But Tagore's individualism is merged in a higher altruism; and while he strongly advocates the utmost possible development is necessary not because of any selfish motive, but because of the greater sympathy it will produce in us for the understanding of other personalities, and of the greater capacity for rendering help and giving joy to all our fellow beings.

It is only by a thorough understanding of his teaching and a sincere determination of carrying it out, and not by any outward manifestation of welcome, that we may deserve the honor of his visit. Perhaps we may say, with a certain degree of assurance, that, as the bearer of this great ethical message, he will not come to us as to a land of stranger. There is always a greater mental affinity existing between the peoples of the two great Eastern nations, than that existing between the people of Indian and of any European country. We have no doubt that he will find among us a greater number of sympathetic followers than that which he has found elsewhere, and that by meeting his soul with soul, and presenting to him, not the mere echoes of his own thoughts or of Western materialistic civilizations, but the true essence of our Chinese culture — no matter how shattered it is, so long as it is genuinely original — we will have no cause to feel ashamed, when he leaves us, that he has brought to us treasure full of gold, but has carried away with him nothing in return.

— *The English Student*, Sept. 1, 1923, 第 9 卷第 9 期

Tagore's Study in Western Education

"The Wreck." by Rabindranath Tagore. 8s.6d.net. (Macmillan) — Glimpses of Bengal." Rabindranath Tagore.7s.6d.net. (Macmillan)

Macmillan. 8s.6d.net.

Rabindranath Tagore's new novel reads as if it had been expressly written for the West. Indian festivals and habits, with which the ordinary Englishman or American is not likely to be acquainted, are explained in the body of the work, whenever reference to one of them first occurs. This method is much to be preferred to that of encumbering a work of fiction with footnotes. The translator has certainly done his work well in that respect. I say the translator, for although no mention of the fact is made on the title page or elsewhere, the novel was not originally written in English by Rabindranath, but was translated from the Bengali. That fact is patent without exposition. Anyone familiar with Rabindranath's style finds it difficult to reconcile the English slang and colloquialism in conversation between Bengali characters, liberally sprinkled thorough the book, with the dignified English of the poet's previous works.

The scene is laid in Bengal. The story is woven around a love affair between a young Hindu studying at Calcutta and an Indian girl, the daughter of a Brabmo (a protestant Hindu) and sister of his college friend. He is married against his will by his orthodox Hindu father to a girl whose face he never sees. Immediately after the wedding ceremony the party embark in hosts to go to the bridegroom's home upriver. There is a sudden storm, a wreck, and he is cast upon the shore along with a girl dressed in bridal attires who later turns out to be, in reality, another man's bride. His struggle to tear himself free from the net that circumstance weaves about him, and the little bride's efforts to find her real husband, make interesting reading.

In telling this tale Rabindranath gives the Western reader glimpses into the transitional Hindu life of today. His characters are typical of their kind — the highly educated Brabmo girl; the hero, with his modern tendencies, unable to express himself because of the strangling grip of old traditions; the orthodox Hindu woman who left her husband rather than lose her caste, and yet who, for her son's sake, inspired by the wisdom of riper years, is willing to have him marry a member of a Brabmo Samaj family; the spirited girl-bride, thrown by a trick of fate into the hero's arms; the faithful servant — all are drawn by a master craftsman who knows his Bengal and who knows also how to tell a story.

The book deserves to be read if for no other reason than for the exceedingly pleasant manner in which it enables one to study the effect of Western education upon Eastern womanhood. Rabindranath puts these words in the mouth of one of his characters in order to sum up the arguments used by old-fashioned people to prove the undesirably of educating women:

"The masculine intellect is like a sword and even without a keen edge its weight makes it a formidable weapon, while woman's wit is like a penknife – sharpen it as you will it is capable of no serious task."

Another character dwells upon the evil which "come of letting girls read English novels," and declares that such girls insist upon love matches instead of gracefully accepting the grooms chosen for them. The author, however, gives a character to his English educated heroine which should convert the most confirmed opponents of such education.

Rabindranath's second work, simultaneously published with "The Wreck" gives additional glimpses into life in Bengal. It serves a still more useful purpose by giving an insight into the innermost feelings and thoughts of the author himself. The pages are instinct with love for Bengal.

— *The North-China Daily News*, Sept. 24, 1921

太戈尔与科学

佛

自印度诗人太戈尔氏来华，中国思想界顿呈活泼气象，欢迎者几举国若狂，万人空巷。反对者亦剑拔弩张，如临大敌。或迎或拒，见智见仁，自由所见之不同而生，然不求甚解，耳食盲从之社会群众，则以目迷五色，无所适从矣。或谓崇拜含利用之意，或谓攻击失敬宾之礼，反唇互讥，舆论界几于满城风雨。记者不敏，窃谓皆不足虑。太氏自谓诗人为无可利用之人，欲利用诗人，其杀风景，违自然，与欧战时以鸽传递战地消息等耳（太氏在沪慕尔鸣路张宅欢迎会演辞）。以一亡国之诗人，在英美贵官富豪之眼中，不为逐世之逸民，则一风雅之清客而已。本无势力，何所利用。吾知崇拜太氏者之无所求，亦犹太氏之崇拜美与自然也。至反对太氏者，其重视太氏之思想，实不下于崇拜之者，因所见不同，发为术道之言论，亦心所谓危不敢不告之义耳。多敌多友，英雄本色，太氏既有所主张，自非阿世沽名之徒，苟一味违心谄谀，不特非敬礼诗人之道，亦非光明磊落之国民所以自处之道也。故今日纷纷以口舌笔墨争论太氏思想之利害者，岂非限于书生好辩之习。惟记者之意，宁愿举国为争论是非之书痴，不愿国人皆成模棱两可之乡愿，故于今日思想界之争，不特不以为多事，且认为吾国思想界之进步。

吾题为《太戈尔与科学》，而泛论国人对于太氏思想之争执乃及数百言，良以国中学术辩论态度往往失当，一涉意气，转滋纠纷，故略贡是非并尊之说。太氏言论最为人所称道与批评者，为其反对物质文明之主张。因反对物质文明时复涉及科学，说者遂谓太氏反对科学。就吾所闻太氏之言论皆无反对科学本身之说，但谓“科学为真理，真理不当利用，故科学亦不当利用。”（在东南大学演辞）其在北京之演说，且有“科学含理至深吾人皆当敬仰”之说。（似在师大演说，大意如此，恐与译文略异。）太氏所反对者为物质文明而非科学之本身也。太氏为诗人，其思想颇近神秘主义，果反对科学亦无可惊异，托尔斯泰尼采辈皆当持非议科学之态度，吾人固不欲独强太氏以信仰科学也。惟其所反对者，止于物质文明，则亦未可厚诬其抹杀一切科学。其所自办之曼谷大学有科学及农林等科（太氏之秘书恩厚之君即为主持农科者），更非痛绝科学视同洪水猛兽之中国顽固学者可比也。吾非谓太氏之言皆是，特谓其守旧复古尚不至吾人所料之甚耳。

科学本无意于应用，研究科学者，不特不为一己之富贵，亦不为人类之功利也。此稍读科学史者，类能言之。然利用非科学之罪，亦犹山水本不为人类而设，然人有饮流食薇者，无害于山水之高洁优美也。且即此利用山水者，苟其以慈悲普济为怀，不为自私自利计，吾人亦但当嘉其善念，不能罪其利用真理也。真理自具不可磨灭之价值，不因人利用而异。科学亦然，吾人岂能因物质文明而薄科学哉。且物质文明亦何有功罪之可言，一切物质皆为生命之工具，其效用有一定之量，过多过少皆足为害。饮食至简之物且然，更况宫室玩好之奢饰品哉。今日欧美物质文明之弊，一在过高，一在不普及。少数人享用无度，多数人衣食不足。多则丧志，少则戕生，此正今日国际战争生民疾苦之源也。太氏所反对者为少数人之过多物质文明，吾人所提倡者为多数人之过少物质文明。结论虽异，动机则一，为针砭流俗计，正可并行而不悖，实无绝对不相容之处也。或者以太氏反对物质文明而仍乘汽车，居大洋房，讥其言行不一，则此不谅太氏矫枉过正之心，遂有吹毛求疵之言也。夫太氏以一亡国之诗人，于举世纷纷逐利之时，独发挥其博爱赏美之言论，视列强之武力与金钱如粪土，人亦不以其为亡国诗人而争相讨论其思想。此其痛快难得，足为被压迫民族吐气，实不亚于爱恩斯坦之过沪。吾愿国人之崇拜与反对太氏者，各从太氏之精神批评其言论，诗与科学本非不能共存之物，吾人但就其性之所近致其努力而已。

——《科学》，第9卷第3期，1924年3月20日

泰戈尔来华的纪念品

市　虎

研究家手捧的之国诗翁来华了。他到华最不可遗留去的，已经有二宗纪念品了：一，赴青年会演讲改期；二，张君劢家二时的会，延到四时后才开。关于第一点，我也难怪他，因为他这样老大的年纪，仆仆风尘，自然劳苦得很，不能即时演讲，是意中事；关于第二点，我觉得这位诗翁，真也太会表现他那祖国懒惰的习气了。

如果泰戈尔不是有意表现他那祖国懒惰的气，他必是有意搭架子。我觉得，这种架子，搭给老大的中国人看，不足为奇，倒是那批捧翁家，足足等了二个钟头，泰戈尔实在有点对不起他们呵！

据泰戈尔自己说：因赴同乡会，所以至四时余才到张宅，然毕竟不守时间。

——《民国日报》，1924年4月14日

诗翁的丰采

文　炎

太戈儿抵沪后，一部分文学界的人捧场捧的很热闹。昨天下午讲学社等四团体在慕尔鸣路三十七号开欢迎会，门首扎了欢迎二字。开会时间本定二时，但这位太戈儿先生至四时余始乘汽车而来。陪乘者为不离左右之徐志摩，和去迎接的张君劢；同来的有英人恩厚之，美人葛玲女士及二印人。

太戈儿下车时，众鼓掌欢迎，太氏以双手合十而谢。旋由徐志摩扶之

至草场中央红色沙发上坐下，太氏须发苍然；发尤多而长，戴黄色帽，仿佛僧道所用者，衣枣色和尚领长服，其状貌，像旧时小学教科书中所画孔子之像。

太氏老矣，精神欠佳，但演说时发音清晰而柔软，不类其态。

会众约六十余人，围坐于此老之前，中有数画家，当场为太氏写生。大概既是到会的人，除了新闻记者外，都是崇拜这诗翁的。

致欢迎词的为张君劢，此君奔走甚忙，最为起劲。欢迎会狠简单，欢迎词毕，太氏演说，徐志摩演说，于是就茶点，散会。

——《民国日报》，1924 年 4 月 14 日

瞿译《春之循环》的一瞥

唐汉森

听说印度的诗人太戈尔马上就要来华了。敏捷的书贾已经在他们的杂志上特出了不少的专号。空气被他们制造到十分浓厚了。生性惯会附和的人类——像 Fabre 的《昆虫记》中的行列虫一样盲从的人类，尤其是我们现在的一般青年，本来早已在遥望西天仅仅勉强满足了他们的崇拜欲的，快要得到可以任情满足欲望的机会了。我想一定已有许多十分崇拜的人，犹如结婚前一晚的青年男女一样，怀了十二分的希望与好奇心，在等待他或她的“最好的女人”或“最好的男子”所将给他或她的启示。

在这样的浓厚的空气之中，我也觉得有点头热起来了。老实说，我是素来不喜欢这位在乐园里低吟的词客的。我老老实实的说，我直至现在还不曾从头至尾读完过他的一部著作。每每被报纸杂志上的狂跳的广告把注意力牵住了，也肯倾了本来很羞涩的钱包买他的著作一读，但据我现在的记忆，似乎我至多读了半部总不免就后悔起来，深惜没有把买书的钱施叫化子，或买一包烟卷吸吸。记得前年从上海经过时，买了他的一部新著 Creative Unity，我还记得我只读了两三页，便怎么也读不下去了。我总觉得他的作品不合我的口味，许多介绍他的文字我读了总觉得有点肉麻。想起了现在有许多的人嚼了一些坏面包似的翻译品也在那边喜极而流涕，我

想我与他们这两种人，必定有一种害了厉害的胃病。当然，他们之中的大部分是一些跟着凑数的行列虫，一部分是装时髦或出风头的俊杰；这些人当然不是害了什么胃病，不过这些人害病不害病却也不是我所愿意关心的。

闲话休题，言归正传。却说太戈尔既已决定来华，一些闲人便忙着制造空气，有的想利用他老先生宣传自己的党网，有的却想跟着他老先生博一个小小的名誉。这种消息传到了古长沙城，早惊动了几位好汉……这几位好汉也发愿要研究他老先生的思想起来，便一齐来访一位隐士。……

这样写来，倒成了新式标点的一段旧小说。我不再这样写了，恐怕有聪明的书贾见了，要拿去累胡适之先生做篇考证。

那是梅花初放的时节，我才从每天做工的地方回来，正在衔着纸烟回想这一天的工作。忽然，我的房门上有敲击的声响。我还不曾说完“请进来”的三个字，时常光顾我这小房间的 M. P. S. T. 四君已鱼贯而入了。他们说太戈尔马上就要来华，报纸上已经有了详细的报告；他们说他们想研究太戈尔的思想；他们说他们特来请我介绍他们看几部太戈尔的著作；最后他们请我分一点时间为他们详解。虽然谈太戈尔不是我高兴做的事情，但是好朋友的请求不可推却，于是我把劫后仅有的一部《春之循环》的英译本从箱内寻了出来，交给他们拿了去。这样，我们于数日之后，便开始了太戈尔的研究了。他们从商务印书馆买了一部文学研究会出版的瞿世英氏的中文译本，他们把两部书对照研究，我时常从旁边给他们一些注解。

这样的研究本来应当是很干燥无味的，然而我们却每每暴跳而喧笑起来，似乎很多趣的样子。这是译者瞿世英氏给我们的帮助。瞿氏译本的错处随处皆是，我们差不多要笑个不停，要时时用力捧着肚子。我从前常对人痛骂错误的译书害人，我这才知道像瞿氏这样的译文有益于人的地方正不少。我想一定有许多人还不曾得到瞿氏给我们的这种益处，所以我现在决定费一晚的工夫抄下来，贡献于我远方的同声的好朋友。

下面所举的便是瞿世英氏所译《春之循环》中的大错之一部。

1. 原文：How dreadful！

瞿译：这样可怕！（瞿译第二面上段第三行）

这句应译为“多么可怕！”瞿译不仅在此处没有一丝，而且把剧中的情调埋没了。

2. 原文：Where can that vizier have gone to ?

瞿译：那国务大臣能到那里去?（第二面下一行）

这句应译为“到底那国务大臣到哪里去了?”

3. 原文：Ah, here is the King at last.

瞿译：呵，这里毕竟是君主。（第二面下十一行）

这句的大意是“呵，好了，君主来了。”瞿君翻出了这几个字。

4. 原文：The joke is not mine, but His, Who has got the whole world by the ear, and is having His jest.

瞿译：这笑话不是我的，是“他的”，“他”以耳得全世界，是有“他的”笑话。（第三面下五行）

这句的大意是：这笑话不是我的，是“他的”，“他”捉住耳朵，把全世界得到了，是“他”在开玩笑。

5. 原文：They, too, want peace — peace from the burning of hunger.

瞿译：他们亦要和平——饥火中之和平。（第五面上九行）

这句的大意是：“他们亦要宁息——饥火的宁息。”瞿君老把 Peace 一词译为和平，于是 I must have peace 成了“我必要和平”，其实应译为我必要宁或宁静。

6. 原文：So why strain our voice in prayer?

瞿译：那么为什么强用我们的声音来祈祷?（第五面下十二行）

这句的大意是：“那么为什么在祈祷中抑住我们的声音呢?”瞿君似乎把前后的意思及 Strain 的意义都弄错了。

7. 原文：One breath of your teaching blows out the false flame of ambition.

瞿译：你的教训的一呼吸间吹出了野心的假火焰?（六面下三行）

blow out 是吹熄的意思，不能这样一个个字译出来译成“吹出”的。并且这句话是国王称赏学士的，若照瞿君这样译出来，岂不是在骂人了吗?瞿君简直没有把原文看懂。

8. 原文：Yet man clings to hope that plays him false.

瞿译：还坚持着去希望做假。（六面下六行）

这句的意思是“但人还坚持着那骗他的希望”。全文是“齿也脱了，发渐白了，但人还……”若依瞿译，岂不是老了还希望做假吗？还不知是不是瞿君的人生观。瞿君翻电码似的译出了，可惜英文有时候是要颠倒过来才通的呵。

9. 原文：How exquisite, So you don’t want any gold, My Master?

瞿译：何其精密。我师，因此你才不要金子么？（七面下六行）

这句的意思是“多高尚。那么你一点金子也不要么，我师？”

10. 原文：...，when poetry brings me this parting message?

瞿译：当诗歌界我以此别离的使命的时候……？（十面上六行）

parting message 是离去的消息即死耗，我真不知什么是别离的使命。

11. 原文：Haven’t you noticed the detachment of the rushing river, as it runs splashing from its mountain cave?

瞿译：你不会注意那急流的河水，当他从山穴中急流出来的支流么？（十二面下七行）

这句的大意是“你不会注意那急流的河水的分歧，当他从山穴中激发出来吗？”这里的 detachment 一词后来还用了两次，都是分枝的意思，暗指创造的作用。在引子中的诗人的议论中，这个字是很重要的。瞿君在这三处却用了“支流”，“分枝”，“分离”三个不同的字，把原字的一贯的意义全然埋没了。瞿君实在没有把原剧看懂。

12. 原文：But it is those who love, because they live.

瞿译：得最终的胜利的，乃是那些因为他们生活着所以他们爱的人。（十二面下七行）

这句的大意是“得最后的胜利的，乃是那些爱的人，因为他们生活着。”“他们生活着”是他们得最后的胜利的证据，不是他们所以爱的原因。这地方瞿君也没有把意思弄清楚。

13. 原文：And if the life within you is not stirred, in response to that call without ,then there is cause for anxiety indeed.

瞿译：若你内面的生命不变动去反应外面的呼声，那就真是烦闷的原因。（十五面上五行）

这句的大意是“若你内面的生命不因外面的呼声而摇动，那就真可以烦闷了。”

14. 原文：But，isn't life inconstant?

瞿译：但是，生命不是不变么?（十五面下二行）

这句的意思是“但是，生命不是无常么?”瞿译恰把北极星拉到南极去了。

15. 原文：Why on earth have you kept me waiting so long ?

瞿译：为什么地球上有你叫我等这些时候?（十六面上十四行）

这句的意思是“到底为什么你叫我等这么久?”瞿君把字翻出来了，也照样排出，我真不知道为什么地球上有这种翻译法。

16. 原文：Why should you dismiss the general?

瞿译：你为什么必要罢黜那将军?（十六面上八行）

这里的 dismiss 是打发的意思。由剧情上说，也没有罢黜那将军的道理，只是打发他去。

17. 原文：In a moment of weakness, I may suddenly find Myself out of my depths in the Ocean of Renunciation, Poet! Don't give me time for that.

瞿译：在软弱的时候，我或者忽然觉得我自己出了“舍弃之洋”的深处。诗人呵！不要让我时候如此的过去。（十七面下八行）

这句大意是：在软弱的时候，我会忽然从我在舍弃之洋中的深处发见我自身（就是说，我会委身在舍弃之洋里）。诗人呵！不要使我有这样的机会。瞿译恰得其反。诗人明明在前文中讥讽过舍弃之洋的，学士挟了这东西来，国王正不愿见他呢!

18. 原文：The youth of these middle-aged people is a youth of detachment. They have just crossed the Waters of pleasure, and are in sight of the land of pure gladness.

瞿译：这些中年人的青年是分离的青年。他们刚刚渡过快乐之水看得见纯粹快乐的地方。（十九面上十行）

这句的意思是“这些中年人的青春，是分枝的青春，他们刚刚渡过了快乐之水，正看得见那纯粹欢喜之地。”detachment 一词，我在第十一条内说过，不能译作分离。pleasure 与 gladness 相差很远，瞿君统译为快乐，把全句的精神全然埋灭了。

19. 原文：The Heralds of Spring are abroad.

瞿译："春之使"出去了（二十二面上八行）

这句的意思是："春之使"散在着。因为他们是要在那里唱歌的。

20. 原文：Yes, the very dust of the earth is tingling with youth....

瞿译：是，地上的灰尘都与青年相接触，……（二十五面上十二行）

这句的大意是"是，便是地上的灰尘都在充满了青春而低唱，……"这句话本来不好译，不过瞿译却是在希望做假。

21. 原文：What a nuisance you are making of yourselves!

瞿译：你们多么妨害你们自己！（二十五面下三行）

这句的大意是"你们多么使你们自己可厌！"

22. 原文：How in the world can you go on writing verses like that, sitting in your den?

瞿译：在世界上你怎么能够坐在你的洞里做那样的诗词呢？（二十六面上一行）

这句的意思是"到底你怎么能够坐在你的洞里那样继续做诗呢？"in the world 是一个强势的成语，与我们的"到底"相似，大一点的字典上皆载得有，瞿君应当多费点力查究出来才是。

23. 原文：There's no holding them in.

瞿译：没有什么把握了。（二十六面下一行）

凡 there is no 之后加一 gerund, 便是"不能"的意思。所以这句应当译为"不能抑住他们了。"

24. 原文：Just one word to make you understand. It means, that if the bamboos were no better than those noisy instruments —

瞿译：只用一个字使你们明白。他的意思是若是竹子不比别的乐器好——（二十七面下八行）

这句的大意是"一句话好使你们明白。它的意思是，若是竹子只不过是那种嘈杂的器具——"no better than 不指好丑而指实质。

25. 原文：What a noise you make!

瞿译：你们做什么声音！（二十九面四行）

这句的大意是"你们多么喧闹！"

26. 原文：We thought it over so vigorously, that people had to run to the

king's court to lodge a complaint.

瞿译：我们很用力去想过就是百姓必要跑到皇庭上去告状。（三十四面下九行）

这句的大意是"我们很激烈地想过，甚至于不能不跑到王庭去申诉。"

27. 原文：Not a sudden becoming. We have been like this from the beginning.

瞿译：不是突如其来的。我们从起头就喜欢这样。（四十一面下一行）

这句的意思是"不是忽然变成的，我们从起头就是这样的。"like 一词在这里译为"喜欢"，瞿君还没有把动词的 tense 弄清楚。

28. 原文：And we have a leader, who is a perfect veteran in childhood. He rushes along so recklessly, that he drops off his age at every step he runs.

瞿译：我们有一个首领，他小孩时是有完全的经验的。他勇往的向前冲去，于是年纪随着跑的步数少。（四十四面下六行）

这段的大意是"我们有一个首领，他对于为童是一个能手。他那样不注意地冲去，于是他每跑一步便把他的年纪丢掉了。"

29. 原文：Go along with you.

瞿译：和你们同去。（五十面十二行）

这句的意思好像我们的"滚蛋罢"，瞿君这样译出来，把前后的情节都埋没了。

30. 原文：All the more reason why you should cultivate our company.

瞿译：为什么你要和我们搭伴。（五十面上六行）

这句的大意是"那么，你更应该和我们搭伴。"瞿译恰得其反，瞿君全然没有看懂。

31. 原文：He never stays with us, lest he should have to keep us in order.

瞿译：除非他必要我们守秩序，否则他决不与我们同在。（五十二面下十一行）

这句的大意是"他从来不同我们留在一块，以便可以不必要我们守秩序。"

32. 原文：We commit all kinds of atrocities, but not that.

瞿译：我们与各种社会交涉，但不是那种。（五十四面下五行）

这句的意思是"我们做一切的坏事，但不做那种。"社会和交涉二字不知从何而来；交涉是 communicate，社会的复数是 societies, 与 commit 及 atrocities 颇有几分相像，我们也许应该为瞿君原谅的。

33. 原文：Bravo, March on.

瞿译：凶汉，向前走。（五十七面上十二行）

不错，Bravo 有凶汉的一义，瞿君很费心翻过字典。不过这里究竟只不过是一个 interjection，没有骂人的意思。

34. 原文：What would our leader think of us, I wonder, if he could hear us now?

瞿译：不知我们首领对我们怎样想，我奇怪不知他能否听见我们？（五十七面十二行）

这句的大意是“我奇怪，若是他此刻能听见我们，我们的首领将以我们为何如？”瞿君连这样简短的文句都没有看懂。

35. 原文：And let us imagine that there we had been before we ever came there.

瞿译：让我们想一想我们从前到过的地方，我们常常到那里去。（五十九面上八行）

这句的大意是“让我们想象我们来到那里之前我们就在那里的。”

36. 原文：Yes, the message that man's flight is not yet over.

瞿译：是的，人的战争的消息还没有过去呢。（六十九面下十二行）

这句的意思是“是的，人的战争尚没有完的那个消息。”

37. 原文：We never knew that we loved Chandra so intensely. We made light of him all these days.

瞿译：我们决不知道我们这样的爱章特拉。这几天来我们以他做光。（七四面下三行）

这句的意思是“我们不曾知道我们这样热爱章特拉。我们平日把他看轻了。”to make light of 是轻视的意思。试问一个人可以做光吗？我们可以把瞿君做光吗？

38. 原文：Then Dada must be near at hand with his quatrains.

瞿译：然则达达手边必有诗。（八十二面上七行）

这句的意思是“那么，达达一定带了他的诗走来很近了。”

39. 原文：What makes you so desperate?

瞿译：你们怎样这般不顾利害呢？（八十三面上六行）

这句的意思是“你们怎么这样颓丧了呢？”

本来至多只想举出三十条来的：不料本书的谬误层出无穷，虽然我沿路把小一点的错误与勉强可以混过的地方丢下不究，然而到底还是超过预算至九条之多了。译者的荒谬，真可以令人瞠目，而他的“希望做假”，尤令人不胜浩叹。错译之外，还有脱落文句的地方三处，即二十三面的“鸟之歌”前，五十八面下段十一行后，与六十九面下段十行后的一段。

太戈尔就要来了，我在上面说过了一定有许多青年在等候狂欢他的高论。翻译成介绍他的高论的人，我想大约离不了是那些曾经翻译或介绍过他的人，因为他们一个个都自以为是研究太戈尔的专门家，当然不免要乘机一显身手。然而他们究竟能不能翻译或介绍他的高论呢？我素来对于这一点是有点怀疑的。这回瞿君的这部《春之循环》的译本，可谓给我解决一件事情了。像这样浅显的书还看不懂，还有什么本领从事于翻译或介绍他的高论？这样看起来，太戈尔这次来华，那些不懂外国文的人，毕竟只好看看热闹罢了。

把《春之循环》的封面过细一看的时候，“瞿世英译”的旁边，有“郑振铎校”的四个字。我这才知道这部译本倒真是应该大错的了。郑君译的几部书早有人指责过，瞿君倒请他校，真不知是问道于什么了。

我费了九牛二虎之力写了这样多，我在前面戏说是分给大众一点提起精神的灵药，其实是我怕别人看了这部译本要闷死在葫芦里面才起了婆心干出来的，我想这倒也不必多讲。但是现在有许多译书的人，稿费拿到了手，便再不管译得如何，别人如何评论，也不倾听，只顾忙着把新的译书完稿。我希望瞿君不是样的，我希望他能够俯纳我这几点刍荛，马上把这部译书改好。

近来常见到批评翻译的文字，这是很好的现象。我以为这种工作虽然是消极的，然而它能鞭策从事翻译的人，使不再欺人欺己，功德确是无量。而且正因为是消极的工作，这种批评家的损己利人的行为，在沧海横流的时代尤为难得，我们应当对于他们表示我们的钦仰和谢意。有一二批评家措词时有过激之处，我以为我们也应当谅解。“指谪一部错译的功劳，比翻译五百部错的功劳更大；因为他的贡献虽微，而他的贡献是真确的。”郭沫若这句话说的好。

近来的翻译品日趋恶劣，我觉得这里面有两种原因。第一是无能的人的滥译，第二是有能的人的洁身自好，坐视不肯动手。我希望无能的人暂时停止翻译，专做培养自己的功夫，让有能的人弄出几部好译本，把文学创作的标准抬高几步。至于有能的人，我也希望他们不因噎而废食。

三月二十一日，长沙。

——《创造周报》，第49，50期，1924年4月19日，27日

太戈尔与哈巴克沁格

玄　庶

两位先生同是印度人：这位哈先生，是新近被上海的英公堂判监禁两月兼作苦工的；那位太先生，是曾经得到诺贝尔底奖金，新近来华，受善男信女风起云涌的欢迎的。我把一个囚徒和一位名震环球的“诗圣”，并在一起，必有人笑我“载人鬼于一车”，诚是，诚是人鬼同车，但哪位是人？哪位是鬼，还要请看官下个判断。

先说太戈尔先生吧！他会作诗，他崇尚东方文化，他反对物质，他鼓吹和平，他不和你们解决什么问题。（这句话是徐志摩先生在杭州会场上代太先生发表的）他所得的奖金，是做成双料炸药发财的诺贝尔先生遗嘱上五分之一的奖金八万元；他得奖的资格，是“文学上的翘楚”，现在他既是和平鼓吹者，照诺贝尔遗嘱的奖励，还有“鼓吹和平最有力者”的一项。现在有许多人称他作“诗圣”。

再说哈巴克沁格先生：他不曾以会做诗出名，他不曾得奖金，他不反对物质，不鼓吹和平，不崇尚东方文化；他说“无论白褐黄色，都是弟兄”。同时又说路透社遮掩了英国印度政府的暴行，他要解决问题。他在上海的英公堂上，说英国的印度政府的暴行，他是一个商人，他在公堂声明“不怕入监狱”。现在他做了西牢里兼作苦工的“囚犯”。

看官们！究竟哪个是人，哪个是鬼？

我依何原因提出这个问题呢？因为我住的地方，前面是商场，后面是陆军监狱，左边是风波桥畔的模范监狱，右边是许多人认为"妖冶湖山娇逸甚，一种三生谁付"的西湖。我在绝不调和的环境中，耳边震得很响"欢迎，欢送"太戈尔诗圣的声浪，同时又有人歌颂他老先生到杭州来连用资都不收的高行；一面又接到哈巴克沁格先生被捕被判决监禁作苦工的消息。

他们同是印度人！我们同是中国人！

——《民国日报》，1924 年 4 月 26 日

太戈尔说笑话

燕 客

太戈儿离沪数周了，现在把他在京消息，介绍一段如下：

很出风头的所谓熊夫人，上次至沪，曾受几个团体热忱欢迎。但欢迎的时候，大家都口口声声的叫熊夫人，可见得不重在伊个人，而重在是熊氏的夫人。这次太戈儿到北京，这曾经一捧的熊夫人，也随着已过第一流人才总理的丈夫去做捧场的，二十五日那天，太氏在应讲学社演说时，忽当向熊夫人一般女捧场的说："余最好与少女游玩，……余之孙女甥女皆为余之最好侣伴。不料来京时乃获与诸女士相见，而其年龄则与余孙女甥女相等，颇觉有趣！余今获坐于诸女士之间，愉快非可言喻。但余老矣，谁肯与余作伴。"在太氏自命为一老诗翁，大家既这样捧场，就把伊们比作自己孙女，也不妨事。但是中国人最怕作别人的子孙——官僚政客除外——那般女捧场听了，很有点不满意。最后太氏说余老矣，谁肯与余作伴几句话，台下的人也太不开通，忽然大笑，这一笑倒把台上的夫人小姐们笑得脸红起来了。

——《民国日报》，1924 年 4 月 30 日

致印度诗哲塔果尔书

金鹤望

震旦诗学后进金天翮，谨致书印度大诗人大哲学家塔果尔先生阁下。闻阁下之名十年矣，道里辽远，文字异趣，不获裹粮相从，并不得藉邮筒以相唱和。然两国文化相通已二千年矣，今阁下复航海西来，将已著作及思想复饷我国学者，诚幸事也。鄙人不能随众欢迎阁下于海潮声中，固以此书代欢迎。其欢迎之心，尤为深至，惟阁下鉴之。窃谓西洋哲学，自希腊以来，至于今日，其受病之根，一语括之曰多差别相。而震旦哲学则物我一体，天人同德。惟其一体，故民我同胞，物我与也。惟其同德，故天人之间，息息相通，此非空言也。贵国自婆罗门诸哲以至佛氏，其道亦然。今佛氏之书，悉入震旦。震旦学者，至今爱之。而阁下之言亦曰西洋人之神在天国，吾东洋人之神在吾心，亦在人人之心，在水亦在火，在千年古木之中，亦在岁岁新麦禾之内。（鄙人不谙英文及梵文此系从译本摘出）伟哉哲人之言，然亦非空言论道而已。近来法国哲学，有佩克森之创化论。德国哲学，有倭铿之精神生活说。其于吾东洋文明，庶几望见其影，而即之犹远。阁下之书出，西洋人惊且欢曰：二十世纪佩克森倭铿之时代去矣。必有其实践之切，鄙人不敢妄测也。吾国大圣大贤，如老子如庄子，其学说德法人能诵之矣，然仅望见其门墙，而不入其宫。况孔孟之博大，与夫佛氏之精微者乎。抑鄙人略涉佛氏之书，佛告诸菩萨以方便随顺，入无上妙觉修习三观，衍成二十五轮。苟修其一，即得正觉。（详圆觉经）其义流入震旦，则南岳大师述大乘止观法，其徒天台智头复演四种止观，曰圆顿止观，曰渐次止观，曰不定止观，曰小止观。止观之法，今尚不绝于震旦，其说乃于吾孔子之言合。大学之言曰：知止而后有定，定而后能静，静而后能安，安而后能虑，虑而后能得。周易系辞曰：夫易无思也，无为也，寂然不动，感而遂通天下之故。夫一心不动而感通天下，此必有实践之功矣。实践如何，曰成既济。六十四卦皆有既济，此非仓卒数言所能盖也。未识阁下实践果用何术，术不一端。譬如百川入海，而同至于海也。愿阁下有以教之也。阁下此来，欲考震旦民族。民族之特性，由先哲文化陶冶而成。则曷先考吾国最高最古之文化，如孔孟老庄之学说，以兴贵国诸先哲，一较同其异乎。闻阁下将赴北京，归途必复出沪上，有与一相晤，作一日夜之深谈否，鄙人亦将以所印之诗相赠，不然亦望赐我一书。书有专词，不能悉译，恨甚恨甚。鄙人二三年后，读佛氏书竟，亦将东航印度，瞻拜佛迹，并参观阁下之国际大学。临书拳拳，书不蓝言。天翮再拜。（此书由吴县陆君谷译述之）

——《新黎里》，第 24 期，1924 年 5 月 1 日

太戈尔与物质文明者

缪　斌

印度诗人太戈尔来华之后，在一片热烈的欢迎声中，却引起了许多人对于他底文明精神的抨击。太先生底精神文明的本身，——用爱来调和人类，——这是人类应该要这样的。那末何以有许多人当它毒枭一般，惟恐防之不周呢？难道人类间用不着爱吗？太先生白白受了这番挨骂，也太冤枉了！我想太先生脑中一定有这些感慨的。以我看来，太先生受这次挨骂，也只好自认晦气：不该把牛头不对马嘴，走坊郎中老套的汤头歌诀，来医治中国今日底虎列拉症呀！太先生现在所极力提倡的东方文化，中国人民也早已受到四千多年的熏育陶养，到现在国家才沦落至于半殖民地的地位，至于东方文化发祥地的印度，精神文明也早已超过了亡国的痛苦，再有了太先生来提倡，真所谓“锦上添花”，也够值得列强们要齐口赞美，诺贝尔底奖金，自然要送到太先生的袋中，可以充他底宣传费。那末，一般已亡将亡的国家底人民，自然可以“曲突徒薪”，在太先生底诗中，找寻些性灵的安慰；都去效法我们颜夫子的“一箪食，一瓢饮，人不堪其忧，回也不减其乐”，否则便驰骛梦想到石器时代；巢居穴住，吟啸叫鸣，觉得真有自然之乐趣。何怪太先生要极力提倡恢复东方文化，精神文明，让东方的国家，一个个像印度般，被西方的物质文明者来生杀予夺，那我们就不管太先生说得博爱——用爱来调和人类——如何动听，绝不游疑地便应当反对！我们固然不认博爱的本身不好，只是弱小民族来提倡博爱，

是一个根本错误罢了。

何以呢？要晓得印度之所以亡，中国之所以弱，并不是没有东方文化，才会亡，才会弱；正因为只有东方文化，缺乏了西方的物质文明，才至于亡，至于弱，还要提倡什么博爱？而不知博爱并不是绝对的，还是要相对的呵！人家假装着来爱你，你真心地去爱他，已经是没有知人之明；设使人家用机关枪来对你，你若还去爱他，那就非死不可。精神文明者，或者还以为死是到极乐国的捷径，所以印度国亡了，太先生还硬要说："西洋文明挟其征服之力，现在压迫了印度，但印度人在精神上，却已战胜了西洋文明。"这是何等笑话！所以太先生也不去管人家国家的亡不亡，拿亡国奴的口吻，到中国来鼓吹东方文化，横竖亡了，也可以像印度般的以精神文明战胜西洋文明。可惜中国人不会是玄学鬼，有血性的人倒底还有，那末太先生就难免不受人家的抨击了。

反对太戈尔来鼓吹东方文化的人，大概是主张物质文明的罢。我们读技术科学的人，犹其是显明的物质文明者。我们所以要反对太戈尔的精神文明，正因为他离开现实不讲，在那里冥想莫测高深的心灵的安慰。那末我们主张物质文明的人，更不应该离开现实，在那里乱喊物质文明。当然我们是中国的主张物质文明者，那就非先研究中国的现状不可了！哼！中国的现状这么样呀？在这种军阀官僚勾结国际资本帝国主义的半殖民地的局面之下，空口喊物质文明，其结果老实说，和空口喊精神文明的，也不过五十步与百步之比耳。恐怕空口的物质文明越喊得起劲，国人崇拜物质文明的心更切。急不暇择，而西洋的物质文明，便格外的容易冲进来了。这是最危险不过的事！现在外货得在中国畅销至于穷乡僻巷，就是一个明显的例证。物质文明者呵！犹其是我们有技术科学的物质文明者呵！再不要离开现实，在那里梦想物质文明，物质文明还是要我们物质文明者去开辟一条路，创造出来，但是谈何容易，这一条到物质文明的路，简实满目榛莽荆棘，毒蛇猛兽。而虎视眈眈，鬼蜮伎俩的国际资本帝国主义，把它们的物质文明猛烈的冲来，压迫我们自己的物质文明的发达，还要勾结了一般率兽食人的军阀官僚来吮吸我们人民的脂膏，使我们无力走上物质文明的路。物质文明者呵！我们须要觉悟我们的进程中，横着有这两个大敌。"庆父不除，鲁难未已"，国际资本帝国主义和军阀官僚不推翻，中国是永远没有希望的日子！物质文明也永远不会达到目的！努力罢！空口说白话，也就是难免太戈尔和一般玄学鬼不要窃笑于我后哩！

——《南洋周刊(上海1919)》，第4卷第9期，1924年5月18日

泰歌尔

诗圣泰歌尔，灵觉傅奕代。
早览雪山云，恒河资灌溉。
游英玩诗律，讽咏入三味。
清歌落人间，恍惚契绝对。
妙语匪所思，一吟百忧废。
远挹印度风，梵神鸟婆队。
吠陀婆罗门，乐化起大块。
童歌与剧曲，深秘沁脾肺。
虚漠忘人我，湛然明五内。
九十六哲人，诸天通声欬。
帝网重重涉，相入了无碍。
却来观人生，草木呈逸态。
当境即乐土，月眉青山黛。
喜舍大解脱，十方虚空碎。
欧哲竟渴仰，摧破堡垒界。
无限接真善，始觉物质隘。
花放天宇新，水流鱼跃快。
交通两洋间，活泼汇万派。
自在乐长生，大我永无坏。

——《佛化新青年》，1924年，第2卷第7~8合号

The Mysticism of Rabindranath Tagore

Lyman V. Cady

PART 1

I. INTRODUCTORY SKETCH [1]

What can mysticism do for religion and for life? Students of religion are seeking for light on this question with a view to determining whether or not it is vital to a developed ethical religion and if valuable, what role it ought to play in the religion of today and tomorrow. It is not the purpose of this article to attempt anything so pretentious as an answer to these questions. It may, I trust, serve to bring as valuable data for such study the mysticism of a great contemporary religious poet and thinker who represents a developed modern form [2] of the religious and philosophical thought of India where mysticism has been characteristic. Nevertheless, whatever relationships, tendencies, and fruitage emerge from the experiences, ideas and activities of Rabindranath Tagore should at least suggest to us some norms by which to evaluate mysticism as a religious type or as a strand in religions experience as a whole.

Biographical study is a *sine qua non* for a sound interpretation of any mystic. It is not possible here however to do more than suggest the background and heritage of Tagore and describe briefly a few aspects of his life intimately related to our special theme. [3] In the case of a figure so well known as that of Tagore, it is possible to rely on the reader for a large measure of acquaintance with the man and his thought. Yet even so, we Westerners must fell the large need of an active, sympathetic, imagination if we are to feel the life out of

[1] 此文保留原始资料的格式，各节标题字母均大写——编者注。

[2] The Brahma Somaj.

[3] For biography and interpretation of Tagore see “Rabindranath Tagore” by Basanta Koomar Roy, and a book by the same title by Ernest Rhys. Tagore’s own work, “My Reminiscences,” is especially valuable for its intimacy and atmosphere. All books on Tagore mentioned in connection with this article are published by The MacMillan Company.

which Tagore has sprung and whose inmost ideals he has shared with us. For he comes to us out of a clime, a stream of culture, a long civilizational past to which we are mostly strangers. Further he speaks from a region of Indian life more than commonly steeped in poetry, where from the event of birth down through each step into adult society, every social experience has interwoven with it an accompaniment of verse expressed in song. Not only so, but Rabindranath Tagore belongs to a remarkably distinguished family which was at the very forefront of the intellectual and literary renaissance going on in Bengal during the past century. His father was one of India's greatest spiritual leaders, honored by the people with the title of Maharshi (great sage).

Rabindranath, after a brief and repelling taste of the deadly formal school life of that time in India, the result of attempted modelling after alien British education, was given a remarkably free and rich education by his own father and by his participation as a youthful poet in the experiences of that unusual home. In the pages of his "My Reminiscences" one gets a delightful picture of the literary and artistic atmosphere which pervaded the place, the constant coming and going of great personages in the home, social gatherings filled with verse and music, art and wit. As a child Tagore was filled a natural mysticism and felt himself utterly one with the world of throbbing beauty and life which luxuriates so marvelously in Bengal. In young manhood came a realistic reaction which held sway over the period of years when he was making every sort of experiment in literary self-expression. He gave himself particularly to poems of love. It was out of this period that he came to that deeply mystical experience which proved as significant for him as a similar experience had been for his father.

In his inner self there had been at work the struggle of the more spiritual side of his nature against the merely sensual and realistic in poetry. This revealed itself in his work "Evening Sons" which won the recognition of the foremost Bengali novelist of the time. This personal meeting with Bankim Chandra Chattopodhya and his unstinted praise spurred the poet on to new heights. Shortly after this time he followed his brother Jyotindra from the family country estate which Rabindranath had been managing to the house in Calcutta. There a momentous revolution came about. Perhaps the memories of childhood initiated the experience. At any rate all of itself one morning there came to hims a great illumination. In the poet's own words he says, "A veil was suddenly drawn, and everything seemed luminous. The whole scene was one perfect music, one marvellous rhythm. The houses in the street, the children playing, all seemed part of one luminous whole — inexpressibly glorious. The vision went on for seven or eight days. Everyone who bored me seemed to lose their outer barrier of personality and I was full of gladness, full of love, for every person and every tiniest thing... That morning in the Free School Street was on of the first things that gave me the inner vision, and I have tried to explain it in my poems. I have felt ever since that this is my goal in life: to explain the fullness of life, in its beauty as perfection." [1] The whole day a poem flowed out spontaneously from his discovered self, called "Fountain Awakened from Its Dream." This experience coming when he was about thirty transformed his entire life. He again felt himself to be part of nature in its universal life and in harmony with her meaning. The theme of his poems before had been human love. Now they are filled with the love of God.

The remarkable and significant thing about Tagore is that contrary to the Indian tendency he did not turn toward asceticism. Living on a houseboat on the Padma River on the edge of the estate entrusted to his care, he came to know the simple and devout Indian peasants, to understand their poverty and helplessness, and to take practical administrative measures for their relief. He differed from the Indian patriot of his day in that he felt that India's problem was not primarily political. It was India's social and mental diseases that needed healing. Out of his pondering on these needs and the sad personal experiences of the loss of his beloved wife and two children,

[1] Quoted by Roy, op. cit.p.76.

came the determination to do something while his energies were fresh for the coming generation. His own unhappy experiences with school education led him to decide upon the establishment of a new type of school at Bolpur where education should be truly liberal and full of freedom and love. Out of this period came the Gitanjali, or "Song Offerings" with which the acquaintance of the West with Tagore began, and which was to eventuate in 1913 when the lectures found in his Sadhana were given in England and America, in his being awarded the Nobel prize for idealistic literature. With this widespread appreciation in the West went a widening of his own horizon to take in the problems of humanity as a whole. Out of the later period when he visited Japan, America, and England in the midst of the great war, he sounded forth by lecture and writing his warning against the perils of nationalism and mechanical civilization.[1]

It must be an unusual school indeed to which a man of such rich personality, world interests and literary fertility would return as his main task. Such is the school of Shanti-Niketan.[2] It goes back to the ancient ideal of the Asram or forest school of ancient India. The place at Bolpur was originally founded by his father who had there a house, garden, small temple and all conveniences for retirement and study. There Tagore's teachers and students live in great simplicity in the intimate relationship of companions and friends. In this school no distinctions of caste are allowed. All discipline is a matter of self-government. There is great freedom from externals in education, the classes gathering on mats under the trees. Thus, the luxurious life of nature about them is an intimate part of their developing acquaintance with the world. In the evening Tagore joins with the students in music and influence is a prominent part of the life of the school. There are definite times in the morning and evening for devotion and meditation. Stated services of worship

[1] In his books "Personality" and "Nationalism."

[2] The significance of this school educationally is indicated by its inclusion in the study of Indian schools by D. J. Fleming entitled, "Schools with a Message in India."

are held twice weekly where the Upanishads praises are chanted and Tagore himself talks to the boys. His personal relationship with the students is most beautiful. He lives alone in the midst of the school, meditating, writing, preaching, but most of all giving his love and guidance to them all. He is always ready to see any boy and they go to him naturally as to a father about their lessons and problems. Together with the quieter side of his school Tagore has combined a vigorous physical life of games and sports in which his students excel. The spirit of social service is alive among them also. Their fire brigade often runs to the town of Bolpur two miles way to put out fires while the less resourceful townspeople look on helplessly. The older students go out in the spirit of brotherhood giving talks on social themes and helping in night schools in the villages around. Thus, a many-sided education is giving at Shanti-Niketan with the purpose of developing full spiritual personality, rich in the spirit of India's past, and yet inspired with patriotism and democracy eager to serve in the social regeneration of the land. Such is the chosen life work of Tagore the mystic.

II. MYSTICISM IN TAGORE'S THOUGHT

In Tagore we have an unusual combination of circumstances and qualities favorable to mysticism; he is a poet, a religious saint, and a Hindu thinker. As indicated above he was brought up under the spiritual teaching of the Brama-Somaj which roots itself in the religious philosophy of the Upanishads. In his "Sadhana", Tagore interrupts these teachings to the West. Indian thought has never made a sharp separation between man and the world of nature in which he was cradled. [1] Man and the world were included as one great truth and the harmony existing between the individual and the universe emphasized. The more man has realized this connection of himself to the living world about him the greater the fruits of success he has reaped from it. The greater the degree of sympathy with the world and realization of the inner meaning of the

[1] Based on the chapter "Individual and Universe," p.5 ff in the "Sadhana."

world, which is spirit, the greater his joy and peace. The glory of man's life is not in its separateness, but in the realization of the wholeness of existence. Man needs the infinite to complete himself.

Tagore points out the contrasts in the ends sought for by the West and the East. The West looks on nature as alien and strives for power over her through the knowledge of science. It seeks efficiency through knowledge. But for the Hindu not the exemplar of power but the Rishi, who realizes his relationship with all things and by union with God enters into everything, is the ideal. Thus, realization is the ultimate end. Not power through knowledge but joy through knowledge, for knowledge is the union of kindred things, the soul in self uniting with the soul in the world, only on the condition of our being at heart one with the inner meaning of the objects of our knowledge is knowledge really possible to us.

In the chapter "Soul Consciousness" he amplifies this theme. "Man must clearly realize some central truth which will give him an outlook over the widest possible field."[1] "We must realize the great principle of unity which is in every man." is "The very essence of the soul is unity. It can only find out its truth by unifying itself with others and only then does it have its joy."[2] Our highest joy is the losing of our egoistic self and uniting with others. The consciousness of the soul is the first step of supreme deliverance. "Man's poverty is abysmal, his wants endless until he becomes truly conscious of his soul." That which keeps man from discovering his soul is according to the typical thought of India, ignorance. Ignorance makes us think that our self as self is real. But this separateness of self is an illusion, "maya" because it has no intrinsic reality of its own. When we come to know ourselves as part of the infinite being and realize him through love do we find what is real within us. Thus, he says, "Through all the diversities of the world the one in us is threading its way towards the one in all. This is its nature and its joy. But by

[1] Sadhana, p.27.

[2] Ibid., p.34.

that devious path it could never reach its goal if it had not a light of its own by which it could catch the sight of what it was seeking in a flash. The vision of the Supreme One in our own soul is a direct and immediate intuition, not based on any ratiocination or demonstration at all. Our eyes naturally see an object as a whole, not by breaking it up into parts, but by bringing all the parts into a unity with ourselves. So with the intuition of our self-consciousness, which naturally and totally realized its unity in the Supreme One." [1]

From this sketch of the bases of his thought in which he does not differ materially from typical Hindu thought, let us go on to consider the paths he proposes by which man comes into the unity with Brahma [2] which is the goal of his life. In so doing we shall see better the distinctive content Tagore puts into his conceptions.

The realization of *union with nature* is beautifully expressed in some of his poems. Tagore himself says the truth of his being is most fully expressed in his poetry.

I quote two of his poems which speak for themselves.

"The stream of life that runs through my veins night and day runs through the world and dances in rhythmic measures.

It is the same life that shoots in joy through the dust of the earth in numberless blades of grass and breaks into tumultuous waves of leaves and flowers.

It is the same life that is rocked in the ocean-cradle of birth and of death, in ebb and in flow.

I feel my limbs are made glorious by the touch of this world of life. And my pride is from the life-throb of ages dancing in my blood this moment." [3]

"Yes, I know, this is nothing but thy love, O beloved of my heart — this

[1] Sadhana, p.36.

[2] It is to be borne in mind that Tagore uses the terms Brahma, God, Supreme One, the All, Supreme Person, interchangeably.

[3] Gitanjali, Poem 69.

golden light that dances upon the leaves, these idle clouds sailing across the sky, this passing breeze leaving its coolness upon my forehead.

The morning light has flooded my eyes — this is thy message to my heart. Thy face is bent from above, thy eyes look down upon my eyes, and my heart has touched thy feet."[1]

The *discovery* of self, the true self, which is the first step to the realization of the Infinite Being receives an unusual interpretation in his book "Personality". He says, "The personal man is found in the region where we are free from all necessity — above the needs both of body and mind — above the expedient and the useful. It is the highest in man and has personal relations of its own with the great world to which it comes for something to satisfy its personality."[2] This is the world of Art, not of Science. Art arose, he contends,[3] because man as above the animals had a surplus beyond what was needed for the satisfaction of his wants to devote to things like knowledge and goodness which are ends in themselves. Art is the outlet of his emotional energy. This is the reason man knows himself, because the efflux of his consciousness is not exhausted in its objects but returns upon himself making man conscious of himself. Therefore, in Art, man reveals himself and not his objects. Further, which arouse our emotions arouse our self feeling. In Art we express our personality which we only know by feeling. The artist as opposed to the scientist finds out the unique, the individual, which is yet the heart of the universal. He creates the living world of truth and beauty. "It is the personality of man conscious of its inexhaustible abundance; it has the paradox in it that it is more than itself; it is more than as it is seen, as it is known, as it is used. Consciousness of the infinite in the personal man ever strives to make the whole world its own. In Art the person in us is sending its answers to the Supreme Person who reveals Himself to us in a world of endless

[1] Gitanjali, Poem 59.
[2] Personality, p.12.
[3] Based on p.18 ff, Ibid.

beauty across the light-less world of facts."[1]

"The consciousness of oneness beyond all boundaries is the consciousness of soul."[2] "Therefore the one cry of the personal man is to know the supreme person."[3] Man has known direct communication of the person with Person, not through the world of forms and change but in the innermost solitude of consciousness. The ultimate reality is in the Person not in the law and substance. Again he writes, "The great Master plays, the breath is his own, but the instrument is our mind through which he brings out his song of creation, and therefore I know I live in a world whose life is bound up with mine."

This is the approach of the poet rather than the philosopher. We are not surprised then to find that instead of philosophical speculation *aesthetic experience* is made a pathway to the realization of the infinite. "What is the function of our sense of beauty in the extension of our consciousness?"[4] he asks. Beauty is omnipresent and therefore capable of giving us joy. In the first appreciation of beauty, it comes to us like a blow in sharp contrast to the not-beautiful, but gradually we realize it in harmony with all. What is unpleasant to us is not necessarily unbeautiful but has its beauty in truth. Through the sense of truth, we realize the law in creation; through our sense of beauty we realize the harmony in the universe. The expression of beauty in our life moves in goodness and love toward the infinite. Music is the highest form of art.[5] In music the heart reveals itself immediately. Music and the musician are inseparable. The world song is never separated from the singer. It is his joy itself taking never-ending form. There is a perfection in each individual strain of this music which is the revelation of completeness in the incomplete. In the beauty we find about us lies a revelation of the meaning of the universe. The scientist sees in the delicate color and fragrance of the flower only so many

[1] Personality, p.53.
[2] Ibid., p.87.
[3] Ibid., p.90.
[4] Sadhana, p.37.
[5] Ibid., on music. see p.111 ff.

facts for his analysis. To the poet they are message wafted out of the heart of the infinite and that is their true meaning.

Tagore before the experience of illumination previously described was the poet of love. The poet of *love* he remained on the new and loftier place. In love we are to realize the union of our finite selves and the infinite being. The problem which is impossible to logic in reality offers on difficulty at all. For in love, we do cross the infinite at every step. The presence of law in the world which seems to drive out the sense of mystery for so many men need be no obstacle. Literature has its laws but we do not stop there. Prosody is not a poem. In the world poem the discovery of the low of its rhythm is a true achievement of the mind, but we cannot stop there, he only has attained the final truth who knows the whole world is the creation of joy. "Joy whose other name is love, must by its very nature have duality for its realization. The lover seeks his own other self in the beloved. The immortal bliss has made himself into two. Our soul is the loved one — it is his other self. We fulfill our destiny when we go back from forms to joy, from law to love, when we until the knot of the finite and hark back to the infinite. Love is the perfection of consciousness. It is through the heightening of our consciousness into love and extending it all over the world that we can attain communion with this infinite joy." [1] "Compulsion is not indeed the final appeal to men, but joy is. And joy is everywhere. Joy is the realization of the truth of oneness, the oneness of our soul with the world, and the world soul with the supreme lover." [2] "Beauty is his wooing of our heart; it tells us everywhere that the display of power is not the ultimate meaning of creation; wherever there is a bit of color, a note of song, a grace of form, there comes the call of his love." [3]

We realize that Tagore while a Hindu seer is yet a modern Hindu seer

[1] Sadhana, p.104.

[2] Ibid., p.115.

[3] The theme of love and the figure of the lover abound in his religious poems. poems 17, 32, 56 in his Gitanjali are some of the best illustrations.

when he puts side by side with realization of the infinite in beauty, and in love, realization in action, which gets an interpretation quite its own.[1] The soul finds its freedom in *action*.[2] The soul cannot find freedom in itself but is ever freezing itself from its folds by its activity. The soul in order to release itself from the mists of indistinctness, to realize itself, is continuously creation for itself fresh fields of action. In action man is engaged in setting free his power, his beauty, his goodness, his very soul. He does not work merely on compulsion. His needs must surpass nature's bare demands for work. He has discovered that he is not complete — that he is greater than his present and that the arrest of life destroys his true function, for life and activity are inseparable.

Life and the soul are not satisfied with an internal economy. There must be commerce with the outside. The soul needs an external object. The truth is we cannot divide Him who is truth into two parts. The true spirituality which combines the emphases of both the East and the West is the correlation of within and without. The soul in all its strivings is to consecrate itself to Brahma. In this dedication lies its joy. We must be able to stay, "In my work is my joy and in that joy does the joy of my joy abide."[3] Activity is the play of joy. By his acting man provides that in which the joy of Brahman takes form and magnifies itself. "He is the fount and inspiration of our work and at the end thereof is he."[4] The same note comes at the close of an exquisite bit in Gitanjali where he writes, "And it shall be my endeavor to reveal thee in my actions, knowing it is the power gives me strength to act."[5]

---

[1] Sadhana, chapter on Realization in Action, p.120 ff.

[2] Tagore's word "freedom" has little to differentiate it in meaning from self-realization, which is the actual content of the world here. He does not touch the moral aspect of freedom which is at the center of Western philosophical interest in the problem.

[3] Ibid., p.131.

[4] Ibid., p.133.

[5] Gitanjali, poem 4. To appreciate how Tagore has developed this side of his thought in intimate relation to his pantheistic mysticism we add part of the prayer with which he closes the chapter on Action.

The pathways of the experience of beauty, of love, of action, finally fuse into the great highway which is the realization of the infinite itself. [1] At the entrance of that highway is the experience of renunciation. Indeed, we only need to give ourselves up to find Brahma everywhere. Daily worship is the daily process of surrendering ourselves, removing all obstacles to union and extending our consciousness of him in devotion and service, in goodness and love. We mush rid ourselves of the fallacy of getting, of trying to add one more thing to our belongings. In face when the soul seeks God she seeks her final escape from the incessant heaping together of things and never coming to an end. "The tragedy of human life is the effort to reach the infinite by absurdly adding to the rungs of the ladder of the finite." [2] Thus by the renunciation of the finite, the outgrowing of his possession, does man progress in the path of eternal life. On the infinite side of our existence our function is to be, not to gain, indeed to be one with Brahma" "In the region of nature which is the region of diversity we grow by acquisition. In the spiritual world, which is the region of unity, we grow by losing ourselves, by uniting." [3]

"Yes, we must become Brahma, we must not shrink to avow it." "Our soul can only become Brahma as the river can become the seal. Everything else she touches at one of her points then leaves and moves on, but she never can leave Brahma and move beyond him. Once our soul realizes her ultimate object of repose in Brahma all her movements acquire a purpose. It is this ocean of infinite rest which gives significance to endless activities. It is this perfectness of being which lends to the imperfection of becoming that quality of beauty which finds its expression in all poetry, drama, and art." [4] Since he is perfect, knowledge which is partial can never be a knowledge of him. "But we can be known by joy, by love. For joy is knowledge in its completeness, it is knowing

[1] Sadhana, p.148 ff.
[2] Ibid., p.150.
[3] Ibid., p.155.
[4] Ibid., p.156.

by our whole being."[1] Such knowledge is immediate and admits no doubt. Indeed, the realization of the supreme soul within our inner individual soul is in a state of absolute completion.

PART II

III. SPECIAL ASPECTS OF TAGORE'S MYSTICISM

There can be no room for question as to the fact that Tagore has a thoroughgoing mysticism. Except for the high notes of extreme ecstasy, he plays the whole gamut of mystical characteristics upon which we may find agreement as broadly typical. Immediacy, illumination, unity, ineffability, and mild ecstasy are all easily found in his writings and experience.[2]

But we are here concerned with pointing out those aspects of his mysticism which are special and characteristic of the man, which lift him out of the general background of Hindu mysticism with which we are already familiar.

Tagore's mysticism is in the first place markedly *aesthetic*. As already noted, he is above all and in all a poet. To his vision, God is the great Poet, the world his poem, the activity of the universe his joy in action.[3] Commerce of the soul with the all-soul is the answer of song to song. The artistic experience, expression, creation, appreciation, joy, are the ways of infinite spirit. Beauty is

---

[1] Sadhana, p.150.

[2] Prof. Coe in his Psychology of Religion pp.268-272 offers as a structural analysis of mysticism the following characteristics:

1. Sense perception of objects not physically present.
2. Systematized control that seems to be self-control.
3. Illumination.
4. Union with God, at its climax rising to ecstasy.
5. Indescribable nature of the experience.
6. When a systematized practise, the withdrawal of attention from sense stimuli to some particular object.
7. Passivity.
8. A generic type of mystical doctrine.

Cf. James classic list of the marks of mysticism in his Varieties of Religious Experience 380-381; Ineffability, Poetic quality, Transiency, Passivity. Cf. also Dean Inge "Christian Mysticism" Lecture 1.

[3] Sadhana, Ch. VII, Realization of Beauty.

the language of the universe and through it we realize the world-soul. Tagore is boldly anthropomorphic. He uses the language of the senses in religious poems of rare spiritual quality. Through this aesthetic quality there is given to his mysticism body, thrill, immediacy, and the joy of full participation in life. Asceticism is a far cry from this realization of oneness with the All.

In the second place Tagore surprises us by the *personal* quality of his mysticism. We do not expect a Hindu who takes his stand frankly upon the philosophy of the Upanishads to put so high a value on personality, but Tagore makes it one of his chief themes. His poems in Gitanjali are full of the personal note. "This is my prayer to thee, my lord." "That I want thee, only thee, let my heart repeat without end. "He came and sat by my side" "Art thou abroad on this stormy night on thy journey of love, my friend?" "My eyes strayed far and wide before I shut them and said, 'Here art thou'." "O Master Poet", "my master," "my king", — with such language does he constantly address his song offerings to the infinite God. In his chapter on The World of Personality he speaks of "the will of a Supreme Person."[1] Again he says, "God is giving himself in love to all."[2] "The one cry of the personal man has been to know the Supreme Person."[3] The individual, he holds, is unique and a unique expression of the infinite spirit which to lose would be to lose something of eternal worth.

Reinforcing this emphasis on personality as he interprets it, is the never-ending theme of love. It is unnecessary to repeat illustrations. It is enough to recognize that the poet of love who finds in love a path of union with God denied to thought, and whose songs are love poems, must inevitably give to God a personal interpretation of a kind, and have a mysticism in which the personal becomes a characteristic value. But Tagore's use of personal pronouns, of personifications and phrases, such as quoted, must not be taken

[1] Personality, p.81.
[2] Ibid., p.89.
[3] Ibid., p.90.

uncritically as the exact equivalents of the highest Christian conceptions of Personality which we have drawn fundamentally from Jesus. The clue to the difference is found in the fact that Tagore's approach in explication of personality is made through the realm of Art. His appreciation of personality is an evaluation of feeling, of self-expression, of creation, of beauty. The ethical note is submerged, though not absent. Whereas with the developed Christian ideal of personality the ethical is made central and constitutive. The will of the supreme person is, to the Christian mystic of the type which has been fruitful for religion and life, a will to righteousness ethically conceived. [1] Love is interpreted as fulfilling itself in ethical and social ends, and not in feeling or joy or even beautiful creation, valuable as these may be. So, Tagore lacks, by this measure, the full content of the concept of true personality, leaving his interpretation of the infinite personality and his purpose weak in ethical and psychological conception. Further his conception of freedom in action does not satisfy the demands of moral living for a real freedom which through real choices actually makes differences in results.

The third special aspect of Tagore's mysticism is its *social quality*. In view of the historic trend of Hindu philosophy and mysticism, the presence of this aspect is the more remarkable. We have already noted that Tagore is thoroughly non-ascetic. On the positive side there is a fine expression of democratic feeling and conviction in his writings and in his work. In his Gitanjali this side of his thought is strikingly manifest. (Space allows but for one quotation.)

"Here is thy footstool and there rest thy feet where live the poorest, and lowliest, and lost.

When I try to bow to thee, my obeisance cannot reach down to the depth

[1] St. Francis of Assisi, John Tauler, William Law, John Fox, are examples of Christians who represent a mysticism in which ethics has been so combined as to make them fruitful sevents of religion and morals. For a discussion of the union of mysticism and ethics see Rufus Jones' "Spiritual Energies in Modern Life," chap.9.

where thy feet rest among the poorest, and lowliest, and lost.

Pride can never approach to where thou walk-est in the clothes of the humble among the poorest, and lowliest, and lost.

My heart can never find its way to where thou keep-est company with the companionless among the poorest, the lowliest, and the lost."[1]

That Tagore should mark out "Action" as one of the ways of the realization of the infinite, is both evidence of his own reaction against asceticism and non-social religion, and his own positive appreciation of social experience and effort in religion. "Who is there," he says, "that thinks the union of God and man is to be found in some secluded enjoyment of his own imaginings, always from sky-towering temple of the greatness of humanity, which the whole of mankind, in sunshine and storm, is toiling to erect through the ages? Who is there who thinks this secluded communion is the highest form of religion?"[2]

This social aspect of religion, of the experience of unity with God and all humanity, gets its widest expression in his later writings,[3] where he takes his takes his stand as an apostle of *internationalism.* He opposes the modern nation as a political and economic organization of a people for mechanical purposes. When this organization, whose other name is Nation, becomes powerful at the cost of the harmony of the higher social life, then it is an evil day for humanity. Nationalism is a cruel epidemic of evil sweeping over the human world of the present age, eating into its moral vitality. Western nationalism has evolved a perfect organization of power but not of spiritual idealism. And against this encroachment of mechanism and power, gorging itself on material gains, he protests in the name of humanity." Man in his fullness is not powerful but perfect. Therefore, to turn him into mere power you have to curtail his soul as much as possible."[4] As for India he pleads, "Let our life be simple in its outer

[1] Gitanjali, poem10. Also cf.8,11, and 77.

[2] Sadhana, p.120.

[3] Nationalism, p.19ff.

[4] Ibid., p.50.

aspects and rich in its inner gain. Let our civilization take its firm stand upon its basis of social co-operation and not upon that of economic exploitation and conflict."[1] Speaking of the removal of the geographic limitations of moral brotherhood and the first reaction of greed and cruel hatred in racial contact he affirms; "Man will have to exert all his power of love and clarity of vision to make another great moral adjustment which will comprehend the whole world of men and not merely the fractional groups of nationality. The call has come to every individual in the present age to prepare himself and his surroundings for this dawn of a new era when man shall discover his soul in the spiritual unity of all human beings."[2] Thus, he gives to the mystical insight of the solidarity of all men through a universal spiritual unity, the widest application to one of the most pressing problems of our modern age.

IV. AN ESTIMATE OF THE ROLE OF TAGORE'S MYSTICISM IN HIS EVALUATIONS AND WORK

A historical study of great Christian mystics reveals how with different persons in different ages, the mystic temper and experience united with other factors to produce a wide variety of types. This combination in Rabindranath Tagore is an unusually rich and fruitful one. A host of forces contributed in his development. Not only was he in line with the finest culture of his people's past, but his own personality and ideals were formed in the midst of the intellectual renaissance of Bengal and in an unusually gifted family. The influences of the spirit and literature of the West, and of Christian conceptions were at work within the Indian movement and also to some degree directly upon Tagore himself. The social awakening in the West and the social fruits of Christian missions in India had generated a new social passion in the Brahma-Somaj within whose circle Tagore moved and labored. Tagore's travel abroad amidst conditions of international contact and later of world war stimulated his gifted and many-sided mind to deep thought on the phenomena of world

[1] Nationalism, p.50.
[2] Ibid., p.153.

civilization. His own experiences with schools as a boy and the privileges of his own upbringing by his father helped in the conception of his school at Shanti-Niketan. The connection of these factors with the social trend in his thinking is very evident. Even his mysticism has its lineage on the side of Hindu philosophy, religion and poetry. In view of this clear recognition of his dependency for much even of what seem unique, we go on to ask what was the special role of his mysticism in this complex of elements, old and new, Hindu and Western.

When we hark back to that great experience of illumination which came to him at about thirty years of age, we see that his mystical experience, begun there and never afterwards really lost, an experience and vision of union with all things and all persons filling him with love for all, actually put him at the center of life and released within him those pent-up energies in a new and dominantly religious direction. It secured for him harmony and insights which brought peace and joy for himself and gathered up into his experience of the divine the currents of culture, of humanitarian effort, of moral earnestness which surged about him, to be poured out in fresh creation in the powerful vehicle of song and verse beloved of his countrymen. While keeping its pantheistic aspect, so rich were the elements melted in the crucible of his experience and so fine the spiritual nature of the man, that Tagore's mysticism has made him one of the creative personalities of modern India and surely of our whole present age. The fact that he has given himself to a creative experiment in education which seeks for well-rounded and spontaneous development of personality for the boys of any caste is evidence of the social fruitfulness of his mysticism. And the uniquely spiritual conception and conduct of the school I believe to be the fruit of his religions mysticism. His own union with the spiritual life of the world in its rich variety and multiform aspects, realized as centrally one, has given Tagore that inner scale of values which makes him put the emphasis always on the human and spiritual. Because of it he does not just react against a civilization which is contrasted with and in some senses hostile to his own, but pierces to its spirit and appreciates its values. He would ally the spiritual resources of his own race and land with these spiritual values in the west to interpret life in such a way as to free it everywhere from mechanism and strife. His mysticism reinforces his largest insights and projects them with the conviction and beauty of his own rare personality into the large problems of India's social reconstruction and the difficult and imperative task of world brotherhood built on a basis of spiritual humanity.

From the fully developed Christian standpoint Tagore has his limitations. We have noted the lack of the fully ethical content in his conception of personality and also an inadequate treatment of freedom. He further seems to fail adequately to recognize the psychological and social conditions for the growth of a personality, making it almost entirely rest on a philosophical doctrine of unity. [1] And he does not escape the limitations of a monistic world view. Evil is conceived rather on the Absolutist fashion as something to be transcended by insight rather than as a moral and social fact to be concretely done away with by effort. He says "Whatever checks the freedom of endless growth is sin, which is the evil which works against man's eternity." [2] This seems admirable till we see what his idea of growth means when we led back to the realization of union." The life in which the consciousness of separation takes first place, this is the life of self. The life in which the consciousness of unity is primary, this is the life the spirit." [3] Thus evil is equivalated with imperfection, fragmentariness, finiteness, and erroneous views of the world. We feel need of a more rugged, realistic and moral doctrine of sin to do justice to the facts.

---

[1] Personality, chapter on Second Birth, p.100ff. For works dealing with function of social experience in the growth of personality and as a necessary condition to any personality at all, reference is made to H. Cooley's "Human Nature and the Social Order", John Dewey's "Human Nature and Conduct", and an article by Spaulding in Scribers, Jan. 1922 on "What Am I?"

[2] Sadhana, pp.47–65.

[3] Personality, p.104.

Again, his view of death, [1] while beautifully philosophic and triumphant over fear, is after all a negation of his own evaluation of personality. Death is the welcome back into the arms of the all, absorption in the stream of eternal a spirit and activity. But this leaves us not only with a frustrated personality, but with a conception which is not after all fully socialized.

A very important limitation on his thought is revealed in his treatment of Science. [2] We feel a hearty response to his message of revolt against the mechanistic and partial views, and their fateful consequences, which science of a certain type has to a large degree fostered in our Western life. But we cannot fail to recognize that he has greatly undervalued the spiritual service of science and her spiritual possibilities when science is true to herself. The Christian seeking the fullest development for all men of spiritual social personality cannot accept a mysticism which is in unrelated antithesis to science, for thereby it fails to serve the full needs of religion in our day.

The limitations we have noted appear to the limitations inherent in a mysticism based upon the monistic pantheism of India. But this does not hinder our appreciation of Tagore's greatness. He is a unique figure with a unique message. At a time when we are trying to revision the world and see it "round", to make fruitful union of the meanings of both Western and Eastern human experience, when we are striving in the midst of an age when power and the multiplication of things threaten to devastate the human spirit, to gain "a just conception of the real ends of life ", to use Bertrand Russell's fine phrase, Tagore comes to us with a new insistance, cast in world setting, on the great truth that "the things which are temporal, but the things which are not seen are eternal." Tagore the mystic knows, feels, sees the Eternal, in the midst of his efforts for his school, for India's social regeneration, and for our divided world life. It is this fact that makes him a prophet in two hemispheres.

---

[1] Gitanjali, poems 84, 87, 91, 100.

[2] The first two chapters of his "Personality" are largely given up to his polemic against Science over against which he presses the claims of spiritual personality.

SELECTION FROM "GITANJALI"

"Where the mind is without fear and the head is held high;

Where knowledge is free;

Where the world has not been broken up into fragments by narrow domestic walls;

Where tireless striving stretches its arms toward perfection;

Where the clear stream of reason has not lost its way into the dreary desert sand of dead habit;

Where the mind is led forward by thee into ever-widening thought and action —

Into that heaven of freedom, my Father, let my country awake."

— Tagore

——《齐大心声》，第 1 卷第 1 期，1924 年 4 月，6 月

泰戈尔来华

沈志昂

千年的枯树，
被人伐了几次的枯树，
永不再丛茂了，
永不再鲜艳了，
更没有人爱重他，
欢迎他。

霹雳一声，
慈善的仁雨，
养活了好多萎谢的植物。
料不到枯树枝上竟也放出一朵美丽而娇嫩的爱之花。
无论什么人，

见了手舞足蹈地羡慕他，
赞美他。

花儿一经开了，
好像千年的枯树发出炫目的光明，
照满了世界，
却惊醒了好睡人。

今朝花儿乘印度洋的大风，
吹到中国来，
那是中国人心悦诚服的表示欢迎他，
可是不多天，
北冰洋的寒风起来了，
怕要把他仍吹回罢？

花儿呀！
当你未开之先，
已开之初，
谁也想到如是的光明鲜艳，
受人们无限的赞赏。
可惜不能常开，
永放光明，
怕不再数十年，
早已寻不到了！

十三，四，十九·自修室

——《江苏省立第四中学校校友会月刊》，第15期，1924年4月30日

太谷尔讲稿

印度诗圣——提倡东方文化——崇尚自然

余青年时代之光阴，多半消磨于恒河两岸，常日默于河畔，在野鸭群中，得心灵之感觉，而一生诗歌思想，亦均从自然中得之。故见山水花鸟，都觉十分自然。若令于正式会场，当众演说，则恐不能自然将所蓄意思，尽情宣泄耳。余最初对于中国之感觉，实于印度大戏剧家嘉利达之剧中得之。盖其中有一场，为风飘旗帜，流苏动荡，而此流苏，即为中国制品。在此种含有诗意之感觉中，即得中国文化极深之印象。中印两国，本有极深之关系。佛教自印度传来中土，即为中印两国文化互换之机关。印度以自身文化作礼品，赠诸中国，中国乐于接受。此种伟大的，牺牲的，包罗万象的精神，充溢于东方，因而造成东方伟大之文明。至余此来，实受一种感动。对于中国目前处境之危险，事端之纷繁，人民之痛苦，均所深知，每为祈祷，希望得安然度此难关。余之来也，非政治家，非传教者，实为求道而来。故余所携，惟敬与爱。余至中国，如居古庙，每觉背后有无数牺牲之精神，因得成就如此伟大之文化。惟世界日趋于败坏，故吾人在任何地方，均得见彼死笨无生气之痕迹，而予吾人以无限之创痛！即如余来上海，在城市间固未曾得见丝毫足以表现中国文化之精神，余诚深以为憾！野草支蔓，损及田禾，此种现象，实所痛心！中国文化，因物质文明而被创，犹之魔鬼展其破坏之舌，尽吞我生命之涎，欲不哀痛，又乌乎可！以言文化与物质，则如谷粒比钻石，谷虽不如钻价之钜，而其真价值乃远过之，物质发达，真趣消失，将来世界，恐徒见闪烁死的光彩，欲觅生的物类，且不可得。即如印度恒河，固世界有名之大河，两岸风景，幽美绝伦。今则烟突林立，机器盈耳，自然真趣，消失无遗，每为之欷歔长叹！惟吾人既生人世，不能完全脱离社会，物质文明，亦未尝无所用。余之所言，盖因物质文明在人生历程中所处位置，颠倒乖乱，遂造成无限之恼闷。余非政治家，亦非外交家，不过一纯粹之诗人，只知心有所感，尽以告人。见兹中国文化，被物质所迫，濒于危险之境，不得不据实以告，深望于人人心中，引起反抗的精神，以维护东方固有之文化，而此种工作之具，尤非牺牲不可云云。

——《中华基督教育》，第 4 卷第 11 号，1924 年 5 月

泰戈尔与梅兰芳之握手

印度诗家泰戈尔氏，近游北京，各界欢迎备至。而梁任公林宗孟二君，过从尤密。一日，泰氏忽云久闻中国梅兰芳之名，欲与一见，二君当即介绍相晤。谈次产遗倾慕。泰氏平日对人不甚作周旋语，而于兰芳则备极赞扬。并谓行装已戒，然极欲一观梅君之剧而行，庶几不负此游。兰芳因订于五月十九在开明戏院特演洛神一剧，特请泰氏及其偕行诸友莅观，而余座则仍照常售票。是日剧座之满，竟无隙地，西人男女尤多。泰氏入座时，座客翘首以观风采者甚众。剧毕后与兰芳晤谈片刻而散。其对于洛神一角，异常赞美，谓其甘如新酿之蜜，其美如七色之虹云云。此老评剧，亦饶诗意，可传为佳话也。

——《新闻报》，1924 年 5 月 25 日

什么话

太戈尔在武昌演说："中国此时并不需要物质的进步，中国此时更急的需要，便是精神的复兴。"

太戈尔的翻译徐志摩说："本来我们对于太戈尔先生，最重要的是瞻仰他伟大的丰彩，亲聆他雷响的声音，至于讲演的内容，倒是不关重要的。"

——《向导》，第 68 期，1924 年 6 月 4 日

精神文明与物质文明

马君武

最近印度诗哲泰戈尔来沪，提倡精神文明，一般信从者，若竟认其说，为可以抵制物质文明，尤大不然。泰戈尔不失为文学家之资格，欲借此以攻击科学，批评科学，榭斩新之帜，未免太拘一隅。世界文明，无论出自东方西方，均为有益于人类之贡献，可供人类无穷尽之研究。简直言之，文明且为世界所公有，精神之文明物质之文明，如身有两翼，并举之前飞，而后其本身可缘之以行，或斩其左，或斩其右，又或以左咎右，以右咎左，皆足以阻碍其自身前途之发达。若云战争剧烈，咎在物质进化，物质殊不任其咎，中印历史，常有干戈遍地，杀人盈野之惨，何所赖于物质，任何时期人类，道德一经堕落，即动杀机，顷刻之间，可致数十百万人于死，言至此，颇多愤慨。末谓诸君求真实学问，无论对于精神物质，务各先有相当之研究，切勿轻信，亦勿轻疑，俟吾良知得到真实见解，而后再下一种相当之判断。

——《申报》，1924年6月3日

服装之美与丑

太戈尔谓女子之心理无一不爱美，而中国女子近今之服装则既短且窄反有似乎爱丑而远不若古装之美然。使今日之女子果自觉其服装之丑，决不作如是之服装也。惟人以为美，而彼亦美之，乃以环境之习惯改变其心理而不自觉，其以丑为美耳。而一入太戈尔之目，则竟以为丑。夫太戈尔固以爱与美为精神者，其几真知美之为美，丑之为丑乎？彼以为丑，或者其果不美乎？余谓爱美恶丑，人情所同。今日女子之服装，可决其必非爱丑而然，并可决其亦由爱美而然。然至爱美而旁观者，适以为丑，则亦一可以研究之问题矣。

——《申报》，1924年6月5日

印度诗圣泰戈尔翁和中国

这回印度诗圣泰戈尔翁，漫游中国，爱国的人士极表欢迎，综合他于各地讲演的大意，“我们东洋人自昔代以来，即受西洋人的压迫，而对我们的压迫专用智力和体力的压迫，因为过度的压迫，致我们无自觉，竟至忘自己的地位，对他们来东洋的时候我们不知道用主人的资格对他，又吾们对乡土的东方有什么人存在，或用什么方法欢迎他们西方人士才好，并至这样方法都没分享，所以我们东方虽是尽有足以他们欢喜的无限宝藏，亦不能够和他们缔好，但看今日的模样，缔好的时期谅将迫近，人类的进化，实可做三期的分别，我们已过第一期和第二期，将近于第三期即凡历史的起初，洪水和猛兽时代，是为初期，那时候人类和洪水战，且和猛兽动开爪牙的战，是争生存的时代，吾们人类虽不能用力胜他，却幸有脑力能够征服他，第二期即用智力和体力行战争的时代，体力和智力弱的人，被强的人所征服，现时西方人士已到达这时代了，我们东洋人士，这时代已自早经过，现时属第三期因为我们经已觉醒于人类是不可徒以智力体力征服人的，以外还有很切要的事，就是发现很光明很深奥而且广阔的世界，足使吾们由极暗黑寂寥的世间而导向光明深奥广阔的世界的明灯，这种思想是不可无的，但是我们欲达这种世界，须有觉悟能尽服从和牺牲的两人，我们欲得最大的自由，不论何事说要能忍耐服从，且我们真欲得最大的光明，更当要觉悟尽大的牺牲，怎样说呢？服从的后面，能够开自由的路，牺牲的后面，能够点光明的灯，这样牺牲，在普遍人观来，就说有极大的损失，但是这不过肉体上的损失，正是留下后来得大利益的缘有称做利益，就是得到达光明自由世界的事，总说一句，将来定体力智力以外，有尊尚悠崇高的生命时代可到，而我们东方人士，经有这种生命，不同他们西洋人现正没头于杀人科学的研究，并凌辱压迫那样智力体力的未发达的徒辈，虽是我们洋人尚被压迫的时候，若肯尽我们的服从和牺牲，要脱他们的压迫，是无难的。”翁这样排斥物质文明，实是要鼓吹精神的文明。翁又常说“惟主义可称做救世方法，欧米的物质文明，为酿成破坏兽欲战争，以外那里有什么价值呢？”物质文明洵是杀人灭道的工具，翁的感叹很类似这样。他又说："印度的恒河为世界有名的大河，两岸的风景是幽美，真属可爱的名胜地方，今日已变成烟突林立，处处机声轰轰，真可聋的那样热闹状况，徒消失自然的雅趣，岂不是可畏叹息么？"翁那样的高说，在中国学者，多表同感。有说，"我们闻翁的说话，不觉怆然自失，我们中华算是极早发达文化，今日变成这样，这不是明明被物质文明所破坏么，翁的话真可促起我们极大的注意……"泰戈尔和中国人士，有极深挚的交游，于中国学术界应有极大的影响了。

——《台湾民报》，第 2 卷第 10 期，1924 年 6 月 11 日

来年之印度诗人太戈尔

苏维霖

太戈尔生于一八六一年五月六日，他的家庭是印度著名的望族，近百年来产生了不少的伟大的人物，为勉加而（Bengal）地方的文艺复兴的先驱者，在宗教音乐政治实业等等都有狠大的贡献，所以印度人，尤其是勉加而的人，一讲起这个家族来，便带着十二分的敬意。他的祖父是一个王子，狠慈善，当时以社会改革家著名。他的父亲受了慈善家的气质，把着牺牲的精神，坚定的主义，不愿意做国王而注了全生的心血去谋社会宗教的改革。这种热诚同奋斗，不知不觉之中得了"大哲"的称呼了。太戈尔自己是一个天才，聪颖的智慧，明断的脑子，活泼耐善的气质，造成他一个诗人，并且是一个哲学家。他的诗歌是自然的结晶，他的哲学是东方精神文明的产物。曾到过英美游历，但是当时反不引起欧美社会的注意。及一九一三年得了瑞典文学会的诺贝尔奖金（Nobel Prize），再得了英国爵士的封位，他的声誉在欧洲简直没有人同他并肩了。他得着奖金那一年，在英国讲演"生之实现"，英美国的人民欢迎他比本国的任何文人还甚些。他又到美国去讲演，题目是"人格论"，美国人欢迎它的盛况，不亚于欢迎英国的皇太子。他也来过日本，日本人敬奉他如神明，称他"圣的太戈尔"。他的作品从此一天多一天翻成美法德日文了。

他在印度办了一个国际大学，丝毫不受英政府的辅助，拿诺贝尔奖金

同作者的报酬充作该校的经费。一九二一年他又渡欧洲，到德国去讲演，因战争疲劳的德国人对于他所称道的东方精神文明极力赞赏鼓吹，奉他为传道的大师。一九二三年秋间，他忽然想访问姊妹行的中国，会晤酷爱和平的兄弟们！中国人——只好中国方面负担旅费，于是乎讲学社就给他送盘费去了，上海商务印书馆的小说月报也因此出版了两本四百余页的太戈尔号，满了他的诗歌散文著作了。可这时候他在加尔加太（Calcana）得了脚痛热病了，非等到翌年春天，他的病好了之后不能来。今年春天到了，他的病也好了，可以到中国来了。但是他的家族同朋友们都不愿意这个六十四岁的老诗人跋涉那么远的路程来中国，所以他的来华好像无期了。但是他们这种规劝，究竟不能阻止老诗人坚决的意志，四月十九号就在上海同中国人见面了。他经过这样长的旅行，身体狠懒了，不得不跑到杭州去安息一下，所以一切的聚会讲演都拒绝了。二十三号继续进北京来，除在清华学校同北京佛教研究会讲过两次之外，在真光电影院讲演七八次，都是北京大学教授徐志摩口译的。太戈尔极力提倡东方生活、东方思想，攻击西方物质文明，因此引起一般青年们的怀疑同反对。青年们反对他是：中国现在物质文明狠低，受外国帝国主义者的压迫非常利害，差不多变成了半殖民地了。太戈尔怎么一倡精神文明，就要使中国人甘于受物质文明发达的国家的羁縻，永远不能脱出奴隶的圈套建设独立国家。所谓东方的生活已经不合时世了，东方的思想有的地方也不合现社会的要求了，太戈尔一味赞美，结果要使东方民族没有向上的一天，怀疑他是受了英国政府的贿赂，在东方游说东方的民族服从帝国主义的国家，永远做物质文明国的奴隶。他受了这一番的反对同怀疑，精神十分懊丧了，再也没有心讲下去，跑到武汉去了。他在武昌讲演的时候把来华的感想说出来，他说中国在今天并不急需物质的进步，而最急需的是东方精神文化的复活。咲！老诗人的确不明了中国的现状，因为他不明了，所以所受的欢迎，总要比他预料的差狠远啦。

——《台湾民报》，第 2 卷第 12 期，1924 年 7 月 1 日

听太戈尔讲演以后

至 精

四月十八号下午四时上海各团体在闸北商务印书馆俱乐部欢迎印度诗人太戈尔，并请他讲演。太氏年六十又四，貌已龙钟，但音调清朗，不如其人，服装古雅，与世俗殊甚。彼是自然之宠爱子，言语行动，均足以表示彼嗜好自然之特性。余聆听其言论，择其一二，以誌吾怀。太氏云彼幼时恒河两岸多高大森林，鸟的鸣声，水的流声，和煦的日光照着，不寒的柳风吹着天然美景如何可爱呵！如何自然呵！今也不然；恒河两岸惟见工厂林立，恒河中皆运送工厂出品之轮船，违背自然，追逐物质，这是何等可怕的现象呵！余以为自然科学昌明，物质文明所给予人们的残酷地方，是无可讳言的；但我们决不能说科学不应当提倡促进，反要回到那太古时代的生活；因为科学的本身非不好，只是人们将他误用了，将它用作少数人的幸福的利器。所以我以为一面当使科学发达，促进物质文明；一面当团结有觉悟的民族，作彻底的社会革命，将目下万恶的私有经济组织完全推翻，达到各尽所能，各取所需的目的，我们不要作资本家的走狗，什么服务社会的名词，在今日不过作为少数资本家驾驰青年的一种术语罢了；真为社会服务是这样吗？望有为的青年勿为彼等所迷呵！大家团结起来，作群众的运动罢！太氏到上海，说在街上看不出中国的真精神，我听了，委实心痛呵！未到过上海的青年，以为上海是中国极文明极好的地方，殊不知上海乃国际帝国主义用经济侵略我国的场所！上海是中国领土，中国人在上海租界内一切行动，反受外人的约束！主人翁的地主，已成为附属品的资格了！有为的中国爱国的青年呀，你们真以上海为中国极文明极好的地方吗？你们若明白这种情形，就应该打破媚外的心理，唤起民众的觉悟，使大家知道真正民族的自决，不是被压迫在国际帝国主义下面的民族所能做得到的；尤应知道我们若要推翻国内资本家和军阀的垄断和专横，非先打倒国际帝国主义的侵略不可；因为后者是前者所依为根据的。中国的青年呀！立足上海的青年呀！你们不要做媚外的迷梦，火速联络起来，打倒国际的侵略者，恢复民族自决的真精神罢！以上两点是我听了太氏讲演后的感想，至于太氏的思想，我以为是中国现在青年所万分不当承受的；不过太氏对自然所生的爱是我们精神修养方面所不可少的。

——《职业市季刊》，第 6 期，1924 年 7 月 10 日

Tagore, Poet of Idealism

H.P. Shastari

Annotated by Z.K.Zia（谢颂羔）

More than five thousand years ago the Hindu sages living in the deep Himalayas and meditating on the deeper problems of being and becoming, leading a life of absolute altruism, discovered the principle of non-dualism, and cried in the ecstasy of spiritual joy "He who sees unity in diversity to him belongs the Truth and to none else." Ever since it has been the chief duty of every Brahman to rediscover the same Truth in himself, and devote the rest of his life to preaching the same, depending on alms for the maintenance of his body. To a Hindu Ignorance means the feelings of separation, and narrowness of heart.

Rabindranath Tagore, father of the world famous poet, Rabindranath Tagore, was a Brahman who in spite of his great wealth and social position devoted his whole life to service of God and man, prayer, silent meditation, and teaching the Truth of Vedanta being his chief pleasures in life. His lectures on Hindu philosophy and devotion are still read by thousands in India.

Rabindranath is the youngest son of that great devotee. He received his early education in Bengali in his home. The atmosphere of his home being charged with spiritual and cultural ideas Rabindranath in his early life showed interest in poetry and devotion. When hardly eight years old he wrote his first poem in Bengalee. He was in school for a short time only as his free spirit revolted against the limitations imposed on him by the authorities. His life has been greatly influenced by one of his early teachers in school, a Spanish Father of the Roman Church who was, according to Tagore, steeped in love of God.

Finding that he was fonder of abstract things than of any secular knowledge, Tagore's parents lost all hope in his career and felt quite pessimistic about his future. Nobody could dream at that time that this boy-idealist would one day be considered one of the greatest poets the world has ever seen.

When nineteen years old Tagore went to England to study in a British university. Materialism has never had any attraction for Tagore and when he saw the people there thinking of their physical needs and material pleasures only, he felt the want of that spiritual atmosphere which was so dear to his heart. He soon discovered that he could not feel at ease in an atmosphere of materialism where little interest was taken in things Eternal and the pursuit of physical pleasures was considered the chief aim of life. He left England without completing his studies and returned to India, to the great disappointment of his family.

His early works were musical comedies and a few operas in the Indian language. He wrote short stories which attracted unusual attention. He now lived in a small houseboat, sailing up and down on the holy river, the Ganges, where he wrote most of his poetical works. It was at this time that Rabindranath realized the unity of God and man, and became a sage or a Rishi. He was so much possessed by God-intoxication that for a few days after the realization of the great Truth Tagore lived semiconscious of his worldly surroundings.

He wrote many novels to teach his countrymen the true ideals of life, the chief of which is Cora. In his devotional poems Tagore follows the Vaish-nava poets of the fifteenth century and "Gitanjali," the book which brought him the Nobel prize, the highest literary honour that a man can receive. This was his own translation of his book "Naivadya." So far nearly hundred works by Tagore have been published.

Tagore is not only a great poet, but also a great philosopher who lives what he teaches. He has not made any money out of his books. His own wealth which was considerable and the income from his publications goes to his University, Vishwa Bharti, at Bolpur near Calcutta. He is travelling in the world in his old age to deliver his spiritual message to the world and create an interest in his International University which has already become a world famous institution.

Gandhi represents the heart of India while Tagore is an incarnation of Indian idealism. His chief reading is the Upanishad. He is also a wonderful singer and the Committee would have doubled the Nobel prize had they heard Tagore sing his devotional songs of Gitanjali. Gandhi and Tagore are great friends and when Mahatma Gandhi was operated upon Tagore offered his personal services as nurse.

Tagore was created a Knight by the King. But his idealist spirit was not satisfied with it and he preferred to be called Dr. Tagore rather than Sir Rabindranath. After the Amritsar massacre by General Dyer Tagore returned his high title to the Government.

Tagore lives a life of extreme simplicity. He eats little, sleeps little, and talk little. His chief pleasure lies in devotion to God and singing His praises. To him the world is a manifestation of God and he therefore condemns none, hates none, and loves both the sinner and the saint. His presence fills one with peace, to talk to him is to forget all the limitations of life. He is absolutely unconscious of his greatness and is always most peaceful. I will never forget the bliss I have had in his company which reminds me of the days of Rama Tirtha and Sri Krishna. Rabindranath Tagore puts the gist of Rama Tirtha and Sri Krishna. Rabindranath Tagore puts the gist of his philosophy in the following verse taken from his "Gitanjali":

"This is my prayer to thee, my lord, — strike, strike at the root of penury in my heart.

"Give me the strength to lightly bear my joys and sorrows.

"Give me the strength never to disown the poor, or bend my knees before insolent might.

"Give me the strength to raise my mind high above daily trifles.

"And give me the strength to surrender my strength to thy will with love."

Rabi Babu, as we Indians love to call him, is a universal poet.

He writes for children, for farmers, for scholars, for women, for workmen, for everybody, and still his theme is the same: devotion and service.

On his return to India Tagore has talked of the Chinese and the things Chinese in terms of high admiration, and his visit to China has brought the two great peoples nearer.

— *Chung Hwa English Weekly*, Jun. 12, 1926

Tagore in China

"Tagore has not altogether appealed to some of the elements in China. He is too willing to recognize the good in Western institutions and too truly international to suit the present phase of acute nationalism in this country." So says Dr. Henry Hodgson of Shanghai in a private letter received in Kobe. However, there was another reason for the displeasure shown by some of the Peking scholars towards Tagore. They understood his denunciation of "materialism" as an attack on science. He explained that it was nothing of the kind, and before he left he received expressions of regret from some who had opposed him.

— *The North-China Daily News*, Jul. 1, 1924

Rabindranath Tagore and Children

On Friday afternoon Dr. Rabindranath Tagore was entertained at Marble

Hall by Mr. E. S. Kadoorie. A large number of people were present. This was the day before Dr. Tagore left Shanghai. After tea, Dr. Tagore made the following speech in which he dwelt specially on his ideas for the training of children.

I am not a speaker by profession or trade, not having that talent I always fell great reluctance when I am asked to speak. I know that I have dealing with language, with words the most part of my life, but this is in silence and in solitude, and then only have they gained their light, their speed and their force, but when I am among my listeners I always feel nervous when I have to talk to them. Though I have had opportunity over and over again of addressing big meetings, I have never got over this "stage fright" as they call it. I am very shy and rather of a retiring disposition. The most part of my life I have lived in utter seclusion away from the crowd of men in my own beautiful countryside near the Ganges and its habitations, quietly for months and months together, and then it was my silent voice which spoke from my heart and which has reached the minds or men in distant shores — but as for speeches, I have not that gift. You know a lion can roar whenever it likes, lying or standing or sitting, whenever it feels like it can roar and it can growl, but a bee can occupy their platform and roar at their audience.

I have to wait for my inspiration and then my voice comes out of the depth of my heart.

I believe most of you have heard that I did speak last night, it was by some chance that it came to me like the wind that catches the sail, and it did come and it was spontaneous and my heart spoke out and I could speak.

Today you want me to say something before I take my leave of you — all that I have to say is this — that is has been a very great pleasure for me to know my host. I have rarely met with individuals who have wealth, material wealth as well as wealth of heart and spirit. I remember only a few whom I have admired with all my heart for the gift of benevolence, of doing good to humanity and also the practicability they possess, and know it is by chance I came to know Mr. Kadoorie. He very kindly sent me an invitation though I was unknown to him. At first I felt great hesitation in accepting the invitation because, as I have said, I am rather shy and I thought that as he is a man of wealth he might not know what I stand for, or what I represent, what ideals I have in mind, what I am working for, and he may not be in sympathy with it, so I had great hesitation before I accepted his invitation, but I am glad I did.

The Children's Demand

You all know for what I am working. It is going against my grain to go about from door to door from country to country carrying my message. It is not the kind of work I am accustomed to for I work in the solitude of my silence. But I did feel the call of the humans, I felt it every day more and more. It came stronger every day. I came out of my solitude and gave up most of my literary work in which I was engaged at that time — I came out and I brought together a few students. I wanted to help them, these students. What was my idea? It was this — that the idea of education which prevails in this world is utterly wrong. I have no doubt it that some human beings will be able to find out that they have been going against nature when they are made to learn their lessons, while they are not in the heart of nature. It is this atmosphere of freedom that gives to them all their lessons, only in human children their minds are tortured, because the adults, the school masters have their own ideas of teaching and the subject they choose, and they force the things upon these young and poor children who are helpless and have had no chance of escaping from the tyranny of these school masters. Nature has provided children with a great fund of restlessness, the children grow up, they run about and through this energy of restlessness they knock their minds against information, he against facts, against lessons. They come with all their force and all their minds and bounce against the facts of the world, and the shock impresses these facts upon their minds, and they gain a great deal of knowledge and from these experiences of utter freedom in the heart of nature, with this gift of life which they have brought into this world, and these poor creatures who love life, who love light, who love freedom, who love their mothers and who love their own people, they are all unfortunately driven to place where their minds have been tortured to keep still.

Torture of Keeping Still

Why should they keep still? They are asked not to move, not to be bad in their talk, not to move their hands and feet. They must move their hands and feet, it is Nature's own bidding which makes them move their hands and feet, and this great world of freedom is set aside, and instead they have this ugly school building, with white walls staring them in the face, no colour, no forms, no beauty and no association of life. And I know for certain that it cannot be right for human children to be forced to accept this life of torture, because they have been born in ignorance that they should be punished for that. No, I was certain that they had to have their lessons in an atmosphere of freedom and in the bosom of Mother Nature herself, where all around them their schooling will come from the sky, from the cloud, from the rustling leaves, from all the facts of life that come to them unasked and unbidden, and with their restless curiosity they will find for themselves their own facts by their own experiences, and gradually their minds will be rested — but this is utterly neglected, they lose their creative faculty from their infancy. Their masters say, "you do this," while they have their ideas of doing something else, and they are wishing and longing to do something that impels them. Don't you know that it is the most important of all gifts that a child derives from the world — this gift of creation? All the time it is the imagination that works to make something of its own minds, but the master says "No, don't do that or this, be still and quiet and behave like an adult." The boys are made to forget that they are children. Is it right? And I know that tyranny if it is constant and persistent can do wrong.

An Education That Kills

I am perfectly certain that the education system which has been prevalent in the world is causing us to lose great gift of knowledge and a great number of individuals are modeled into an average type of standardized, education which helps them to become clerks in some Government office, but it does not help them to find out their own personality or their own soul. In fact, this education utterly kills their own sense of their personality and the reasons of their existence which gives them their freedom, and I said I would give them freedom, and I offered them freedom.

I have my children in a building bringing them up in an atmosphere of freedom and culture. Unfortunately, I am not alone — I have my own teachers who have been brought up as others. I gave up going to school when I was 13 and that saved me! Most of teachers were not wise enough to leave off early, they persisted till they got their M.A. and B. A. degrees. There are some who have failed in their examinations and in what they call discipline and all that. Now, I know of course that there must be something of these taught. I tried to give them as much freedom as it is possible, and I know from my personal experience that this freedom has saved many of people of institutions, and boys from going wrong, and I came out with this love of freedom. And what happened to me when I was in the company of these children? I found out the eternal child which dwells in every human being, the child has the creative gift, and child wants to build his own world, that Child has creative gift, and he has the eternal spirit of growth. They become wise and fixed in their doctrines. When I came into touch with the children I found the child within me. I say that when I was 40 years I began to grow, I am still growing and I have not come to the end of it. Lessons come to us as daily surprises. Surprises come to us in our joys, our sorrows and games, they all come upon us as great surprises then we are thoroughly roused. We come to understand greater problems and because these things come as a shock and surprise, then death comes which we don't expect.

The Life of Surprise

All lessons should come like surprises, but our education and institution lose absolutely that spirit of surprise and wonder, its every subject is definitely fixed, the hour is fixed, the teacher is fixed, and the poor child has to suffer the monotony of this dead education which is imposed upon them. And the cry of the children comes to me, suffering children — they say "Poet you can save us, you have faith in child life, you love children, save us."

What is freedom? Freedom is only perfect relationship between our fellow beings, because when we are in a strange place why do we feel constrained? Because the relationship is not perfect, we are pulled back, but directly the perfect relationship is established which we fell among our brother, among those whom we love — then we gain freedom. Freedom is not negative, but it is positive. It is with the freedom of perfect relationship that we come close to each other. I have me come to you, supposing you were not kindly to me I would be like a prisoner. The least little kindness you show to me you offer freedom to me, because that helps then that atmosphere of kindliness and hospitality, my friends, and this is pleasure, this is happiness, but everywhere this is thwarted, and the whole world is suffering from this, and I said to myself. "This is not the time for you to remain in your solitude — come out." Though I am weak, I am old and I have no strength of the young though I have the confidence of the young, for it is a sign of senility to want faith in ideals—I am fortune, I have all these.

The Cry of the Age

But as I say, the cry of age has come to me and I go from door to door, from country to country urging people to come to close to each other, because it is from the meeting of hearts through the meeting of souls, of ideals, that great streams of truth flow.

You do not know, that your people, I mean the Jewish community, you occupy a particularly locality where the East and the West did meet, where all these great ancient civilizations had their conflicts, their fights — Egypt on one side on Palestine of the other side, and Rome — there was this great churn of mind, and you did produce a great civilization and ideals and the same thing has happened with Japan and China. And now the whole world is waiting for this. The human races have not met in their right spirit and therefore this great fact of coming into close touch with each other is not carried out.

Who am I — a poet! I have turned out my thoughts through the medium of words. What have I to do with buildings and institutions, with practical men who are experienced and prudent and far-sighted. I did call from my mission and found that nobody would believe me and I had to take upon myself this work. I felt that no one would come to my help, that I must walk alone and so I go from country to country carrying this cause of truth which I have taken up, and when I meet with people who are not intent upon profit-making and who have still got the freshness of faith in their minds, I feel rested. There are people who come round me and who profess admiration for me and say I am a great poet. I do not accept their homage because they do not accept my ideals. They don't work with me — their hearts are elsewhere, and I am alone and struggle with my weak strength and my weak voice, going from door to door.

The Search for Ideals

I appeal to you, if ever you feel this call also — as you must, it is in the air, you must listen to it if you want to be saved. These countries which are only occupied with their own local problems they will lose this great opportunity of this present age when all the problems will have become the world's problems, and you must listen to them, and when you don't forget this old man who is struggling to find idealist to the call which he has heard, and I am glad to say that in my wanderings I did meet men who have the enthusiasm for idealism.

Therefore do not deal with truth with mere curiosity, with superficial curiosity but with deep enthusiasm which truth claims from us — do not deal with truth in that supercilious manner of patronage, do not be proud of your gifts, try to bow your head down when the message does come — forget your narrow self and bring out your best. Never come to it in the spirit of curiosity, not with that modern spirit of something which is very difficult to define, something fashionable, or believe they have their fashionable sentiments which are of no use to anybody. Either reject truth with all its thoughts or you accept them and know right in the proper manner of spirit and humility and self-sacrifice, otherwise I can tell you, my friends, that it is this which makes me feel so reluctant to speak. I know there are very few people who will accept this ideal if they do not, then truth is tarnished by being used in the market place and places where there dwells indifference of mind and cynicism. Therefore, I feel great reluctance to speak out what I have in mind here. Forgive me if I have said anything which seems to you rude, you must know it is not my own personal self that speaks out. I have the call of the great truth which has been given to me, and I have come to offer this before you. If you accept you help me materially my friend, if not — well, I go my own way, alone.

— *The North-China Daily News*, Jul. 1, 1924

太戈尔莅晋演说补志

太戈尔氏是以五月二十一日莅晋，二十二日在文瀛湖畔自省堂讲演，听讲者万人空巷，自省堂竟无隙地。太戈尔氏来时，几无路可走，乃由旁门而入，直上讲台，由冯教育会长略为报告，即由太戈尔氏讲演，讲时约三十分钟。讲毕，由徐志摩君翻译。因人数太多，翻译声浪较小，词句多带土音，大半不能明白。所以翌日太原各报，皆未见登出讲演稿之全豹。记者位次于讲台相近，对于讲演大意，自信尚不误会，因特补志于此。但据听讲之日已久，又未必不无舛错，阅者请谅之。记者载：

我（太戈尔氏自称下仿此）这次由印度来到中国，又绕道来到山西，得与诸位在此谈话。我的心中，实在欢喜的不得了。中国与印度在世界上，都是东方的古国，而中印的文化关系，亦发生较早，所以我到中国来，好像走到了第二故乡。可是东方的中印两古国，到现在都成了被西方物质文明压迫的国家。不仅中印两国，以外许多的弱小国家，都被少数国或少数人压迫着。世界本是无尽的宝藏，世界所有的物产，尽可以供全世界人之享用而有余。近被少数人利用种种力量（水利电力汽力），总而言之，科学的力，尽量的探掘开发，攫为己有，把持独占，作为资本。又利用之以奴使群众，或压迫别的弱小国家，因此使全世界多数人的生活，都沦到水平线以下，他们却大享特享其非分的过分的福。现在说一譬喻，世界上是起了蝗虫，农人们辛苦力作的禾稻，满山满地青枝绿叶蓬蓬勃勃的禾稻，都被蝗虫咬的咬掉了叶，折的折断了枝，噬的噬去了心。那么世界的强者优者，即所谓世界上的少数人，他似居于征服者的地位，侵略者的地位，世界上物质想用，几都归他们独占，他们自必可以锦衣玉食修其身，享尽天下无穷之福。但以我推测，如此贪得无厌，以少数人奴使群众的局面，长久下去，于他们未必有利。试看自欧战后，军国主义资本主义之将就崩坏，物质文明之渐归破产，便可知道。在这里又可说一譬喻，比如一个母羊，生下若干小羊，本来这个母羊的乳，是足够那若干小羊吃的，可是其中有一小羊，特别恃强，往往把持母羊的乳，不给别的若干小羊吃，自己一味的想多吃。那若干小羊因营养不足，自终归于饿瘦，或饿死。但那恃强的羊，因吃得太多，或者也要胀死，或饱死。这种局面，如何能永久支持呢？所以我以为人类世界，本来是极美丽的极和谐的，因世界上少数人的私欲抗进侵略残杀竞争妒忌，把极美丽的世界，弄得极丑恶了，极和谐的世界，弄得极紧张了。世界又本来是充满了生命活气洋溢的，又因少数人利用政治经济的势力奴使群众，压迫弱小民族，把极有活气的世界，弄得死气沉沉，大多数人皆失其有望之乐了。由此看来，我们多数人，凡是被征服的，被压迫的，被失去生命的，都应该联合起来，把本来美丽的世界，还他一个美丽，本来和谐的世界，还他一个和谐。本来充满了生命的世界，拿我们的生命，并且还须要把无尽宝藏的世界，很节俭的使用，俾我们的生命，永久在这无尽宝藏的世界里，美丽和谐地生跃躍着。我自信我是带有这种使命来到世界，我希望大众赞助我这种使命之成功。

——《来复》，第305期，1924年7月13日

泰戈尔来华给我的感想

顾惠人

欢迎泰戈尔来华的声浪，去年我已听见了。后因当时中国的气候不适诗哲泰氏的身体；所以不能如约来华。一般抱着热烈欢迎的人们，大失所望，到了今年四月十二日的那一天，他竟惠然驾临，上了我国的岸；于是欢迎他的歌，唱得不绝。在泰氏没有来华之前，早有组织委员会，准备着欢迎泰氏，这种兴高采烈，轰动一时的欢迎，弄得我莫名其妙，人们如发狂似的热情，究竟为什么？是不是为了他是当代有名的印度诗人？所以要一瞻丰采；还是为了他曾于一九一三年得诺贝尔奖金？所以我们大家来聚个热闹，向他说些恭维的话，我们倘为了这些缘故，而向他表示欢迎，实在没有一些价值，这都是为了受一时感情上的冲动所发生的，等事过境迁，泰氏回府后，欢迎从此亦了结，那末，这种欢迎有何意思呢？而且我们将来怎样对得住这位高年白发的诗人，不辞辛苦，跋涉艰难，来到吾国呢？

倘以上述的理由，而去欢迎泰氏，仍然不免带些势利的色彩。据我个人的眼光，看他不仅是一个诗人，更不是为了他得了诺贝尔的奖金，所以身价十倍，他是个纯粹朴实的人，没有丝毫卑鄙的行为。泰戈尔之所以为泰戈尔，就在这一点！他的伟大的人格和主义，而我们所以要欢迎他的缘故，亦正在此！

我们中国现在是不是在人格破产，物质势力横行的时代？上自总统，下至平民，都是贿赂公行，不加顾忌，大家尔诈我虞，能骗得过则骗，选举大总统有什么贿选，开国会有什么卖票，种种奇形怪状，层出不穷，加之工业制度传入我国，工厂一天一天的加增，一般工人受了经济上的压迫，不得不入工厂作工，那些厂主竟有的以奴隶牛马待之；于是那些工人

时思反动，但无实力，所以他们只有饮忍痛苦，终日呻吟于资本家之下，在这个人格沦亡，物质势焰的当儿，来了一位人格的提倡者，精神的安慰者，那末，怎么不使我们以热烈的爱情和诚意去欢迎他呢？

泰戈尔的人格，我们可从他所流露的诗中找出，至于他的诗集早经国中有名的人士介绍和译述，不容我这个不学无术的人来多说，但以我个人对于泰氏的人格所见到的和诸君一谈：

要讲诗哲泰戈尔的人格，我们先要懂得什么是人格，人格的界说本是很难立的，因为人格的定义有从心理学立论；有从社会学立论；亦有从伦理学立论的，它们各有各的论调，而且各有各的着眼点，我们暂且不用它们，但我们可以说人格乃是自我的表现：从情感方面；意志方面；和意识方面，我们现在以这条解说，而窥察泰氏的人格：

（一）美！美好乃是人格表现的初步，一个人要造就伟大的人格，必须知道什么是美？到哪里去找它？美不都是愉悦人目的，乃是提高人的心灵的，加之美只有主观的评决，没有客观的标准，这样说来，我们一时不能断定什么是美？然而我们不能说世界上没有真的美，真的美乃人类心灵上和精神上的兴奋剂，现在上海大马路伟大洋房的美，不是真的美，乃是矫揉造作的人为的；美所以不能感应人生的精神，有时反觉得厌恶。那末，真的美在那里？我可简单的回答："它是远在天边，近在眼前。"我们可以到围绕我们的大自然中去找它。泰戈尔一生人格的美的表现，是受天然中的美的感化，我们可以从他所作的诗中可以见到：

当早晨你寺里的钟声鸣时，男人们和女人们急急的走下森林地的小径，带着他们的贡品！鲜花。

但是我躺在树荫下的草地上随他们过去。

我想，我还是躺着为是，因为在那时，我的花儿正含苞待放哟。

及至天将暮，花都盛开了，于是我乃去行我的晚祷。

歧路第六十二首　泰戈尔著 / 雁冰译

天色晦暝，雨淅沥的下着。

愤怒的电光从破碎的云幕里射下来。

森林如一双囚在笼中的狮子，失望的摇着鬓毛。

在这样的一天，在狂风虎虎的拍打他的翼膀的中间，让我在你面前找到我的平安吧。

因为这忧郁的天空，已荫盖着我的孤独，使你与我的心的接触的意义更为深沉。

歧路第二十首　泰戈尔著/郑振铎译

读了以上泰氏的二首诗，我们知道他常流连于自然的当中，与它结很深的缘，自然是他的伴侣，他的生命的寄托所，这样，他还不为受天然的美化么?

（二）真！人格的价值的高下，可以“真”去估量她，舍弃“真”而不能讲人格，因为人格是“真我”的表现。人们人格破产的大原因，就是为了他们鬼鬼祟祟，口是心非，没有把他们的真人格表现，他们有时，有意作无病的呻吟；亦有的时候，他们的病已入膏肓，但他们有意的装硬好汉，说些面子上的话，但我读泰戈尔的诗，不禁使我想见他的人格。这亦许是他的“真我”的显示，我可节录二首在下面：

我的歌去掉她的装饰品，她不宝贵那衣服与饰物，装饰品要阻碍我们的联合；他们要横梗在我和你的中间；他们的玎珰声，会掩捏你的微语。

我的诗人的虚荣，在你面前羞耻得死了，呵，诗人的主，我在你的足下，请你只要使我的生命简单而正直，如一管芦笛，被你贯注以音乐。

这里是你的足凳，你足所放的地方，就是那最穷苦的，最下等的以及迷途者所在的。

当我想对你鞠躬时，我的敬礼竟不能下达于那最深处，那最穷苦的，最下等的以及迷途者的中间，你的足所放的地方。

骄傲永不能接近于那个地方，你穿了谦抑之服，在最穷苦的，最下等的以及迷途者走着的地方。

我的心永不能找到他的路走到你与无伴侣的最穷苦的，最下等的以及迷途者为伴侣的地方。

前二首：迦檀吉利第七，第十　郑振铎译

（三）爱！爱乃是泰戈尔人格的结晶，他有很多的诗，都是流露爱的情绪；但他的爱的对象，不是物质，他所爱的乃是纯洁的，高超的天然，没有一点污浊的思想夹在里边，可怜啊，多少有作有为的青年误解了爱，而中它的毒，我们读了泰氏的诗，可以使我们懂得爱的真情：

我爱这些沙岸，这个地方有些寂静的池沼，鸭子在那里呷呷的鸣着，龟伏在日光地下曝着；黄昏时，有些漂浮的渔舟，藏在茂草中间。

我爱那有树的对岸，那个地方，阴影聚在竹叶的枝上；妇人们捧了水瓶，从湾曲的小巷里出来。

同是这一条河，在我们中间流着，它对它的两个岸，唱的是同样的歌，我在星光底下。一个人躲在沙上，静听着水声；你也在早晨的光明里，坐在斜坡的边上，静听着，然而我从它那里向你说的密语。对于我也永远是一个神秘。

爱者之赠遗　泰戈尔著/郑振铎译

我从你底甜密[1]的束缚中释放出来，我爱！请不要再加这接之酒了。

这重香之雾竟室塞了我的底心了。

把所有的门都统统打开，使晨光可以进来。

我迷失在你里面，拳缠在你宠爱之怀抱里面。

把我从你底诱惑里释放出来，为我反到人性里去，我将赠你我底自由之心。”

我爱，我底心日夜渴望着和你会集！那好像全般吞灭了的死亡的会集。

好像一阵暴风一样的把我扫开；拿了一切我所有的；惊醒了我底睡眠，抢夺了我的清梦，在我底世界里将我抢去。

在那蹂躏里，在那灵魂的极裸赤里，让我们成了美中之一。

哀哉我底空虚底希望呀！除出在你里面之外，何处是这协和的希望呢，我的上帝？

园丁集第四十八，第五十　徐培德译

[1] 现规范写法为“甜蜜”，“甜密”引自原文。

我们已由泰氏所作诗集中得见他的伟大人格的实现，和写照，因其他有这样的人格，所以他能抱尊高的主义，他的和平恬淡的主义，不能不使我们佩服到五体投地。我前读他的传记，其中提及当他的一九一三年接得诺贝尔奖金的电报的时候，一般人们听见了，都为他欢天喜地的在街上唱着歌儿，敬祝他的荣誉，但他老先生住在家里不动声色的叹着："啊！我以后没有安静的日子了。"从此可知他对于功名利禄不稍顾及的。

现代的文学大家，曾于一九二三年得诺贝尔文学奖金的爱尔兰人夏芝，他曾为泰戈尔作迦檀吉利集的序，内中夏芝说："我每日对泰戈尔，读他的一行，便可把世界上的一切烦恼都忘了。"我们虽不能像夏芝那样的受泰氏的默化，但至少我们亦要得到些他的人格上的感应，才不负此次泰氏来华的一行了。

——《心灵》，第 29 号，1924 年 10 月 1 日

太谷儿的笑画

寓

太谷儿的诗情，是从小窗里送进来的。太谷儿的真理，是从地下掘出来的。这话并不是我胡说，因为太谷儿最爱的是他房中的窗。他曾说，"当我在窗前和母亲接吻的时候，是我最快乐的时候。"他的杰作《远途之鸟》和《新月集》。差不多完全是从窗中窥望的情感。他在小的时候。常常用竹竿挖土。别人问他你挖什么。他答道："我挖地下的真理。"

——《笑画》，第 1 卷第 12 期，1924 年 12 月

泰戈尔

布景：轮船埠头

人物：泰戈尔及翻译人

欢迎之中国人士：甲乙丙

印捕：丁

码头扛夫：戊己

小儿：庚辛壬

甲：好荣幸啊，世界大诗人泰戈尔，居然来了。

乙：好了，中国得救了。

丙：这是我们东方全体的光荣啊。

泰戈尔携翻译缓步同上，一律头裹红巾身穿印服。甲乙丙趋与握手，极表欢迎。

印捕趋上照料，驱逐闲人。

小儿一群及码头扛夫围拢近旁。

印捕：打上海白，慢慢吽。

戊：这个新来的阿三蛮有样子。

己：恐怕是大英派来的巡捕头，所以中国人也去拍他的马屁吧。

庚辛壬："快看"，"老阿三"，"阿三"。（一阵乱呼。）

翻译向地上连唾数口。

泰戈尔满面欢容，口称有趣有趣。

翻译人暗白：有趣虽有趣，已经赠了你一个"阿三"的头衔了。

——《笑画》，第 1 卷第 12 期，1924 年 12 月

太谷儿名著《天文家》

《天文家》是太谷儿作的一首诗，载《新月集》里面。我把它演绎出来，聊作《笑画》的资料。

新月当空，皓魄满地。太谷儿和他哥哥在门前玩耍。太谷儿道：

"哥哥，我们来捉月亮吧。捉下来收到我小箱子里，明天我们俩拿出

来玩。”

他哥哥道：

“你这傻小孩子，月亮离我们不知多远，一个人就能捉吗？”

太谷儿道：

“哥哥，你真傻。母亲很远的站在那地望我们，你也觉得远吗？”

他哥哥道：

“笨小孩子，不远，你能够着吗？”

太谷儿道：

“我们不会爬到喜马拉亚山上捉去么？”

他哥哥道：

“呆小孩子，喜马拉亚山你能爬吗？”

太谷儿道：

“不会叫父亲做一个梯子吗？”

他哥哥道：

“更笨了，你的小手能捉吗？”

太谷儿道：

“叫母亲打一个网子。”

他哥哥道：

“月亮很大，网子是罩不下的。假使你要高一点看，爬到喜马拉亚山上，你就要觉得月亮大了。”

太谷儿道：

“啊，哥哥你真呆了。当我们爬到桌上，不是高一点吗？何以和母亲接吻，不觉得母亲的脸大些呢？”

寓一道：“太谷儿从幼年的时候，就因爱情而忘却了高大的思想。虽是笑话，确有至理。更可称为爱情的天文家。”

——《笑画》，第1卷第12期，1924年12月

郑译《新月集》正误

成仿吾

太戈尔的《新月集》The Crescent Moon 本来早已由王独清君译出，为创造社世界儿童文学选集第二种，郑振铎君以为王译太不易懂，有再译之必要，于是参考王的译文，再把这部书译出来了。这部书的原文本来极简洁明了，王译又无大错，所以郑君这回的工程，在常理应是事半功倍的；然而事有出人意外的，郑君的译文不仅不比王译易懂，不仅许多地方跟着王译弄错，而且有许多地方王译本不错的他颠倒错了。郑君的英文，我是领教过来的，然而这回我因为他有王译可以参考，极希望他不再弄出笑话来，使人齿冷，不料他依旧发挥他的个性，而且错到使人怎么也不能为他辩解。我们的翻译界离林纾的时代已近十年，倘使我们现在还只能译出这样的东西来骗人，我真不能不为我们的翻译界羞了。

郑君的译本已经出了两个多月，我至今没有闲工夫去买它，这回倒是一个朋友拿了一本来给我看。郑君的英文程度本来是人所共晓，我原不必扬他人之恶以显自己之能；不过我既看见了，颇觉得有点像胸中作呕，非吐出不行，而且郑君既然译错了，我由他的学力断定他是不能看出他自己的错处的，那么，我为读此书的诸君的利益起见，似也不可不把郑译的几处大错改正一下。这种工作决不是有趣味的，反之，在我自己是万分寂寞而心苦，况且我这几天正因眼痛的缘故封了一双眼，现在只靠着一双痛眼在这里写呢。

我现在依郑译的顺序，把我一路看下时所看出的几个大错写在这里。

1. 来源（郑译第三面）

郑译：是的，有个谣传，说它是住在森林荫里，萤火虫么朦胧的照着的仙村里，在那个地方挂着两个会幻变的懊怯的蓓蕾。

原文：Yes, there is a rumour that it has its dwelling where, in the fairy village among shadows of the forest dimly lit with glow-worms, there hang two shy buds of enchantment.

此节以王译为是，

王译：是呀，有个谣传，说是它的住处，是在那萤火的光儿所暗暗照着的森林影中的仙村，那儿挂着两个羞怯魅人的花苞儿。

“萤火虫朦胧的照着的”是林荫的形容词，像郑译那样译出来，就好像一个人把帽子挂在脚上了。“会幻变的”也与原意还差十里。

2. 孩童的世界（第七面）

郑译：在那儿，理智造了她的法律的纸鸢而飞放，……

原文：Where Reason makes kites of her Laws and flies them, ...

什么是“她的法律的纸鸢”？郑君不知道 make...of 是一个成语吗？此处也是王译不错，郑君大约不知王译正对，反以为把它直译了出来，便不会有误，殊不知竟大错了。郑君以后可以牢记“make...of”是“以……为……”的意思。

王译：那儿，理智以她的律令为风筝而飞放……

3. 审判官（第十三面）

郑译：只有我才有权去骂他，去责罚他，因为他只许爱他的人惩戒他。

原文：I alone have a right to flame and punish, for he only may chastise who loves.

此句的后半又译得大错了。who loves 是 he 的形容子句，此处的 he 是泛指一般人的，郑君却把他看成指小孩子的去了。王译并没有错，不知郑君参考的时候，究竟怎么看起的了。

王译：我自己才有责备他的权，因为只有能爱人的人才能惩罚人。

《新月集》只是儿歌集（Child-poems），所用的文法和字句极简洁明了，学过一两年英文的人大都能够了解；以上所举三例在原文也并非难懂，而郑君竟至大错。郑君的译书资格已经自行取消了，亏他还自夸“很忠实，且不至看不懂”。忠实到那步田地，而且还有能看懂的自信，无怪乎他要说“王君的译文，太不容易看懂了”。以下我再来举几个奇异的错误。

4. 对岸（第二十四面）

郑译：厚的芦苇的（？）在岸边四围生长，水鸟藏他们的蛋在里面。

原文：thick reeds grow round the margins where waterbirds lay their eggs.

此处的 lay eggs 是“产卵”的意思，仍以“不容易看懂”的王译文为不错。

王译：茂盛的芦苇生在水鸟们下卵（子儿）的池塘周围。

5. 对岸（第二十五面）

郑译：日已完了，影子俯伏在树底下，我便要回到书桌上去了。

原 文：When the day is done and the shadows cower under the trees, I shall come back in the dusk.

郑君竟把“dusk”弄成“书桌”去了！书桌是“desk”呀！一个字看错，本来可以宽容，但前置辞是“in”字呢，我们如将错就错，岂不是钻进书桌里去了吗？此句不消说仍以王译为不错。

王译：当白天完了，阴影藏在树子底下，我要在黄昏里回来的。

6. 花的学校（第二十六面）

郑译：从无人知的地方

原文：from nobody knows where

这也是一个成语，在此是“Whence do they come? Nobody knows.”的意思；照郑译便成 from a place where nobody knows 去了。此句仍以王译为是。

王译：没人知道是来从何处。

7. 花的学校（第二十六面）

郑译：他们是要罚先生站壁角的。

原文：their master makes them stand in a corner.

郑君的译文恰好把主客颠倒，成了俗语所说的“拣个狗来打石头”了。这样浅显的字句，何以会错得这样奇离？令我百思不得其解。

8. 商人（第二十八面）

郑译：再想像着，我的船已载了满船的东西，预备要登岸。

原文：Imagine that my boat is ready at the landing fully laden.

此处 landing 一词是码头的意思，船儿满载着货物已停顿在码头的地方，是预备出发，并不是“预备要登岸”，郑君跟着王君同样地错了。王译作“预备到上陆的地方”，这个错处是完全不能隐讳的。王君在同诗中还有一个奇错：

王译：真珠都撒在发狂的海浪旁边底水花里的砂子上。

原文：pearls are scattered on the land in spray by the wild sea-waves.

意思是："真珠被狂暴的海浪撒在砂上成为水花"，scattered by 是相连的，in spray 是形容 scatter 的副词读，王君全盘弄错了，伯奇与沫若为他校改时亦同未注意到，这是我很引以为遗憾的事，但是郑君也还是错了的。

郑译：珠子都散在被汹涌的海浪所吞的沙滩上。

9. 小大人（第三十六面）

郑译：十一月里放假的时候。

原文：In the holiday time in October.

郑君竟把 October（十月）记成"十一月"去了，外国的十二个月的名词真是不容易记得清楚呀！假使他是错成八月的时候，我还可以说他懂拉丁文呢，但是……。

10. 我的歌（第五十一面）

郑译：我的歌又好像一双到了你梦中的羽翼，……

原文：My song will be like a pair of wings to your dreams.

此处的"to"是表示附属的意思，是说："我的歌将如双翼附丽于你的梦"，郑君也跟着王君一道错了。

王译：我的歌儿要像一对翅膀向你的梦儿里，……

这不消说是大错。

以上我把郑译的是十个大错举了出来，同时也把王译的错误纠弹了几个，此外郑译中小一点的错误尚有几处，现在只把我所偶然发见的几个列在下面。

（1）孩童之道（第四面）中的 to learn mother's words from mother's lips

郑译为"去学从母亲的唇里说出来的话"是不对的，还是王译"从母亲的唇儿上学母亲的话儿"好。

（2）同章（第六面）中的 weave the double bond of pity and love 郑译为"编成了怜与爱的两条带子"，"条"字应该为"重"字，或依王译改为"股"。

（3）偷睡眠者（第八面）中的 to fetch water from the village near by, 王

译的"到近村处取水去了"多一"处"字，郑君竟也跟着错了。

（4）审判官（第十三面）中的 he becomes all the more a part of my being, 王译为"他几几乎成了我自己的一部分"，这"几几乎"三字是"更加"之误，郑君又跟着错了。"几几乎"在英文是 almost。郑君只知道跟着他人弄错，到了这篇的末句偏不知跟着他人学好，足见根基薄弱的人是没有判断好丑的能力的。

（5）玩具（第十四面）中的 I am busy with my accounts, adding up figures by the hour, 郑译为"我正忙着算账，整整几个小时在那里加叠数字"，这"整整几个小时"直是杜撰。by the hour 是以小时为单位的意思，王译亦仅勉强可以通过。

平心而论，王译也还未到完善的地位。译笔过直，在许多名词之下加上一些"儿"字，在王君或者是想保存原文的风格与儿歌的神情但是我们读的人实在有几分慊厌，虽说不是"太不容易懂"。而且我校看郑译时，便同时发见了郑译没有错而王译错了的两处。那便是：

（1）"追唤"中的"没有人会觉得失了他的"，原文是 no one will miss it，王译竟弄成"没有一个人会不满意的"；

（2）"雨天"中的"故意要恼她一样"原文是 to tease her，王译竟弄成"去扯了他母亲之后"。这些都是很奇怪的错误。不过我们可以替王君原谅的，他译《新月集》，在郑译出世之先，他无译本作参考，而他的译文比较还无甚大错。郑君不满意王译，既自行挽起袖子再来选译一遍，而且还把王译本来做过参考，竟自人错亦错，人不错而自己再来弄出些大错，自己看不懂原文而还说别人的译文"不容易懂"，这种诬人欺世的行径，我真为我国的翻译界羞，我的痛眼要被眼泪涨破了，我不愿再多说了。

十一月二十七日夜。

——《创造周报》，第 30 期，1924 年 12 月 2 日

几首太戈尔底诗

顾苍生

太戈尔底诗早已公认为有价值的了！我们中国文学研究社，也已经出版了不少的译本，如《飞鸟集》,《园丁集》等类，文艺界早已得到极大的应响了。我在今年六月里，英国剑桥底一个我底朋友邵询美君，寄给我许多近代诗集丛书；我便乘着暑假期中，将太戈尔底一本，翻译了。但是经着许多朋友底批评讨论之后，觉得很多不满意的地方，所以样子也印好了，仍没有出版！我认为太戈尔这本诗很深奥，不是看一二遍就能领会的！我很喜欢选出几首，借着《天籁》底篇幅来介绍给读者，并且附着原文，还在翻译之后，说明我底意思，对于那首诗底好处，读者倘若有暇，也不妨共同研究，我是很表欢迎的！

书原名：“The Angustan Books of MODERN POETRY” by Sir Rabindranath Tagore

篇原名：“Epigrams”我译它叫“短诗”，这篇在原书底十九页上，共分十二小节，我现将几首较为容易领会的来介绍。

第一首原文：Labour and Rest

Labour and Rest are bound by closet ties,
For rest falls lidlike upon labour’s eyes

我底译文——工作和休息

工作和休息，都是被最紧密的结所束缚，
因为休息像眼皮一般的盖落在工作底眼睛上。

我底意见——这首诗底命意，虽然很浅，但是很不容易立刻领会的。他的意思照，我想起来是这样：“工作和休息，是有连带关系的，休息多了，工作将无用的。”因为他说工作底眼睛是被眼皮盖的，眼皮犹之休息；休息时，眼睛盖落了，就看不见东西了；倘若永远地休息着盖落着，那工作就好像一个残废的盲子了；岂不是没用了吗？我底翻译对于末一个 Eyes 起了许多疑惑，因为我想 Eyes 是多数，但是他底多数只要加一个 S 就够了，翻译中文却是大大的艰难。我后来想翻译“……两只眼睛上”。但是后来我知道太戈尔底用多数是为了要 ties 和 eyes 同韵。并且多数和少数都可用的，（因为譬如我们讲话，他说："你底眼睛好像秋波！"我说："你底两只眼睛好像秋波！"这两句是同一个的意义，绝不会因着缺少了"两只"二字而那个人底一只眼睛是秋波，一只眼睛是瞎子！）这句话在英文上是用多数的，因为大多除非不是生眼睛，眼睛是两只的！但是现在 Labour，太戈尔是以为它是一件有生之物的；而我说倘若不是韵底关系，用少数也不要紧。总言之：我译的是中文，而中文中多少无甚分别，所以我译作"……眼睛上"。也没写一只，也未写两三只！这本是无甚紧要的话，但是我以为很有价值贡献！

第二首原文：Kindness and Gratitude

"Who art thou, silent one?" Eyes tear-bedewed Give Kindness answer, "I am Gratitude."

我底译文——仁爱和感谢

"你是谁，寂静者呀？"眼睛露湿了泪水

而回答仁爱，"我是感谢。"

我底意见——这首诗底意思，是说仁爱的人决不自己说出的，决不要得人感谢的！这诗中的两句话："你是谁，寂静者呀？"和"我是感谢"。都是感谢说的。因为，感谢看见仁爱不说话——便是不要得感谢。所以它感激仁爱得很而哭了？"你是谁"是感谢有意说的，下面称它寂静者，便晓得感谢是已经知道仁爱是仁爱了！末一句"我是感谢"，愈足以证明感谢底看得起仁爱，仁爱底真仁爱！仁爱也不会不知感谢，但它自己仁爱了，感激也用不着了！在译这几首小诗，我也得到了许多有价值的讨论，便是"Who art thou, silent one""你是谁，寂静者呀！"一句。这句底直译，应该是"你是谁，寂静者？"但是这一译，意思便变成你是什么人是不是寂静者？因为寂静者下面有了一个问句符号。现在我要使这句与原著意思一样，所以只得加了一个"呀"字，倘若加一个"吗"字，便和上面"你是谁，寂静者？"同样的误会了！若然说："寂静者，你是谁？"便是不说话的是谁，那一句装在头上有些情形不同了。因为装在上面是感叹的意思，上面有命令性质。换一句说，我们可以照着原文底格式译，较为好些。

第三节　原名"The Inalienable"译为"难移者"

原文 Says Death: "I take you son;" the thief: "Your gold;"
Says Fate: "I seize on all you have and hold;"
"And I," the Slanderer says, "Your name destroy."
"But who," the Poet asks, "Can take my joy?"

译文 死亡说："我敢取你底儿；" 窃贼："你底金；"
命运说："我把持你所有的所握；"
"而我，"诽谤者说，"你底名破败。"
"但谁，"诗人问，"能取我乐？"

讨论 这首诗底命意很简单，一看就懂了，无非是说各种人底性情和诗人底真乐而已。我以为这首诗不宜于直译，像前面的译文，虽然于文法上没有差误，但是我们读书自然是看他的意思而读下去，若然不乘，很觉乏味的一件事；所以我将他底意思，译成一首诗歌在后面，希望阅者有一个极诚实而满意的批评！照我自己底评论，以为我们翻译的东西，不必太拘泥于形体的整齐，有时竟然弄得所翻译的，人家看不懂，并且翻译不是查字典，查着字典而翻译下的东西，不足称为美满的翻译的！因为大都读过一些英文的，都会查字典的，他们自己会，也用不着你去多费手脚，或者你有差了，人家看不出，也跟你差了；那你要人看了你底翻译而便利，反而人家受你底害了！所以我的解释非直译式底这篇诗，极愿意介绍！

死亡曰："取汝之儿兮！"
窃贼曰："取汝之金钱！"
命运曰："取汝所有兮！"
读者曰："取汝之名誉！"
诗人曰："我乐兮！
谁能取！"

上面底三首诗，便是我所介绍的，如若有不对的地方，我极愿意领教而研究的。我还有几首太戈尔底诗歌也愿意介绍给读者，下次有空，再当贡献！

末后一句话，便是我极希望读者诸君不弃而共同研究，因为研究者，便是完全之母！

——《沪江大学月刊》，第15卷，第2、3期，1925年10月16日，11月1日

太戈尔作品之初次介绍至中国

秋　山

太戈尔之作品，传遍中国，约在民国八九以后，其前中国文坛上未尝闻太戈尔之名也。然据余所知，太戈尔之作品，初次介绍至中国，乃在民国五年，介绍者为欧阳仲涛。其时欧阳仲涛有《介绍太阿儿》一文，刊载于梁任公主任之大中华杂志上（民国五年二月号）。除介绍太戈尔之身世及其学说外，并载太戈尔诗数首，此为太戈尔作品初次出现于中国文坛也。今录其爱国歌云："皇皇祖国，吾灵魂之所领，吾先人之所建兮。忠则尽命，吾身当为之献兮。吾喜则作而歌，歌为祖国曼兮。有时背被而泣，泣为祖国怨兮。吾腕虽弱，搀扶祖国，力弥健兮。谁尔执者，吾决断之。腰间太阿，孰云钝兮。皇皇祖国，吾灵魂之所领，吾先人之所建兮。"又有两首。原文题名曰箴。其一云："汝当师蜂，飞游太空。酺啜万华之业，酿造佳蜜，故不能深伏久蛰夫巢孔之中。"其二云："而毋居囚，逼仄而秽幽，猥曰廓治之，亦新狱耳，岂得逾圆垣而自由。"译笔亦用散文，然甚简洁可读，不得谓非最佳译。然在当时，则无人注意。谁知所谓太阿儿者，则即后数年名满吾震旦之太戈尔也。

——《民众文学》，第 14 卷第 7 期，1926 年 8 月 13 日

Talk with Rabindranath Tagore: The Malady of Unrest East and West

Aldo Sorani

Rabindranath Tagore has paid his second visit to Italy, this time in response to Mussolini's personal invitation, and Mussolini welcomed him in Rome with all the honour. The poet was much feed not only in Rome, but also at Florence and at Turin, where great crowds came to hear his public lectures on "The meaning of Art" and on his "School" lectures he will repeat in London. In the meantime, he proposes to make a sojourn in Switzerland and Austria, and also to consult some specialists about the heart trouble which impairs his health at present.

In Florence I was privileged to have quite a long talk with the poet. We met in the sunny sitting-room of his hotel that dominates the Lung Arno, and the poet talked with me in a low and sweet but rather tired voice, sunk in a deep armchair, caressing of the last novel by Selma Lagerlof.

"Italy appears to me ever more beautiful," he said, "and Florence fairest among Italian cities. But I would have preferred to come to Italy not laden with years and fame, but in a neophyte's pilgrimage, even as Shelley and Keats came. Youth would have appreciated better still the message Italian poetry conveys. Yet, neither celebrity nor old age are of my making or fault!"

The Burden of Fame

Tagore returned to the burden of his world celebrity. "I am not made to run about the world and to be pointed out to the crowd, especially the European crowd. My life and its message are interior; all true life in interior. The multitude gather to behold the Poet, to hear the Poet, yet, having seen and heard him, it does not know him, for the Poet remains concealed, and the louder the clamour and the larger the multitude, the more deeply will the Poet withdraw himself within the shelter of his soul and rest unknowable. but how can I now rid myself of the burden of renown?"

I asked him, pointing to the novel by Selma Lagerlof, if he read many European authors, and he replied that he read many of the English, like all the pupils of his school, who devour English books with ardour. Nordic literature makes the strongest appeal to him, and especially the Russian; above all, Dostoevsky, Tolstoy, Turgenev, and also Gorky.

The Inner Discord

Almost inevitably our conversation touched upon the relations between

East and West, the two civilization.

"I always think," said Tagore, "that the two civilizations can and should remain distinct, and, at the same time, complete and harmonize each other. In Asia we are already too much apart and divided into countries, races, and cults of diverse origin. You in Europe, despite many divisions and many struggles, have succeeded, after long efforts, in attaining to a unity of culture, and this unity has an element of the miraculous especially in the field of the organization and coordination of scientific knowledge, and hence has a supreme importance."

"But does it not seem to you that the world war has interrupted and menaced even this cultural unity?"

"Maybe, but not forever. You are more crude, more willful, more exacting and even after the war, more aggressive and at variance. Yet the greater of danger for you would lie in the acquired habit of belief in discord as an ineluctable and fatal law of life, and, above all, in believing necessary and beautiful the interior discord, that is to say, the warring of man's soul with itself. There are people who hold that true life lies precisely in this continual contradiction with themselves, this intimate fight of ideas, sentiments, passions. It is a dangerous error. The ideal life consists not in a state of perpetual contradiction with ourselves and with others, for life should achieve harmony with us; it should radiate peace and union."

"It is true, however, that catastrophe of the war suffices to explain this restlessness within and without, which nevertheless cannot endure forever. The day will come when it will be borne in upon you that the desire for exterior benefits and their accumulations is useless and dangerous, and you will feel the need of a true peace and to put order in your houses and in your souls."

"You will then recognize that much you held as goods as not so in reality, but are the rubbish of centuries, and then you will set yourselves to sweep away the dross that hampers and oppresses you. Then indeed, you will possess, both within and without, a new land of promise whereon to build, wherein to sow the seed of coming harvests, and you will reach a higher plane of civilization and neighbourly life with others and with yourselves."

"Do you share the belief of some others that assistance for this necessary work of clearance and rebuilding could profitably come to us from America?"

"No; America is too far away, too much a prey also to the very same ills that agitate Europe, too preoccupied with this world's goods and too rich. One could quote to her the words of Christ: 'It is easier for a camel to pass through the eye of a needle than for a rich man to enter the kingdom of Heaven.' For America to prove of aid and inspiration to Europe, it would behove her also to have gone through the deep waters of calamity. Moreover, America is not free. We in India are, it is true, under a foreign domination, but we are freer men by far the Americans — spiritually freer." — "Sunday Times"

— *The North-China Daily News*, Aug. 23, 1926

Tagore on Western Civilization

Rabindranath Tagore, India's poet-laureate, has declared that the depiction of night life, sex relations, crime and undignified scenes in American films released throughout Asia are "a libel on Western civilization." These sensational films are partly responsible for misunderstanding between the East and the West, and are keeping the two civilization apart. Whilst the proper authorities are urged to exercise a vigorous censorship so as to do away with the evil effects of such misleading motion pictures, the producers should be reminded that they would earn the gratitude of Orientals and Occidentals if they should be more careful in the selection of plays for the silver screen and try to give a truer and more exact portrayal of life in the two Hemispheres, the fact remains that truth should be more respected than the almighty dollar obtained from the production of sensational scandalous, libelous and harmful representations.

— *The North-China Daily News*, Jan. 25, 1927

Dr. Tagore's Mission to Far East

Calcutta, July 15.

Despite his age, Dr. Rabindranath Tagore, India's greatest poet, is an indefatigable traveller. His most recent project is a visit to Java and French Cambodia, where his main object will be to study the influence of Indian culture in the Far East, with special reference to its architecture and literature. On this subject he had much to say at a farewell gathering on the eve of his departure, held at the Calcutta University, which assem-diverse points of view. India true rural Ambassador as one of the speakers described him. The message of India which they inherited from the past, and which they wanted to realize in the present age through increasing cooperation of cultures and mutual understanding said the poet, was to study the mind of man in its realization of different aspects of truth from diverse points of view. India's true self manifested itself not a narrow, self-centred existence, in self-glorification, or economic exploitation, but in kindling all the higher instincts of the inhabitants which had been visited by the missionaries of old. But it would be a false reading of their past history and an insult to the soul of India if they merely took pride in the achievements of their ancestors, and did not practice in themselves the true immortal spell of ancient India by merging themselves in the greater world outside and recognizing everywhere the Universal Man.

— *The North-China Daily News*, Aug. 16, 1927

An Opponent of Tagore

Robert Merrill Bartlett

Mr. Wu has been an outspoken opponent of Tagore, and during the Indian poet's visit to Peking, Wu Chih-hui's rough satire was too much for his delicate sensibilities. Mr. Wu's style is characterized by the use of common language, slang, vulgar comparisons, keen humor, bold satire and audacity. In the *Controversy Between Science and Philosophy of Life* he attacks Chang Chun-mai, the chief defender of the spiritual interpretation of life, and other half-hearted friends of science, calling them Tagores of China. One of the longest and most original documents in this discussion is "*A New Cosmology of God and Philosophy of Life*." Here Mr.Wu denies the existence of God, arguing that the material basis of life is more acceptable than the spiritual, and concluding that the philosophy of the anarchist is his faith: "Every one does what he can and gets what he wants." Wu Chih-hui is like Browning's heroes, fearless, idealistic, striving for progress. In *Personal Blind Talk* he writes: "Some one has asked me: 'Have you become pessimistic? Have you retired from work?' It is true that I have retired for a time, but you never find the word pessimism in Wu Chih-hui's philosophy dictionary!"

— *The China Weekly Review*, Nov. 19, 1927

太戈尔的灯蛾

印度诗人太戈尔，最近以他在中国日本间人们求他在扇面书页墙壁上的题句，印成一本集子，叫做《灯蛾》Fireflies。有人说他大概是以灯蛾比自己，以灯火比中国与日本的他的崇拜者的热诚，而他则将因此而送掉他的老命。但说这句话的人尚未读过那本集子，不晓得究竟对否。

——《狮吼》，第 11 期，1928 年 12 月 1 日

时代的太戈尔

扬　鞭

在现时代为我中国人所最鄙视之印度国，居然十步之内，必有芳草，

产生一太戈尔，号曰诗哲。太戈尔行迹所抵，其地之民众即若狂，即吾向所最鄙视印度人之中国，亦竟视为大成至圣。一般未来的中国太戈尔，捧之搂之包围之，犹若孝子之于牌位。太戈尔给予印度之光荣，猗欢盛哉，蔑以加矣。或曰：犹太之耶稣，大中华民国之孔仲尼，视太戈尔得乎高出一筹乎。然去年南京孔仲尼游街之日，上海反基口号高呼之时，又岂彼二千年来捧孔捧耶稣者所能预料。太戈尔之今日，特时代的一种工具，为一般未来的中国太戈尔，取作傀儡，捧之搂之包围之，为己身造成将来太戈尔之地耳。十年廿年百年后，反太欤，游街欤，都将归纳于符号中矣。哲云乎哉。

——《大晶画报》，第 3 期，1929 年 3 月 27 日

欢迎印度诗哲泰戈尔先生并祝六旬晋三寿序

张叙忠

征人早行，图绘见新诗之贵。佛幡入梦，旌幢来异客之光。望者明星，飞者健士。萃北方之学者，共听梵音。觇西域之化人，多惬春目。相与议论上下，低昂古今。虽有驿馆，睹舍星之照远。岂无玉笛，让清角之声悲。慨自东土生民，惟好懿德。西极天马，惯逞雄威。热极草干，南国既已邈矣。榱崩栋折，华夏不其殆而禅有野狐。孽生爱骏，是以同心之曲。响应当时，密独亡国之音，哀怨动众哉。然犹忆舜乐凤鸣，禹图龙负。卢牟六合，亭毒八荒，海水不波，问摩诃无使者。青云干吕，知中国有圣人。蔡博士求仙，正摩腾来汉之候。梁骑尉持节，是天竺尊唐之时。或取梵经，或图神像，或录霞表风土，或者询国外里程，奚必盐谷之官，译传天朝安乐。亦假释迦之道，度尽苦海众生。缘送迎而写新潮，弥来往而存大信。心乎爱矣，情在于斯。文献可征，山河忽易。遇金人于梦里，灵境犹通。指铜驼于棘中，洛宫苑在。共愤心以磨剑，怜被辱于仇鞭。遗臣归尸，何来田横之岛。顽民作气，先剖比干之心。愿精神既郁屈于当年，则文化比废皇于异日。剥极必复天之数，有开必先理之常也。于是泰戈尔先生先得藏地积气，独为希世传人。疏狂年少之时，慷慨立身之

始。县知用不藏者仁不显，身不隐者道不全。卜宅荒原，阶上苔绿。授徒近市，槐下风清。面壁澄新，得灵感于间静。望日度树，妙达欢于自然。宜其咳唾皆成珠玑，歌声若出金石也。顾或谓才为世出，世亦才难。鼓骇浪者长鲸，何不金箭以拔。去宿垢为大洁，可许银鹄先奔。至于无聊之诗鸣，宁作前驱之敌忾。岂知劫到白虏，别有慧心。口非黄龙，不吐毒气。和声可以鸣盛，不怒而威。寰海赖此壮游，闻音有喜。所愿抟抟大地，鸿迹留泥。煌煌神都，客车投辖。恰是斗炳东指，有地皆春。又道方辉西经，此人主寿。学海回澜于震旦，法雷大响于坤舆。天鉴下民，不教阴风怒作。心重与国，会当净土复名。维时五色浮香，信传四月八日。八纮再燿，兆自周甲初元。猗欤盛欤，皇矣裔矣。某何梁携手，罔陵陈辞。天下苍生，愿共锡无疆之祉。海外难老，已先见维岳之尊。虽然人事何常，胜会不再。持钵而至，护珠而回。窃愧臧旻之才，遍数三十六国。感增朱普之句，不尽千百万言。

中华民国十三年甲子四月初六日

——《军需杂志》，第2期，1930年2月

太戈尔小时的故事

显　伦

全世界震名的印度大哲学家大诗人太戈尔氏，他在小时，曾有一件很有趣味的故事，我今天特介绍在这里。

他家住在恒河附近，恒河是印度最大的一条河，同我国的扬子江是一般，在印度古书上，对于恒河有很多神话，而且恒河风景最美丽，所以太戈尔小的时候，就常喜欢在恒河两岸玩。有一天，他很顽皮的拿一根木头，立在河边，对水面上打去，被打的水面，泛起很多好看的浪花，他想拿木头再去打那浪花时，那浪花老早就到下面去了。

他的脑筋，忽然的异想天开，他觉得水这种东西太顽皮，当你打他一下后，他便急急的跑开，再想打他时，已经是来不及了。他回头在岸上摸一块瓦片来，将木头连打上去，瓦片动也不动的给打个破碎不堪，于是他

恍然的大悟了！

他恍然大悟的是："水因为活泼，所以受了一下打就赶快跑开，不再受第二下的打击。瓦片因的呆板，所以打一下也不动，打两下也不动，到以后，终于打得稀烂了。足见一个人是要活泼，不要呆傻，因为活泼得到便宜，呆傻的就要吃亏的"！

太戈尔这段妙想，倒真有点意义，我们不能忽略它！拿中国人和外国人在一块儿比较一下，就会马上看出，外国人比中国人活泼得多，所以到底中国人受到外国人的欺，整个民族国家，弄到这般地步！我们从今以后，要把呆板的气味脱去，极力表现出活泼的精神，个个人都是活活泼泼的，生气勃勃的，我们的国家就会马上强盛起来呵！

——《民众教育半周刊》，第1卷第16期，1930年5月1日

泰戈尔之"图画诗词化"

曲人尽知印度之泰戈尔为大诗家，为教师，著述家，而鲜有知其为美术家者。泰氏近来致力绘事，极有心得，并设女子美术学院于印度，提倡指导，不遗余力，其所作画，异乎常法，非新非旧，不东不西，融汇贯通，固其然矣，而随意所之，独创一格，使个性尽情表现，尤不失巨哲之特征。泰氏于绘事，盖有"独得之秘"，其理论綦长，亦颇深奥，愧未克遂译其梗概，惟有一言，足资介绍者，则其所谓"有许多天然美丽的线条不断地在那里活动着，然而唯有最适当的始有生存之可能。……我的画是'诗词化的'。……要是标出题目来，不过求其能以辨识；首要的是韵律的意义，形式乃在最后；并且我的画决不是用以描写一种思想，或表现一件事实的"云云。兹将泰氏近作数种，按期刊登北画，想亦景仰诗圣者之所乐睹欤！

——《北洋画报》，1930年8月5日

想起了泰戈尔

印度诗哲泰戈尔民十三年到北京受各界欢迎，大看中国戏，大谈中国戏而且自编一戏令中国人演之。兹将当日诸友与泰氏之谈片集录，以记当时之热闹。

泰戈尔说："余最初对于中国之感觉，实于印度之大戏剧家嘉利达之剧中得之。盖其中有一场，为凤凰旗帜，流苏动荡。而此流苏即为中国制品。在此含有诗意之感觉中即得中国文化极深之印象。"

王小隐云："大抵诗境主流动，无闻中外。所谓心性独发，神韵大然，断非上帝视角所能演事。公孙大娘舞剑器，惹出诗翁一大篇，岂亦流苏之为用欤？观蚯蚓出泥而悟笔法，亦何以异是。昔社里传闻瞿菊农试界碑，而讥其为沙场老将之哀昏，声之感人如是，不审老诗翁能领略一二否？"流苏动荡，得无"胭脂所拉"否？旗帜风飘，得无"龙套所举"否？谓以此而得中国戏剧之全艺，太仓一粟，而况乎文化之全体，然大诗翁而如此垂青固当张臂，低头，躬身，以谢。并特笔以书曰："中国剧中之一小物，有足使世界有名大诗翁，窥见中国文化之伟力。"

协和礼堂盛会记事（红叶）

中外名流，在协和医院礼堂为泰戈尔先生庆寿。扮演先生自编的剧本（独幕剧）。印度某国公主向安基耳国王求婚。国王自负英雄，矢守十二年内不婚主义。公主不胜哀戚。所感于爱之神及春之神，二神云：他的主义全是虚伪。因借与公主美的面貌一具，以一年为期。国王果心动，转向公主说爱求婚，公主教训他说你的不婚主义是假的，你的爱也是假的，我的面貌也是假的，一年之后要退付别人，你当如何。遂将其斥退。

扮公主者林徽因女士，扮爱春二神者林君宗孟徐君志摩。国王系某某二君扮演。梅君兰芳到场参观。鄙人为之介绍于泰先生。先生又云到中国如到故乡，青山绿水恍惚觉得旧地重游。在印度年虽衰老，在此中国则如婴儿初生。请君当为我染红蛋，设汤饼，语多谐极，座中指为之解颐。梁任公为赠一名曰竺震旦。以国为姓于古有征。

泰戈尔与中国剧(宝县)

戏剧原始与印度化

现代戏剧之成分观

梁任公演说吾人所以欢迎泰戈尔，提起“印度与中国文化的亲属关系”，并举出精神结合的之副产物十二种，“音乐”以外。还有戏剧。

他说“中国古代之歌舞剧，如揆头（节头）其实为拔豆。北魏志谓自印度传来。……”

我就这一点推论起来，以为中国戏剧之承受印度的赠品。确确不止这一端。在编制和取材上，有很重大的遗迹可寻，并且可以认定印度文化（或者单说佛教）对于中国戏剧有极大的一次贡献。

中国戏剧的原始（狭义的）究竟是什么时代？（这个问题是君青向我要求答复的，顺便在此处说明。）据我所知道，最早要算“梁朝的大云之乐”，是扮一老翁演述西域神仙变化之事。清人纳兰成德考定此为优伶登场扮演之始。（渌水亭杂识）但要晓得此时所谓“西域神仙”，便是“印度诸佛”的化名。

西历五〇二——五九四，正是梁武帝到敬帝的一朝时期。武帝本身就占去了四十七年（五〇二——五九四，）大云之乐定然做在这个时代。这个时代却又是佛教异常活动的一个时代。

梁武帝既然是个信徒，又当那“达摩老祖”自天竺来华演讲。（五二七）不仅梁朝是这样崇仰佛法，就是北部的魏朝，也正在大刻云岗石窟，雕镂庄严妙象，又象“禅宗”这件东西也是这时候的一个出品。可知道当时所谓“神仙”大概不能尽数为张道陵一派所凶办，必定要有些“智慧神通”的人们在内。况且自来“西域”两个字地面非常广漠于闻，姑坛，龟兹，安息，固然在内，即使印度，也不出这个范围。（后汉书卷一百十八，西域传第七十八，……至于佛道神化，兴自身毒。……是以印度为西域也。）

在佛教极盛的时代，而演述西域的神仙变化，我便说：“中国戏剧的原始，与印度文化确有关联”。

总还不算胡扯！

这话可又说回来了，泰戈尔又和中国剧有什么关系？此话不是这么说，因为泰戈尔想到印度文化，从印度文化想到中国戏。若说是中国戏要得泰戈尔提倡，或是简直说中国戏是从印度传来的，固然极不像话。便拿泰戈尔的当做了“佛法的伽蓝神将”，希望他来弘震旦之宗凰，却也是一样的错看了人了。题目理清以来，再来谈谈现代戏剧的成分。我们晓得清朝乾隆时代，戏剧最盛，在那当时的四本大戏：

一，九九大庆；

二，法官雅奏；

三，劝善金利；

四，昇牛宝筏。

据《啸亭续录》皆是张文敏（张照?）奉旨所撰，这前二节是一吉祥神戏，仿佛“赐福”、“献瑞”、“麻姑献寿”一类东西。（别外一种应节戏，叫做月令承应。）其下三四两种，便目连救母的故事和唐玄奘取经的故事，玄奘取经还算一种相关的历史，这目连救母确实采自大般若经，是直接取材的。（按目连本从母姓，译者莱菽，称为刘青提，则不知所本。）当时搬演须时一月余，（四川演全本，闻须运台两月。）至今虽存遗的故事很多，而“游六殿”、“滑油山”、“目连救母”（单指酆都相会一出）依然是老旦的本工重头戏。却是这本《劝善金科》的一二点结晶体了。（中间又经了由昆曲变二簧的一番变化。）

高腔的“目连救母”内中存留的部分，比较“二簧就多得多。此外若“渡江”（达宁事）思凡（全本名《孽海记》)，水漫（《白蛇传》）都含有极深厚的印度色彩（或者说是佛化。）更有一部《归元镜》传奇，简直合基督教的神戏，是一班用。

——《大公报》，1930 年 10 月 8 日

甘地太戈尔之我见

杨世昌

单拿我来讲：甘地，太戈尔都是我崇拜而信仰的，我只有拿他俩的精

神人格来作模范，来改造我的一生命。谈至于到我的学问经验看来，对于他俩可说也无从见解起，现在我且不自量力的来瞎说一下：

天意是在黑暗里面固封，在人们眼前，你如感着的是困苦黑暗……你不妨把他揭破——要魂魄上有生气的。——那么？黑暗里面的执灯者自然会出来！

印度就是个证明：

帝国主义与弱小民族是不相对待的，所以印度屈服于英国，并不足为奇，这场买卖交割以后，偏又闪出个甘地来，一着之下，大有转败为胜的希望，咦！他就是黑暗里领导的执灯者！

他们睡梦里惊醒所要求的目的，眼睁睁的看见甘地努力的帮助他们推送到面前来，所以印度复活及同时为世界上帝国主义下针砭这个重责，甘地能够肩着，固然是足以钦佩的；但是全印度民众，却也不是“不肖子”，数百十万人的趋向进行奋斗，同是以民族独立，民众解放为目标。

这里却有个疑问：“假使当初的印度，和现在的印度一般，那可以断言：大不列颠也难以入手，推想数十年前印度；定是与朝鲜不相上下的。”

这一个魂魄上有生气，心腔热的民族，是否变种？这又是一个大大的疑问。

“不是！”

这是个离死差口气的人，得了华佗扁鹊著手回春的良医救回来的。

这个我不能说是甘地了，因为当时做人工呼吸，打强心针，确是有一个抱了伟大深刻的意志，下了一番苦工的人生。

这就是现在远遁在英国的太戈尔先生。

太戈尔，当然也是印度特产之一，现在印度的有如此程度；印度同胞们亦应该纪念他。

他所抱的主义，正是现在大家所反对的国家主义，但是；这么个印度，欲得到个自治殖民地位尚不可得，安有国家，民族依国家而存，欲脱离羁轭而自立，亦不得不以国家为单位，可是印度有八种不同之宗教，有二百二十二种之方言，文字又不如中国之统一，社会阶级多至二千三百层……所以印度之欲达到民族团结；统一独立治地位，其所遭困难，有较世界任何国为大，所以我们应该注意到太戈尔怎样的提倡国家主义。

太戈尔，他是个印度著名的族，他是个软弱的诗人。

人家不留意他，软弱看他，他正有他常常深住在印度群众心中的，就是把他压到最低层去；他口里还是极纯熟的念着底“国歌”在呢!?

“你的祖国在竞斗着，在受苦着，唉！她在饥饿着，仅有肯尽责任的儿子才能解母亲的忧呀!”

朝阳耀着它金色的光彩……清晨的路上便有人唱着这歌——加入神与祖国的祈祷。

年潮满涨时，牧童在榕树下游戏，他也对着树枝上的鸟，田野中的牛……都唱着这些歌。

国会与会议中唱着。

王子宫中唱着，乞丐口中唱着。

结婚时与祈祷时唱着。

……

死睡般的印度，他已病愈了，他已睡醒了，他已能够悟到他们所唱的“国歌”，他已有了智识和经验；他已认清了目的和观念，他们，他们唯有夺出黑暗；向着光明努力!

说到这里，又不得不提出甘地，我没法，把他俩下个批评，太戈尔是个慷慨好义的义士，甘地是个忠勇善战的将军。

未战以前，感到军士粮草的缺乏——他——我尽我的所有来协助他们。冲锋杀敌呀！怕军士们临阵畏怯——他——我尽我的心力，死和他们一块儿。

由此看来：太戈尔已根本解决了印度民族，他在印度人心灵上已创造了新观念，已改正了他们旧有的错视，同时注意到他们的“心理”和“教育”。甘地他已为印度人造成了新生活。他天天在和他们实地经验着，他更是在每个印度人本身上要求的。

假使印度有太戈尔而无甘地，我不能说印度永不翻身；但恐迟点罢?

或者；有甘地而无太戈尔，怕也迟点罢？

归根也就是因果的道理——拿天意来讲——奄奄一息的印度，魂魄上生气；是太戈尔给他打的，黑暗中的印度，长夜中的明灯，是甘地照他们的。

一九三〇，十，四，作于盐中。

——《盐中学生》，1930 年 12 月

India's Poet Waits the Dawn

A wise man has come from the East, but the gifts that he bears are not gold and frankincense and myrrh, for to him these things mean little. It is song of the sun's glad gold that he brings, that and the music of the clouds and forests and of the mellow moon. His gifts are intangible, yet incalculable — lyrics of love and life, a rhythm of unity a value of being, a harmony of design in all creation.

It was in a great drawing room that I first saw Rabindranath Tagore, a room filled with gorgeous furniture and large modern portraits. On a huge sofa, swathed in a dark blue robe he sat, almost huddled in one corner. In the half light his body was lost. Out of the shadow loomed his white hair and beard and his dark eyes. The portraits, good in their way, became realistically banal, the masterpieces of Chippendale and Sheraton lost their significance, even the leather-bound books in the cases which rose majestically to the ceiling were too loud and patent in the calm which he seemed to suffuses.

His movements are slow, almost stealthy, and the quietness that overwhelmingly surrounds him makes even the thought of a sound of his footsteps inconceivable. His voice not much more than a whisper, is musical and low, and as if it came from far off, while the caressingly languid movements of his small hands accentuate his murmured musings.

My charcoal grated loudly on the paper as I worked. It was the mention of India that seemed to draw him out of his remoteness.

"There are two kinds of Indians," he said: "those that you call Indians, the dead Indians, and my people, who are vitally alive and pulsing with fervor, but who, nevertheless, are in a miserable state. I have been away for a year now and so I do not know the exact state of affairs. But we have had a sad history, a history of desires, delusions and dreams.

"At one time our villages were in close contact with the manifold culture of Indian. They were cherished and served by all capable persons with the best that their minds produce. Today they are fatally neglected. They are fast degenerating into serfdom, compelled to offer to the ungrateful labor for work carried on in an unhealthy and impoverished environment. They clouds have blotted away the stars, and we wonder when the dawn shall begin. For we are humble and suffer and bear the burden of power, and hide our faces and stifle our sobs in the dark. But the morrow shall be ours.

"I have lately been in Russia. Ten years ago, the Russian peasant was in much the same condition that the Indian peasant is today. But now that is no longer the case. I found education where there had been ignorance, and I found what is the essential basis of all education-self-respect. That is what our great Mahatma in India is endeavoring to do to teach people to respect themselves to realise their own part in the great scheme of the universe."

"Does this mean you favor Bolshevism?" I asked.

"I am not interested in it." he replied, "All I can speak about is what I saw. I am opposed to an force. Liberty can never be obtained by it; it is only by means of education that can be secured."

When I mentioned the suppression of religion in Russia, he turned toward me. His sinuous fingers curled his beard.

"Religion cannot be suppressed. It is not a fractional thing that can be doled out in fixed measures as among various subjects in a school curriculum. It is the truth of our complete being, the consciousness of our personal relationship with the Infinite. It is the true centre of gravity of our life. This we can attain by daily living in a place where the truth of the spiritual world is not obscured by a crowd of necessities assuming artificial importance; where men live with a perfect faith in the eternal life before them.

"I am sure that those peasants in Russian today with their education and self-respect realise more fully than the downtrodden, illiterate serf of a Czarist regime that the multitude which moves in this ever-moving world is permeated by one Supreme Truth."

His eyes roamed around the room, their whites showing lustrous in contrast with their dark pupils and his tan skin. But it was evident that he did not see what he was looking at. He went on:

"It was with the desire to help my people realise this supreme truth that I founded Visva Bhrati. It is a school and university combined where the classes are conducted in just such surroundings as those in which the ancient forest dwellers of Indian realised the spirit of harmony with the universe.

"When I was thirteen years old I ran away from school, for I could not tolerate the traditional methods which were employed, in which individual traits and tendencies were ignored. One cannot grow a lily from the root of a carnage seed, nor a cabbage from a lily root. It is with this in mind that the teaching is carried on in our haven of peace, and these children for the most part are permitted to follow their natural bents.

In addition to the school and college there is also an institute of rural reconstruction whose object is to bring life in its completeness into the villages, making them self-reliant and self-respectful, acquainted with the cultural traditions of their own country, and competent to make efficient use of modern resources in improvement of their physical, intellectual and economic condition."

In order to accomplish this the poet has turned over to the institute, his estate at Santiniketan, the Nobel Prize money and the income from all of his Bengali works. The Quakers have helped him and so have one or two private individuals, but for the most part it is his donations that have kept the undertaking going.

As he had spoken of the economic condition of the villages in India, I asked him what he thought was the cause of the economic unrest throughout the world today.

"All of the nations of the earth," he replied, "are sad because bigness alone is the object which they pursue. People are searching for something without, which they can only find within themselves. The goal that they seek is the wrong one and when they attain it they find it is a worthless bauble not worth the pursuit. And in this mad pursuit they care not what means they use, forgetful or ignorant of the fact that true happiness can only be obtained by sacrificing one's self and not by seeking what belongs to others, that is to say, by contributing to the universal and not robbing the individual."

I mentioned that I had heard that he was drawing now instead of writing. He smiled.

"Yes," he answered "for two years or so I have been making drawings with colored inks. I cannot claim any merit for my courage, for it is the unconscious courage of the unsophisticated, like that of one who walks in a dream on a perilous path, who is saved only because he is blind to the risk.

"The only training which I had from my early days was the training in rhythm, the rhythm in thought, the rhythm in sound. I had come to know that rhythm gives reality to that which is desultory, which is insignificant in itself. And therefore, as I was writing I found myself annoyed by the erasures. The scratches in my manuscript cried like sinners for salvation, and assailed my eyes with the ugliness of their irrelevances. I would take my pen and begin working over them; they began to take form. What they would be or why they took the forms they did. I did not know. But often I found myself taking more time in rescuing them into a merciful finality of rhythm than in carrying on what was my obvious task.

"In the process of this salvage work I came to discover the fact that in the universe of forms there is a perpetual activity of natural selection in lines, and only the fittest survives which has in itself the fitness of cadence. I found lines that were crying out for their mates. I feel that to resolve the unemployment problem of the homeless and heterogeneous into interrelated balance of fulfillment is creation itself."

"These are some of my beginnings," he explained as he showed some pages of his manuscript with designs spread over them. "In them are the germs of my later work. They are versification in lines. Whatever merit they have is a rhythmic significance of form, which is ultimate and which does not depend upon any interpretation of an idea or the representation of a fact."

I asked him what connection there was between his work as a poet and as a painter.

"None," was his answer. "When I start to write a poem. I have a vision before my eyes, a mental representation. My verse attempt to communicate images seen or created. But when I draw I not know what I am going to make. I have no preconceived scheme in my mind. I take my pen and begin to draw and suddenly I see a head or a flower or a cloud."

He was carried away by his subject. "Sometimes I make mistakes. It is as if I broke the stem of a flower trying to bend it. Then the curve dies. I have led it on to its destruction. For all these forms are like so many little souls which expect their salvation from me."

In reply to the question as to whether he believed it was some higher force that directed his hand, he replied:

"No, for if it were a higher force the results would be more perfect than they are. I believe that each one of us has two beings within him. One of these is quite above the other in intelligence and feeling; in fact, one of these beings is quite a stupid follow. It is the other one who does the work. If the stupid fellow gets the ascendancy, nothing is accomplished, but if we can only take this fellow and hold him in subjection and not let him interfere with our subconscious self, then we can reach heights seemingly unattainable."

“After a poem is written or a picture drawn the stupid fellow in me does not understand how it was accomplished. In fact, often I have wondered at some of the things which I have written and could not understand whence I had obtained the ideas, and I cannot tell you what some of the meanings in any own pictures are.”

— *The China Press*, Jan. 5, 1931

画家泰戈尔

卢生（译）

泰戈尔（Rabindranath Tagore）之为诗哲已为国人所尽知，殊不知诗哲于诗之外，更有画家之目。此印度老人从事绘画不过两年。我们在他的原稿之中，找到许多订正品；这些拙劣的绘像来启示画的起源；即画由于装潢的精华中产生出来。

这位诗人的绘画不啻是继他的诗品而作。他们盖即启示他胸中所蕴蓄迷恋而不得解决的东西。看了这些画品的人切莫说泰氏于此自衒其能，——因为在这里头纵然有时见到手法不灵，然而这并不是讲究他的笔法；这是表现泰戈尔的真面目，是暴露一种被支配的气力，一种柔韧的活力，一种戏剧的表现力，它潜伏在抒情的恬静之后——阻断的笔势在不言中对于作者只晶莹透彻的精灵不啻有欲言不尽的表示，其意若曰：幸勿扰醒我的沉思的生活（vita contemplativa）！

他借这些人物的形状以表示他的言语，和印度人借佛像以表示的恰是相同。我们看到他的绘画中的山水，动物以及装潢的作品，便会联想到东方的毡氈，联想到印度的神秘的细密，画联想到锡兰和爪哇的傀儡形像，至于外国派的工巧却只点缀这些绘画所自出的文化领域之轮廓而已。看了这些画品的人，如其不识其作者，或许会认为出于诺尔得（Nolde）的手笔，看了这些——极似哥德人在那里努力表现其艺术的——图案的人，却会生出这个疑问：即欧洲的文明是否也把古代文化在绘画中的最后遗泽灭绝了？

泰戈尔的作品虽然这样和他人的相像，可是在其中却没有一张是折衷派而作的。一般的都具有较深的根底。大凡虚伪的“模范者”往往属于那些以其艺术从头开始的人们与时代。在七十岁时代才开始绘画的泰戈尔这样画法，好似必定由他才发见出画理。

除开那些粗陋的模拟的画像之外，泰戈尔的画像就是抒情诗，或且照这样表述出来，就是“线中的诗句”。哲学家泰戈尔的思想不特浸淫于其诗人，甚于且其画家。这话并不是对画像的内容，对现实的世界而说，却是对支配世界的自然律，对维持世界的秩序而说。在他的起笔中寓有诗的节拍，在他的结笔中现出泰戈尔的智慧。他的丰富的幻想之连续不啻供认他的心灵在和宇宙之灵合致着。画的笔法合于诗的节拍，画的色泽却带着诗的音调。

——《中国新书月报》，第1卷第9期，1931年8月

太戈尔的印度国歌

罗耀武

最近所读的作品中，最能使我感到无限慷慨的，要算是太戈尔的印度国歌。这歌不但能唤醒人民起来反抗，而且是青年们的指导原理，其“如果没有人响应你的呼声，那么，独自的，独自的走去吧！”这句话尤其是现在的青年所应接受的最好教训。

我们青年，当事业开手的时候，心的热度常同火一般的强烈，所发的言论，所感到的思想，都是很正确的，很壮勇的。可是经了某种挫折，或受人的诅骂，讥讽之后，不免中途灰心。能够不为险阻，贯彻始终的，竟是很少数很少数。因此，幻灭之感，常常笼罩一般青年心头。多少伟大的事业，每成昙花一现。其主要的原因，在乎因循观望，不能认定目标而“独自的，独自的走去！”

要知道社会上的多数人们，是被因袭的网所束缚着的，他们是随波逐浪的；他们的诅骂和讥讽，都是盲目的，是没有合理的根据的。只要你能用你的高温去消灭它们的冷酷，用你的忠诚去破灭他们的邪心；如此世上

谁不是你的保护者，你的信徒？朋友啊！只要努力的“独自的，独自的走去吧！”成功之神就能给予你满足的成功。

附泰戈尔印度国歌（略）。

……

——《回浦潮》，第 6 期，1931 年 10 月 30 日

太戈儿的恋爱观

情 怡

太戈儿是印度的大哲学家，也就是世界的大文学家，他的历史，他的著作，久已远振，用不到我来多说。不过他对于恋爱，也有独见之处，并且太戈儿是情场的过来人，更有切身的经验。青年男女愿听“恋爱的福音”的，请向下看：

（一）恋爱的意义

宇宙的爱与男女的爱，在太戈儿眼中看来，只有对象大小的分别，没有绝对的不同。他以为宇宙有神灵和物质两方面，情人的恋爱，也是灵肉一致和合的关系。他说“不，我决不关闭我的感官之门，听觉视觉触觉的欢喜快乐要生出你的欢喜快乐来。”他又说：“‘性欲’受了恋爱理想的驾驶，就化成了一种的完成，这种恋爱的最高表现，便是人类对于‘无限’的爱的象征了。”

因此太戈儿对于恋爱的定义是“恋爱是理想化，美化，精神化”。进一步说，“爱不是一种单纯的情操，爱便是真，爱便是欢喜，这种欢乐是在世上所有创造物的根株上。”概括起来，太戈儿认为恋爱是两性在实现灵肉一致的和合中“互相创造人格”的欢乐。

（二）了解与障碍

太戈儿说：爱是由两方才能成立，不过仅是双方面的相对立，一时意惹情愫，心动神迷，也未可算做真恋爱，真恋爱要排除一切障碍物，而远于互相了解的境界，爱是以灵为对象，要了解这个灵，只有用爱，爱是爱对方的灵，了解是了解对方的心。由心灵的相互了解，再加以肉体的结

合，才成了真正的恋爱。

不幸世上常有许多事物，足以阻碍心灵的相互了解，这就是美貌，金钱，名誉等。太戈儿对于受以上势力影响的人，很不以为然。他说爱就是自身的目的，别的事可以引起“为什么在我们心里，并且须得个理由去答他。但是我们说‘我爱’的时候那就没有问‘为什么’的余地了。因为他就是自身里的最后回答”。如果我们懂得恋爱不是成就别事的手段，为恋爱而恋爱，目的即在自身，这样就可消除那使心灵不相了解的障碍了。

（三）舍弃与占有

排除障碍在不得已的时候，不可不有一种舍弃的精神，这就是牺牲的精神。这种舍弃并不是因为厌恶，而是因为要实现一种更大的欢爱——喜。

太戈儿说：“我们在历史里可以随处看出，舍弃的精神就是人类灵魂最深的真实。当灵魂对于任何东西，说‘我不要这个，因为我是在这个之上’时灵魂就将存在内中的最高的真实表白出来了。譬如一个女孩在各方面知道她是高过于所玩弄的傀儡时，她会把这傀儡舍弃了。有了这种觉悟，我们知道我们是比我们所占有的东西较伟大。”又说：“不论何物，如果我们为自己储蓄的，便使我们和别人隔离了，我们的占有物就是我们的限制。”由此，我们可以知道太戈儿对于舍弃认为是应有的精神，就是自身也在舍弃之列。对于占有不满意的，认为是惹起烦恼的根源。

（四）自由与束缚

太戈儿说：“在爱里，束缚与自由并不是矛盾的”。在爱里，我们其实并不是被束缚者。当我们舍弃自身和一切占有物，而与爱人相和合，真正的爱便实现了，在这爱里，我们可以得到意识的自由，而不使灵魂囚禁于小我之内。所谓意识的自由，就是把意识活动的范围扩大，跳出个人欲念自私的圈子，为着爱而活动。而意识不被自我所限制。关于这点，他说：“我们在圆满的爱里，找到我们自我的自由了。无论引起多少痛苦，只有为爱而做的都是自由做的。因此为爱而做的工作是爱里的自由”。我们要知道。在爱里虽然有束缚，但我们却借着这些束缚以表示一种欢乐，已经超越了限制而受自由兴趣了。所以太戈儿说：“在这里，是极自由，同时又极束缚，不过束缚与自由是一样有光辉的”。

（五）结论

恋爱是一种初步的爱，从这步起，引到爱社会，爱人类，爱宇宙，使爱达到无穷大的实现，而自我与宇宙大家融合无间，这才是太戈儿“爱之福音”的根本意义。现在引他一段说话，做本篇的结束：“我们爱子女，朋友，或其他心爱的人，这种爱往往阻抑我们灵魂更远的实现。这能够放大我们意识的范围，是没疑惑的，但却又限制这意识最自由的扩张，虽然，这不过是初步，所有的奇异都在这初步自身里。这能够指示灵魂的真本性给我们看。由这里使我们确实明白，我们最高的欢乐，是在乎我们能抛弃为我的自私，而与别的联合。”

——《斗报》，第 2 卷第 33 期，34 期，1932 年 12 月 10 日

诺贝尔文艺奖与亡国者

穆木天

昨天，同一位杂志的编者谈起诺贝尔文艺奖金，接着作了一点戏谈，说：

——你们贵刊出不出“满洲文学专号”?

——那么，你就是最大的作家了。其次，还有李辉英，他笑着说。

——还有一位就是杨晦。我们算是“满洲”三大“文豪”了。说着我笑了笑。

这是一段笑谭。可是他引起我无限的感伤和好多的疑问来。

据说，这一次的诺贝尔奖金获得者蒲宁，是一位“流亡者”，现在住在巴黎。我觉得我的境遇同他有点相同。虽然，我不敢把“流亡者”这个荣衔钉在脑袋上，可是，从“九一八”以来，我总算是一个“亡国者”罢。而且，蒲宁住在西方的巴黎，我住的则是东方的巴黎。这次，蒲宁得奖，我觉得自己也似乎沾到一点光。诺贝尔奖金委员会总算看得起“亡国者”。

印度的泰戈尔老人得过了一次奖。他也是一位“亡国者”，因为他住在印度，所以，我们也没有意识到他具有“亡国”的悲哀的。所以我们也看不出诺贝尔奖金的委员会是如何地高看了他。可是，这一次，把奖金颁

给蒲宁，确是委员老爷们“另眼看待”了。

我想将来如果委员老爷照准这种“体恤”“亡国者”的原则继续下去，那么，“亡国者”也会有一条出路。不但受封，又可以发财，名利双收，岂不是两全其美。美国的黑人作家，非洲的黑人作家得过，将来就是最后，轮到“满洲”的话，无论封的是我们“三大文豪”的那个罢，我总可发一笔洋财，虽不加官，也可进禄。那时，至少，我可以多吃一点牛肉。因为都是好朋友，无论是杨晦受封，或是李辉英领奖，我是总可以揩一点油水的罢。

然而蒲宁并不是一位了不起的作家似的。库蒲林 Kuprin 人所共知的库蒲林，并未受过封。如果问世界有没有尚未受封的大作家。在法国不是有着纪德 Andre Gide 么？在俄国还有高尔基。可是，不给纪德，又不给高尔基，而偏偏地给了蒲宁，这足证明奖金委员会，是不以作品，而是以身分取士了。那么，“满洲三大文豪”不是更有希望了么？

奇怪的是自从泰戈尔受封之后，其他的亡了国而未曾作“流亡者”的作家并没有得过奖。去年诺贝尔奖金给的是美国的路易斯 Sinclair Lewis，黑奴作家休士 Hughe 等没有一个受过奖。这是怎么回事呢？若不是以作品的价值分，就是对“亡国者”的待遇，是不等的。

可是，为什么对于“亡国者”的待遇会不同呢？“亡国”，在什么地方，都是“亡国。”大概是因为“亡国”的方式不同，“亡国”的性质各异。那么，“满洲的三大文豪，”也可以不要希冀了。

像我们这样的“亡国者，”恐怕不是诺贝尔奖金委员会所能同情的。

——《申报》，1933 年 11 月 19 日

太戈尔与国际大学

胡明春

太戈尔略传

太戈尔先生于一八六一年生于印度朋佳利，他是王族的后裔，但是愿

意放弃尊贵的王位，做一个东方民族解放的诗人，哲学家，美术家。其祖其父皆为一代圣人，在印度均有远大之声誉。先生幼年当居加尔各答及喜马拉亚山脚之乡村中，先受印度式之私塾教育，后得加尔各答大学文学博士。二十四岁始出外游历，一九一三年得世界最荣贵之诺贝尔文学奖金，先生之大名始轰传天下。一九一九年，先生有英轮之游，时欧战告终，于和平运动心颇有感触。一九二四年（民国十三年）受中国之聘，毅然来华讲学，我国文艺界亦曾热烈欢迎，时先生已六十三岁矣。太翁著作初用印度朋加利文，后渐译成英文，凡读其著作者皆有一种清快爽漫之感，其著作之富，世罕其匹。中以诗歌、小说、戏剧为最多，他如哲学、美术、文学、宗教、政治、教育等论文亦甚丰富。加檀吉利一文为得诺贝尔奖金之伟大著作，先生即将此奖金全部概归他所创办之国际大学作为基金，故国大（国际大学之简称）内部则日见充实，其校誉亦日益远大矣。一九三零年（民国十九年）太先生乘遊欧之便，到处展览其美术作品，颇得各国大美术家之好评。先生一生最大之事业为沟通东西洋之文化，求东西民族互相了解，基此以实现世界之和平，故对于圣底尼克坦学院之希望甚大，圣地尼克坦即有求和平之意义，但该学院已于一九二一年改称国际大学矣！

先生之日常生活，非常俭朴。饮食以牛乳蔬菜为主，有时亦略进肉食（印度人大都皆禁吃猪肉，而回教徒禁律尤严），服饰多为印度自纺自织之土布，西装洋服视为耻辱（此点与甘地主张同），故国大学生多服布装，形式简单只求身体舒适，即为满足。太翁每晨四时起床，诵诗祷告（不是做耶稣天主的祷告），日中除读书写诗外，并时作文绘画，每有新作必对国大学生演讲，声如宏钟，神气凛然。每年春夏之交，欧美名流不远千万里之遥，来印度一瞻东方诗圣之丰采者，络绎不绝。对我国人赴国大求学甚为优待（如减免学费，住特别宿舍等），太先生对甘地之革命运动亦深表同情，并时有抗英言论之发表。太先生今年（一九三三），已为七十二岁之高龄诗人，尚屹然生存于被压迫群众中，说一句公道话，给英国人打一棒使他们不可侮的印度民族。印度虽亡于英，而印度必将独立，为太戈尔近游苏俄时之壮语也。

国际大学概况

国际大学最初始基，创设于一九零一年，梵文原名为婆罗门黉舍，或译作婆罗门书院。其初范围极狭小，一九一三年太先生游英伦始扩大发展，改和平学院；有成东西文化中心之计划，国际大学之带有国际性者即在此时开始。

风景：国际大学位于东印度孟加拉中点，离加尔各答九十九英里，火车行五小时可达。校址地势略高，周邻低垂，举目四瞩，空旷无际，校之四边茂林修竹，葱翠如锦，四季花谢又花开，香无间断，椰树榕树随处成荫，真令人陶醉，加上太先生所领导之美术生活，更觉人生之无穷乐趣也。

设备：国大学生多课外之活动，故正式之课堂甚少，常以青天为盖，绿树为墉，在自然之园林中即为国大之课堂矣。学生教授各携坐毯一方，盘坐草地，或演讲或诵读，书声鸟声每相和应。图书馆为国大最贵重之设备，内藏有二三千年前之木叶古书数千卷，为稀世名贵之古物，中国书文现备有二十四史，太平御览，资治通鉴，佩文韵府，全藏佛经，十三经等。除图书馆外以艺术院为最优美，房屋是新近建筑，为半欧半印之式样，适用且美观，院内陈列绘画，雕刻，古币，古物及印度古代乐器等。而学生对于美术科之成绩，亦可算首屈了。国大自备有马达一具，全校电灯都由这发电所供给，校中亦备有汽车一辆以备学生教授及东西外宾往来之用。国大尚有医院一所，规模甚小，若患疾病随时均可就医。政府特别为国大设一圣地尼克坦邮电局，所以外国发去的邮电只要写一圣地尼克坦的地名即可收到。

讲到国际大学的教授生活真是菲薄极了。他们都感受太戈尔先生的和平精神而来，教授除印人外，各国国籍数亦不少，对印度都有很深的信仰，他们在各大学教书每月都可得一千三四百元的薪金，而在国大者只得二百罗比（约国币二百五十元），教授们穿的是土布，吃的是箪食瓢饮，每天只进一点粗茶粗饭，还有两印度教授自己打水，自己煮饭，以自己劳苦当做美德。国大学生之生活亦如此。而诗圣太戈尔先生之生活亦如此。吾辈青年对七十二岁之老先生该抱一种什么观感去做我们的忏悔呢！

——《艺风》，第2卷第2期，1934年2月1日

泰戈尔的政治哲学

Sinha, S.（著） 徐咏平（译）

泰戈尔底天才是深入于多方面的。採句罗曼罗兰（M. Romain Rolland）所习用的话来说，是“像歌德般的”（Goethe-Like）。除了文学之外，近代印度各方面很不少受其影响的。在音乐方面，他底影响，达最高度；因为他底文辞是大众的，在识字的人们间，泰戈尔底诗歌，充满印度各处，流行极广。教育在印度之改革，莫不受泰戈尔底影响，他可谓是印度的大教育家。在他底晚年，他所播下的教育理想之种子，开始渐渐萌芽了。种子们并不曾落在岩石上呢！

泰戈尔在印度教政治底演进上之贡献，也不是不深刻的。他那Swa eshi节的一首纪念辞，每年此日都给印度青年一种兴奋。有为的青年领袖之一的尼赫拉（Pandit J. Nehru）曾说：“泰戈尔给我们底民族主义一种国际主义底景色，并且以艺术音乐及其诗歌来装饰它，使成为印度底醒觉了的精神徽章”。

泰戈尔底政治理想的贡献，均深藏于一九〇五至一九一〇年狂飚时代底许多演说中。下文吾将详述。这时代之情感底激动，虽不甚受人注意，可是在印度却没有失去其效力。在印度政治改进中，泰戈尔底思想，灌溉了印度政治意识之土。甘地的不抵抗运动来了，虽然有若干缺点，许多失败却比任何先乎此者成功的多了。

印度底政治醒觉，不再是虚面现象了，它刺激印度圣魂的深处。其机密为何？为什么甘地成功而别人失败？这回答是别人底政治改革採自外洋，而甘地底却取自印度本国底文化之源——他底真实的张力。在这里泰戈尔与甘地相遇了。

许久以前，泰戈尔曾说及印度的政治解放，必为一种自然的发展，必得采用印度人民之法则的印度佛教（Dharma）。任何政治运动必与印度底过去有关，印度底社会制度有关。这是泰戈尔的大发现。他说明印度人之“宪法”热的不确定性。“英国人已决定，无论如何都要保持其在印的统治权，假使他们看到有些不稳便加上两三个钉，钉的牢牢的，使勿得脱法。

仅因我们会说一口漂亮英语或者满嘴逻辑，他才不打算放弃其商务习惯”。甘地向泰戈尔同样的路走，泰戈尔底梦经甘地底向导而实现了。甘地之成功，虽不完全，却非不合式的，顺事之自然性。在精神方面：泰戈尔与甘地又是同一范畴的。

泰戈尔的发现是什么样呢？一言以蔽之，可称之为印度史底开门咒：（The open-sesame to Indian History）（请参看天方夜谭“四十大盗”）印度数千年旧文化之秘密。印度文化不如他国文化般的受外国文化之猛击，它是在它底宏大威严的路上发展前进的，吸收许多外来的元素，造成一种自己的文化。“印度不接受许多异端而扰乱，也不探索每个外来者底敌人。所以她无所拒，无所毁；她弃绝不法，认识一切观念的伟大；所以她把他们都带进来成一和谐的东西”。

印度并没有失去她底特质；这话怎么讲？锁匙躺在印度社会组织中。印度底天才者，发现社会基石在作用层中，在各个社会单位及其经地方议会底平权底极度发展中。这种共生有机体关系不仅增加社会各要素底张引力而已，且能造成社会协调。每个人都有其特殊嗜好；每人都有其信仰范围。简言之，印度是个乡村共和国，虽然在崩溃底磨难中，将来将不失如此。“在我国中，国王作战以保全其领土；执行法律，但是社会组织牵及一切，自水的供给以至于知识的供给，如此之简单自然，统治权虽可变换，却不足克服我们去破坏佛教，毁灭我们底社会机构叫我们散亡漂泊”。“国家生存于小茅屋中”最确当也没有了。在这里印度文化生命兴旺起来了。

印度社会组织中之明显的半轮，是印度社会基石与不灭的印度文化中。“……各种不同的文化生命，放在各种不同的政治集体上。在那里那激动人心的人民底责任存在着；而且假使一阵风而吹倒了，整个民族也受伤而死了。在英国国家的倾覆，也就是民族的败亡，但是只当我们底社会我们底佛教跛脚不灵时，危害才真正能颠灭我们底国家。这是我们所以不作孤注一掷，用一切去抵抗统治权底改换，而不惜任何牺牲去保持我们宗教的自由的理由了”。

但是这种社会与国家间底优美的均势，靠两种主要情势，第一，是自治单位之经济自给；其次，是保证国统治者，尤其是外人统治者对社会观念的尊敬。及至现在，这两种情势全充分发达了。

印度与西方文化的接触，各方都属有利的。机械的交通工具，打破印度传统习惯，使农村的经济为世界经济的一部分，使失却过去的保守性。都市的发展，介绍农村一些最良的元素。印度旧文化的崩溃，退化与贫穷，为不可避免的结果。墙壁中抽出一块石头，整个社会自然难免起动摇呀。

那末到什么地方去找的一个新社会基石呢？这成问题了。缀起他们才遗留着的残丝是可能的吗？或者必得从事建立一个新的吗？没有绝对的回答是对的。显然，传统势力不能完全推倒，任何组织也不能支持与新时代违背的精神。要把印度社会阶级制度取得社会平等制度，显然前者不合时宜的。泰戈尔之政治贡献为合作——合作复兴印度农村经济与文化脊骨。

泰戈尔一如爱尔兰诗人乔治·罗素（George Russell）相信人口之减少，退化，衰弱为国民贫穷与忧郁的结果，冒险进取精神衰退了，农村社会组织散漫了。减除贫穷为主要问题。开拓“民族之心很快衰颓去的沙漠”为主要事业。一切便跟着解决了。饥饿的胃没有吃饱，赤裸的背没有穿衣之前，一切改革与宣传都属无效。所以泰戈尔不单宣传驱除贫穷而已；且实际从事在他自己办的逊提干塔大学举办合作，工作者在校训练后，带回农村去以合作理论与技术，并帮助农人办理合作，解决一切困难。

这是泰戈尔救助一个古国衰亡的灵魂的方法。泰戈尔还教育未来的国家主人翁——儿童。“印度的政治解放，在她自己儿童底手里”。

——《汗血周刊》，第 3 卷第 23 期，1934 年 12 月 10 日

泰戈尔的《覆舟》

宋清山

《覆舟》是一部长篇小说，它的作者就是大名鼎鼎的印度文豪泰戈尔先生，泰戈尔八年前到过中国，并且都在许多地方演讲过了。关于他的事迹，他的性格，在中国已经有了专集的记载，无须用我来介绍。我现在所

要介绍的，不过是他的作品中的一种——《覆舟》。《覆舟》最初是用印度的彭家利文写的，由著者自己译成英文，所以英文的译本，也可算是原文了。英文名称叫做“The Wreck”，大概最初的出版是在伦敦，但是我所见到的译本，是德国 Tauchnity Edition 翻印的。

泰戈尔著名的作品，大半都是诗，因此别人都称他是印度的诗圣。但是他的诗中，都含着很深的哲理，所以我们读了很不容易了解他的真意。他的小说中，如《家庭与世界》(Home and the World ）之类，也多有含高尚的哲理，要不是明白他的背景，读的时候，往往使人“如入五里云雾中”，简直是莫名其妙。但是《覆舟》一书，就与他别的作品不同了。我们读这部书，虽然不明白他的背景；但是，也能够了解他的深意；而且从这散文的里面，可是看出诗人描写的天才。这个原因，大概不只一端；一方面固然因为书中的大意比较的浅鲜，另一方面就是因为书中的背景大半和中国的情形相同。

关于《覆舟》的背景和作者的动机，我在八年前在北平也听过作者的演讲。我现在照我的记忆力之所能及的，将它写在下面，或者对于想读这部书的文友们，不无小补呢。泰戈尔那一次的讲演，专门是为帮助各大学生了解他的作品。他开始就说中国和印度，有许多礼节和习惯。印度的婚姻制度的不良，较中国有“过之无不及”。中国的婚姻，虽然注重“父母之命，媒妁之言，”但是除了回教徒以外，关于对手方的宗教观念，差不多是没有多少人注意的。印度则不然，除了婚姻的择配须完全由父母主持之外，还要对手方是与自己同教的，否则，虽然是门当户对，这门亲事，也是作不成的。印度的宗教，大别分为三派：一是印度正教，二是婆罗门教，三是回教。如果印度正教的人同婆罗门教或回教的人结了婚，叫做卖了祖宗，是同教的人所不齿的。

印度结婚的日期，也是和中国一样，必须要由星象家择定的。这个日期，必须上不犯父母，下不犯子孙，方可算得吉日良辰。一经择定之后，就视为天经地义，虽有种种重大的阻碍，也不能改期的。往往因为这个原故，发生了许多惨剧。但是，印度人的命运观念，比中国人的还要深，所以只恨自己的命苦，从来不会想到星象家择错了日子的，至于因风雨或大水而延期的时髦话，更是谈不到了。

我现在所要介绍的《覆舟》，就是专制婚姻的惨史，也就是印度的旧礼教和习惯的写真。作者的动机，本来非常简单的；但是，他对于印度旧礼教的不满和悲哀，就决不如他对我们口述的那样简单了。照泰戈尔亲口所讲的话，他写这部小说的动机，就是因为有一次起大风的时候，看见恒河里面翻了几艘船，淹没了两对新婚夫妇，以及他们的家族和朋友。动机虽如是简单，可是书中的内容，就非常的复杂。全书的内容，依我个人的意见，可以分为三大部分。第一部分是讲少年律师雷米舒（Ramesh）的婚姻惨史和礼教专制的遗毒。第二部分是讲雷米舒和玛拉（Kamala）的假夫妻生活，以及他同寒梅（Hem）的婚姻破裂史。第三部分是讲一切的秘密发现，和两对夫妻的破镜重圆。但是其中的形情过于复杂，严格的说来，真是无从分起。全书的布局，俨然与美国影式的影相像，而奇情节之离奇，又与沙士比亚的喜剧同出一辙。

《覆舟》情节介绍（略）。

……

（介绍者附曰：此部小说背景与动机，很合乎于我国的婚姻制度。可惜未有人把它翻译成中文。但是译成中文并不是很容易的，往往看着就未有头绪，脑筋就散乱如麻。这篇介绍不过将它的大意写出来，如果将他的详情介绍出来，那恐怕再写这么十篇八篇的，也未必能写明呢！）

一九三五,四,二十三，作于故都。

五,六，录于琴岛。

——《文艺月刊》，第10卷第2期，1937年2月1日

太谷儿关于人生观底三封信

太谷儿氏前年夏天间游历欧洲，旅行中有致其国内友人书多通。述其感想。最近发表于印京喀尔格答新出版之月刊《近世评论》中，书中所言，大致不满意于西方之物质文明，而重视精神生活；其言皆含有哲理，足以发人深省。兹择其尤耐寻味之书函节译于后：

（一）五月二十日寄自亨堡

吾人将于明晨离此赴科本哈根。吾非理想的旅行者，吾从未预想到以异国不断的盲撞意外之事与意外之人为乐。今日之飘泊生涯，已使余厌倦，而追维平和安乐椅中之宇宙不置。（中略）……今日世界处处失其常态，空气中充塞不解决之问题。能歌者不以歌自遣，须大声为他人传命令。然而吾之生活，果必为永久之北极的生活，不断黑暗之生活，责任无尽之生活，而永无一灿烂星晨之夜，来吾之眼前，以导我入上帝之门乎？人死果仅为生活之休止乎？非告吾人爱国主义域限之外，尚有一广大无边之境界乎？何时我可最后调整吾之生命，而招接"精神"以临兹尘世乎？西方之小学教师，尝诏吾人，谓世上除表示与国民学校地图中者以外，别无重要之事物，只有我之国家为我之天地，吾之生与死只在我之国家内得以连络。而东方之人，苟亦自尊其国，而图拒斥西方者；即如一窭子，以胠箧之术，施诸西方也。虽然，我东方人之祖先，较明白真理；较悉自由之真面目。知自由之为物，不可剪其羽翼，而以地理上之樊笼范围之。我今觉实现此真理之日，已不甚远；我求我死时，不为一爱国家，或一政治家：而为一自由精神；不为一新闻记者，而为一诗人。

（二）五月二十七日寄自斯笃呼姆（瑞典京城）

（上略）……欧洲人无限之傲心，已突遭遏制。彼等之意识，似正在退出其所自开之路矣。巨人饱受创痛，疲极思眠。和平之泉，本自东方流出，涓涓不绝：备甚之欧洲，自然移其面目而向东方；如小儿然；因逞身手而受伤，遂避众而寻其母；而东方者，非向为人类精神之母，惯以其自己之生命，分于人类者乎？惜乎我人在印度者，尚未知此欧洲之呼救声，已达吾门；负此可以普拯人类之荣耀，而不自悟，诚大憾事！我以所到各国，备受欢迎。辄欲求其真因。——有人谓因我爱人之故，此说信耶？吾不敢知。吾向来所谓文字，固时时流露爱人之意，谅能普达全世界之人心。然则，果前说而确者，吾愿以此爱人之声，为我毕生之南针矣。日者余独憩于亨堡之逆旅中，忽有德国妙龄郎二人，姗姗而入，以玫瑰花一束相赠；一女操断续之英语谓余曰："我爱印度。"余询何故？曰："因君爱上帝耳。"此盛大之赞美，吾不敢承。特其言实为一种福音，使我欣喜；彼之意，殆印度爱上帝，故彼爱印度耳。今日国民皆自爱其国，此爱国观念，徒养成国与国间之猜疑怨恨；世界今正渴望一不爱己，而爱上帝之国；——唯有此国可要求全世界各国人民之爱。吾人高呼爱国，不啻谓邻国之人，非我之弟兄。实则此并非真理，唯此可以最后解决之。

（三）六月十日寄自大姆斯他德（德国）

德国各地之人，皆集此间，与我相见；开会于海斯大公之园邸中。来宾各以问题相质；有不解英语者，由凯塞，林伯爵为我翻成德语。第一问题，为坎拏大籍德人某所提出，曰："此科学文明之将来若何？"余作答后，彼又问："人口过多之问题若何解决？"继复有人问；"佛教之真谛。"余解答此三问题，足费两小时之久；彼等状至恳切，使我愉快。盖德人惯于思考严重宏博之问题，善为深思。吾人在印度，只从新式学校之教科书，得知若干理想；供考试通过之用。而新式小学教师，均为英人；英人在西方各国人中，最与理想不相容。彼等为人，非不善良正直而恃，但含有过强之兽性，时时表现于赛马，猎狐，角力，及其他运动中；而对于一切理想之接触，则顽强抵抗之。德国之政治野心，今已遭一猛烈之制止；其人民几一致向精神方面寻求安慰，以代其惊外之成功。德国今日似已上一精神的旅行之途，虽经济困窘，已达极点，其思想殊不仅专致于纺织，机器，或政治上之新运动，有颇努力于"内心的自由。"此"内心的自由，"即予吾人以超脱一切环境变化之权力者也。吾尝遇英大使于柏林，谈及余在德之工作，彼深致赞美；并谓望余供给一种哲理，以安德人之心。余知彼此言盖自英人的观察点而言之，盖彼以为哲理乃一种安眠剂，可以缓和德人之躁动，使之酣然入梦；而战胜者乃得安稳享受其以武力夺来之物质利益，揣彼之意，殆背人窃笑以为此宗交易，吾英人获利也：抑知此等利益，就精神的究竟而论，固贱若粪土耶！

——《互助月刊》，第 1 期，1937 年 3 月 15 日

泰戈尔为西班牙内战发表宣言

印度大诗人泰戈尔，最近以印度反战反法西斯同盟主席的资格为西班牙事件发表宣言，号召全世界进步人士主持公道，援助西班牙共和政府。

“世界文明目前正在西班牙受到威胁与践踏。弗朗哥高举叛旗反对民主政府与西班牙人民。国际法西斯蒂用兵西国，接济叛军金钱。摩洛哥人和外籍军人泛滥全国，到处是死亡饥饿和贫穷。

玛德里，文化和艺术的圣地，目前正在炮火包围中。它那无价的艺术作品为叛军的炸弹毁坏了。甚至医院和托儿所都没有幸免。妇女和儿童都死在了血泊中。

不要让国际法西斯蒂大破坏的洪流继续泛滥了。要给不人道的放荡行动、种族偏见、掠夺欲望和战争野心一个迎头打击。要把文明从野蛮的洪流中拯救出来。

在这决定的一刻，在西班牙人民蒙受伟大痛苦的一刻，我向全世界有良心的人士呼号。

援助西班牙人民阵线！援助西班牙合法政府！打死反动！拯救民生政治，拥护文明和文化！”

泰戈尔，纯粹的诗人，埋头于学术的哲学家兼教育家，从不参与政治生活，这次他热烈的号召自然能格外引起世人的注意。

——《时事类编》，第 5 卷第 12 期，1937 年 6 月 16 日

市商会及青年会致函泰戈尔

广州市市商会，广州基督教青年会函泰戈尔爵士云，报上得读阁下联合奈赫鲁先生及印度国会，对日本抗议，盖以日军阀不顾人道，轰炸我中国平民，此种维护正义之精神，吾人深致感激。尚希阁下传达奈赫鲁先生及国会会员，申述余等之谢悃。吾人坚信抵抗日本，乃为我国及全世界保全正义而奋斗。迩来日机屡袭广州及近郊，屠杀非武装平民，复用潜艇毁灭中国渔舟及渡船，无辜被屠杀者为数不少，吾人已饱受痛苦，然深知前途艰苦，更为深重。今蒙贵国同情，则余等一切痛苦，亦易于肩负。中国现已决心抵抗，惟仍须贵国与其他国家之协助，实施对日经济绝交。日军阀非仅威胁中国，全世界且将受其害，即日本本国亦难幸免也。十月十六日。

——《广州青年（1931）》，第 24 卷第 39 期，1937 年 10 月 18 日

不做泰戈尔

枫

在第九期的《战斗旬刊》上，我们读到了武大同学的沉痛的报告，并且读到了一段非常滑稽的消息，就是，武大的文学院长陈源教授，劝学生安心读书，莫问国事，将来国家亡了，大家还可以做中国的泰戈尔。

陈源教授的这段话，我想决不是戏言，因为陈教授是正人君子，决不肯随便开玩笑的，而且，陈源教授一向奉行的教育路线，便是亡国主义的路线。自从在北平时办《现代评论》和鲁迅先生笔战的时候起，一直到现在为止，他无论在言论上和行动上都从没有违反这个路线。

他劝青年们做泰戈尔，自然不成问题的，他自己应该以身作则了，但是，我看，陈教授还没有这个资格。首先，他不是一个诗人，他和诗人隔着十万八千里的距离，他除了翻译过一本《父与子》和写了一本乱七八糟的《西滢闲话》以外，在文坛上没有一丝一毫的功勋。其次，泰戈尔这位老翁，究竟还有些正义感，他对于西班牙的叛乱，公开发表宣言，反对德意法西斯强盗，对于中国抗战，也公开发表宣言，反对日本法西斯匪徒。但是我们的陈教授呢？他除了谆谆告诫青年去做亡国奴以外，还曾说过一句人话吗？

尽管陈源教授苦口婆心地劝青年做泰戈尔吧，但是中国的文学青年，都在斗争中觉醒过来，而要学习着去做高尔基，巴比塞，向着这些巨人的足迹去追踪。至于陈源教授的屁话，除了讨“皇军”的欢喜以外，还有任何作用之可言？

“保存文化根源”

前天我们的王教育部长，在武大训话，训词大意，报上已经登过，想来大家已经看到了。王教长的这次训话，无论从那方看，总算有了进步。他承认了战时教育的重要性，认为“战时大学教育，当以战时需要而定”，不像某大学校长那样的顽固，说是“翻遍了欧美的教育辞典，都找不出

‘战时教育’这个名词”，因而对于战时教育，顽抗到底。

可是，王教长的另一句话，却使我们不懂，他认为目前教育，“当以适应需要，保存文化根源为原则，兼筹并顾，双管齐下，不可因噎废食”。所谓“文化根源”究竟是指的甚么？和“保存国粹”的话，究竟有甚么区别？是否抱着书本不放，便可“保存文化根源”？这些问题，王校长都没有替我们解答。

但我们可以大胆地说，目前的抗战，便是保卫文化的战争，日本帝国主义想消灭我们的国家，还想消灭我们的文化，因此，凡是真正承受中国文化传统的人，应该是坚决的起来，为保卫文化而战斗到底，因此，全国各大中学，应该赶快把学生从死的牢笼中解放出来，让他们参加保卫文化的战斗，从实际的斗争生活中去学习，去受教，如果王教长所说的“保存文化根源”的真义在这里，那当然是应该为我们绝对拥护的；但如果王教长的意思是在另一个方面，是在劝青年读死书，在劝青年接受亡国教育，是在劝青年们在炮火中“抱残守缺”，是在劝他们在亡国以后，去做泰戈尔，那么，这种办法，事实上只会断送中国文化的根源，事实上是宣传亡国的文化，事实上恰恰做了中国文化的罪人！我想我们的王教长，该不会是这样糊涂吧。

——《文化新闻》，第2卷第1期，1937年12月10日

宝贵的同情

印度伟人同情中国抗战
泰戈尔谓中国绝不屈服

据大陆报云：印度三大伟人，热切同情中国抗战；此三人中甘地为提倡不合作主义者，尼鲁[1]曾两次担任全印国民大会主席，至少为百分之九十印度学生崇拜之偶像，太戈尔为著名诗人。马德拉斯国际教会大会代

[1] 即“尼赫鲁”，本文下同。

表，于十二月间曾访谒此三大领袖。大陆报记者访问甫自印度归来之中国代表，据称甘地虽然确信不抵抗主义，但于特殊环境下予抵抗行动以援助，并非过失。渠称：自渠参加印度独立运动后，在南非波尔战争及世界大战时，曾担任救护工作。渠信援助英人可获英人之同情。太戈尔对于中日战争之态度，可于其与日本诗人函内见之，该函称："中国为不可征服之国家，人民精诚团结，正为其国家创造一新时代。中国继续抗战，一时之失败决不能摧毁其抗战精神"。尼鲁为印度著名政治领袖，渠谓印度拟与中国物资援助，全印领袖当已通过议决案两项：（一）谴责日本对华"侵略"；（二）采取抵制日货步骤。

——《大众（上海 1939）》，第 1 卷第 2 期，1939 年 3 月 15 日

泰戈尔访问记

我们几个人于去年十二月底，在印度马都拉大会闭会后就去访问甘地，泰戈尔，尼赫鲁三位领袖……（略）。

离开了华特我们便到波尔坡附近之善特尼吉丁学院去访问诗哲太戈尔。他年近八十，白发长髯，道貌岸然，因为不敢使他过于疲劳，我们只和他谈了三刻钟，虽然我们在学院住了一天。我们没有和他谈中日问题。因为他很客气地说，"我不懂得政治"，可是他的书记给了我们一份他给日本人野口米次郎关于中日问题的信，我们看过之后，觉得他头脑非常清楚，说话非常坦白，其中有几句说："我们替你们日本民族忧愁，因为你们的军阀向中国所造之孽，还不如他们向日本人民所造的孽之大。中国是不能被征服的……他们是忠勇的，是团结的，现在正在艰苦的奋斗中，创造出一个新时代，日本虽然武力较胜，但中国的抵抗，表示了更高尚的道德能力，我现在更相信日本前进思想家冈仓的话，中国是伟大的。"我们读了这几句话，一面是愈觉得感奋，同时也对这位老诗人，表示无限的敬仰。

——《东方战友》，第 6 期，1939 年 4 月 1 日

诗圣太戈尔与中日战争

雪　尘

当卢沟桥事变发生以后，不可避免地，我们神圣的全面抗战展开了，这战争，是为国家之独立，自由，民族之生存，恒永而发动，是为世界的公理，人类的正义而发动。我们的民族性和国策是和平的，而我们的人力，物力，财力，却为日寇的破坏和平而牺牲，所以，不但我们酷爱和平的人民，一变其遗传的天性，对日寇深情惆怅，下了抗战到底，胜利第一的决心，就是全世界的公正人士，亦莫不痛心疾首，深抱不平和愤慨，而印度诗圣太戈尔先生，便是为人道正义，严辞谴责日寇的一人。

先生为近代提倡东方文化，宣扬东方文化最有力之一人，亦倡导世界和平，拥护世界和平最有力之一人，他不知替东方文化出了多少气，争了多少气，又不知替世界和平出了多少力尽了多少力。因为他要提倡东方文化，宣扬东方文化，所以对于为东方文化最大柱石之一的中国文化，特别表示爱好，尊重与赞扬。因为他要倡导世界和平，拥护世界和平，所以对于我们最爱好和平的中国人民，特别表示亲敬，友善与爱护。又为他要替东方文化出气争气，要为世界和平出力尽力，所以对于日本人民近几十年来之发愤图强，努力振作，也特别表示欣慰，称许与期望。但不料日本军阀，毕竟根性卑劣，气量鄙小，既不能高瞻远瞩，复没有大国宏愿。甲午之役，侥幸战胜了腐败的满清，即趾高气扬，不可一世。十年之后，再侥幸战胜了老大的帝俄，便更野心勃发，狡妄思逞。迨至欧洲大战，又趁火打劫，暴发了些财富，虚涨了些声势，更是狂妄猖獗，不可理喻。太戈尔先生早已看出了它的危机，于十几年前到日本讲学的时候，即对日本军人提出了一个严厉的警告，他在那里讲了一篇《国家主义在日本》，对日本军人的偏狭的国家思想，及其自私自利的野心与企图，很严厉的揭发与教训了一遍。但短见的日本军人等，不但不知有悟，从而改勉，反而起了许多逆感，使他对于日本的深厚期望，便日渐减少，乃至于消失。而日本军人，更变本加厉，如此大举侵犯其文化祖邦之中国，更在中国如此野蛮横行。且不但要亡中国的国家，并要灭中国的种族，这无异于掘发日本自己祖宗的坟墓，来埋葬日本自己的子孙前途，使先生特别感着惋惜，悲悯与哀痛，在激动的心弦和颤慄的手腕之下，写出了本书内所载的几件在这次中日战争中最可宝贵的文献，并可说是在人类正义与暴力奋斗之中几个最尊严有力的颁告与书笺。

本书的目次是这样的，（1）诗圣太戈尔与中日战争，（2）太戈尔先生致蒋委员长及中国人民书，附蒋委员长后书，（3）太戈尔先生给日本侵略者之训诫，（4）太戈尔先生第一次答复倭诗人野口信。

第一篇是叙述译著者在上海大战的时候，方由国际大学到南京印度安达拉大学去演讲“中国近代政治经济社会史”，太戈尔先生忽然害了一场重病，且有过一次最危险的时期，及至由南印度演讲回来，先生的危险时期已经过了，且在渐渐康复，恰好中国中印学会理事主席蔡子民先生与监事主席戴季陶先生拍去了一个电报，慰问太戈尔先生的病状，他把电报译好了送去读给太戈尔先生听，并因先生的问及，约略告诉以日本军人在中国底疯狂，太戈尔先生听着很是伤痛，立即叫他的秘书，按照口授，拟了一个复书，致谢蔡、戴两先生在我国在生死存亡奋斗之际，犹能以深思远念及他的慰问，并对我国人民，此欧战于所关于伟大和平国土之非法无理的侵略，作英雄勇武之抵抗，表示钦敬，并且祷我国的胜利。这个电报发出之后，同时在印度各报纸发表了，于是顿时便被路透社记者，把它广播于全世界，日本侵略主义者看见了，便想法买动了一个亡命在日本的印度人名拉什伯哈里波斯的，由东京打了一个电报给太戈尔先生，请求他不要发表反日言论，并设法劝阻印度国民大会及尼赫鲁氏，不要做反日举动，太戈尔先生接了他这个电报非常激怒，当即寄了一个快邮代电给他，驳复他的申请，这个代电也给印度各报发表了，并经路透社记者把他广播了，于是日本侵略者，又指使在印度加尔各答已无声无臭的印日协会的一个什么会长，特地托人送了一个很精致的古瓶给太戈尔先生，想要结纳他的欢心，使其对于在这次日本侵略、中国反抗战争的局面下，退出他自己的伟大的立场，停止他拥护和平与东方文化的呼声，放弃他维持人道与正义的主张。可是，不论日寇如何央求，鼓吹，太戈尔先生的立场与主张，总是不为所动，不为所变。同时，他对于日本人民，又始终是一样地慈悲，一样地爱惜。因此，他对于这位所谓“印日协会会长”也者，也写给了一封婉而有力的信，说明他对于日本帝国主义的侵略政策，不能赞同。

去年四月底，译著者为的要对于祖国抗战的情形，有所了解，有所尽力，并为的国际大学中国学院及其他种种事情，告假回国一行，太戈尔先生特地写了一封信，交他带呈蒋委员长，并另外写了一封很长的"使音"，交他带呈蒋委员长转致中国人民，表示其同情与敬意。在译著者回国之后，中日战事的演变，一天一天地剧烈，太戈尔先生的焦心，悲愤与呼号，也一天一天随之增长，而日寇则用尽了方法，向太戈尔先生纠缠，总想把他骗过去，有的向道长诉短，有的要请他到日本去，又有的要求他出来做个和事老，并有一个倭诗人野口者，曾一再写信给他，为日本的侵略与暴行作辩护。于是，太戈尔先生，便以慈悲与仁爱，祥和而又庄严的态度，把这野口剀切诚恳的训诫了两遍，于是便产生了一字一泪与一字一血，并字字含有一个大慈大悲的心与至真至正的理的两封答复野口的信。

这是第一篇文字的梗概，可以说是本书的一篇序，因为作者与太戈尔先生亲炙甚久，所以对于太戈尔先生对于我国抗战的同情与希望，写得非常动人。

第二篇的大意已在前面略述了，兹不赘及。

第三篇太戈尔先生给日本侵略者之训诫，里面有这样的话。

"假使你能够使中国人民信服你们的军队轰炸他们的城市，使他们的妇女儿童等成为无家的乞丐——且借用你自己的词句，即那些尚未被炸成（泥鱼的残骸），——假使你能使这些牺牲者信服，他们所遭受的只是一种仁慈的待遇，此种仁慈的待遇在末了将拯救（他们的国家民族），否则你殊不必再来游说我们相信贵国的高贵目的，你的正当的愤慨攻击你所谓那个（亵渎不自爱）的人民，他们走在焚毁他们自家的城邑与艺术宝库，（臆测的话，也许还在爆炸他们自己的人民）藉以诽谤你们的兵士，使我想起拿破仑进兵至莫斯科时眼巴巴望着莫斯科城市宫殿在火光熊熊中的高贵暴怒，你是一个诗人，我很希望你至少能有那种想象，一种人民到了使其必须甘愿把他们自己许多年，实在是许多世纪，所辛苦缔造的许多事物，不惜付之一炬，那是出于一种何等非人的失望。……你的控诉，是，当那些（不诚信的）中国人，广播他们的恶毒的宣传时。你们的（诚信的）日本人，却是守着静默的。我的朋友，你不知道，没有那一种宣传是能胜过一种高贵与善良的行为么？如果这种高贵与善良的行为是属于你们的，你又何需畏怯你们的牺牲者的狡计呢”。（P19）

“那必使我过于悲伤与痛苦，我若在那里眼看着他们一群一群的给他们的统治者运到一个圣国去，作种种无人道的罪恶，而那些罪恶，将在人类的历史中，把他们的名字印上一个永久不可磨灭的污点。”（P21）

是的，太戈尔先生不仅是个诗人，而且是一个哲人与圣人，不但有极深厚的感情，而且有明察的理智，任日寇怎样的污蔑我们，而为自己的侵略行为诡辩，但是圣哲的灵心慧眼下面，总知道“事实却显然不是如此”。

现在我在把第四篇里面野口的原信和太戈尔先生驳斥他的信，对录几段在下吧。

“这次的战争，并非一种杀人的疯狂，而是为得要在亚细亚大陆上建立一个伟大的新世界不可避免的方法，虽然这方法是很可怕的，盖（亚洲为亚细亚人之亚洲主义）必须实现，相信我，这是一个（亚洲与亚洲的战争）。”——野口（P29）

“人类，虽遭受了许多的失败，毕竟相信一个社会的基本道德的结合，因此，当你说到（手段虽然极端的可怕，为得在亚洲大陆建立一个新的伟大世界，却无可避免），——我想你指的对于中国妇女儿童的轰炸以及对于古代庙宇与大学等毁灭，是为了亚洲而拯救中国的手段，——你实在是以在兽类之中尚非不可避免的一种生存途径，发诣于人类，——你是在塔顶，建造你的亚细亚的观念，我相信亚洲所负的使命，诚然如你所指出，但我决未梦想，是与那帖本尔杀人的恐怖势力的行为，可以一致的。”——太戈尔（P24）

“但是你如果知道，日本人民的邮政储金，已多至五十万万日元，与政府的经济繁殖相呼应，你将表示惊叹，为应付战争所引起的各种困难，我们是一文钱都节省，并连一废弃的破片都要好好利用。”——野口（P31）

“你说及可怜的日本人民的储蓄，与其缄默的牺牲和苦难，而以为得意，殊不知这种可悲的牺牲，显然暴露其为被劫取而供大炮的奔放与侵略其邻人的家室并劫掠伟大的人为财富而为非人的效用。我知道，宣传已成为一种美妙的艺术，在非民治国中的人民，要抗拒那时时刻刻的麻醉毒

剂，几乎是不可能的。”——太戈尔（P25）

“中国是不可征服的，他的文明……是正在表现着惊人的才智，他的人民的誓死忠诚与其空前所未有的统一，是在为那个国土创造一个新的时代，没有准备而为一个巨大的机械化战争所投入，中国还能保持着自己的立场，没有暂时的失败，能破坏他的完全兴起了的精神，对着日本军国主义所剽窃的西方科学，中国的立场，显示着一种固有的优越的道德的崇高，今日，我才更能了解我从前所本了解的那位心量广大的日本思想家冈仓郑重对我说：‘中国是伟大的’，他那种的热忱与意图。”——太戈尔（P27）

我年来因为心绪忙乱，无论看到什么书，总索然寡味，那怕是一本一二十页的小册子，一拿到手里，便感觉得厚沉沉的，只是这本诗圣太戈尔与中日战争，买来之后，不但一口气把它读完了，并且已读过了五遍，只觉得它是太少，太少，翻到尾页的时候，不自禁要把书壳翻了转来，下意识地，希望它后面还有几页没读完的，是的，它是太少了，似还有一些散见于报章上面的太戈尔先生关于中日战争所发表的文字，都还没有收入，我热烈诚恳地希望译著者在本书再版时补充一下，或其他文化工作者来从事搜集，汇印成一册为人道正义说教的完整的福音吧！

——《新新新闻每旬增刊》，1939年10月11日，第2卷第11期

三种角度下的太戈尔

东方式的传道师　现代气息的诗人

方　企

佛教在中国所发生的思想，中译佛典给印度所保留的文献，够充分证明中印关系的密切，而在密切关系中，也很见得中印文化精神的不同，印度人所具的，是传道的精神，而中国人所具的，则是求法的精神。这说明的充份证明，不是这里所能提出的，只为既然要谈点太戈尔，恰正用得着这种说明。太戈尔曾两度来到中国，虽然这和他的赴欧，赴美没有多大差

别，但他对中国确特别寄与希望，他当然以为东方人自然更易于了解东方精神，中国人眼中的印度诗哲因而以为他的理想也就比较以中国人为最易于接受，他在中国的演讲，就颇带一点传道的企图。固然他的影响很小，第二次且几乎只引起相反的效果，但文坛上到底一度流行过太戈尔式的诗，并且很有几个人迢迢地跑去国际大学读书了。就这么小小的范围，授与受的精神，似乎也显然分别着。去年，读书于国际大学的谭云山发刊《太戈尔与中国》的小册，今年，有人给太戈尔祝八十高龄，（他生于一八六一年今年作八十岁算是东方式的吧）。他的已就黯淡的影象似乎又将重渐浮现。自然这并不因为他新有了什么特别值得注意处，而是因为整个印度正逐渐吸引我们的注意，而他自然是想到印度时所必想到的人物的一个。今年的印度，不仅我们天然会注意，并且全世界的目光也都很注意地集中着。单说三四期来的亚细亚杂志的书评栏中，所介绍的，就都以关于印度的书为多数。就涉及的印度人物说，固然全只讲甘地和尼赫鲁，而太戈尔似在忘却之列，但不久西方必有对印度的更普遍的注意而那时西方人趣味所趋，说不定倒转是太戈尔。可是太戈尔也并不是一个纯粹东方式的教道师。他虽具有宗教气的哲学观念，但并不曾企图成为一个宗教家，他虽也该称为圣者，但并不因为他像隐居森林的修士；他的国际大学虽然带精舍想建设的，却是一西方式的民主国家。太戈尔的著作，虽披着东方式的外衣，而实际却是要把古老的印度文学，渐引得和现代精神接近。他的所以能意味，也所指向这只是现代教育的目标。甘地所用的是东方式的反抗方式，而所在诗人多于鲫鱼的印度跃出为特殊的诗人，正因为他的诗已含有现代气息，所以前人不能与他相比。而且他也并不想多造就出几个东方诗人，他在教育上颇注重实际生活。

——《申报》，1940 年 4 月 7 日

本会代表印度泰戈尔大学征文

印度泰戈尔大学委托本会征求“泰戈尔对于中国新诗的影响”一文，长短不拘，中英文皆可。此次中国抗战，印度民族及泰戈尔本人对中国甚

表同情。泰戈尔的作品对初期的中国新诗也有相当的影响。凡对这问题有兴趣者请踊跃参加，稿寄本会转交或径寄。

Cheena-Bhavan
Santiniketan,
Bengal, India.

——《大公报》，1940 年 4 月 30 日

泰戈尔大学访问记

Fouguet, G.（著） 潘君拯（译）

在巴黎，罗马，瑞典，开罗，及德黑兰等地，泰戈尔和他的长袍以及响亮的声调都曾给我们留下热诚的印象。世界各国的学生们都乐于以诚意结交代表法国青年男女的我们。我们曾经真的遇到未闻泰戈尔大名的人——地中海港口一位法国领事，当我们告诉他将取道赴印度访泰戈尔时，竟如此回答："泰戈尔！泰戈尔，加尔各达，旁拿勒斯，谋索，那些都是可爱的城市啊！很好，我的朋友们，愿你们在泰戈尔快乐！"

我们从加尔各答起飞，穿过孟加拉富饶的乡村，直到我们看见诗人所住的寂寞旷野上两个熊熊的火盆。他的父亲是一位神圣的人，驻居该地，建了一个隐居的别墅，后来他的儿子回到故乡，开了一所小小的学校，这所学校逐渐扩大，蜕变为今日举世皆知的著名文化中心——圣地尼加敦大学。

我细察地平线，搜求圣地尼加敦八百学生的学校，游戏场，教室，以及宿舍，我仅看见散布在棕榈叶中的茅屋。我们开始下降，我看到一大群人穿着五色缤纷的长袍，全都昂首仰观飞机着陆。我们踏上诗人所居住的土地了，但是圣地尼加敦在那儿呢？

受到学生们一阵热烈的欢迎后，我们被导入诗人的屋中——一块遮蔽的台地上一间质朴的房屋。莱平突兰乃斯·泰戈尔正在屋中等候我们，他高寿已届七十二岁，是一位脆弱的老人，他的脸庞已起了白色的皱纹，在我们行近时他笑着迎接，我们试行着有趣的印度额手礼，向他致辞，然后

坐下来聆听异常悦耳的声调。泰戈尔操着英语，迂缓而谨慎，我想像假使他操着本地语说话，那声调应如何温柔啊！——据云孟加拉语是世界上一种美丽的文字。我们的谈话是普通性质的，诗人告诉我们当他访法时，女诗人故诺爱里伯爵夫人穿着中国服装来欢迎他，在谈话的时候他颇具一些文雅的幽默。

那天我们离开泰戈尔后曾与教授们一同进膳，这是一次仪式上的聚宴；席上备着匙叉，以备取食咖喱时用，这颇使我们失望，因为我们极想像土人一般用手混合食物，然后取食。

教授们都颇饶风趣——年青，而快乐。不久我们就随着他们去访问大学，但是我们始终没有看到过大学所在。我们走至室外时就问："教室在那儿？"

"教室吗？"他们回答："这儿是没有教室的，我们在芒果树下聚会，在露天上课。"

第一次使我们惊愕以后，倒颇为自然了。学生们成群住在散布在乡村各处的小屋中。十八岁以上年龄较大的学生随心所欲地自行组织起来。年轻的学生——从九岁或十岁起——则在他们所选队长的管辖之下，但是队长必须循规蹈矩——他的职权是很容易转移的。黎明时，钟声响了，学生们从床上——四条板，三条板——一跃而下，高唱泰戈尔所编制的歌辞来欢迎朝日。接着他们在香蕉树下仓卒地洗水淋浴。半小时后学生们穿着洁净的白色长袍，臂下挟着用方布包着的书籍，向选定的树下走去，教授们就在那儿等候他们。他们成一半圆形踞坐着，而功课即在鸟语宛啭中开始。学生得任意插嘴，询问各种问题。在欧洲此种无礼的举动是该受责的，但是在圣地尼加敦却应嘉纳。功课完毕后学生全体回室，教授们则参加我们在途中所组织的游戏。

我询问此种不寻常的熟稔是否会损及师长的威信与职权。

"第一，"学生回答说："我们的教授不是我们的主人，他们解释每一件事，但是他们不发命令，他们是我们的兄长，他们知道每一件事，而我们的事也从不隐瞒他们，我们爱护他们，他们也爱护我们。"

圣地尼加敦的教授们都具有非常的品格，泰戈尔把他们从印度各地——实际上说世界各地亦不为过——搜集拢来，文学教授也许是近代印度最伟大的文学家，有一年圣司格列脱[1]的教授是一位世界闻名的法国人，意大利皇家学会副会长亦是泰戈尔的一位教授，那里并且还经常有英，德，中，日各国教师，课程完毕后卒业文凭亦如寻常，学生虽度着自由的生活，但是仍可以毫不费力地，修毕学程。然而在圣地尼加敦的生活最着重培养清醒，亲睦独立，慷慨，和合时代的精神——依照泰戈尔的哲学。

我们被导入回廊绘着壁画的宏大建筑，这就是图书馆——印度最佳的图书馆，全部藏书，从最古的印度方言——空前绝后地收集着各种无价的手抄本，以迄今于近代加尔各答，伦敦，与孟加拉各地的科学评论，图书馆对面另有一所白色建筑——雕刻术，跳舞术，演剧术的教室。因为演剧的艺术在这里是极负声誉的，所以青年学生每星期编着他们自己的剧本——歌剧，喜剧，或趣剧，在剧本中他们可以不怀恶意地戏谑任何人，常常有“教师”的剧本上演，但是常常并不是最成功的。

我们去访医院，看护因为工作轻松，所以都在睡觉。在圣地尼加敦是不大容易患病的。我们又看到邮政局，为不在家用餐者所设的食堂，出售练习簿，墨水，钢笔，照相用具的互助合作社，我们甚至在一丛香蕉树下找到一家咖啡馆，出售茶，牛奶，以及柠檬水。

教授们的生活一如学生，他们的家在棕榈树荫下的小屋内，环绕着芳香扑鼻的花园，这处远绝尘寰的洞天福地，结成了一块包括一千人以上的部落。

最值得我们赞赏的是艺术学院（Kala Bhavan），大量搜集着世界各国的文件与照片，游客常常出资购买这些青年艺术家的作品，得资即用以建造印度大城市中的陈列馆。与艺术学院毗连的是几间小小的工作室，学生们得开窗对着岑寂无比的乡村，孤独而缄默地在内工作。

上课的时候我们爱在圣地尼加敦附近徘徊，我们颇欣赏嚷嚷群蜂辛劳的工作景况，每处芒果树下功课都在进行着，每棵树下都有孩子在读书，男子在工作，女孩们穿着五彩缤纷的“纱丽 Saris”，她们的头发经过浴后都是湿淋淋的，注视他人上课，这与我们在欧洲教室中的惨淡景象恰成一个奇异的对比。

[1] 圣司格列脱（Sanskirt）是印度东部的古代文学。在东方文学中占一地位，至今南部人士尚传承此种文学。

傍晚在功课完毕，运动（足球，曲棍球，网球）告终，沐浴竣事，一餐俭素的晚饭用过后，学生们都作日常的散步，成群学生在夕阳的斜晖中手携着手出发至乡间路上，谈着笑着，他们常讨论的主题是文学艺术，和哲学，他们引吭高唱泰戈尔的最新一曲，重复地唱着他的最新一首诗，他们到小小的圣德尔村中去访问洁白无尘的农舍中的农人，在农舍中他们和婴儿游玩，和村人嬉戏，野蛮的阶级观念和残酷的宗教迷信这两件蹂躏全印度的恶事，在圣地尼加敦是不复存在的。

我们在暗中回到各人的屋中，在十点钟唱过赞美诗后，静默笼罩了这部落。

当我们逗留在圣地尼加敦的时候，艺术学院学生特地为我们举行了一次野餐，艺术学院学生全体步行出发，而蔬菜食品用一辆牛车载着，随在后面。途中我们访问一处属于圣地尼加敦的模范农场，那儿的学生当农人的面试验及批评他们工作的结果，他们的工作完全遵照最新式的科学排水灌溉方法，饲养动物，耕种田地亦复如是。仍旧以为泰戈尔仅是一个梦想者的人，可以在那儿看到药房，那儿疟疾问题的研究极为缜密，所以在那一区域内此种疾病竟完全绝迹，最后应提及的就是那儿有一家合作农业银行，在那一区域内遍设支行，厥功甚伟，学生们为全体农民所景仰，在我们经过时农民们均极热烈的接待我们。

星期三是圣地尼加敦的星期日，在那天到处都有一种欢乐的感觉。泰戈尔所司祭的一所庙宇是一间像温室般的大屋，由铁与玻璃造成，是一八八零年式样。那里的窗镶着各色玻璃——蓝红，绿，紫，橙；地板则黑白相间——样子是怪难看的，然而星期三早晨这地点为众学生所挤满，他们穿着杂色的长袍，还沓而入，令人忘身之所处。我们在里边找不到丝毫空隙，他们全伙都在地板上，赤脚，肘触着肘，穿着白，蓝，绿，淡红各色长袍，诗人本人乘着一辆小车赶到，把草鞋脱在门口，像一个预言家般的走了进来，拖着白发，远远地一瞥，态度从容，凛然不可侵犯，他坐在一张小凳上，引导一简短的仪式，读一段忧婆尼沙（Upansihads 为吠陀经一部之梵文论说集），然后注释经句。

泰戈尔虽年事已高，然而仍矫健异常，他日出而作——写作，绘画，作歌。他一个人管理全部大学和农场，二者他是同样爱护的，他与教授，舍监，书记，以及技师们谈话。学生们每次演剧，他都到场，批评，赞誉，及忠告。每天他总来访问他的学生，与他们谈话，或教导他们，他并且口授他的秘书作谨慎而恳挚的回信——他从世界各地收到一千封信。他教授一班年轻的唱诗班，接待无数跋涉千里为求一见的宾客，并且竭力想予每一个人良好的印象，但是种种俗务仍不能妨害及他的读书，他每日规律地阅读所有的印度文学评论杂志和英、美主要的文学评论杂志，并且加以注释，这还不够，他并且投稿十家至十二家刊物，继续写他的传记，处理他和世界名人往来的私人信札，修改他的著作的英文译稿，他每天仅在一张硬床上睡一些时候，翌日拂晓他又在伏案作书了。

一天傍晚当我们谈及诗人时，一个年轻的书记走进来，给我们看一幅奇异的地图。这地图是他设计的，为了要表示圣地尼加敦的令誉是如何无远勿届，这是一具大型的印度模型，上面插着许多金头的钉，地图四周围着各国的小国旗。

“这些国旗代表在此地工作的教授和学生们的国籍，共有二十八个，遍布全印度地图的针，则表示圣地尼加敦毕业生所居的村镇，共有一千多个。”

我们必须要告辞的时候终于要到了，在最后谒见诗人时我们请他说几句话。

“告诉欧洲，”他说，“印度正在苦痛地忧虑着暴风雨的降临四方，但是我们相信将来欧洲会联合起来，正如我们相信将来印度会联合起来一样，那时候才能融合印度的古老智慧和科学的近代欧洲的新力量，建立伟大而和平的文明！”

——《天下事（上海）》，第1卷第18期，1940年10月15日

泰戈尔印象记

Newson, R.（著） 潘君拯（译）

奇妙得很，我在印度所化的几个月中，从没有看到男子或女人的笑貌。可是，从这个人的观察就武断上帝没有把笑的本能赋予印度人民也许

是谬论的见解。然而，我曾广泛地读过泰戈尔的卷帙浩瀚的著作，但我仍必须在他著作的一部分中找出惟一的致笑的企图。

我的住所离泰戈尔的小茅屋 Shyamali 仅一箭之遥——这所小屋位在他儿子壮丽的住宅的园中，在这儿我度了许多日子，但是我从没笑过。一天我走进我的起居室，发现一只勤勉的山羊坐在我的安乐椅上，寂静地凝视着。于是，最后我放声大笑，长而响。据我所知，这是第一次可闻的愉快的声音，至少在印度——泰戈尔的故乡——这一部分地方。

莱平屈伦纳·泰戈尔（Rabindranath Tagore）并不是一个不幸的人。他并不是一个失意的文人或潦倒的天才。他的仪容较西方诗人的传统模型大相径庭，因为他的养尊处优的生活较大多数诗人均为优美。这儿没有盲目的乞儿，虽然也没有来自露凯庭君岛（Leucadian Rocks）的鲑鱼。泰戈尔业经获得非常的令誉，在他的本乡他是像一位神祇。印度边省中的农夫们在劳作时都唱着他的歌，而在他的家乡他更为善男信女们所包围——在他们的宗教中他是信仰的中心。现在他未去世以前，已成为孟加拉（Bengal）及圣地尼加敦（Santiniketan）两地的神话中的人物——在那儿他曾兴筑了奇异的隐居屋舍，成为一个神圣不可侵犯的人物。旅客们从印度各地来到此地，专诚访问诗人。一列印度小诗人聚集在他的门口，直至晚间我仍听到这些无情的泰戈尔的崇拜者用孟加拉语或印度式洋泾浜英语高声吟诵他们的诗篇，泰戈尔坐在略高于往来不绝的访问者之上的宝座似的坐椅上假寐。他的红色的长袍和尊严的须对于圣徒们是一种强烈的讽示，所有的眼光都注视着他，似乎他是一位哲人，一位国王，或是在这独立的太阳系中一位最尊贵的人。有时他的眼皮张开一会，有时这诗人用孱弱的超俗的声音嗫嚅地发出缓和平凡的谈话，但是他从不笑。在这时候他很少讲话，即使最热心的崇拜者也以为他是一个拙劣的谈论家，冷漠的小说家，以及无足轻重的政治家，在谈话时印度女诗人奈德（Sarojini Naidu）就能容易地控制他，虽然印度妇女至今仍保存着尽人皆知的怕羞心理，莱平屈伦纳对于谈话的理论正与亚林匹克诸神之王（Olympian Zeus）对诸小神的相似，声音在地下面和四周杂然并作，但是他却坐在宝座上颔首或假寐，接着，这千载难逢的机会突然到了，低垂的眼皮举起了，孱弱的声音听到了，诗人发表着缓和平凡的谈话，在圣地尼加敦是毋需波斯威尔

（Boswell）（注一）的。

泰戈尔在本乡的声誉原寄托在他的诗和奇异的魔力上，这魔力是诺贝尔奖金带给他的。宗教狂的国家主义需要一个国家的中心人物。他们已经找到这个教皇授予的贵族，富而有田地的哲人，智慧的诗人，和本地许多乐曲的著作人。哲士，圣人，作曲家，国家领袖——就是他一个人，但是尤其重要的，对于孟加拉人民而言，他是诗人，我们一定应该记得：在印度——人民在街道上吟诵伟大的咏史诗（Epics）来接待宾客的地方——诗人仍是为人民所歌颂的。

除了印度文学界中最前进的理论家外，泰戈尔诗人的地位是毫无问题的为一般人民所乐于承认的。在事实上，若是你想欣赏他那众多的诗篇，你必须懂得孟加拉语。但是即使在译文中，仍保存着萦人心怀的美丽的思想。

“我以为我将享受死的滋味，因为生的滋味我已享受得够了，”他歌唱着。又说：“假使我去世以后，让这算是我的诀语罢：我所看到的一切都是不可超越的。”又说：“世界是更富于爱情了——这爱情是曾经失去的。”

除了声誉卓著的西方诗圣最伟大的诗篇外，我以为这几行是最能令人感动的了，即使翻译——这不适当的媒介已夺去了它们真正的特色和音乐。但是泰戈尔的诗骨中包含着一种奇异的自贬的味儿——是东方的特色。当我们听到这些虔敬的诗篇的一卷卷译本时，泰戈尔在西方的声誉显著地低落了。在他的许多著述中，我以为 Gitanjali 的几段和悄静美丽的 Post Office 全部或能继续保持它们的名誉。但是叶芝（W・B・Yeats）（注二）将诗人介绍给西方读者时所加的热情的赞美却证实不虚。

据说泰戈尔本人认为圣地尼加敦是他的主要的，最永久的诗。在半野蛮的圣泰立（Santali）人中他已建立了这学校，教授青年本地和西方学术。乐谱用 Arcadian，课业在大而多枝的芒果树下教授。体罚绝对禁止。每级都是男女同学，虽然两性自然地会分成很清楚的两队。印度青年并不勤勉。当诗人从宝座上向坐在他足下席上的孩子或成人们发言时，他们并不注意。但是我们不得不承认圣地尼加敦的学生们因不注意学业而遭受损失极少，因为学者们对于他们所授的科目难免有不正确的观念。

多么美丽啊！印度青年们穿着传统的古典服装载歌载舞，男孩女孩们头上都戴着花，在树间出没。当然在某一时期泰戈尔的学生们将走出学校，进入世界，而即使在印度，他们所受的缓慢的乌托邦教育与日后生活的重担亦将格格不入。我记得一个泰戈尔制的产儿曾真正经营着初步的商业。他开设了一家小店，一切货物均可以二倍市价购得。他常以极大的耐性坐在我的床旁，那时我正患着危险的回归热。一天，我赞美他的热心，他解释他一眼正看着我的牙膏管。后来，当我挤出了最后半寸牙膏时，他极愿意为我做一些事，他并且告诉我他的名字是苏杰（Suji），意义为“太阳之神”，“看天堂的面，请出去罢！”我说，于是他穿上鞋子，离开了我的卧室。这时，我躺倒在床上，想到了泰戈尔。

几步以外，这伟大的孟加拉诗人或许又循例坐着冥想茅屋的廊道，或想象昨夜梦中的景色和生物。像一个学术家一般，他自有宏伟壮丽的地方。然而这天赋在他生命的后期方始到临，在那时候他的乐曲和诗久已驰誉全印。他的诗在体裁和内容方面是救世的，他的乐曲散发着起伏不平的孟加拉地方小丘上的牧羊人的气息，或许还具有本地牧人的简单的旋律，因为他的全部知识，都是从拜黑（Bach）（注三）和悲冬汶（Beethoven）处获得的。他的容貌和仪表酷似慈变的部落神——本地的云师或造物主。甚至有人隐约地把他和耶稣基督相提并论。但是在他所有的图画中都有着狂暴的，像晚间的沼泽般的乖僻，这点使学术界中最野蛮的巴黎安那其主义者也会感觉他可爱。

因此，在我讲话的时候，我躺在圣地尼加敦医院中的床上，想到这伟大的创造者。我想到他的颇孩子气的自负，极易由谄媚而满足的骄傲，对于放弃自己的生活，在圣地尼加敦为理想服务的教授们苛刻地待遇一头蜥蜴，将它钉在墙上，对面墙上挂着一幅栩栩如生的泰戈尔的肖像。邻床一个小孩开始在唱一曲孟加拉歌，曲谱均系泰戈尔所作。在请求他停止歌唱时，我的声音较平常所用的任何英语或孟加拉语更为亲切动人。我的祈求发生了效果。在一段时间中静默统治了整个病房，于是我闭拢了眼，向着这位可敬的穿着红袍的哲士和诗人的肖像。

他们是奇异的圣地尼加敦的人氏——这些泰戈尔的信徒！他们赞美诗人和他的事迹。他们赞美他的歌曲中的音乐，和他的表演的才能。（在他手编的戏剧中，尤其在扮演上帝一角的时候。）甚至他偶然踏进舞蹈界，也未曾遭到任何非议。他的教育制度中显而易见的缺点亦受到人们的大度宽容，然而学术家泰戈尔本人在那几点上并不欠缺。在本乡，艺术家泰戈尔是一位并无声誉的哲士。他的书是模糊的被称为“火山爆发”。而这位诗人，这位哲学家，仍机敏地躲避着谈话。

从这样的观点上我的同情心油然而生。在我以为这位隐然的东方华资华斯（Wordsworth）（注四），但尼生（Tennyson）（注五），或惠脱门（Whitman）（注六）并不在宣述印度人民或印度风景自卑的禅味是过去传统观念的反响。这些图画，虽然是生涩而粗莽，却能表示心灵的真诚——至少它们能泄露几件隐藏在面具和传奇后面的事。（译自伦敦水星杂志一九三八年十二月号）

注一：波斯威尔（James Boswell）苏格兰传记家（1740—1795）。

注二：叶芝（William Butler Yeats）爱尔兰著作家及诗人（1865—　）[1]。

注三：拜黑（Johann Sebastian Bach）德作曲家及音乐家（1685—1750）。

注四：华资华斯 (William Words worth)。英格兰诗人（1770—1850）。

注五：但尼生（Alfred Tennyson, 1st. Baron）英格兰诗人（1809—1914）。

注六：惠脱门（Walt (Orig. Walter) Whitman）美诗人（1819—1892）。

——《西洋文学》，第 9 期，1941 年 5 月

印度诗哲：泰戈尔

强　生

一九四一年八月七日在印度的加尔各答地方陨落了一颗巨星，一个为实现他梦想的哲学家与政治家。他是谁，他就是给中国最熟悉的印度诗哲——泰戈尔。氏享年八十，生前会获诺贝尔一九一三年度文学奖金，其名著有《园丁集》及《新月集》等。

[1] 原文空缺，此处年份应为 1939——编者注。

氏于七五寿辰时，世界各地贺电纷至，尊泰氏为大诗人，大小说家，社会改革家，及宗教大师等。今年五月，英国牛津大学打破先例于氏所住之乡举行授赠氏以文学博士荣誉学位。

对于这位巨人，我们很想给以详尽的描述，介绍。然而在中国关于他的材料及其著作是如此之少，因此，从另碎报章上，东拼西凑，缀成文章，总算我们对这伟人的一些纪念。

泰戈尔的生平思想

泰氏生于加尔各答，出身名族，他的父亲是有名的宗教家，家境颇富，从小便有优良教育。稍长，随父亲到喜马拉雅山旅居十年，时与自然接触，受自然的陶冶。十七岁，游学伦敦，毕业后归国，在恒河流域开辟农场，创立国际大学。

他生平到过中国，日本，欧洲，美洲与苏联，其足迹所到之处，颇受一般之欢迎。

他的日常生活习惯：食物以牛乳，糖果，蔬菜为主，但不戒肉食。四时早起，祷告世界祈求和平。日出，至户外散步，寒暑不辍。日中工作非看书作诗即作诗绘画。晚间，召集男女学生，歌唱其所作诗曲，声音溢于四外。新作完成，辄作讲演声调嘹亮，如黄钟大吕。

泰氏的思想颇为优异卓绝，分析起来，可以分为三方面的来源：他在贵族生长父兄等都为哲学家和艺术家，当他侨居高山时天天与大自然接触，融化在大自然中，造成他对于自然的爱好，表现在诗语间便是清丽，飘逸。其次，他早年留学欧西，接触了西洋物质文明，民主思想，归国后，正是宗教改革运动，新文学运动和国民自主运动抬头的时候，他处于这样狂风暴雨的时代，虽然因他本身的诗人气质使然，但是或多或少给予运动推动的却也不小呢!

泰氏的文学功绩

人们都知道泰戈尔是一个文学家，尤其是在诗上的成就，其伟大，给人以巨大影响，在文学史上所造就的功绩，是值得歌颂的。所以泰氏的诗会如此给人以魔力，因为他的诗可以说没有一篇不含有清美，平和，自然，朴真的素质，和优雅的词调，因而人人欢喜，歌诵。有一个印度人说过："我每天读泰戈尔的诗，读他一行，可以把世上一切的烦恼忘掉。"

中国五四时的文坛健将冰心女士，也受了泰氏的极大影响。他的诗集自序为说到："这是我读了泰戈尔的诗以后作的。老实说，我看泰戈尔的诗更十倍于我看自己的作品。我觉得他的诗是用异常的，内在的，沉毅的情绪，用音乐似的词句写出来，给我们的感动太深了……。"而对于中国来说，泰氏的作品在五四时代确给予中国文坛一个巨大的影响。泰氏的诗是在中国的诗从旧五律七绝到山诗风格上一个有力的刺激。当时王独清郑振铎翻译了《新月集》《飞鸟集》到中国来，当一九二二年三月泰氏到中国来，受到了我国文艺界热烈的欢迎。

泰氏的事业

当一九二一年七月泰氏从英国回来时，他规定了三种伟大计划。他以后的一生就是根据了他所规定的目标努力的：一、在国际大学提倡东方文明；二、在国际大学附近实验农村改进工作；三、在国际大学提倡人类大同调和东西文化。

所谓国际大学就是泰氏一生努力的事业结晶品。因为国家主义的流行，泰氏从日美回国后深觉印度古代的文化有提倡的必要。所以他与一九一八年年底，在和平乡召集了他旧时的学生，及朋友的会中，泰氏发表他的主张，改组原来的学校，使成为提倡东方古代文明的中心，至将成为 Visva-Bharati 集合世界学术于一堂的意思（即国际大学学义）。

在国际大学中，是特别注重在学校造就一种国际空气，常常请东西各国闻人来校演讲，因为这样就可以使学生狭窄的胸襟渐渐可以扩大。在国际大学中尽量让学生有自由发展的机会，竭力引起他们对于自然，音乐，艺术及乡村的兴趣。在大学里的人数增加时，不得不有相当改变，如收费的办法等。因为旧时印度的理想，教师不但免费供给教育，而且系担负学生一切生活上的需要。等到人数增加，这种办法自然无法继续。在教学上保守着师生必须共同生活的一点，而且各种活动上，师生必须合作。在国际大学的附近还设立了许多夜班，使学生们担任夜校教书的工作。同时他们可以在他所举办的农村事业中，获得许多练习的机会。这样教育与生活就可以打成一片了。

关于他的提倡东方文明及调和东西文化和他在中国时对清华大学学生谈讲可以作证：

“我们生长在这个大时代，应当庆贺自己。你们中国青年应首先认识自己的文化，有人说，中国文化唯实的，唯物的，我并不相信这句话。你们固有的社会组织处处表现出不自私的精神。你们的民族并不崇拜金钱，也不崇拜武力。我不相信你们的文化是唯物的。我游历中国各地，看见土地培养的很肥美，一切日用的器具都表现艺术的美；这些都表现精神文化。我以为你们能当物质却不为物质所累，这是你们伟大的地方。从你们固有的文明，并不难看出物质文明与精神文明的区别。现在东西两洋的文化主流，快要合流了，你们应当赶紧做你们的贡献。”

为了他的负起国人文化的使命，对于苏联的新实验，自然也要去看看。在他到苏联的第一次招待会上就说明：

“将我的目的，是来贵国学习你们怎样处置世界文化问题的经验。近代的文化使人类违反自然增加了人类无穷的痛苦。现在你们对于人类文化问题，做大规模的解决，其成功与失败，将来历史自有定论。我不愿在此作无理的批评。不过你们的魄心，是值得佩服的。我的教育理想是在创造自由的人格，发展人类的创造力，我相信你们的理想与我无异。”

对泰氏的论定

他出生在名门有很好的教养，能留学于英国，同时，在当时国内又是三大运动在此起彼伏中，泰氏从伦敦归来，已授有极大名望与学识。他也在对于新文学运动在起作用。他固然反对一切侵略战争，主张调和东西文化，主张国际和平，对于国民运动表示深切的同情，佩服甘地的人格及领导民众的才能，并且赞赏尼赫鲁认为是“后起之秀”。然而泰氏是一个诗人，正因为他是一个诗人，所以正如他自己说过一样，他已经老了，而且到底是个诗人，所以对于这个伟大的民族解放运动不能多做贡献，这是使他觉得抱歉的地方。

——《益友》，第4卷第10期，1941年9月1日

和平诗人泰戈尔

子　长

八十岁的白发诗人泰戈尔于本月七日离开了这战云密布的世界去了，泰戈尔一生崇拜自然的美，提倡人类相爱，他整个思想以和平为出发，极力反对战争。

泰戈尔的幼年在一个极有家学渊源的环境中，父亲德贲德那拉次Devendranath Tagore系印度大哲，住在加尔各答，是当时该地大隐士之一，但泰戈尔讨厌学校的刻板而和大自然隔绝的生活，所以在十三岁那年，从学校中逃出来，此后永远不再进学校了。

泰戈尔自己说："从学校逃出之后，我开始自己研究，隐居在靠近恒河的一个地方，多半时间住在一只小船上，在那儿写诗写小说，写剧本，做着甜蜜的梦。"

那时候的作品多半系描写恋爱的抒情诗，和描写大自然的田园诗，他的恋歌大胆而率真，有深刻的情绪，有乐曲般美丽的外形，极为人所爱读，差不多没有人不沉醉于他的诗，而受他的感动的。

他的田园诗则表现了他对大自然的崇拜，不过印度是热带地方，树木高大畅茂，到处是树林，所以他更为酷爱森林，他会说："森林是活的，它养育着人类的生命，"又说："森林是伟大的，但它未使人感觉渺小，它的环境，刺激了人类固有的创造性，扩大了人类的同情性。"他的森林哲学就是他崇拜自然的产物。

泰戈尔不但系一代哲人，而且又是一个教育家，这是很奇怪的，为什么他从学校逃出来，自己又提倡教育呢？原来它的教育并不像我们学校的教育，更不是上海的弄堂鸽笼教育。他的学校建筑在广大的田野之上，环境是幽静而美丽，他的教育是师生间的共同生活，学校教育与社会教育打成一片，不是叫学生刻板地背教科书，而是叫他们有自由发展及发表的机会，叫起他们对自然，音乐，艺术，乡村，发起兴趣。他的学生爬在树上预备功课，在森林里听讲，在田野中遨游，每日旦夕，均在树下祈祷，唱诗。

这一所学校就是和平乡，现在改为国际大学。泰戈尔教育的理想是创造自由的人格，发展人类的创造力，怎样才可以达到这个理想呢？则非有一个和平的环境不成。

如此，泰戈尔的学生不是和社会脱离了关系了么？不是的，泰戈尔自己做过隐者而做不成功，他怎么可以叫他的学生们走上这没有出路的出路呢？泰戈尔在国际大学附近，举办许多农村事业，又设立了夜班，学生们就负起教育乡人的责任，又在各种农村事业中训练自己的学生。

因此泰戈尔不但是一个诗人，哲学家，教育家，而且又是一个农村改革者。此外，泰戈尔对于印度人之迷信宗教，也是坚决反对的。

泰戈尔的宗教思想也是自由的，纯高的，他反对各种宗教的繁文缛节，他本人的家庭实行过印度教的改革，我想他自己也许不会在恒河中沐浴以求神佑吧？那本是印度人所视为神圣的。泰戈尔的宗教是崇拜大自然的反映，完全从大自然所给予他的美感中得来，他在大自然美之背后发现了大灵之存在。

泰戈尔足迹遍全球，他到过中国，日本，美国，英国，苏俄以及欧洲大陆。一九一三年得诺贝尔文学奖金，今年一九四一年，英国牛津大学在泰戈尔所住的和平乡赠他文学博士荣誉学位。

泰戈尔年高体健，每日均祈祷和平，他会说过：“在天空中，在无限的空间里，和平之神坐着，似乎是在默想。众星环绕和平之神，似乎要静听神之教训……”

是的，和平之神正在默想，默想世界为什么这样乌烟瘴气，众星环绕和平之神，我们更应该模范他们静听教训——

和平诗人已经离我们去了，但和平的种子已经撒满人间，和平的花朵在不久的将来将灿烂地盛开了。

——《市声》，第2卷第3期，1941年9月1日

泰戈尔：一个维护人道主义的老人[1]

张若谷

最近病殁加尔加答之印度诗哲泰戈尔，生前二度来华，观光我国文物，此孟加拉之老诗人，歌颂东方精神文明甚力，且为一热诚之人道主义维护者。彼对于中国遭非人道之惨劫，深表同情。民国二十八年，至函一日本诗人，颇不直日本文人之为军阀作辩护者。原函略称："余对日本民族抱无限痛心，余相信日本民族终必从幻梦中觉醒过来。中国不能被征服，人民忠心爱国团结统一。中国虽为一毫无准备之国家，但作战至今精神始终不屈。日本今日藉重西方军事科学，但与中国比，中国民族道德人格均超出日本以上。前日本思想家冈仓曾告世界人士曰：中国民族伟大，此语日本人当信之。"

中国为卫护世界人道主义而奋斗，故能激发世界正道人士之热烈援助，泰戈尔亦为维护人道主义之一员，且为世界智识阶级之领袖，彼感中国自古多忠烈志士，杀身成仁，舍生取义者比比皆是，此种民族人格不朽之精神，直可视为获取真实人道主义永久胜利之征兆，故剀切为日本拥护人道之同志言之，而尽友谊之忠告也。

——《永安月刊》，第 29 期，1941 年 9 月 1 日

泰戈尔的生平与成就

黄道明

在世界文学家列传中，泰戈尔要占着顶重要的地位，这话大概不算誉之过实罢。记得郑振铎教授作《文学大纲》，特别提过印度诗圣泰戈尔。与甘地，托尔斯泰这些伟大的文学革命家同提并论。当年清华大学吴宓教授主编前大公报文学副刊的时候，也曾为文介绍过这位名震瀛寰的世界诗

[1] 原文名为《马相伯·泰戈尔·萧伯纳——三个维护人道主义的老人》。

人。因之，泰戈尔，这个名字便普遍的深刻的印入我们的脑海里。

泰戈尔于一八六一年生于印度恒河下游唯一都市加尔各答城贵族的家庭，于本年（一九四一）八月七日逝世。享年八十岁。这老头子曾于一九二六年（民国十五年）遍游中国各个都会，并来北京，接受各大学的邀请，作公开的文学哲学演讲，倍受我国学术界的欢迎，亦被加以攻击。这在我们的回忆中，还模糊的残留着泰氏的伟大仪表。因为他是一个“唯心论”者，提倡“东方的精神文明”是“人道主义”的说教者，主张陶醉于自然的怀抱中。又因为他坚决的强调东方精神文明的价值，崇拜精神文明，与中国的老庄自然哲学，不谋而合。故对功利主义，侵略主义的英国，仇视极深。在印度与甘地同属“不合作主义”的领导者，而不讨英国的喜欢，时时受着英国当局的监视与放逐压迫。

他的爱好自然的个性像陶渊明似的来自幼时的生活环境。景慕自然，憧憬自然的乐趣，使他不能受学校教育规律生活的束缚，而常常到自然原野森林中去寻找真理。十一岁时与其父同登喜马拉雅山，给予他后来作诗一极大启示与动力。由于他天生爱好自然，崇拜精神文明，形成他的歌咏自然，推崇东方本位文化，反对物质主义的伟大哲学见地。在印度，他开有“国际大学”，即一本斯义而创立设教者。他十三岁时，即学作诗，十九岁发表处女作小说。去英国留学，努力专攻英诗的韵律。他的一生学问也就此奠定了博大深厚的根基。

一九一二年，泰氏年五十一岁，游英美，曾受英美学术界人士热烈的欢迎。翌年，获得世界驰名的“诺贝尔”文学奖金，一九一四年，英皇赠以荣誉的“爵位”，于是，泰戈尔之名，遂震动了世界哲学，文学界，而被全世界知识阶级所景仰。虽然，他是个被征服民族，落后民族的诗人，叫那些鄙视印度民族有成见的优越感的英国学术界，不能不打破自尊心，而维护泰氏的身份地位。这实在是难能可贵，替印度民族争光不少的地方。

正如我们知道的一样，泰氏生平喜爱文学，努力使诗歌决定其伟大的文学成就。他著述计（一）论文：生之实现，人格，国家主义。（二）诗：园丁集，新月集，採果集，飞鸟集，爱者之赠与，歧道。（三）剧本：春之循环，邮局，暗室之王，牺牲。（四）杂著：我的回忆，家庭与世界等。这些作品，在现在世界文学的遗产中，由于泰氏的物化，已变为非常珍贵的历史资料。我们纪念泰氏的逝世，同追悼许地山教授一样，心理上泛起莫名的悲痛，为世界文坛折一巨星而惋惜。泰氏今后安静的长眠于地下，但其贡献与精神，将与天地争光日月并明永垂不朽，这是我们敢以断言的。

——《中国文艺（北京）》，第 5 卷第 1 期，1941 年 9 月 5 日

反英的太戈尔

士　奇

太戈尔未死之前一月余，以英国官方竟发表声明，非难印度人对于战争之取消极态度，于六月十四日愤然而起，力斥英国之非，其反驳语略云：

“英国榨取印度人已因此濒于饥饿，印度因以食粮品供给英国，故印民中今已无盈握之粟，而英国本身方以印度流血惨事为忻幸，英国人之招印民之嫌弃，实英国本身之失败。盖英国人，反乎印人之信赖，牺牲多数印民幸福，图饱自己之私囊也。英国人对此等事实，应知所愧也。”至于太戈尔的反英态度，则他认为印度该要自治，倘然英人因此而施以压制手段，则万不屈服于大势之下：他并且说：“他们越是束紧他们的索子，我们越是要咬断这索子，他们的眼睛越红，我们的眼越要张开，现在是你们去工作的时候了，不要再做甜蜜的梦了，他们越是叫喊，我们的睡梦也可以更快更快的治好”；——他是希望英国再不要有那做世界的主人翁的迷梦，一国与一国的文化，风俗，人情皆不同，欲强力统治是一件不可能的事。

太戈尔的最大决心是把印度人的礼物奉献出来（他认为这也就是印度人对于世界的使命），这礼物是什么呢？是“精神爱，美和自由。”

——《政治月刊（上海）》，第 2 卷第 3 期，1941 年 9 月 10 日

谈泰戈尔的《黄昏之歌》

柳 川

泰戈尔是最喜欢冥想的诗人，他有许多没有原因的感情和没有目的的渴望，他写道：

有一片广阔的荒野，他的名字是“心灵”；它的交错的枝柯摇摆着黑暗。像一个婴儿，我在它的深邃处迷路了。[1]

这表示他对于自己的心灵活动爱慕并沉溺到何等程度，而他的《黄昏之歌》最足以代表这种倾向。

一八八四年以前他的兄嫂离家远旅的时候，他们三楼的房间和阳台都留给他，他便过起孤独的日子来，而他写诗的态度忽然改变了。从前他写诗是要取悦某一些人的，常以那些人的诗的趣味为标准。现在他可以完全自由了。他用一块石板写诗。从前，他用稿本的时候，总不免有一种与别的诗人竞美之意，而一块石板是固然适合于一时的心情的。它似乎对他说道，“不要怕，你想写什么就写什么吧，擦一下就全掉了。”于是，他非常高兴地写起来。他的心灵说道，“好容易我所写的都是我自己的了！”这并不是他的骄傲，父母对于第一个孩子的高兴不在于孩子的相貌如何，乃在于它完全是他们自己的。如此，泰戈尔达到了快乐的高潮，以致对诗的音节也不太固执了，他的自由诗似乎打破了规律，同时却也造成了独有的规律。他把那些诗念给他的友人巴布听，得到了无限惊奇和赞赏。他自信力渐渐增长起来，觉得从前完全是在别的地方白白寻觅自己内心所有的东西，觉得如同从束缚的梦中醒来一样。这是泰戈尔的诗人生涯中最可纪念的时期。他自认《黄昏之歌》里的诗都是粗制滥作的，无论在音节文字和思想方面，惟一的好处便是纯真，即使诗篇没什么价值，写作时的乐趣还是值得珍贵的。

《黄昏之歌》这一部散文诗集在形式上虽不十分整齐，想像的丰富和魔力却无人可及。诗集出版不久，泰戈尔有一天去参加朋友的婚礼，有些

[1] 见《晨歌》。

人正在给号称“孟加拉的斯科特”的一位诗人加花环，那位诗人却接过花环来套在泰戈尔的颈上，对主人说道，“你没念过他的《挽歌》吗，那第一篇诗[1]就比英国诗人科林斯的《黄昏颂》还好。”——

黄昏之灵啊！

独坐在无涯的天空下！把世界拘在你的膝头散开你蓬松的头发，俯视着它，你的脸充满了爱，充满了娇美！极其轻柔，极其轻柔，啊！你低语的是什么呢？你对自己吟哦的是什么歌子呢，当你睇视着世界的脸的时候？

一天又一天我听过那些字句，而今天我不了解。一天又一天，我听过那些歌吟，而我未曾学会。只有沉睡压倒了我的眼帘，思想的负担压迫着我的灵魂。然而……在我的心之浓处……更浓些，更更浓些，在它的核心……有一个语声和你的语声相应答。

一个从我不知道的乡土来的为世人遗弃的流亡者在和你同声歌唱。黄昏之灵啊，似乎是你自己的乡土的一个邻人，一个居民，几乎是一个弟兄。在我的灵魂的异邦失了路，他徘徊着哭泣着。听见你的语声，似乎他听见故国的歌，而忽然他从远方应答了，他张开了他的心。他向四周窥探；像是寻觅你。他徘徊，不安而且急切！好像是他曾经住在彼方的星辰之间，曾在那儿哭和笑。在孤寂的深夜，在那些星辰之间，他也许坐过，唱过歌；然后他睁开眼睛，看见周围的世界。这些我想他都记得，泪便从他的眼中流下来。啊，何等的希望，何等的朋友，或竟有何等的爱情，他都遗落在那儿！他的心极愿意回去找这些，却徒然地寻路。多少往昔言谈的记忆，多少失去的歌吟，多少他的灵魂的叹息——赧颜的半露的爱微笑，温柔的爱抚，爱情的低语——啊，黄昏！都失落在你这黑暗里！它们飘动的一群充满了你的黑暗，它们在“永久”的平静的心中徘徊像一个破碎的世界碎片。我坐在你的脚下，在这河岸上，它们便在我周围聚集，环绕了我。也许有一个字，一段半说出来的言辞走进我的耳朵，不断地，从世界的四角。也许有一个微笑，或一个半露的微笑，飘浮在我眼前，时而

[1] 指《呼召》。

显现，时而隐灭。一个灵魂，一个面孔的幽灵，睇视着我的面孔，然后默默地走去。啊，黄昏，有爱心的母亲！一天又一天，我来到你的梦幻的膝前！你用你那有爱意的裙裾裹起来我的灵魂，你引回来过去的记忆！

今天，黄昏啊，我来了。我开了眼坐在你的黑暗中。我要唱；轻悄地，柔和地，要让你听一两个歌。如果没有人听见这些歌，如果这些歌失落了，黄昏啊，你千万谨慎地把它们藏在你的暗影中，在一个荒凉的隐秘的所在：在一切古老的歌，一切失落的笑，一切被遗忘的梦所在的地方，给它们建立一座坟墓。我深知你的爱心，黄昏啊，我深知你的爱心；我知道你会秘密地把它们的尸骸葬入土中，你会在墓上守护它们，免得有人以残忍的嘲弄揶揄笑它们。那儿只有温柔的露珠会降下，轻悄的风会叹息。静默会坐在那儿用手支着它的腮；那儿也时时有一颗颗星辰坠地。

写《黄昏之歌》后部时泰戈尔住在恒河畔的一所别墅，过着欢乐得发懒思慕得发愁的日子，和流过了树林荫蔽的两岸间的哀吟的水声相应和。那孟加拉的天空，那南风，那从东到西，从草原到碧空的广阔的闲静，对于他都像是饮食对于饥渴的人一样。他那些河畔的可爱的日子像荷花片片地从水上飘流不去，有时候阴雨，他便独自狂歌，天气好时他和他的兄嫂划一只小船，他的哥哥用提琴为他伴奏。回来后他们坐在临河的阳台上，寂静笼罩了河水和陆地，船只几乎完全没有了，树末的边际沉入暗影之中，月光便在平静的水上闪耀起来。那所别墅的最高的屋子在一座圆塔上，周围都有窗子。泰戈尔用它做了写诗的所在。从那地方只看见的四面的树顶和天空。他曾有两行诗写道：

在那儿，云雾安卧在无限空间的怀里，
我为你造起来我的屋宇，啊，诗神！

不过后部的诗作似乎反不如前部佳胜。在梦幻的美这方面全集是一致的，而早期的充满了狂热和精致，次期的各有些单调之感，因为泰戈尔很喜欢用排比的写法。

怜悯是世上的风，
怜悯是日月星辰，
怜悯是世上的露，
怜悯是世上的雨水。
像一个母亲的爱之河流，
正如这恒河的流动着，
轻轻地对它两岸的湾流和角落，
低语着叹息着一样——
这纯真的怜悯，
倾泻在心头；
减轻世上的饥渴，
他用怜悯的声音唱歌。
怜悯是树林的阴影，
怜悯是黎明的光阴，
怜悯是母亲的眼睛，
怜悯是爱人的心思。

《黄昏》一首恐怕是后部最好的了，在这一首诗中他造出一种空气来，他想像到一个母亲和一个孩子，于是这有魔力的催眠歌成功了，读起来恍惚觉得这些诗句向人招手。最美的是末一节：

来，黄昏，轻悄地，轻悄地，来！
你的臂上挽着梦的篮子！
低诵你的迷人的言语，
织成你的梦的花环！
把它们戴在我的头上吧！
用你的多爱的手抚慰我吧！
河水睡得沉沉的，将喃喃地唱
一支睡中织成的半歌；
群蝉将弹奏出单调之曲。

在《心的哀歌》中他觉得不该再为那朦胧的悲哀吟咏了，他责备起自己来，诗中的“鸽子”便是朦胧与悲哀的化身：

在我心的倾圮的基石上，在静静的日午，
一双鸽子独自坐着，唱它的唯一的歌曲，——
没有人知道它为什么歌唱，
听了它的悲叹，寂静带着低泣扩张了，
回声也哭起来。
心啊！你什么也没有学会，
除了这唯一的歌，
在世上千万的乐曲中。
只呻吟着这一个！

没有人倾听你的歌！
他们不听算得什么？
或者听见了也没人哭，
他们不哭算得什么？
休止吧，休止吧，灵魂！这么长久
我再也听不下去了——这支不变的歌！

这显然的表示了诗人从非真实的幻想的世界中走出来了。他开始批判自己，觉得自己如同迷失在黑暗的森林里，需要天光和空气。终于他把“内在的自己”投入外面的世界，而他的心思健康起来自由起来，而“黄昏之歌”便结束了。他在他的回忆录里写道：

有一天早晨我偶然站在阳台上。太阳正从多叶树顶中间升起来、我继续注视的时候，忽然一个屏障似乎从我的眼前落下去了，而我看见世界尽在神奇的光辉中，到处涌着美和快乐的波流。这光辉即刻贯穿了累积在我的心上的层层的悲哀和失望，让它充满了宇宙之光。

——《中国文艺（北京）》，第5卷第1期，1941年9月5日

印度·世界诗人：泰戈尔研究

金　丽

泰戈尔深慕中国文化底优越，他在民国十一年，曾一度来游我国，之后，他更尽瘁于沟通大亚洲文化，他渴望我国当局建立一个中印学院，以为沟通中印两大民族文化的核心。

他对中国抗战，表示最大的同情，曾写诗痛责日本是毁灭亚洲文化的罪人！——编者

是诗人，是爱国诗人，是哲学家，是领导印度民族抗争，一直做着实际工作以至于死的革命伟人——被称为“世界诗人”的泰戈尔，在去年（一九四一年）八月十日与他苦难的祖国作着长辞了！呵！东方的这群疯狗，在他死后的第六个月，他也许是料到的吧，已叩他那祖国沃野千里的外门了。

侵略者是绝不会舍弃这一块肥肉的土地的。

我们将看到印度人民，今后接受新的历史课题，英勇地在国防前哨上，温习着泰戈尔悲壮的诗句了。

罗曼罗兰说过：——无论人们用怎样的荣誉来纪念你，但最美丽的最神圣的坟墓却在我们心台！

诗人呵！你的坟墓建筑在千万人的心里。

泰戈尔传略

泰戈尔是在一八六一年诞生于印度的加尔各答，他的父亲是一个有名的宗教家，家庭环境不能算差，但他不幸的，在幼时就丧失他的慈祥的母亲了。

幼小的泰戈尔，跟他的父亲是住在喜马拉耶山山麓的一个村落中，于是，十多年的童年生活，陶冶了他酷爱大自然的性格。

一八七七年，当他在十六岁的时候，创作了一首长诗加惠加尼，这首长诗可以说是泰戈尔的处女作。十七岁他第一次到了英国，并且得以泛游欧美各国，他早期的文学与思想的修养，便开始有了丰美的收获。

一九一二年，泰戈尔是五十二岁了，他携他的心爱的诗集园丁，再游欧美，这次他大受世界各文化团体的欢迎，并在各个著名大学里演讲，他的声望得所益隆，翌年，他写成了一部哲学巨著——《生之实现》，曾获得诺贝尔奖金。

他的成功的诗集，除园丁以外，尚有恺当乔利，新月，邮政局，卡俾之歌，拾果，迷途之鸟，以及还有一个剧本暗室之王等。

泰戈尔与祖国民族运动

一个诗人，绝不甘服自己的祖国，在外来的暴力统治下，他却可以回避现实作闲世翁的！泰戈尔自不能例外。虽然泰戈尔平常所主张的为国际主义，为与自然偕一；在他所著的民族主义一书里，也屡有微词，实则正言若反，我们看他的诗歌对颂扬印度往哲底智慧，鼓励他底国人奋斗以求精神上的自由，是一个显明的铁证。

泰戈尔主张世界各国应共同合作，以同登于觉悟之路为鹄的，是以他说："持有正义博爱的眼光的人，一定知道全人类应该休戚攸关的，今诸君所持以凌人的行为，他日必将还治在诸君的身上"！然而泰戈尔对于英人暴力的统治，也何尝有过一丝的忽视，所以他接着说："……我们虽身处于被统治的地位，但一息尚存，这颗心是不会死的！"又说："我之所以讲这话，不仅单指着印度问题，激于我亲爱的同胞被虐待底哀情，实在，人类的前途，是有莫大的关系的呵！所以无论印度是否为不列颠政府；只要是他组成的国家，其目的是为了榨取自利的，都在我们所应该痛恶之列！"由此，我们更可以概见泰戈尔那种悲愤的情绪了。

近代印度的各派民族运动，泰戈尔是不大满意的，他也说："印度国民会议所采行的政策为半推半就的政策，而其方法为摇尾乞怜的方法。"对主张独立行动的极端派，泰戈尔更诋他们"避重就轻，给印度前途是不负责任，……他们的建筑理想于西方历史上，仿行西化是多么削足适履啊！"

依照泰戈尔的意见，他说："我深信以为我们同胞如果不要恢复印度就可不管，如果要恢复印度的，那么必需从改良教育着手。"又说："今日我们所应该焦思而力行的，首先在改除社会的恶习问题，那种因循苟安的心理，因袭着的印度传统观念：所谓盛行门族的制度，举凡一切的大事小事，没有不秉承（权贵）的，于是养成盲从怠惰的习惯，没有一点点独立自治的精神，所以此风一天不改革，任那有五花八门美丽的理想，都是不着边际的。”

他对于经济方面，痛诋近代的工业，对印度固有的工业为英人无情的摧毁，表示深深的悼惜——他就是主张，一面从事减削每个人的物质的欲望，不为因陀罗天——财富——所引诱，一面恢复旧有的工业，以顾全农民生活。他所手办的“平和学院”，重要训条，就是：“生活简单”四个字，他说：“也许有人以为我们的学校生活过于简单，这正是我常说的实的理想化，……从教育的眼光来说，我们更能不承认（实）为我们必经的一个学校吗？”

泰戈尔的诗生活

泰戈尔，他学习写作的心，而是热切的，夜里，他甚至不睡觉，也可以一个人坐在房里，在微光下念书，写诗，或者让自己孤独的影子在树荫下月光中移动着。很多的诗篇，常常在这个时候结下了因缘。

他青春时期所写下的恋歌，是抒情的，那泼辣的情调，会引起来印度道德家的反对和攻击了，不过对这伟大的诗人，这如日月之中天，光明绝不会为微风所吹得熄的。印度固有的诗的格律是给他破坏了，但他却创作了许多新的优美的韵律与新的活泼的形式出来。

春光明媚的日子里，他常常陪着他的侄儿们，深深给天真的儿童去领会了祖国的国土的鲜丽与可爱，他伴着他们生活在山水之间，而泰戈尔看到侄儿们正在自由地玩得高兴了，他呢，就坐在海滨岸石上，或是森林的深处写着他的优美的诗句。他有时也和同嗜好的友人歌唱，或演做他自己写的剧本，在这种快乐的空气中，喝完了他少年时代的浪漫的甜酒。

泰戈尔是二十三岁时结婚的，他底结婚使他底诗慢慢地舍弃了恋歌的调子，一度从事于神的颂赞。步程着向新的觉醒的路上，他热烈地爱着自然，也爱人间，他听见了自然的呼声，而更与世界相接近。之后，他对自然的爱，成熟而为对千百万被压迫的被损害的人的爱了。

是饮多了人类欢乐哀悲的酒吧，泰戈尔到三十岁左右，对自然与世界的情绪益加沉挚深刻了。他的宗教诗，取得了“世界诗人”的美誉。许多祈祷者在早晚念他的歌，且含着热泪当作赞美的诗唱。

给祖国争取自由的浪潮里，他写了许多崇颂爱国的与牺牲个人的诗。他的爱国诗歌激励了全印度人的心灵，路上的行人唱着他的诗，牧童对着牛羊唱出他的诗，船夫，农夫也唱着他的诗，王子，乞丐大家都唱着他的诗。泰戈尔自己也唱着：

我的祖国，我对你贡献了我的身体，我为你牺牲了我的生命，我为你而哭泣，我的音乐也将为你祈祷而歌唱！

多少富有爱国热诚的青年，为祖国唱着他的诗歌微笑地走上了断头台。

他爱国的诗歌所孕育的，是爱力，鼓励，和牺牲的精神，没有一点愤怒，嫉妒，或憎恶世人的暗示。

他非凡的喜欢儿童，把他们这般天真的小天使，认做祖国自由最有希望的新芽。他带着一群“平和学院”的儿童，穿着白丝袍合唱着诗歌。有一天，泰戈尔摆摇着他多须的头正在写诗，一个孩子偷进房里突然叫道：

“简直像一个疯子。”

“是的，我的孩子，诗人是比疯子更坏的，你是什么时候跑进来的？”

“你做了那么多的诗，为什么不教我做诗呢？”

“我的孩子！诗歌的负担是非常之重的，我不欲使你有这种负担。”

“是的，我自己会去学，他们似乎都很喜欢你的诗，虽然你是担负重一点。”这孩子到十岁时也会写诗了。

当泰戈尔第二次在欧洲漫游，在他的讲台上，人家也给他布了一个森林景致。他到郊外森林中游散时，早有人在预先等候他，更有许多孩子手执鲜花跳舞在泰戈尔的面前。

到了晚年，泰戈尔想逃避名誉，他自己说的：“是倦了，我只愿休息在星光的下面，我不欲再得国人的赞美与责备。”但名誉仿佛又像黑雾似的把这位诗人包围着，于是，他自己拼命的听喊：“诗人，你在哪里？”

泰戈尔的哲学思想

泰戈尔的哲学基础是建筑在邬波尼杀昙“梵我一如”观之上的。他解释：“梵是宇宙的意识，万有之生命和光明都为他所产生：人们的肉体精神，都潜于它意识之中，太阳的吸引地球，是通过他的意识，光明从太阳传到行星，又从这行星传到那行星，都透过它的意识才可能的。他是遍满于宇宙的实在，无论在广大的世界或在内包的心灵界都有他的住家。”所以他又说：“梵是永远地实在，虽然超越时间，但也活动于时间之中。它虽是绝对完全的存在，但常理想于不完全中而创造不已。梵是完全的无限的理想：为爱，为真理，为欢喜，为美，为善。总括一句话，梵是万物创造之神，为全知而充满周遍于法界的存在。”这似乎是泰戈尔的哲学思想把一切都看作“你当因舍而得，你其勿贪”！把相对的东西看做相互一致（一元论），就是把宇宙事物看成一元（梵）来解释的。

但泰戈尔一面虽尊重为宇宙原理的梵，同时又认特殊的个性尊严，他说：“我是绝对独尊，我是我，我是唯一无二，便是以宇宙的全量，也不能粉碎我的个性。这个性在外貌上看来，虽然似乎是很弱小的，但在事实上看来却很伟大，能和一切力量抵抗”。他虽然这样说，但并不是无条件肯定自我的，乃是以“自我”根源于梵而求尊严的。

泰戈尔的哲学，又有所谓，“再生的方法”之举。在印度“再生”的意义为鸟，因鸟生了卵，卵孵化才为雏，是有二度的诞生。所以泰戈尔假借这个名称来证明说：“如果雏不自破卵壳，怎能出现于自由世界呢？”所以“卵之壳虽美，但为了（再生）不能不破。我们的生活也是这样，舍弃自我，才得生活于真正的自我。所以人不应该有满足，如果有，那是很可悲的事。我们应当速去假我，直参于梵的世界，浴于充溢底爱中。”

把泰戈尔的话，我们归纳起来，他的哲学思想，可以分作三点：就是一为梵（神）底观念；二为个我底问题；三为再生底方法。

末后，我重复地以心灵底呼唤：“诗人呵！你的坟墓建筑在千万人的心里。”千万人的心里，有你复活的影子，你不是在你哲学思想里，解脱着“再生”的意义吗？诗人呵！

——《诗歌与木刻》，第 8 期，1942 年 4 月

太戈尔先生与东方精神

张道藩

一

诗人是人类的灵魂，哲学家引导人类走向圣境。太戈尔先生是大诗人，也是大哲学家，他的诗就含有他的哲学，他的哲学也就是他的诗。

我国诗经序文开章便说：“诗者志之所之也。在心为志，发言为诗；情动于中，而形于言，言之不足，故嗟叹之，嗟叹之不足，故咏歌之；咏歌之不足，不知手之舞之，足之蹈之。性发于声，声成文，谓之音，治世之音，安以乐，其政和；乱世之音，怨以怒，其政乖；亡国之音，哀以思，其民困。故正得失，动天地，感鬼神，莫近于诗。”当我们诵读太戈尔先生的美妙动人的抒情诗歌，或是哲理深邃的哲学论文，或是精心结构的小说戏曲的时候，无不感动心震，便使我们完全证实了这些话语的真确意义。他的诗的人格是和谐而完美的，像一株高耸入云的古树，在晓风里幽欢的，愉快的颤动着，吐着轻盈的声音，放着晶莹的光彩的，就是他的诗句。那一点极微妙，但极真实的灵机，是永远不可模拟的，正如一张音弦调正了的琴，有轻微的触动，他那里就有微妙的声音。这是他自己的诗句：

“如同树，它的样子，我脱落我的字刻在地上，
让我的不出口思想，在你的沉默中开花。”

二

本来，诗是宇宙的音律在人心中的反响，惟有健全的心灵，强烈的生命，崇高的情绪，才能产生真正的“诗”。

虽则诗的目的，不是把哲学告诉我们，正如哲学论文不一定写成诗的形；但是如其一首诗，不包有哲学的幻想，便很难完成它的目的，也像哲学不能启开人类的锁着的心扉，便完全失却它的价值。黑格尔说：

"诗的目的，在把谐和的宇宙的究竟，理想的形式，放进想象的形式里。"亚里斯多德也讲："诗是一切文字中最有哲学思想的，它的目的就是真理。"所以诗的真使命，不单在供给欣赏的快乐，不单在表现人性，和人生的感情，它的使命还在理想的真理的默示。诗之所以为诗，只因为它是哲学的。

身体的享受与快乐，固为印度人所极端反对，对于没有精神的自然，也为印度思想所排斥。所以太戈尔先生反对唯心论，也不同意功利主义，在他看来，灵魂与物质是一个东西，不能分离的。外形是内在的表现：外形而适合内容，则称之为美。他认为美是主观的，一切东西的达到精神的和谐，都靠我们自己。

在这里，一个直觉的哲学家，他超越了小我，已经得到意识的真自由，他听得灵魂的密语，他听到宇宙在不停息的流转，于是打开束缚，发为音节，从和谐里得到快乐。这就是古印度的哲人，也是现代伟大的太戈尔先生。他是古代印度的子孙，现代印度的母亲。

三

太戈尔先生的诗，所以能激动印度人的心灵的原因，就是因为太戈尔先生不但是古时代印度哲人的承继者，而且是现代印度的先知先觉。他的诗歌已经变成了印度的国歌，那种充满了生气的字眼，燃烧的思想，和光明的启示，早已深深的灌溉在印度人的心里。

太戈尔先生相信一国的诗歌与一切艺术文化灭亡的时候，便是这个国家的灭亡。这话也就是我国孟子说的："所谓故国者，非为有乔木之谓也"的意思。他早年受了印度文化的爱国教育，在少年时代，便常和爱国同志秘密讨论改革印度政治社会的方法，后来便开始写他歌颂献身报国的诗歌。老年虽渐渐于冲淡的境界，正是诗哲的化境；要知道，他的内心却依然是火热的。

当清晨的时候，朝阳耀着金色的光彩，印度的民众便在街上唱着他的诗歌，唤人起来，加入对于神与祖国的祈祷，他们唱的是：

"你的祖国在竞争斗着，在受苦着，

唉，他在饥饿着，

仅有肯尽责任的儿子，才能解母亲的忧呀！”

所以印度之有太戈尔先生，乃是印度历史文化，加上时代精神的最高成就。是东方民族的光荣，也是人类将获得永久和平的朕兆。

四

太戈尔先生的爱国诗歌，所孕蓄的是爱恋，是鼓励，是牺牲的精神，但没有愤怒，嫉妒，或厌憎世界的暗示，正与我国古诗所崇尚的“乐而不淫，哀而不伤”的理想相符合。这是他与许多标榜“铁与血”的军国主义的诗歌不同之处，也是有些人反对他的主张的理由。殊不知，真能感动人的，而且永久激荡人心灵的诗歌，就是这种诗歌。虽然带了充分的宗教性，却没有游离现实；虽然没有激烈的指出整个民族的出路，却明白地昭示了时代的动向。所以惟有能够认识东方文化的人，才能了解他。

对于上帝的爱与祖国的爱，是他生命里两个主要的特征。上帝是他灵魂的伴侣，祖国则是他人生的对象；他是一个具有世界主义理想的印度国族主义的倡导人，他相信人类的国族，因其分而益显其繁复，他以为人类是超乎一切国族之上，国族的份子以及她们在人类社会里的合作是，宇宙和谐的发展的要着；正如人体的各类机构，它们的区分与合作，为人体健康的发展的条件一样。他有一次在英国人与爱尔兰人联合欢迎他的宴席上说：

“虽然我们的言语不同，我们的习惯不同，而在根底上，我们的心是一个。……东方是东方，西方是西方，但这两者必相遇于友爱、和平与互相了解之中。”

他又曾经说过：

“我们要确认只有经过种族的个性的发展，我们才真能达到普遍性；并且只有在普遍性的精神的光明里，我们才能完成个性。”

我们觉得很奇怪的，这不就是总理主张的：世界主义是民族主义的理想，民族主义是世界主义的实行。的确，同是国族思想最高的指标。我们有了总理，中国已经得救，因此相信：印度有了太戈尔先生，印度也将获得自由与光明。

五

印度思想的最高点在于优盘尼基（Upanishad），太戈尔在他的哲理诗中所唱的，在他的“生之实现”的论文里所说的，也就是这个优盘尼基哲学。在优盘尼基中有几句话：“世界是从爱中生的，世界是被爱所维系的，世界是向爱而转动的，又是进于爱之中的。”这个真理，太戈尔先生是要完备的把它发挥出来，他也像总理发明“民生是历史进化的中心”一样，相信人类永久的和平与自由发展，即存在于这个和谐之中。

当第一次大战后，大家都认为欧洲须要采取东方的理想，太戈尔先生也很荣耀的说：

“你的光明与欢喜，是潜在东方去解放世界的灵魂。”

可是侵略国家受了第一次世界大战的惨痛，并没有觉悟，变本加厉，又酿成了第二次大战；现在虽是战争方酣，但终必有一天，他们会想到太戈尔先生的话，觉得懊悔莫及。而且也终必有一天，实践了太戈尔哲学，那就是世界永久和平的实现，也就是中国抗战，和同盟国家联合抵抗侵略者胜利之后，人类真正的光明与喜欢降临的时候。

六

无疑的，太戈尔先生是现代世界一位最伟大的诗哲，他的作品加入印度文学内，印度文学立刻复活了；他的清新的译文加入英国文学里，立刻树立了一种特异卓越的文体。同时他的哲学思想也像他的诗歌作品一样，独特的跳出了近代的一切争辩与陈腐的空气，如清晨的曙光照耀于世界久居于黑暗中的人的眼前。他曾漫游欧洲，也来过我国，我们看熟了他皓白的头发，听惯了他妙曼的歌声。但是他的崇高思想，伟大的国族主义精神，以及蕴藏在他内心的美化了的热烈的战斗情绪，恐怕只有今日的中国人民才能彻底了解。记得他曾经说过：

“他们越是束紧他们的索子，我们越是要咬断这条索子；他们的眼睛越是发红，我们的眼睛越是张开。……”

对于印度的政治，太戈尔先生以为即使有好的政府的各种便利，仍不能讲为自由，因为自由不是离开人生和国族的独立而能得到的。他明瞭一个文化风俗人情完全不相同的国家，断不能做这个国家的主人翁，他对于本国是如此看法，对于友邦也是同样的态度。所以当时日本开始侵略我国，我国奋起抗战，他便立刻对我表示最大的同情；因为太戈尔先生代表的是东方精神的升华，也是现代人类思想的圣化；印度有了泰戈尔先生是印度的光明，世界有了太戈尔先生是世界的幸福，虽然在人类永久的和平尚未来到，世界正在炮火弥漫之中，太戈尔先生已经在八十高龄上离开我们而逝，但是我们深信只要爱好和平的民族，加紧共同努力，打击黩武的侵略国家，则真正的世界和平，不久必将实现。那时候，大家也许才能真正理解太戈尔先生的东方精神！现在请让我借用印度的祈祷词来结束本文——

“让我们为了善，为了真，为了人人的永久，为了你（上帝）的心的联合的天国，为了灵魂的自由，坚确的立定，并且努力的忍受。”

三十年十一月，重庆

——《文艺先锋》，第 1 卷第 5 期，1942 年 12 月 10 日

中印学会召开年会

中印学会为泰果尔先生与蔡孑民戴季陶诸氏所创设，酝酿经营，远在十年以前。二十三年成立迄今，亦已八载，自迁移陪都后，尚未集会，经若干日之筹备，始于本月三日举行年会于中央图书馆，出席会员极为踊跃，由戴季陶氏主席讨论修改会章，扩充组织，确定工作进行计划，及征

求会员，筹备经费等办法，并推定朱家骅，张道潘[1]，谭云山，陈大齐，太虚等为理事，吴敬恒，戴传贤，商震，王宠惠等为监事，并以中央研究院院长朱家骅，中央大学校长顾孟余为正副理事长，陈立夫，张道潘等为常务理事，戴传贤陈布雷二氏为正副监事长，王宠惠，白崇禧，商震，王世杰为常务监事，戴氏在开会时有一长篇演说，极为学术界所重视，而到会诸氏相继发表重要之报告与意见云。

——《图书月刊》，第 2 卷第 7 期，1943 年 2 月

中研院征文纪念泰果尔

中央研究院拟征集国内作家撰著专文译成西文由中印学会出版精印一巨册，以纪念印度故诗人泰果尔。

——《图书月刊》，第 2 卷第 7 期，1943 年 2 月

泰戈尔的东方文化观

印哲太戈尔氏，在战前曾莅我国讲学，对我国文化备极赞扬，曾在一次公开讲演上举出三个譬喻，形容我国文化的伟大之处，并进而说明西洋人士不易了解的原因。语极中肯，足以发人深省。

第一个譬喻：认为我国文化，像是一个具有天才的乐师在弹着钢琴，一位西洋的客人，聋了耳朵，他却听不见和谐婉转的声音，只见乐师的手在不停的动着。

第二个譬喻：认为我国文化，像是一颗数合抱的大树，今年看它不见长大，明年看它亦不见长大，实则它的枝干上是更见充实。

第三个譬喻：认为我国的文化，像是一条波浪滚滚的大江，江水总是向着东流——流向海里去。但是遇着一阵逆风，水像倒流了，实则它还是

[1] 即“张道藩”——编者注。

日夜不息地向着海里流去。

——《十四年》，第1卷第2期，1946年12月1日

泰戈尔的音乐

茵底罗（作） 山灵（译）

我感到万分愉快，得以尽我所能把我所知道的一点关于我们最敬仰的民族诗人和音乐家。也是我所最亲爱的叔父，泰戈尔的音乐写出来。使亲爱的中国朋友们借着这篇小文多少得先了解方面的便利，我知道中国朋友们对于诗人的品格和他的创作非常尊重。诗人也曾和中国朋友们努力在把这两国间在过去已经中断了的关系重新联系起来。

但是，我总觉得，直接去听音乐，要比阅读写下来的文章易于了解。比方说，读者们如果爱好音乐而稍稍读些泰戈尔乐谱的话；那，一定会比从我所能给的这决不完备的说明中去领会要直接得多了。

有人说，音乐是宇宙间的一种共同语言。不过，我想即使它是一种和世界语一样的共同语言，但是在应用它作为相互表达的工具之前，总要必须经历一番学习和训练。同时我又感觉到奇怪，为什么过去中国的经书，刺绣，建筑，以至于文艺作品的翻译，在外国不必过分精研便可欣赏，而中国音乐却始终如同一本密封着的书似的，我们毫无所知，至少我个人是如此。是因为音乐不能翻译呢？还是因为在中国之外不容易得到听中国音乐演奏的机会呢？说老实话，我虽然大半生消磨在世界上的大城市之一——加尔各答——中，却从来没有耳福欣赏过中国音乐。我有时在漫想，也许是因为中国的乐理和其他国家的不同，又许是用眼睛直接去接受不常见的景物美，比用耳朵去反应不常听的调子，纵令声律调协的乐曲，要容易得多？这又是心理问题了。上面的话并非与题无关，而这足以说成我的主要论点：欣赏外国音乐的条件是一定要去听，不是一次，而是反复地，仔细地去听。在这篇小文里，我并不想提示实际演唱的方法，而只是做一种理论上的说明，同时指出泰戈尔所贡献于印度音乐方面的特色，并且引用一些人们所熟习的东西音乐比较两者之间的异同。

若是让我仅是避免引用音乐上的专门术语，同时还要叙述得简单明了的话，那么我觉得印度音乐与东西音乐的不同之处可以归纳做两点：第一，是印度音乐中有所谓“曲调”（Raga 旧译“情”，“色”。相当于中国昆曲的“宫调”，皮广的“板”，更像唐宋以来燕乐中的“管色”）的存在和共在演唱方面的重要性。“曲调”的艺术精髓，需要极长的时间去研究，而且很难通达，不易操纵自如。第二，所谓东西音乐的灵魂，“旋律”或“和声”，在印度音乐中是没有的。印度歌曲的特点是没有任何约束，比欧西音乐更多自由而丰富的发展机会。唱歌的人在演唱的时候，可以利用许多颤音和声去掩饰那支曲子——当然不能越乎曲调节奏的范围。同时，还有选择演唱的机会，允许省略和删削。这种演唱会的自由，构成了印度曲调独异的特色。现在我再把泰戈尔的音乐拿来和传统的印度音乐各做比较，看看泰戈尔音乐的特征。否则，若是泰戈尔对于印度音乐并无特殊贡献，那就无需浪费笔墨了。泰戈尔和其他世界上的伟大人物一样，他的创作也是基于传统的。他的传统则是坚固的建筑在他那加尔各答的丛林旧宅中。那儿，常常聚集了印度的著名歌者，泰戈尔幸运地能从他们的口中听到印度最好的音乐。他虽然不曾正式做他们的学生，可是，他借着领悟和聪慧却吸收尽了他们的长处，正像一颗小树的吸取四周环境的营养而繁荣滋长一样。他从幼年便开始作曲，和他的写诗一样早，有些他的早期诗作是用婆罗遮士语（Braja）写的“爱的抒情曲”，他用笔名“日狮子”（Bhanusinha）发表出去，歌曲的题材则是采自牧童偏人天和少女罗陀的恋爱故事，一个为印度诗人永不厌倦的主题。我在小的时候就唱会了这些歌。

毫无可疑的，泰戈尔的早期歌曲，沾染着浓厚的儿时所受到的传统歌曲影响的色彩。他的第二期歌曲的开始，是他住在莲花河上船室里督查乡下地产的时候。在那儿，他熟悉了那些市民和士人的生活和音乐，虽然音调简单，那种民歌式的赞美诗，兼具古典气氛和通俗情调，吸引了他。这是泰戈尔之在印度传统的音乐中能有独创之处的主要构成因素。以后，他扩张固有的成分，增加更新的节奏和韵律，逐渐凝合，逐渐实验，这便成了他的第三期，也是最后一期的音乐。这种真正“泰戈尔派”的歌曲，他一直也在改善，创作，持续到死。

我再谈谈泰戈尔歌曲的一般性质：

自然，这么一位伟大的诗人，不必说通常流行的孟加拉歌曲的文字不能和他的辞藻比拟，而且他更有一种给许多声音铿锵的字加上适切的调子，经组织以达完善的手腕。他还具有把孟加拉语言填入印度坦斯古典曲调中的技巧，非常熟练。他的歌曲包含万象，印度各个省份的音乐特殊成分没有不被他吸取过的，融化过的。他作曲的数目不可数计，题材和内容亦广泛无垠，包括了人类情感的最精妙的面面。不过，为了便利他自己却粗略的把它们分作：恋情歌，宗教歌，季节歌，爱国歌和杂歌五种。

谈到曲调，泰戈尔则是打破了严峻的音阶制度，以增加组织音色上的自由。当然，传统乐歌的主要肩架仍在保存。同时，他的每一支歌曲的处理方法都预示着个别而明显的不同。所以，在他的歌曲中，唱的人没有像在传统的印度歌曲中的能有过多的自由。在传统的歌曲里，歌者可以自由润饰，而主要的目的反倒是对于所唱的歌曲，不论是某个特殊的“曲调”或是某种“象征歌”，仅仅加以轮廓的描画；并不是一个创作歌曲的整体阐发。泰戈尔反对这种部分表现对于整体铨述的危害，也反对由某一部分做主脑而剥削其他部分自由的怪相。

谈到韵律，泰戈尔则是鄙视拙笨，顽梗和迟滞，而赞成清爽明快的风格。他的歌曲里的节拍都能与舞蹈相和。他在歌曲方面的成就，给予被人弃舍而濒于绝境的印度歌曲一付灵剂，把他拯救出来，得到社会上新的估价。韵律轻快而简朴是他的歌曲所以解放的理由之一。和这对立的是我在前面谈到的印度古典音乐所特有的不可胜数的“席间诗章”，为了要有演唱可以伸缩的自由，这就只得用缓慢而所谓严肃的节奏了。

泰戈尔在十几岁的时候便到了英国，他很早就和欧西音乐发生接触。后来，他还一直在常常唱英文歌。虽然他在他的歌曲里时时增加新的营养，但是却不曾受到欧西音乐多大的影响，这种奇异的现象倒是值得注意。他具有一个气力充沛的男子高音的好喉咙，他一直唱到衰老得不能再唱的时候。

读者如果真对泰戈尔的歌曲感觉兴趣，那么我愿意推荐一本唯一可靠的乐谱，那就是法国巴黎刊行的伯克教授的《泰戈尔二十四篇》(Twenty Four Songs of Rabindranath, by Prof. Arnold Bake)。

译者后记

我希望把泰戈尔翁不为我们所知道的方面向国内做一番报道性的介绍，例如，他的音乐，绘画，乡村建设等等。这里，我不自己讲话，免得主观的色彩过于浓厚而掩盖了事实的真相，所以只愿以选择可以信赖的印度人的文章翻译过来。这篇《泰戈尔的音乐》的作者茵底罗（Indira Devi）女士是泰戈尔翁的侄女，孟加拉著名小说家和文艺理论者乔萹黎（Indira the Chaudhurg）的妻子，现任国际大学乐舞学院的名誉院长。她曾在一九四五年获得全孟加拉省妇女对于文学艺术著有殊勋的学会金牌奖，今年整整七十五岁。她的这篇文章本来是给中国中印学会泰戈尔纪念特别刊写的，当时由我译成中文，然而始终不曾印出。

——《现代知识（北平）》，第 2 卷第 12 期，1948 年 4 月 16 日

Tagore's High Place in Indian Art

Rabindranath Tagore holds an unique position among the living painters of Indian today. He is recognized as the father of the modern Indian renaissance in painting.

Tagore started his career as a painter after being trained by two European masters, Mr. Palmer and Signor Gillaidi, in the Western technique of painting. His inborn genius began to blossom forth and his early paintings revealed a sharp sensitiveness which was able to assimilate the best forms in nature and in art. After some time, however, the well-known authority. Mr. E. B. Havell, saw the futility of imposing a foreign style of art on an Indian painter, and persuaded Tagore to draw his inspiration from things Indian and to cultivate his own style in painting.

New Idealism in Art

The artist did not find this a difficult task. His was the first effort in modern times to effect a synthesis of the refined delicacy of Mughal art, the glorious colour effects of Rajput painting and the inimitable elegance of Ajanta frescoes to a new idealism in Indian art.

When he set out to accomplish this interesting task of reviving and resuscitating the languishing art of India. Tagore was faced with the problem of finding the secrets of Indian pictorial language. He therefore collected and studied representative specimens of the Mughai, Rajput and the Pohar schools and tried to derive materials and elements to build up a modern language of Indian art.

His early paintings revealed a passionate plea for the expression of art through indigenous forms. He turned the old vernacular art of India to a truly national one, representing many phases and varied facets. His studies are full of divergent moods and flawless expressions, which surprise even the most critical of connoisseurs.

Tagore's painting, "Radha and Krishna" is characteristic of his genius. Done in a style delightfully his own, it combines all that is best in Indian painting. The general treatment, pictorially speaking is Ajantan. The features retain the typical Rajput — Pahari style of profile and the colour effects are blended in a sublime manner.

Amalgam of Varied Styles

Two other paintings of Tagore have been hailed as great works of art. They are, the "Banished Yaksha", and "Siddhas of the Upper Air". These were executed immediately after he revolted against the realistic style of the west. They revealed for the first time the intensely Oriental character of his art.

For some years Tagore painted after the best manner of the Mughal masters. It was amazing how close his style resembled those of such masters as Mansur, Mr. Hashim and Vichitra. His three masterpieces in this line of painting are — "The Dream of the Taj", "The Building of the Taj", and "Shah Jehan's last glimpse of the Taj". They portray Tagore at his best in this particular phase of his mood.

Not being satisfied in reviving the Indian style of painting Tagore, with his uncanny power of assimilating methods and manners from all schools of painting, freely adopted the secrets of the pictorial art of Asian and European masters, off and on.

Mystic Miniatures

Consequently his "miniatures" combine an intensely romantic and lyrical quality with a dreamy and mystic treatment of his subjects which lift them on a far higher level than the planed of a mere literal naturalism.

The subtle grace of his "Illustrations to the Meghaduta", the "Cloud Bessenger" of Kalidasa, "the Illustrations of the Rubaiyat of Omar Khayyam", his "Bond-Slave", "Aurangzeb" and many more, all reveal his wonderful range of vision, the refinement of lines, and the breadth of his palette.

Tagore's work is an amalgam of different schools of painting. Yet he is distinctly original — a wizard and a magician of colour.

— *The North-China Daily New*, Jul. 21, 1949

第三章

缅 | 怀 | 与 | 追 | 思

泰戈尔荣哀

唁电雪片飞来

（孟买八日路透社电）印度诗人泰戈尔于七日逝世后，其子已收到吊唁函件甚多。在所收之唁电函件中，有印总督、孟买省长、印度司法部长、甘地与其他印度要人。一般对泰戈尔，多称颂其为哲学之思想家，尤足称颂者，即为彼之长期服务，由高尚理想鼓励，以高贵之观察，与不倦之探讨，“足为后世之模范”。

——《大公报》，1941 年 8 月 9 日

泰戈尔逝世噩耗

英各界同声哀悼

路透社八日伦敦电：英国各界闻印度诗哲泰戈尔逝世消息，自廿四岁起即发表其文章于报端，英国之研究文学与哲学者皆推崇之，认为当世知识之领袖。一九一三年曾得诺贝尔文学奖金，印人获此荣誉者以泰氏为第一人。泰氏讲学于英美德与远东诸国，到处受人欢迎。一九三七年十月日本侵华，泰氏大愤斥其野蛮，而对于日本之轰炸中国平民谴责尤力。伦敦泰戈尔学会近曾接其最后一文，内有“西方人类未能保持其千百年来所造成人类文明与尊荣之价值，使余心悸，此皆人类不以道德价值引导国事而信一切皆取决于暴力所致。此种邪恶信念之第一试验，始于满洲见之”等语。今伦敦各界定下星期举行追悼大会，届时与会致词者，将有萧伯纳、韦尔斯与赫胥黎等名流。

——《申报》，1941 年 8 月 9 日

All Indian Mourns Death of Tagore

Bombay. Aug. 9

The entire country is mourning the death of Sir Rabindranath Tagore and there are spontaneous demonstrations everywhere in memory of India's great leader, thinker and philosopher. Tributes are being paid to the memory of Tagore from all quarters.

The Viceroy in a message to the poet's son states: "I am deeply grieved to learn of the death of your father. This marks the end of a long life of service inspired by high ideals nobly conceived and actively pursued and will be an inspiring example for generations to come."

The Governor of Bengal said: "In Tagore Bengal has lost a son whose long distinguished career has been inspired by service to his fellow men."

Mr. Gandhi said: "In the death of Tagore we have not only lost the greatest poet of the age but an ardent nationalist. There was hardly any public activity to which he did not lend his powerful personality."

—*Reuter*

—*The North-China Daily News*, Aug. 10, 1941

诗悼泰戈尔

黄枯桐

（曲江十日专访）印度名诗人泰戈尔氏，于本月七日逝世，世界人士，同深痛悼；粤参谋会副议长黄枯桐氏，特赋诗一首以悼之。黄氏古诗，名闻海内，氏襄任中山大学研究院主任，现乡居从事教育，多有创作，其悼泰戈尔诗云："卧佛无言独惘然（十七年前余曾参拜锡兰岛卧佛），文星今忽殒南天。明王□[1]作风流尽，新月（氏诗译本有《新月集》）凄迷弓柄弦。衰凰惊传已堕云，清风千载炳遗文（氏新著《生之现实》论者谓乃森林哲学也）。声闻菩萨原空相，目断恒河夕照昏”。

——《大公报》，1941 年 8 月 16 日

印度诗人泰戈尔病逝

顷接孟买八月七日电报，印度名诗人泰戈尔已于今日上午病故，享年八十岁。

泰氏履历。泰戈尔，印度诗人，哲学家，一八六一年五月六日生于加尔各答，父亲著名宗教家。氏幼年丧母，习于沉思，十六岁作长诗《加惠加尼》，是为处女作。二十四岁卜居西西伊密，过田园生活。十七年间，成诗颇多，还皆歌颂大自然之作。一九零一年，在和平庄创筑学校后发展为一国际大学，名 Vlava Bharti 为氏终身事业之一。一九一二年，遍遊欧美，并至各大学讲学，声名远播。一九一三年著《生之实现》，是年得诺贝尔文学奖金。一九一六年曾来我国，在平沪各地讲学。氏反对人为的文化，而挚爱大自然之美，故常同情印度民族运动。甘地宣谓与英不合作时，氏立即参加此种运动。我发动神圣抗战后，氏对我大为同情。生平著作有诗歌六十卷，并有散文小说颇多。《恺当乔利》（一九一二），《园丁集》，《新月集》（一九一三），《邮政局长》，《琪泰拉》（剧本一九一四），《卡俾之歌》（一九一五），《拾果》（一九一六），《迷途之鸟》（一九一七）等。均堪称杰作。

——《教育通讯（汉口）》，第 4 卷第 31 期，1941 年 8 月 16 日

[1] 原文缺失——编者注。

Death of Great Indian Poet

London, Aug. 8

In wide circles in Britain the news of the death of Sir Rabindranath Tagore, Indian poet, dramatist and social reformer, has been learned with profound grief. For several days successively less hopeful bulletins had prepared the British public for the passing of India's great and honored sage.

He will always be remembered in England, where he enjoyed the greatest esteem of all who care for letters and philosophy as one of the most distinguished intellectual leaders of our time.

The only Indian poet to be represented in the Oxford Book of Modern Verse, this is but one indication of the unique influence exercised by Tagore on English thought and poetry. In Oxford — the home of English culture — he was a well-known figure at one time.

Many Englishmen will continue to treasure the memory of his venerable appearance, which radiated goodness and quiet strength, and of his voice, which had an almost magical beauty.

The debt of gratitude which countless thousands of Englishmen feel to the great figure who has just passed away is for the great part Tagore played in bringing to the West and understanding of higher thought of the East.

Memorial meetings to pay a last tribute to one of the noblest and finest personalities modern India has produced will be held in England next week, when due expression will be given to the feelings of sympathy felt by English leaders and lovers of thought and art and letters with the family of one upon whom worldly honors were showered but whom worldly things left untouched.

The Tagore Society in London, through its joint secretaries, Messrs, P. B. Seal and B. B. Ray Chaudhuri, has sent a message of condolence to Santi Niketan, Bengal, on the death of Tagore.

Tagore's death "is a great loss to the world and the greatest loss to India," the cable says.

A condolence meeting to be held in London next week is expected to be addressed by Bernard Shaw, H. G. Wells, J. B. Priestly and Aldous Huxiety.

His Last Message

In his last message to London received by the Tagore Society here, Tagore said: "Failure of humanity in the West to preserve the worth of civilization and dignity of man which they had taken centuries to build up weighs like a nightmare on my mind. It seems clear to me that this failure is due to men's repudiation of moral values in the guidance of their national affairs, and to their belief that everything is determined by a mere physical chain of events. The first experimental in this diabolical faith was launched in Manchuria. Those who build their power on moral cynicism are themselves proving its victims. Nemesis is daily proving more ruthless."

Tagore was 80 years of age. He belonged to the family of Tagore, well-known in the literary, artistic and social life of Calcutta. When he was about 24 years of age he started to contribute articles to the vernacular press.

He became one of the most successful exponents of the neo-renaissance spirit in Bengali literature and portrayed the simple lives of the peasantry and middle-classes of Bengal. He also wrote many successful dramas, including "The Postman."

Fondest Dream Realized

In 1901, he founded a university at Shantinakatan, near Calcutta; it realized one of Tagore's fondest dreams, by bringing together boys and girls, not only under one "Alma mater," but by conferring on them the benefits of a common life in the little community at Shantinakatan. The school sought to develop the love of a healthy open-air existence in the students; they were taught to draw their lessons and inspirations for life from nature, which constituted a drastic departure from the cramped, crowded atmosphere of schools in

Calcutta, and represented a revolution in educational system in India.

Later, Tagore laid on it the impress of his international outlook, by developing the school into a sort of international university. Since then Visva Bharati, (the Sanskrit name by which the University is known), has attracted many savants and distinguished men from all parts of the world.

Regarding himself primarily as a poet and social performer. Tagore managed, after a few tentative incursions into it, to keep clear of the welter of Indian politics. He criticized the revolutionary movements in very strong terms, and sought unsuccessfully on many occasions to bring about that complete Hindu-Moslem unity which he considered to be the only remedy to "check the evils which may bring on the unfortunate country the disgust and derision of the whole world."

Ambassador of Friendship

His brilliant gifts as a writer of English have made him one of the most successful ambassadors of friendship with England.

He lectured throughout Great Britain, the United States, Germany and Japan, and his audiences never failed to be influenced by his obvious sincerity, his stately figure, clothed in flowing robes, and his fine head with penetrating eyes and patriarchal beard.

The year 1912 witnessed the first appearance in English of "Gitanzall," Rothenstein (as he then was) and "Chitra." These works caused a sensation and among the honors showered on him were the Nobel Prize for literature in 1913. He was the first Indian to be so honored.

In 1914, the King conferred a knighthood upon him.

During a lecture tour of the United States early in 1923 he was accorded a warm welcome at Yale University.

Shortly after his return to India he flew from Calcutta to Teheran, where he was received in audience by the Shah.

World wide Acclaim

In May, 1936, on his 75th birthday Tagore received messages of congratulation from all over the world, acclaiming his work as poet, dramatist, novelist, political thinker, social reformer and religious teacher.

He fell dangerously ill with erysipelas in the summer of 1937, but made a good recovery.

The Japanese invasion of China stirred him deeply and in October, 1937, he issued a broadcast message to his fellow Indians condemning "the barbarity of Japanese militarists in their dealings with China."

To the Japanese poet Yone Naguchi he sent a dignified but poignant rebuke of the Japanese bombing of defenceless Chinese.

At the age of 77 Tagore suddenly began to paint and an exhibition of his pictures was held in London in December, 1938. They were strange fantastic sketches less of any given subject than, as it were, the random musings of a poetic mind jotted down on paper. Two of these sketches are in the possession of the Borough of Croydon.

Doctor of Literature

In his 80th year Oxford University conferred on Tagore the degree of Doctor of Literature.

It was conferred by Sir Gwyer, Chief Justice of India at a special convocation of Oxford University the first ever held outside England — in the village of Santineketan in Bengal.

Sir Rabindranath Tagore was a man of extraordinarily venerable appearance, tall, massively built with a splendid head and thick silvery hair clustering on the sides in heavy curls, a beautiful face and long white beard. In his long sweeping robes he seemed like one of the Magi.

He had a beautiful voice, an irresistible power in speaking, radiated calm and goodness.

With none was he seen to greater advantage than with children. Indian or British, Chinese or Japanese, they all alike instantly succumbed to his magnetism and love of them.

— *Reuter.*

—*The North-China Herald and Supreme Court & Consular Gazette*, Aug. 20, 1941

对于泰戈尔逝世的感悼

叶恭绰

泰戈尔已永辞此浊世而去了！泰戈尔之死为全人类之一大损失，不止文艺界学术界之损失，尤其不止东方与印度。吾国人知泰戈尔之名甚多，于其死，当然表示悼惜，而与之有接触及契合者，自必尤然。今只叙余之经历及感觉。

十年前，余居沪时，老友姚弗堂（华）自北平以所译《飞鸟集》属为作序，将原作悉变为无言绝句，而情理曲尽。余因是益有感于泰戈尔之为人，其襟抱渊深，在在表现东方哲学之特色，尤足吸引同情。未几，泰戈尔东来过沪，徐志摩招致于其寓所，款以极美之中华筵，时沪上文艺家多列席，谈叙甚欢。泰戈尔不多言，则出口成章，殆若诗歌。余叩以佛学，则逊谢未研究，亦不愿谈政治。其仪观俊伟，褒衣长髯，实令人过目不忘。时笔会同仁，亦欢迎之，甚热烈。顾我国政府，似未有何表示，或偶未注意也。既泰戈尔返印，于其所办国际大学，设中国学院，又欲为我国学生专辟宿舍，其自捐款达百万卢比，欲我国有所捐助，以示提倡，属谭云山回华，商之戴季陶先生及余，戴与余为之部署筹集图书款项，云山奔走多次，迄未能满吾等初愿，而九一八事起矣。余避地到香港，泰戈尔与余等尚书问不绝，并赠一摄影，亲自署名，即上刊者皆是也。泰戈尔为我国之良友，人多知之，无待阐扬。顾念中印文化之灌输融化，阅千余年，占世界文化史之特殊位置。其间并非偶然。谓吾国任何人之精神上，皆有印度文化之结晶，良非过论。今兹世界第二次大战后，全世界文化，将发生剧变，应如何定向以适应今后之需要，而弥将来之祸患，此正哲人鸿儒所当努力从事者。而东方固有文化之精髓，如何方能炼冶提供于世界，此亦深有待于精识如泰戈尔者，共相探讨，兹一旦溘逝，真令人不能无高才凌替天地悠悠之感也。（姚徐二君亦先数年逝世）吾国文化所浸渍于印度者至深，而印度文化，经吾国之咀嚼融化，复自呈其特色，论理吾国应有反哺之谊。但今日吾国所能贡献于印度者为何物乎？此又可为太息者也！国际大学，有吾国学生数人，其程度及成绩何若？余不之知，深望其间有人崛起也。

卅年八月八日

——《大风（香港）》，第 96 期，1941 年 8 月 20 日

悼太戈尔先生

太戈尔的逝世，是东方文化界的严重损失。太戈尔一向是同情中国的抗战的，他曾在谈话里和信札里，对于中国人民寄托了热切的愿望。我们常常记起，离得很近的东方印度，有一位崇高的诗人，他们的同情的眼在注视着我们，我们常常记起，离我们很近的东方俄国，有一个民族诗人麦布尔，常常用他清亮的喉咙，为苦难的中国歌唱。如今光辉的星座之一已经陨落了，我们的悲哀也只有用歌声才能传达出来："当红色的罂粟花开遍了中国的大地的时候，我们从麻痹里，得到了一个清醒的解放！"太戈尔的作品在中国有郑振铎译的《新月集》，《飞鸟集》，太戈尔到中国来的时候，他自己起了一个中国的名字，叫"竺震旦"，他对中国的爱是殷切，中国的人民应该纪念他。

——《时代文学》，第 1 卷第 3 期，1941 年 8 月

纪念太戈尔

沁　人

听说太戈尔在今年七月间死了，我非常难过，难过的泪都阻塞住。

我们伟大的诗人，东方的一颗星，终于陨落了，永久的陨落了，但他遗留给人间的爱之火炬，我相信，将更灿烂的照耀起来。

不过，他毕竟是死了，黄金彭加尔的景色，失去了它的情人，喜马拉亚耶山峰上的青碧无垠的天空，再也受不到幽美的灵的抚摸，全印度的人们，再也听不见他那热情的爱感的新歌……我也仿佛在看着夕阳的沉沦，为着宇宙将从此失掉光耀，而深深地感到说不出来的心头的破碎。

我爱的他的歌，更爱他的伟大，因为他已不是平凡的人，是一团诗魂。

为了纪念诗人的死，为了排遣我的悲哀，我写了他的一生。

（一）生平

拉实特拉那斯·太戈尔（Rabindranath Tagore）在一八六一年五月六日生于彭加尔地方，印度是一个“诗的国”，他的家庭是一个“艺术之宫”，所以他的诗才幼芽，吸收了清新之路，很容易滋长起来。

他童年的时候，不曾踏出大门一步，只和别的两个孩子一起读书，所读的东西，他早已忘记，只“雨淅沥的落下，潮水泛滥到河上来”一句，还没消减，这是他与文学的第一次接触。

虽然他家里有花园，有池，有大榕树，有鸭儿，但他一天一天的长大，便渐渐渴望到家宅以外去，于是先后进东方学院，师范学校，彭加尔学院，但都不合他的意思，这并不是他不喜学问，是他不喜欢强迫的和规定的课程，他心中一味充满了诗的冲动。

所幸，在师范学校时，有个教师和他很好，常常教他作诗的方法，或者给他出题目，或者自己先写一二行，然后再叫这十岁左右的学生接下去。

他诗的天才便一天天发展起来，在童年时代就有诗童的声誉。

在他的一封信上说“我的童年时代，已经不大记得，但我却很记得，常常的，在清晨的时候，我心上总不知不觉的泛滥着一种说不出的愉快，全个世界对于我似乎充满了神秘。每一天，我总拿了一根小竹棒，在那里掘土，想着也许可以发现那些神秘的一个这个世界的一切美丽与甜蜜与芬芳，一切人民的走动，街上的歌声，鸢的鸣声，以及家园里的可可树，池边的榕树，水上的树影，清晨的花的香气——所有这一切，都使我感得有朦胧的认得的人物，幻化了这许多形态，以与我为伴”。

一次，他陪着父亲，坐了家艇到恒河上去，父亲所带的书中，有一部约那地瓦（Jayadeva）的吉塔哥文达（Gita Govinda），那诗句不是分行写的，当他读到："黑夜走过寂寞的林屋"一句时，他心里感着一种隐约的美，他便把诗韵照音分开，将全书重抄了一遍，预备着自己读，这种工作使他得着很大的快乐。

后来，他父亲带他到喜马拉耶山旅行，他们走上山坡，春花在路边岩隙中盛开，瀑布在森林中挂下，太戈尔的双眼，几乎没有停视，心中涨满了新的爽快，最后他们住到了一个山顶上，和山林作了伴侣，这幼小的充满了怀疑的诗人，常常独自由这个山峰跑到那个山峰，自然对他显示出无穷的神秘，瀑布从悬崖倒挂下来，水声潺潺的响着，大树像祈祷者，兀自立在那里，太戈尔用心的爱感去温存它们，觉着胸襟益发扩涨起来，像河流之泛滥——这种自然的美的赏赐，加之他父亲的人格的感化，使他终生印着憧憬的痕迹。

回来以后，他便觉得学校讨厌，他的家庭教师，便给他解释战神之生及莎士比亚的麦克伯（Macbeth），他同时还自动的读了许多彭加尔的书和杂志，并且常在日记簿上涂一些诗句，有许多夜不睡眠，一个人在书房的微光下读书，远寺的钟声铿然而鸣，夏夜的月光静泻在地上，他便如幽灵似的，到花园的树荫下去散步。

在十七岁时，他的二哥，要他到英国去留学，经父亲允许，到了白里顿（Brighton），后又到台房萧（Devonshire）去，那里有山有水，有汪洋的大海，有草茵，有松林，眼中所见的都是美，心里所有的都是快乐，所以他常常带了伞，坐在海岩上，海涛澎湃，日丽风清，望着松林的影子发呆，于是他写他的诗。

还有十八岁至二十三岁，是他的浪漫时代，这时所作的抒情诗非常好。例如：

"我跑着，如香麝之在林影中跑，闻着他自己的芳香而发狂。

夜是五月的夜，风是南来的风。

我迷了路。我浪游着，我寻求我所不能得到的东西，我得到我所不寻求的东西。

我自己欲望的印象从我心里跑出来，在跳着舞。

耀耀的幻象闪过去。

我想把他紧紧的握住，引我到迷路。

我寻求我所不能得到的东西，我得到我所不寻求的东西。”

太戈尔在这时是最自由的，他随意写诗，随意毁了它，他不是写了博朋友的喜悦而写诗，乃是如闲云之舒卷，流水之淙淙，完全是为自己快乐而写的。

到了二十三岁，他的放浪生活便终止了，和一个女子结了婚，灵的感觉渐渐的在他心里占了优势，他舍弃了清新的恋歌的调子，而从事于神的颂扬。

及至太戈尔到了三十岁左右，他的人间的经历愈深，他饮得人类的欢乐与悲欢的酒愈多，则他对于上帝与自然与世界的情绪愈为沉挚深刻，才成了伟大的世界的诗人，他所作的诗歌，所发的音乐，虽然复杂，而他的琴弦却只有一条，即上帝的爱。

他的诗集白拉摩格特（Brabmo Sangits），是宗教师的集子，出版后，就成为彭加尔人所崇拜的中心。

他的英文诗集吉檀迦利（Gitanjali），在英国出版时，不仅感动了以热忱介绍这诗集的诗人夏芝（Yeats），且感动了全英国的人，全欧洲的人，一九一三年瑞典文学会以诺贝尔奖金奉给太戈尔，这是东方人第一次在欧洲得到的荣誉，立刻全世界都认识了他。

以前，他曾到过英国，美国，但他的来去，不为社会所注意，自得诺贝尔奖金后，生活即不自由了，走到一处，一处的人便带着热忱欢迎他，要求他的思想上的赠品，后来还到日本，民国十三年到中国讲演和游历，他的讲词，都由徐志摩记录起来。

还有一个时期，他父亲叫他到西莱蓬去管理产业，于是他便和农民和自然更接近了，他常常乘舟在柏特马河，对自然的各方面，加以观察研究恋念，爱惜，他说：

“我没有旅游相特马之前，很怕因为常常相伴之故，我对于它不能觉得有趣味，但当我一浮泛在河上时，我的一切疑虑都消失了。水波汩汩，船身微荡，天空光洁，柔缘的水灏莽，河岸上树林的枝叶新鲜——颜色，音乐，跳舞，及美丽集合而使自然的高起的和谐，照耀着光彩，所有的一切，在我心里惊醒了一种敏锐的趣味，与沉挚的愉快。”

在西莱蓬的许多年里，太戈尔的文学收获很丰富，他的大部分的短篇小说和诗，都是在那里写成的。

当一九一七年世界第一次大战告终以后，世界上到处都弥漫着和平的新觉悟，太戈尔便想用那伟大的爱，让人们把纷纭扰乱的都溶成“一个甜蜜的调和”，以此宗旨来往欧洲各地，传布东方文明了，并且还为印度民族向英国政府请求自由，但恒河的风光，总是敲着他的心的门，唤他回去，所以他总是舍不了他的故乡。

回来以后在鲍尔甫（Bolpnr）办了一个学校，名为和平之院（Shantineketan），把他的文学奖金及著作的代价，全部用在这上面，以很自然的教学方式，绝不抑制儿童的天性里的自然的快乐，所以学生的学业与性格的成绩都很好，在其他学校里八年才能预备好的课程，在“和平之院”只要六年就够了。之后又改为国际大学，他到德国讲演时入场券所售得的钱，都捐给他的国际大学。

这不朽的诗人，始终是为了人类的幸福，在祈祷……

（二）思想

太戈尔是一个大哲学家，印度的精神爱国领袖，一个戏曲家，一个编辑者，一个教育家，而还有超此外的，他是一个爱的诗人（The Poet of Love），爱情从他的心的灵魂里漾溢出来，幻化了种种的式样，母的爱，子的爱，妻的爱，父的爱，情人的爱，自然的爱，上帝的爱……都在他的优美的歌里，曼声而恳挚的唱了出来。他的歌声荡漾在天空下，轻轻的触动人的心弦，使人们快乐的笑着，眼里汪出兴感的泪珠。

太戈尔，是以伟大的人格，濡浸在印度精神里面，尽力的表现出东方思想，同时却受了基督教的精神的感力，他说世界是从爱生的，是靠爱维系的，是向爱运动的，是进入爱里的，宇宙之创造是爱，而人生之目的亦是爱。

他对于教育的意见是：“教育的目的，不在于解释意义，而在于敲打那心的门。如果我们问一个儿童，叫他叙说出这样的敲门时，他心里所惊觉的是什么？他也许要说出些非常愚笨的话来。因为内部所发生的感觉，是比他所能用言语表白的更为巨大的”。所以，在他创造办和平之院时，有这样一段话：

“我为了要复现我们古代教育的精神，决定创办一个学校，学生在那里能够在生命里，感觉到一个比现实的满足更高尚更光荣的东西——熟悉生命它自己。我想把小孩子们的奢侈除去，使他们复返于朴质。所以因此之故，我们的学校里，没有班次，也没有凳子，我们的小孩子们，在树下铺了席子，在那里读书，他们的生活力求简单。这个学校建立在大平原里的原因之一，即在于要远远的离开城市的生活，但在这一层之外，我更要看孩子们与树木一同生长；因为两者的生长之中有了一种和谐……。”

从此证明，他并非是遁世厌世的人，乃是入世爱世的，且非常爱他的印度，他相信“一国的诗歌绘画及音乐灭亡时，便是这个国家的灭亡”的话，所以才专心去做一个诗人以重兴印度。他做的国歌，使印度人永远深铭在心里，当唱到“你的祖国在竞斗着，在受苦着，唉！她在饥饿着，仅有肯尽责任的儿子才能解母亲的忧呀”！其影响实较唱“醒来，快醒来，战胜，而且把压迫者的暴力冲到地下去”为更大。他的爱国的诗歌，乃孕蓄着爱恋，鼓励，牺牲的精神，却没有丝毫的愤怒，嫉妒，或是憎恶世界上任何人的暗示。

太戈尔的著作里所表现的精神主义的理想，都是印度哲学的真理。所以他是宗教式的理想家，他对印度大喊：“败比不名誉要尊贵的多，忧愁比愤恒要好的多，受苦比使人受苦要好得多；让我们学习受苦而不恨，牺牲而不失望，让灵魂除了永久的正直以外，不像别的鞠躬”，这就是太戈尔对于印度的使命。

至晚年，很想逃避名誉，虽然名誉的石碑，已重压在他的身上，所以他眷恋在柏特玛河上，目的即在诗人的成功，就是诗人的寂寞，诗人的名誉，则如黑雾似的，使他不能找到自己。

（三）著作

已译成英文的，有二十几部，都由英国和美国麦美伦公司一家出版。

（1）诗歌：吉檀迦利（Gitanjali），采果集，园丁集，新月集，飞鸟集，思余，情人之贻与歧路，飘流和路旁。

（2）戏曲：邮政局，暗室之王，齐德拉（Chitra），春之循环，牺牲和其他。

（3）小说：饿石和其他，姨母和其他，家庭与世界，沉船，哥拉（Gora）。

（4）论文：生之实现，人格，国家主义，创造的一体。

（5）自传：我的回忆。

（6）信札：彭加利的景物。

（7）译文：葛拜耳诗集（Poems of Kabir）。

（四）结论

总之，太戈尔的诗的目的，是在把人类从他们的欲望中的束缚上，解放出来，他生命的节奏，就表现在他诗的节奏中间。

他把他的爱，献给整个的人群，让人们的心境幽美，快乐，让人们的灵魂，浸在自然的和谐中，这就是他的伟大，这就是他人格的太阳。

现在，他虽然在青松绿萝之间，昏昏的睡，也许仍要做着春池碎波的梦，但他在大地上撒遍的爱的种子，将要更繁盛的开出有力的智慧之花。

一九四一，八月十六日

——《大风（济南）》，第 4 期，1941 年 9 月 1 日

悼泰戈尔

夏烘秋

曾记得你到中国来游历时说：“我爱中国人，也爱西洋人，
但中国人对我的爱，我却感得比西洋人更诚挚而情深。”

啊，泰戈尔——伟大的诗人，

你的诗，是我们胸中的呻吟，
你永远爱着世人（正如同世人永远爱着你）：
然而你死了，
世界上，失掉了一位慈祥的母亲。

印度是英国的殖民地，
中华是万国的殖民地。
伟大的泰戈尔啊，
我们爱你的诗，
爱你个人，
也爱你的民族。
我们用热泪来读你的诗歌，
我们用哀嚎来追悼你的灵魂，
我们用强大的呼声。
呼唤着同中国人受着同样痛苦的
亲爱的印度人民！
然而，慈爱的母亲终于死了。
抛下一群可怜的孩子们。
在这吃人的社会上，
有谁再来安慰这群可怜的孩子们的心？

然而——
地球一天天的回转，
地球面上的一切在演着新陈代谢。
泰戈尔啊，你的死。
也同旁人一样，
是件极平常的事。

伟大的泰戈尔啊，
你静静的死去吧，

我们还活着呢，我们将用“力”来
扩大你的“爱”
你放心的去死吧。

好，别矣！
你在天之灵，
看着我们“干”好了。

——《大风（济南）》，第 4 期，1941 年 9 月 1 日

泰戈尔翁也长逝了

铁　笙

了解印度思想的地山师殁后三天，印度诗哲，亚洲唯一获得诺贝尔文学奖金曾代印度民族在精神上吐一口大气的泰戈尔翁，也溘然长逝了，是印度和中国的不幸？还是他们两位大师的不幸？我不配对泰戈尔翁的死说什么话，因为我不会像跟地山师那样有过绛帐受教的机会，但一想到地山师的死，泰戈尔翁的噩耗便也不期而然地引起一些悽然的感觉来。在我们这些民族里，培养一位伟大的学者或思想家不是一件易事，所以一位伟大的学者或思想家的凋零，也越值得我们扼腕：泰翁的死，就给了我这样一种感觉。

还在高小时代（一九二三），《北京晨报》便异样被我喜爱着，泰翁的大名也在那时开始认识。他长发披肩银须飘拂的神情，曾和耶稣圣像一样，同在我小小的脑海里泛起一重微波，报上载着他和徐志摩先生到处讲演，受人欢迎，同时台下也有人发散传单，请他回国，两种对泰翁不同的反应，会使小小的脑海纳闷多时。后来慢慢读了郑振铎先生们的介绍和翻译，对泰翁的思想和生活，才稍稍了悟一点，他诗文中所涵蓄的情绪，给一个笃信基督的孩子。也才能体悟起来，人道主义和国家主义的种子，也借着这两种力量渐渐扎了根，虽然泰翁的思想情绪，毕竟是站在辅助地位的。

年青人都有一个时期喜爱热烈火爆，高中时代对这位老人的怀念便慢慢疏远了，虽然偶尔也拿起他的诗集或剧本读读，究竟不再像高小及初中时代那样虔敬，最“激烈”的时候，连对圣雄甘地的作风都有点反感，对于歌咏自然鼓吹人道主义，精神文明的泰戈尔翁，自然不屑一顾。抹杀一切，用一个思想模型来范围全人类行为是每个青年会有的思想阶段，所以泰翁和耶稣一样，是会被我践踏在脚下污泥中的，年龄和阅历将一个人从完全幻想中提出来的时候，才可以比较广大点欣赏自己以外的一切，也才能明白世界不单需要汗流浃背除草刈莠的田丁，也需要默默撒种，或晨曦灌溉的农夫，而人间之真正的可爱，也就在不但有流乳与蜜的丰美粮食，同样一株小草，一涧浅水，也是人类生活上所必需的，泰戈尔翁给我们的，至低限度有像仙草灵水那样美丽。那么一朵代表人类精神思想美丽的花之陨灭怎能不使我们怃然叹息呢！

泰翁出之印度贵族，又受了英国人的教育，所以好些朋友咒他为“奴隶的诗人”将他的成功一笔抹杀，这在现在的我看起来，觉得是太不应该的，一个人不能不受环境的影响，也不能不有他应付环境的方式，这种影响和方式是不应该也实在不能被固定的。泰翁受英国文化的熏陶和影响确是实事，他也没有像彭佳尔其他爱国的人一样拿手枪炸弹来对付灭亡他祖国的人，但他一样热烈地爱着他的祖国，而且天地也许有末日印度文明也许有毁坏，泰翁留给他祖国的一颗热烈的心，却永久不能消灭——印度的国歌，泰翁心灵之吐露将永远伴着朝阳晨旭，同其光辉。

郑振铎先生说的好：“‘你的祖国在竞斗着，在受苦着，唉！她在饥饿着，仅有尽责任的儿子才能解母亲的忧呀！’其影响实较唱‘醒来，快起来，战胜，而且把，压迫者的暴力冲到地下去，’更伟大。”这是实在的。他没有喊“起来”对灭亡他国家的人怎样怎样，却用温柔的歌词，多方面的热情，将祖国植到每一个印度人，每一个爱好自由而深受压迫的印度人的心灵深处了！“我对你贡献了我的身体，我为你牺牲了我的生命；我为你哭泣，我的音乐也将唱歌者为你而礼拜。虽然我的臂弯无助而且无力，而他们仍将为你——仅仅为你——的缘故而去做事：虽然我的刀不庄严而污锈了，而它仍将斩断束缚你的链子，我的甜蜜的母亲。”这是他对于祖国的讴歌，这是他永久不灭的灵魂，“奴隶的诗人”能如此吗？

"兄弟不要灰心，因为上帝并不曾在睡，绳结愈紧，你的束缚的时期也将愈短。咆哮之声愈高，你也将愈快的从你的甜睡中醒来，压迫的打击愈厉，他们的旗帜也将愈快与地接吻。不要灰心。兄弟，因为上帝并不曾在睡！"使印度爱国青年昂然走上断头台。领受一刀成永诀的死刑，而口中还高唱着不辍的，是这样的泰戈尔的歌！泰翁是仅仅在讴歌自然吗？是仅仅在享受英国人送给他的爵士的富贵吗？是仅仅向森林说教向飞鸟、田园星月吐出哲理的"奴隶的诗人"吗？泰翁不死！"印度也绝不死！

泰翁留给世人的精神之花，将永照日月和任何其他民族伟大的作家将同垂永久。

——《中国文艺（北京）》，第 5 卷第 1 期，1941 年 9 月 5 日

由许地山的死谈到泰戈尔

洗　耳

这几天接二连三的噩耗，纷至沓来：八十岁的老诗翁泰戈尔和将近半百的许地山先生，在本月四日和七日，相继羽化而登仙了。在这剑拔弩张，枪林弹雨，举世乌烟瘴气，天下纷纷大乱的时候，这一老一少，兰摧玉折，溘然长逝了。我们这世界上，本来容不下许多好人，他们都是老早就该撒手归去的，泰戈尔虽然多活了几十年，却是过了多半世的亡国生涯。天底下没有好人走的路。这个地球上的生物，离着文化的境界，还差得远呢。他们去了，也是应该的。

或以为此二人不当相提并论，因为泰戈尔的资格，修养，名誉，声望，和年岁，比许地山的，都大得多。这话虽不错。然而他们乃是同类，他们彼此的理想，抱负，气质，风度，全是一样。他们是沙漠地上的同路者，向着同一的目标而行。泰戈尔是灵活的泉水，许地山就是其中的湍流：许地山好比一颗金刚钻，泰戈尔就是一块大钻石。二人所差，不过一个是八十年的修炼，一个是四十八年的修炼，只差那三十二年的道行而已。

这一老一少是两个人间之瑞。他们与耶，佛，老，孔等等，都是亚洲

之光。他们如今不约而同，前后仅距三日，离开我们而去了。

关于许地山先生，我在贵报附刊上已说了些话，暂时不想再说，如今单就泰戈尔再说几句话，况且谈泰戈尔，也就是谈许地山了。

泰戈尔生于弱小民族的印度，他的思想是从印度原有的婆罗门教与佛教的教义上又融合了基督教与西洋哲学的意识而成的，有东西文明调和的意味。他崇拜“自然”而求精神的解放，能彻底了解人生的价值，超脱世界一切物质的束缚，而生活于充满的爱力之中。所以他所作的诗歌，都是慕“真”与爱“美”的感情之表现。他所竭力提倡的是精神生活，主张个人与宇宙调和在一起，来培养精神生活，才不致于作物质的奴隶。但是要达到个人与宇宙和谐的境域，必须使自我解脱，以求“真自我”。欲发现“真自我”，必在“爱”里下工夫。“爱”能渗透一切，融合万物。没有“爱”，就没有“同情”，那么作人的根本就消失了。继而言之，人生必得有“爱”，才有意义。所以他的哲学，可以说是以“爱”为归宿。向来传为厌世思想的印度精神，他在这上边给加上了进化论的新解释，而鼓吹入世爱世的主义。所以他是一个绝对赞美人生，而不是厌恶人生的人。

可是他的人民太不争气，太没出息，不团结，不合作（不是甘地的对外不合作，是在内部自己的不合作），在社会里分着严格的等级，于是他的祖国灭亡了。他空口念空时，用一般人认为是老生常谈的博爱精神，是到底敌不住英国人的枪炮的。所以有些人会蔑视他，说他那“反对物质文明”的主义是无济于事，是自取灭亡。上次欧战之后，他虽亲身到英国去为印度人民请求自由，也无效果。但是他和甘地始终相信他们自己的博爱主义，领导着印度民众，在黑暗中和侵略者对抗。他们相信他们终有胜利的一天。他现在虽忽然而逝，但是他的精神是不会随他而终的。因为他把他的工作，已经完成。现在的印度，没他也行。咱们也许会看见他的博爱主义战胜了英国科学利器的那一天。

这不是说泰戈尔能用武力来战胜英国，我想印度的武力，也许永远不会胜过英国。这是说等英国受了严重教训之后，他们就会低首于泰戈尔的精神之下，那才是泰戈尔真正的胜利呢。在历史上，基督教手无寸铁的博爱主义，和古罗马帝国的穷兵黩武，两相抗争的结果。就是个最好的例子。当时罗马对于基督教，真有灭此朝食的决心，但是到后来，在罗马的京城里，却高高地树立了十字架。直至今日，基督教的教皇，不是还盘踞于古罗马帝国的老巢里么？我并不是宣传基督教，现在一般教会里的教徒们，还说我是教会的反驳哩。

所以泰戈尔的精神没死，他的人民必能复兴，因为他们现已悔过，在它们的血管里，已经奔流着泰戈尔的血了。

泰戈尔的人格之力，比机械化部队，力量更大。它不仅是诗人哲人，他实在是圣人！

在民国十三年（一九二四）的春天，他受北京大学之约，曾到中国来过一次。那时他身体不健，而且有病。在未来之前，他的家属，亲戚，朋友，和他的医生，都不教冒险远行，连他的法国朋友，罗曼罗兰也写信反对他来。他自己也着实踌躇了好久。后来中国文学研究会徐志摩先生等人。连连地写信催他，他就毅然决然的来了。他说他到中国来："只是代表印度人民向中国致十二分的亲爱。"

可是没想到，在他来到中国之后，在全体的知识分子热烈的欢迎之下，有少数的青年，竟对他老实地不客气起来，弄得大杀风景。那正是曹昆贿选，直奉再战，冯玉祥倒戈的那一年，也就是孙总理逝世的前一年。那时中国因为受够了精神文明的苦恼，要用物质文明的劲头来干一下。那几个青年大概是出于爱国之心，就对这位超世的贵客，不讲礼貌。有的说："泰戈尔先生你作诗吧！你管不了人家的国家，请你莫谈天下事！我们的陶渊明先生，他不知有汉，无论魏晋，那是你的好模范。"那几个反对泰戈尔的人，无论他们的动机是如何，我相信，他们是没有读过他的作品，不明白他的主义，不认识他的人格。

泰戈尔于一九四一年八月七日归西去了。现在让我们拿徐志摩关于他的几句话来纪念他："他是灵活的泉水，一颗颗颤的圆珠，从地心里，兢兢地泛登水面，都是生命的精华……他是百灵的歌声，他的欢欣愤慨响亮的谐音，弥漫在无际的晴空……他永远指点着前途的光明……现代的文明，只是贪淫与残暴，自私与自大，相猜与相忌，倾覆了人道的平衡，产生了巨大的毁灭……在这荒惨的境地里，他肩上扛着铲除误会的大锄，口袋里装着新鲜人道的种子，不问阴晴地努力工作……同时他口唱嘹亮的新歌，鼓舞在黑暗中将次透露的新芽……无论在何处，他永远是青年人的最忠心的朋友！”

（转载自《吾友》三日刊）

——《中国文艺（北京）》，第5卷第1期，1941年9月5日

和平·自然，相爱·真美：东方诗哲太戈尔逝世

彝

印度大诗人太戈尔氏八月七日在加尔哥答患肾病逝世，享年八十岁。此白发诗人曾于一九一三年获得诺贝尔文学奖金。

扬溢着真和美的情思

这位曾经给予中国诗坛相当影响的东方白发诗哲，竟这样恬静地脱离了干戈纷扰的罪恶世界，也许正是他的幸福吧？

太戈尔是一个大诗人，也是一位大哲学家，他的哲学思想，就包含在他许多优美的诗文里。

太戈尔是崇拜自然，爱好和平的，他彻底了解人生的价值，是超过世界一切物质的效能，而生活在充分的爱力中，所以，他竭力提倡精神生活，在他的诗文里，是扬溢着爱“真”和好“美”底情思的。但他也不否认物质方面，他是绝对赞美人生，以为人得了“爱”才能有意义。因此，他底哲学，可以说是以“爱”为归宿的，以“爱”为全体，而知识为部分的。“爱”是全体，所以经过爱，即能遇到真理。这一点，他和法国哲学家格柏森底直觉主义是极相类的。

充满着哲学和诗意的家庭

太戈尔所以能够成为一个大诗哲，他底充满着哲理和诗意的家庭环境，是有着很大关系的。在童年时代，他跟了被印度人尊为“大哲”的他底父亲德宝德那拉次，和一个著名哲学家底哥哥名德威琴德那拉次生活在一起，自然是受到了良好的陶冶。据他后来告诉人，有一次，他父亲教他

读一部书，书名叫什么，早已忘怀，可是他深切地记着两个富有诗意的句子，即是“雨花溅着树叶震颤着”及“雨淅沥地降着，春潮泛溢到河上来”两句。从此，他便爱好文艺而开始和它接触了。

少年时代的太戈尔，最好做描写爱情的抒情诗和关于爱底文艺作品，他的恋歌，曾引起印度许多道德家的反对，以为他的诗歌要破坏印度固有的旧道德。另外，一些守旧的女人也攻击他，说他破坏了彭加尔诗的故有格律。虽然如此，他却在无意中获得了一位名震文坛的知音者，这就是彭加尔著名小说家雀陀巴驼耶，他们不期而然地相遇于一个历史家陀特底结婚宴会上，当陀特将一个表示敬意的花圈赠给雀氏时，雀氏却将它转赠于太戈尔，说这花圈应该送给这位青年诗人。这意外的荣遇，使太戈尔深深地感动了，流着泪接受这位小说家底敬意。

太戈尔底诗，可以说没有一篇不含有和平的，自然的，相爱，真美的思想，和幽雅美丽的词调，所以人人喜欢歌诵。有一个印度人说：“我每天读太戈尔诗，读他一行，可以把世上一切烦恼都忘掉”，这也可见太戈尔诗歌的感化力了。

影响到中国的诗坛

一九二二年三月，这位白发诗哲，游历到中国来了，他受到了我国文艺界热烈的欢迎，请他演讲的，请他题字的，做诗的，使这位年将花甲的老诗人，忙得不亦乐乎。尤其是那个正在编辑“北京晨副”被称为“中国诗哲”的徐志摩，特地星夜乘车南来上海，向太戈尔膜拜执弟子礼，而且设宴替他洗尘，还当众演说：

> 我昨晚为太先生作伴，致全夜未睡，可是深觉有味。太先生为人，我人极崇拜之，可以称之曰美，曰圣，曰伟大，是出乎超人以上的伟大呢——

这可见徐诗哲对于太戈尔底倾倒了。的确，太戈尔给予中国诗坛的影响，实在相当大的。

当文学革命运动以后，是在开始一个文字解放的时代，但做惯五律，七绝的中国文人，对于诗的革新，感到有些茫然。虽然胡适之毅然地发表他的第一部新诗《尝试集》，那毕竟是“放大脚”，遗留着许多旧诗词底气息。此后，沈尹默，刘半农二氏，以西洋自由诗的风格，致力于中国诗底改革，可是，他们也是受旧文学教养相当深的人，所以，他们底诗，在外表上，固然进步了，内容方面，却部分地保存了中国律绝的影子。

直到知堂老人，以精炼幽恬的笔触，翻译了日本的短歌和俳句，一时仿作者很多，这才使中国诗走了另一个新底途径。不久，冰心女士也发表了《繁星》和《春水》，她在一部诗集的自序里，有这样几句话：

这是我读了太戈尔的诗以后作的，老实说，我爱太戈尔底诗，更十倍于爱我自己底作品。我觉得他的诗，是用异常的，内在的，深刻的情绪，用音乐似的诗句写出来，给我们的感动太深了——

接着，王独清和郑振铎也翻译了太戈尔的《新月集》,《飞鸟集》,(《新月集》有二种，王译为泰东出版，郑译是商务出版）这就是所谓哲理诗，小诗的又一派，不过后者的影响于中国文坛，似乎更较大些。

太戈尔的文学著作，可以分为三类：

（1）诗集——有《园丁集》,《新月集》,《采果集》,《飞鸟集》,《爱者之赠与》等。

（2）剧本小说——有《牺牲及其他》,《邮局》,《暗室之王》,《春之循环》等。

（3）论文——有《人生之实现》,《人格》,《国家主义》等。

总之，他是一位伟大的诗人，一个和平底天使，对于他底死，实在叫人非常悼念的。

太戈尔的生平（略）

……

太氏著作中译

《飞鸟集》,《泰戈尔诗》,《吉檀迦利》(均郑振铎译）

《新月集》(郑振铎，王独清各有译本）

《诗人的宗教》（胡愈之译）

《泰戈尔的诗与文》（黄新民译）

《短篇小说集》（沈雪雁与叶如音译）

《泰戈尔小说》（王谙译）

《泰戈尔戏曲集》（瞿世英，邓演存，高滋合译本及朱枕薪译本）

《谦屈拉》（吴康译）

《春之循环》（瞿世英译）

《散雅士》（景梅九译）

《家庭与世界》（景梅九，张墨池合译）

《沉船》（刘笃实译）

《印度故事》（郑振铎译）

《东印度故事》（孙席珍译）

——《政治月刊（上海）》，第 2 卷第 3 期，1941 年 9 月 10 日

忆太戈尔

今　吾

是十四年前的事情，那时笔者在山西某中学读书，学校当局因钦慕太戈尔先生的文学盛名，于是特地邀请他老先生前来讲学，尤记得太先生穿着一袭黑色印度绸的长袍，雪白的胡须，长长地挂在胸前，端直的鼻锋，高高的颧骨，两目炯炯有光，态度祥慈和蔼，语言深沉动听，不失为一代诗圣的仪表。某天晚上，笔者和几位爱好文艺的朋友，举行了一个游艺会，先是请太戈尔先生讲述他从事文学研究的经过，最后由我们表演他的剧本《牺牲》，太戈尔先生一面注意着我们剧中人的动作，一面在作着笔记。剧终请太戈尔先生指正批评，我们获得了不少的知识以及一切舞台经验。从那时起，太戈尔先生便留给我一个深刻的印象。

岁月蹉跎，倏忽间又是十四年的时光了。在这期间，虽也不时读过太戈尔先生的名著，可是，他个人的生活行动，便渺无所闻了。

日昨惊悉太戈尔先生的噩耗，又使笔者泛起十四年前共话一堂的一

幕，曾几何时，一代诗圣的太戈尔先生，竟成了我们沉恸回忆的一位古人呢？

——《政治月刊（上海）》，第2卷第3期，1941年9月10日

挽印度诗哲泰戈尔

曹纕蘅

嘉伦堡上重携手，诗客庞眉系我思。浩劫讵期今日烈，深悲微许故人知。伦交并世传双鸟（余于去夏过印访君海外各报多载中印两诗哲会谈记），讲学横流失一夔。中印文明沾溉远，恨君不见大同时（君谓西方文明缺点是在太过视物质与权力余极韪其说因语君中印同为文化最古之国吾人应倡导东方精神文明沾溉世界共登康乐愿以共勉）。

附注：君晤余时，已患足疾，然言笑如常，语及北平旧游，辄惓惓不置。并极称吾国园丁庖人技术之美。余谓俟时局稍平，当为君力致之。君云，余老矣，此生恐不能再履中土，言次怅然。

——《大风（香港）》，第98期，1941年9月20日

泰戈尔逝世了

八月七日为印度大诗人泰戈尔逝世之日，享寿八十岁。他的贡献是印度所能贡献的，就是真、善、美。他的英文也说得很流利，记者会亲聆他的伟论，十多年前他在闸北商务印书馆东方图书馆演讲，希望中国青年勿受西洋唯物主义的麻醉，记者很受感动，但他的言论不为那时的一般激进分子所欢迎，因此颇受打击。

记者对于泰戈尔虽然不十分认识，但他那种超越的审美思想与大同主义，确乎为二十世纪一般领袖们所不及。

——《明灯（上海1921）》，第293期，1941年10月

泰戈尔公子电谢戴季陶

印度诗圣泰戈尔逝世，戴院长曾慰其公子离谛达拉那。兹日前泰公子复书致谢云：戴院长阁下，家严业养，荷承电唁，毋任感激。尊敬予鄙人以特殊之慰藉，因先严对阁下最大之友爱与尊敬，虽在卧病床第之际，尚频念及。前次阁下之光践圣地施克坦，迄其生命最后之一瞬，犹当众宣称其对中国伟大前途之信念，以及对伟大中华人民之敬爱也。谨致敬礼。离谛达拉那，兹泰戈尔拜启。一九四一年申锐。

——《新闻报》，1941 年 11 月 4 日

陪都文化团体追悼印度诗人泰果尔

中央文化运动委员会，中央研究院，北平研究院，西南联合大学，中央大学，中印文化协会，中央图书馆等七团体于十一月二十九日举行印度诗圣泰果尔追悼会，会场设有中央图书馆阅览室，各长官及要人等赠送挽联花圈甚多，并有林主席题颁“文化导师”横额一帧，及蒋总裁送“诗圣云亡”挽纬一帧，场内颇为严肃静穆，先由戴院长傅贤领导主行公祭，按中国旧仪式行礼，次于哀乐声中举行追悼会，由朱部长家骅主席，并由朱部长介绍诗圣身世，颇为详尽，谓泰氏不但为文学家及诗人，且富于爱国爱群爱人类之热忱，而于我国抗战，尤表关心云。

——《图书月刊》，第 1 卷第 7～8 期，1941 年 12 月 31 日

忆泰果尔长者

戴传贤

民国三十年八月

天竺摩诃泰果尔长者脱涅槃于圣地尼克坦之兰若，鸣呼哀哉，世间眼

灭众生失怙，何其速耶，追念前岁，仲三仰慈颜于加尔各答大城间慧启于圣地尼克坦大学观天女之散花，受香积之法食，维摩之文宝，俨然曼殊之说法尚在，曾几何时，而长者之觉灵遂归睹史多天，世界众生更入大苦，聚矣含识，定业如是，如是然自古圣哲身谢道隆生尽法头。

摩诃长者之慧灯法命其承离无疆，长作世界众生济定迷津之宝藏，盖可心也，震旦诸道友集会于陪都重庆于长者像前，献花供养，备极至诚，敬作此篇，聊表微忱耳。

巍巍顼弥峰　浩浩恒河水
钟灵降圣哲　慈悲真善美
正法遍十方　圃音震邈迩
善济诸众生　文学余事穷
至德垂万代　世界蒙福祉

附：编后

印度哲人泰果尔，声诗播于五洲。盖深入乎礼乐之原，有得乎性情之争。世涂未夷，天继先觉，国未可量也。挽近中印两民族之文化交亲，当用为后世所纪念而不谖。《忆泰果尔长者》一篇，有历史意义存焉。

——《图书月刊》，第 2 卷第 2 期，1942 年 2 月

追记泰戈尔先生纪念会

葛一虹

对于泰戈尔先生，这一位，印度的大学者的历史和他的作品，我都不十分清楚。不错，我曾经读过他的《新月集》，但那是十几年以前的事情了，并且当时所得的印象也很模糊。仿佛他那所特有的，带着宗教的和平的气息，对我并无什么了不起的引吸力，不但如此，根本上我是不同意于他的那种哲学思想的。我的稍显稚气的直觉，不用说，是由于那时候我们的时代精神造成的。泰戈尔先生曾一度来到中国，他不能普遍地受到欢

迎。我想，大概也因为不得其时的缘故吧？

九一八事变以后，泰戈尔先生对于日本军阀发出了严厉的质疑，从遥远的土地上传来的这一种使人感到温暖的同情，是值得人们宝贵的。几乎在我脑海中退去了的这一个大诗人的形象，这个时候却又浮现了出来。但它之在我到底还是不十分亲切的。而在此后的十年中，我也没有更多的机会，使我这位人道主义者和他的作品接近起来。关于他的消息很少，在文坛上也不常被提及，就是曾经受过他的诗的风格的影响的那一种中国新诗也已绝迹了。我记得只曾看到徐悲鸿先生替他画的一幅半身像，双手垂胸，一个慈祥而又庄严的老人。似乎一直到去年他的死讯传来的时候，才引起了一点注意。偶然也听到疏落地有人在讲。就中印文化关系上来说，泰戈尔先生实在是极有贡献的；我们的确对他太疏远了，我们是不够了解他的，我便是其中之一。

我的参加这次纪念会的动机便在这里，我希望能够多知道他一点。另外呢，无论怎样说，这一举世所重的现代诗人的逝世，自然也有足以纪念的。

一九四一年八月的某日，香港 SCMP 的广告栏刊出了一个启示，说将有一个印度大诗人泰戈尔先生的纪念会要举行，欢迎参加。具名的是一个叫做朋乔的先生。于是写了一封信去表示愿参与这个盛会。接着便寄来了几张印得很精美的请柬。

“聪明人咖啡店”，香港最华丽的咖啡店之一，时间是午后四时，我和三位朋友准时到了会场。在我的想象里，今天到的人应该不会过于少的。可是在会场上除了主人朋乔先生和他的几个朋友以外到的很少。香港是一个讲生意经的都市，关于泰戈尔这样一个人，自然没什必要支付过多的关心的。不过，我想，虽然如此，这一个机会假使不是朋乔先生来办，而由一个喜欢风雅之类的“皇家爵士”或所谓，“港绅”出面支持，那么今天的会场一定会挤得满满的。

幸而会众到的还不多，殷切的主人便有较多时间和我们这几位中国宾客来谈话。当他明白了我们是从事文学工作者之后，他不知不觉之间表示出更多的欢迎，朋乔先生是一位年约卅岁左右的结实印度人。元气充沛，神采很好，穿着一身白色的圣洁的西装。说得一口漂亮的英语，他是泰戈尔的学生，最近才从祖国到香港，预备赴美国取道。

到会的人陆续来了。四十多人在摆成山字型的桌子旁边，倒也不算冷落，却颇显得十分严肃的。印度籍的不过五六个，中国籍的也不过十个上下。此外大多数英国籍的。新闻记者相当多，女宾很多。和我们同去的那位大小姐被主人延请至上坐，算是最尊贵的客人。平时她是以勇敢见称的，当主人过来不断请她起来谈话和频频劝饮的时候，“冒险家”与这个意外的殊荣似乎也显得有些不好意思。

朋乔先生的致辞非常真挚，他动人地诉说着泰戈尔先生的生平。泰戈尔先生在印度不仅是一位大诗人，大学者，大教育家，他受到印度广大人民的爱戴。他是印度新文化创造者之一，文化运动中的一位权威的领导者。他的活动是与印度民众的独立解放运动始终联系着的。 所以，他的不幸的死亡，实在是值得全世界进步人类所敬悼的。

接着，一位中国的老教授起来说话。他曾经到过印度，是泰戈尔先生的一位朋友。他们的交集是异常的和谐的。从他的话语里，使人们知道了泰戈尔先生对于中国文化的珍视，以及他创办的中国学院的艰苦奋斗过程。

此后是二个英国人讲话。

最后是一个印度青年的激昂的演说。他是学习工程的，才从卡尔加达来，候船赴美，更求深造。从外形来看他和朋乔先生是不同的。粗鲁一点，直率一点，他没有朋乔先生那样的绅士气，他也不会说流利的英语。他说的很急促，他对于他的没法掌握的语言来表示出他的所要说的话，显得十分着急，然而，即使如此，听的人也还是很感动的，我以为，谁都很同情他。

他说的关于泰戈尔先生的倒不多，主要地他却说了许多关于印度民族解放运动的事情。印度人民的苦闷，他们的愿望，他们奋斗情况等等。从他的笨拙的言语里面，闪耀出这一个民族的光明，热烈的掌声寄予了无限的期望。

“聪明人”的代餐原来是丰富的，新从印度来的主人还献呈出了他珍贵的土产，许多不知其名的精神食物使宾客在赏到兴味之余，对于那遥远的文化古国更增加了些神往。

泰戈尔先生是一个伟大的人道主义者，他生在那个环境，他便有了那么样带有和平主义色彩的思想。这，在本质上，是革命的。现在，伟大的印度民族解放运动的成功时期愈益近了，这一位老战士虽未及目观其成，但这一果实，他是有份的，他曾经参与过劳作与耕耘。

一九四二，七，十六，重庆

——《文化先锋》，第 1 卷第 7 期，1942 年 10 月 13 日

诗人的最后——记泰戈尔死事

Chanda, A. K.（著） 山灵（译）

本文作者阐陀先生（Anil K. Chanda）是泰戈尔翁晚年的私人秘书。现任印度国际大学的大学部主任。他的散文写得别有风致，而且又是泰戈尔翁的近人之一，所以我把这篇记事译成中文拿来发表。

——译者

一九四一年七月二十六日到二十九日，师天（Guru-Deva）[1] 住在加尔各答的双桥住宅（Jorasanko）；三十日，医生为他施行手术，他死在八月七日十二时十三分，活了八十岁零三个月整。

在二十九日的傍晚，他向主治的医生圣底大夫（Dr. Jyoti Prekes Sirkar）询问在施行手术的过程中要感受到什么样的痛苦，最好是毫不隐瞒地讲了出来，他可以自己准备一下。圣底大夫和师天谈话的态度是相当自由而不拘束的——师天很喜欢他的机智和幽默——他笑着告诉师天说："先生！没有什么！我只给你施用局部麻醉，你会完全清醒的。可是，你却不会感觉到有人在开你的膛，破你的肚。中间再挂上一条幔帐，不用看我们这群讨厌的家伙。你想写诗的话，就写；写出诗来我都不会引以为奇迹的。"师天听到末一句话，便笑了起来，回答道："要真是不比写诗的痛苦更甚的话，那么我早就准备好了。"圣底大夫为了使他更安心起见，便又添了两句："我既不弄险也不摒弃一切可以的防护。做医生不能忘掉孟加拉的这句'防范永远没有终点'的格言。"师天立刻把圣底大夫的引

[1] "师天"（Guru-Deva）是甘地先生送给泰戈尔翁的美赞，现在印度人都以此称呼他而不名。

证翻转来回答了："可是你也别忘掉'从来就没有防范能够超过终点的'呢！"过了一会儿，师天把我的妻子叫到床前，替他记录下来一首口占的诗，诗是这样起头的。

烦恼之魔的暗夜

再再地

爬向我的门楣。

师天逝去之后，报上把这首诗刊载出来，还加上《死亡》做标题，说是诗人的最后一首诗，事实上，在这之后，他还留下了另外的两首诗，都没有题目的。

夜，平静地过去了。

那一天终究到了。从早晨起，人们就忙碌起来，家宅变成了医院的样子，临时的手术室，在东廊下、正对着卧室的出口。虽然大家忙成这个样子，师天却是毫无所知，他躺在床上低吟出他的最后的另一首诗。

你，在你的创造的路上

遮着了一张斑斓的迷惘之网

你这……

一如往日，一行一行地吟咏出来。我妻子把它抄好，朗诵给他听。他并不十分满意，说还有几个韵脚不够铿锵，想要修饰一下。但，他却疲倦的不能再构思了。他说："这些日子，我真容易困惫啊！医生们告诉我说行完手术，便会复原的。算了，放着以后再改吧。"这首诗竟没有得到润色的机会。

她的儿媳在寂乡患病挣扎着给他写了一封信，刚好在开刀之前寄到。他读了，叫别人写了回信。在信尾上，他用颤抖着的手亲自签了"爸爸"两个字。那是他的绝笔，以后他就不得不放下那只曾经用来克服一切的武器了。他的绝笔是写给一个让他在最后三十年中活得安逸而不岑寂的女人，笔封得真是再合式没有了。她值得接受这样贵重的纪念品。

十点半钟开始施行手术，十二点三刻完了。医生公告：经过良好，尤其是他的体力之强为医生们所没有想到。我们把消息宣布出去，同时传电通知甘地先生。傍晚，医生再来检查，慰问他："这次开刀您定感觉很痛苦！"他惨笑着回答："没有的话！你干嘛逼着我说谎呢！"

夜间他不能安然地睡。三十一日是开刀后的第一天，病状突然恶化：体温上升，脉搏加速，他不时地忍耐不住精神的苦闷，在诅咒伤口的疼痛。医生们来得很多，做了缜密的诊察，会商的结论是“不很乐观”。其实，我们倒不曾把这种现象看得过分严重，以为是施行手术之后应有的反应。果然，夜中的情况就好多了，他能有一会熟睡。八月一日，病状大见轻减，体温脉搏全都恢复到正常，还饮用了相当数量的流质，夜里更好得多，于是，我们便在八月二日，决定请他的儿子罗谛（Rathindra Nath Tagore）先生回去照料患病的妻子。但，不久师天就感觉到不能安息，肠胃作痛，晚间，又增加了噎嗝的现象。当夜，病势并不和缓，他始终没有能够入睡。八月三日，从早晨起，我们也惶恐起来，觉得如果他的儿媳能够挣扎着病体来的话，最好是赶紧来。过午忽然有了转机，夜里的情形也好，我们的一线希望之火又再一次地燃烧起来。可是从四日起就不行了，病况是决定性的恶化。早晨，他的儿媳赶来看他，他已经不大能讲话了。五日，新的症状越来越多。不住口的在咳嗽，噎咳从无一刻曾间断，药物不能直制止。夜间依旧由医生们不休息地做各种的努力，夜便这样的过去了。

六日破晓，我们的希望之光跟着太阳从东方慢慢地升了上来，师天略为安定了些。可惜我们的希望只是闪电的睐眼，他的病势突然急转直下，一会不如一会儿。口，连一些水都咽不下去，眼睛也浮肿起来（我们的眼里可全是泪珠了）。过午，医生们嘱咐我们办后事。时光拖着迟滞笨重的步伐踱去，留给我们的是一片漆黑。死神把它的暗影抛掷在我们的身上和心上。从午夜直到次晨三点钟，他只反侧了一次。之后，便只有等待那不可避免的来临了。太阳又从东方慢慢地升起来，这只是八月七日，师天却剩下了哮喘。直到午前十时，医生们还不肯向死神献剑，再度施行了氧气治疗，但，不曾发生丝毫效果。哮喘，一声比一声微弱，过了十二点钟不大会儿，便完全停止了。

在这与死神的激烈争夺战中，我们自认全线崩溃，死神从我们的阵地里把师天掠夺去了。

——《时与潮副刊》，第 10 卷第 2 期，1948 年 8 月 1 日

第四章

英 | 伦 | 足 | 音

New Books: The Indian Poet

Lascelles Abercrombie

"We call this the epoch of Rabindranath." The distinguished Indian gentleman who made this significant remark to Mr. Yeats probably meant by "we" Bengal rather than India at large; possibly he only meant the elect and cultured fellowship that obeys the movement called Brahma Samaj — a lofty, eclectic creed singularly combing rationalistic reform with mystical revival. But, at any rate, the poems of Rabindranath (and, it seems, the melodies the poet has composed for them) are enormously popular and influential wherever Bengali is spoken; and it would be strange if some of those who delight in them did not consciously recognize in them the qualities most noticeable to a European-qualities which unmistakably have the air of marking the climax of some great spiritual and mental rhythm, of marking, in fact, and epoch. The age of Shakespeare, however, did not call itself by the title; and it says something remarkable for the alertness and vividness of Indian consciousness today that the sonorous name of Rabindranath Tagore should have been already acknowledged as the name of the present Indian epoch — perhaps one should even say of the present Oriental epoch. For it seems not unlikely that this poet may win himself a spiritual empire comparable with that of the classic Persians; the future may see in his work the expression not merely of his race but of the East — at least, of the non-Turanian East. Certainly, we Occidentals can scarcely fail to perceive in these exquisite and noble poems that peculiar artistic greatness which seems necessarily to imply a general great condition of life surrounding and inspiring the artist; we, from the midst of industrial triumph and commercial supremacy — we can scarcely fail to perceive this envious admiration. The abundance and simplicity — to borrow two of Mr. Yeats's epithets — the inevitable ease with which profound things are expressed, the mingling of delighted sensuous imagery with keenest spiritual experience, the mingling, too, of intense personality with the sense of a whole community's impulse and activity, the formal shapeliness of the poems (extraordinarily noticeable in the beautiful English translation made by the poet himself, and sure sigh of an elaborate and masterful technique in the original) — these are qualities which, in co-existence, have perhaps never yet appeared as the result of individual genius alone. The poems of Rabindranath could not credibly come except on the crest of some large and vital impulse moving thorough a nation; the milieu for such work as this must either be the youthful vigour of a new civilization achieving again some positive ideal mastery in life, realizing in itself at large an active sense of mystical or metaphysical significance in life. Mr. Yeats excellently puts this, the most obvious and exciting quality to a European mind in Rabindranath's poems, when he says that to read these lyrics today must surely give something like the sensation an Englishman of the time of Richard would have had on reading translations of Dante and Petrarch.

So, the epoch of Rabindranath is not simply a literary epoch. "He is the first among our saints" — this is another significant remark made by the Indian gentleman already quoted, — "he is first among our saints who has not refused to life, but has spoken out of life itself; and that is why we give him our love." Certainly, there is no "refusal to live," accompanying Rabindranath's austere sense of some mystical, super sensuous reality in life; rather that seems to have made his sense of immediate familiar life more glowing and joyous. And as this is his obvious greatness to a European, and admittedly his most notably characteristic to an Indian, it may be worthwhile to see if it is explicable. No oriental poet could be more abstrusely mystical; no European poet more aware of the sweetness and brightness of common everyday life. Moreover, the perfect continuity of thought in his lyrics is like nothing that can be found in the lyrics, say, of Hafiz; whatever the form of Rabindranath's poems may be in Bengali, it is evident from the translation that he does not rely on rigid continuity of form to get unity. In fact, there is no radical difference between his lyrical art and that of Europe. The strangeness we find in him is entirely in his matter and his impulse; he does not give the sense of a strange art which practically all other Oriental lyrics give. In a word, Rabindranath seems to be an Oriental profoundly influences by European thought, but not in the least disorientated by the influence; we should rather say that the European influence has been completely Orientalised in him. The old and distinguished Tagore family has a long tradition of English scholarship, and of interest not only in Indian but Anglo-Indian affairs. And his father, Devendra Nath Tagore, was a great figure in the theistic movement of the Brahma Samaj, which seems itself an expression of desire, local at first but soon widespread, to add the vigour of European reason to Indian mysticism. But when the former threatened to oust the latter Devendra Nath led the conservatives in the schism, and insisted on keeping the Brahma Samaj an essential Oriental religion; and so his son, Rabindranath, whatever Europe may have done for him, is Indian first and last. It would, no doubt, be going too far to speak of Rabindranath as an outcome of the Brahma Samaj, which is itself probably the outcome of a much larger impulse. But the characteristic of the epoch of Rabindranath is plainly mysticism "speaking out of life itself," so speaking, in India at least, for the first time. And it seems unavoidable to see in this some fusion of Western thought with Eastern. The East maintains its alert sense of what is behind life, but the West brings its vivid sense of the intermediate value of life itself. A poet appeared just at the critical moment to voice this characteristic in noble and astonishing lovely songs — songs that leave one with a vision of life standing enraptured amidst its marvellous world of sensuous experience, but always tense with expecting the awakening out of this coloured, musical dream into the real ecstasy of seeing its mystical Brother and Master.

— *The Manchester Guardian*, Jan. 14, 1913

Recent Verse

Our two volumes of Indian poetry represent, the one an Occidental culture working in an Oriental atmosphere, the other the pure inspiration of the East. Mrs. Naidu's charming *The Bird of Time*, for which Mr. Gosse has written an appreciative preface, gives in the classic measures of English verse the classic passions, but with an exotic colouring. 'A Rajput Love Song" is not different, except in its metaphors, from Western love-songs, and the beautiful "The Call to Evening Prayer" shows a catholicity of religious feeling which is cosmopolitan rather than Indian. Sometimes, however, as in the folk songs, in "Vasant Panchani" and "In Salutation to the Eternal Peace" we find a mood which is different in kind from our own. *The Gitanjali* or "Song Offerings" of Rabindranath Tagore are wonderful in their way, though Mr. Yeat's introduction is perhaps written in too hyperbolical a strain. The author is a thinker of the Brama-Samaj school, and his poetry, Mr. Yeats tells us, is widely read and reverenced among his countrymen. Even in a prose translation it is possible to realize something of the spacious wisdom and joy of the original.

— *The Spectator*, Feb. 15, 1913

An Indian Drama

A Reading by Mr. Rabindranath Tagore

The Indian Art, Dramatic, and Friendly Society is little more than twelve months old; but during its short career it has already made several serious efforts to fulfil its professed intention of bringing the East and the West into closer touch and of giving each a better understanding of the other. The latest of these efforts took the form of a meeting yesterday afternoon, at which Mr. Rabindranath Tagore, who is described as India's "world poet" — a man of great accomplishments, whose claim to the title of poet is undeniable, and who, by his works, has established an influence that is altogether remarkable over his fellow-countrymen of every class-read has own translation of one of his own plays.

Before a large and deeply interested gathering that included many Anglo-Indians and many well-known men of letters, Mr. Tagore leant over his reading-desk — a tall, slim, figure dressed in tight-fitting garments of black; a face with finely chiseled features and with the deepest eyes and a flowing beard in which grey is taking the place of black; and a strangely thin, but musical, voice. In the dusk of late afternoon the shaded light that was directed upon his manuscript was reflected in a copper glow upon his face; but he read with hardly a gesture, without a break, and in the accents of a refined Englishman from the beginning of his short prose-poem to the end.

There were two gods in his caste — Madana, the god of Love, and Vasanta, the god of the seasons, of spring, of youth. The hero, Arjuna, was a great warrior and the descendant of Kings. The heroine, Chitra who gave her name to the play by way of title — was a princess. That she was a girl was a mishap not easily accounted for, since Shiva, the god of Life, had promised her grand-sire none but male descendants. By way of repairing the mistake so far as possible, her father had brought her up as a boy, dressed as a prince, skilled in the use of arms, and worshiped by her people, to whom she was a valiant protector.

When Chitra saw Arjuna she regretted, for the first time, her manly costume and her manly ways. She threw herself at his head, but was received very coldly; for Arjuna had taken a vow of celibacy that was to bind him for a dozen years. She turned to the two gods for their aid; and from Vasanta she obtained the gift of beauty that was to remain to her for twelve months. Thus, armed she renewed her attack upon the hero; and this time she proved irresistible. His vow was forgotten; and though she warned him that she was "an illusion" they began together a life of idyllic happiness.

Chitra's happiness was not complete, though. She feared that this borrowed beauty alone had made an impression on Arjuna, and that, as she put it, her body was her own rival. She begged that the gift might be taken from her, that she might reveal to him her "own true self, a nobler thing than this disguise." There was no escape from the terms of the gift, though; and before the year was up Arjuna began to tire of the beauty that alone made any appeal to him. The villagers came to his for protection from marauding robbers — their princess, Chitra, who had been their protector, had gone on a mysterious pilgrimage, apparently, for none knew where she was. Chitra's hopes of winning him in her real person and her fears of losing him altogether were described in language that was full of passion and of real feeling, and embellished with descriptive touches, many of which, even in their translated form, were delicious. Eventually, when the last hour of the year had come, Chitra made her confession. She became again the warrior princess, and wondered, almost hopelessly, if Arjuna could still love her as he did when her beauty was a thing to marvel at and she had little else to commend her. "My beloved," he replied, "my life is full." And that was all.

The reading was received with enthusiasm by the audience; and the poet — a quiet, almost a shy man — was overwhelmed with compliments by the many admirers who crowded round him before he could escape from the room.

— *The Westminster Gazette*, May. 10, 1913

Platform and Stage

The production of Rabindranath Tagore's play, "Post Office," at the Abbey Theatre tonight, should attract considerable attention in Dublin, not only because of the charitable object for which the performance is being given (the Building Fund of St. Enda's College, but for the play itself. Gordon Graig's scenery will be used in the play. Besides "The Post Office" the pupils of the St. Enda's college will perform "An Ri," a play in one act, by P. H. Pearse. This performance will be the last given by the Abbey Company until the autumn.

— *The Irish Times*, May. 17, 1913

Performance in Aid of St. Enda's College

A performance in aid of the building fund of St. Enda's College, Rathfarnham, took place in the Abbey Theatre on Saturday night. The appeal met with a generous response, there being a large audience, and additional interest attached to the occasion on account of the inclusion in the programme of a play entitled "The Post Office." This was the first production in Dublin of the piece, which consists of two acts, and has been written by Rabindranath Tagore, an Indian writer, some of whose work has already attracted attention in portions of Western Europe. Mr. Lennox Robinson was responsible for the production. Mr. W. B. Yeats and others associated with the Abbey Theatre have already expressed a high opinion of Tagore, and their judgment was confirmed by the appreciation and applause extended to this specimen of the author's art by Dublin play-goers, as it was presented in its English dress on Saturday night. It is not a very imposing play, but it has many attractive and, at the same time, pathetic features. What it conveys is the call of death — the invitation from this world to the Great Beyond; and the medium used is the life of an adopted child, who is wasting away under the influence of some disease in an Oriental district. The malady defies the science and skill of the physicians, and death is figuratively represented by the receipt of a letter from the King — the Ruler of all realms — delivered through "The Post Office," which has recently been extended into the locality where the scene is laid. Though the play is designed to convey a solemn lesson it is not devoid of other aspects, and there is a certain element of humour blended with the pathos in which it abounds. For the

Abbey players (the second company were the exponents of Tagore's art) there were some unusual circumstances associated with the production, the garb used for the pose being the principal one. The performance was realistic in a marked degree. The central character in the play — that of the child — was sustained in a sympathetic and impressive manner by Lilian Jagoe, hers being an outstanding triumph in the presentation, for she revealed a fine conception of the part. The death scene was especially good, and the audience expressed strong approval of the work. The other principal characters were presented with credit by Philip Guiry, Charles Power, Michael Couniffe, Thomas Barrett, and Sean Connolly. The scenery (composed of Gordon Craig screens) was arranged by Mr. J. F. Barlow, and provided a very fine setting for the presentation of the piece.

The second portion of the entertainment also provided an interesting attraction. It consisted of the presentation of "An Ri," a morality, in one act, by Mr. P. H. Pearse, the performance being in the capable hands of the students of St. Enda's College. It met with a very cordial reception, and both author and players were warmly applauded. At the close of the performance Mr. Pearse was called before the curtain, and, in the course of a short speech, acknowledged his thanks to the audience for the support extended to the appeal.

The Abbey orchestra, under the direction of Mr. John F. Larchet, played some enjoyable selections of music during the course of the entertainment.

— *The Irish Times*, May. 19, 1913

Nobel Prize for Indian Poet

In awarding this year's Nobel Prize for literature to Mr. Tagore the Nobel Committee have established their reputation for catholicity, for the same body but a few years ago awarded the prize to Mr. Kipling. Mr. Kipling and Tagore are the only British subjects who have been thus honored. Both, by an odd chance, are intimately connected in life and work with India. But India could not very well express herself through men more different in spirit and craftsmanship than this rough rider of Imperialism and this delicate artist of the most intimate nationalism. Perhaps there is here evidence of a change in the temper of thought, for the opinions and tendencies of writers are not disregarded by the Nobel Committee when they are weighing their literary merits. On no other hypothesis can be explained the persistence with which the claims of Anatole France, assuredly the living writer with the most universal reputation, have passed over. Or, again, their blindness to Hardy's preeminence; for Hardy is no longer a purely insular classic; no Continental critic worth his salt or heedful of his reputation now dares ignore Hardy. The Nobel Committee is a conservative body, and the scepticism of Anatole France and the pessimism of Hardy are too unorthodox to find favour. Within the limits of choice, they allow themselves they have made a fine and bold selection. They have shown that art knows no East and West for ever sundered by a mutual unintelligibly. The great themes are same for Orient as for Occident, because they are the humanity which in many essentials is the same everywhere.

— *The Daily News and Leader*, Nov. 14, 1913

An Indian Poet

The announcement that the Nobel Prize for Literature has been awarded to Mr. Rabindranath Tagore, the Indian poet will, we believe, cause some surprise, but no dissatisfaction. A very short time ago his works, although long famous in India, were quite unknown in these countries. They were first discovered for England by Mr. William Rothenstein, who is to deliver the Hermione lectures in the Alexandra College next week. He brought the poet to London, and was primarily responsible for his rapid leap to fame in the West. Afterwards Mr. W. B. Yeats became the sponsor for M. Tagore. He spoke in public about the beauty of his Indian poems, even when they had been translated into English. He lectured about them, and even staged a play by this author in the Abbey Theatre. It did not, if we remember right, quite conform to Irish notions of drama. But we cannot deny, even if we would, the merits of Mr. Tagore's poetry, for authorities so far apart as Mr. Yeats and a Daily Mail reviewer are ready to vouch for it. We welcome the honour which has been best owned on him, not only because it is an appreciation of good literature. It is also a sign that we are drawing a little nearer to the East, although we live in Europe. For centuries the literature and thought of India have been quite beyond the ken of all but a few scholars. We have realised vaguely that there were Hindus of high education and culture, but we have seldom even made an attempt to get to know their work. Our soldiers and officials have lived side by side with these men without discovering their literature. We must hope that the award of this prize to Mr. Rabindranath Tagore will prove to be the beginning of a new era in this respect. There must be many masterpieces of literature lying hid from the eyes of Europe, although they may be famous in India. It is our business now to enrich ourselves by discovering them. Mr. Tagore has shown that Eastern poetry need not always lose its savour because it is translated into English. We owe our thanks to Mr. Rothenstein for opening to us a door which may lead to a region of unsuspected beauties.

— *The Irish Times*, Nov. 15, 1913

The Nobel Prize for India

The choice of the receipt of the Nobel Prize for Literature has furnished more than one surprise, but so far no selection has been quite as startling and significant as just announced. Mr. RABINDRANTH TAGORE, the most eminent of living Indian men of letters, has an immense reputation among his countrymen, especially in his own province of Bengal. But his fame in the West is entirely of yesterday. Until his visit to Europe last year hardly a line of his writing was known in the English-speaking world, and although at this moment a number of other volumes — poems, dramas and essays — are appearing in Britain and America has been gained entirely through the little collection of mystical religious lyrics done by the poet himself into English prose and published twelve months ago under the title of "Gitanjali" (song-offerings). Now, surely that is an extraordinary thing. A poet of high renown in India but known to English readers only through one little sheaf of lyrics, and presumably not yet even a name to the educated world of Continental Europe, is awarded the single international prize for literature — and that a handsome sum of money bequeathed by a Scandinavian captain of industry. The force of contrast could no further go. That the choice is fully justified is nevertheless beyond serious dispute. He is a poet and a seer of genius. For more than thirty years (his age is 53) he has been producing, philosophy, and music. There is, indeed no modern Englishman who could properly be compared with him, and if we would find a parallel we should have to go rather to the countries that have given birth to men such as BJORNBON and D'ANNUNZIO. For Mr. Tagore has toughed the life of his people on almost all sides. He is the typical singer and interpreter of modern India, but he is more — a religious leader, a constructive critic of society, the most admired of all exponents of Indian nationalism on its ideal side. He belongs, moreover, to a family from which, for several centuries, has come a succession of scholars and thinkers, jurists and theologians, artists and men of affairs. The work of RABINDRANATH TAGORE was certain in any case (after the revelation of his genius in "Gitanjali") to make its way in the West. The other day Mr. W. B. YEATS, to whom the English reader owes his introduction to Mr. Tagore, predicted that the mind of India was destined to be increasingly "the sweetener of our life and deepener of our thought." The award of Nobel Prize in the poet of Bengal will unquestionably help to bring about the fulfillment of the prophecy.

— *The Manchester Guardian*, Nov. 15, 1913

Books and Bookmen

There is little doubt that what some people are largely calling the "Indian Renaissance," but which may be better described as the rise of Mr. Tagore upon the West, is, as yet, the more striking event in the poetry of the century. The contrast between the work of Kipling and Tagore, the two English recipients of the Nobel Prize, is too obvious to dwell on, but one might almost think that Tagore had been raised up for the express purpose of refuting Kipling's best-know line, "East is East and West is West, and never the twain shall meet." Here is a member of a race different from our own, of a civilization not only different but antithetic, one summed up in the word "meditation" as ours is in the word "energy," and yet no sooner do the accents of his voice fall upon the ears of the Western peoples than they recognize it and hear as if "the voice of their own soul heard in the calm of thought." Beneath the distinctions, which although they seemed fundamental prove to be superficial, that separate the races, Mr. Tagore has struck down to the principles that unify the race. His themes are of the sort that have gone to the making of literature in all ages, but no one has handled them recently with the immediacy and intensity of vision and feeling that are his. They are old, but in his hands have the freshness of dew upon young flowers. They are majestic and yet are set forth with an inimitable delicacy and tenderness. In the West they have been subjected to all the apparatus and feeling. It is all to the good that a literature that has found its way with such astonishing directness into the heart of a civilization engrossed in its science, its commerce, and its machinery should be rapidly on the increase. Close upon "Gitanjali" came "The Gardener," close upon the latter came the charming and winsome "Crescent Moon" and now comes "Sadhana." Certain words in the preface to "Sadhana" are exceedingly illuminative.

"For Western scholars," says Mr. Tagore, "the great religious scriptures of

India seem to possess merely a retrospective and archaeological interest, but to us they are of living importance, and we cannot help exhibited in labeled cases — mummified specimens of human thought and aspiration, preserved for all time in the wrappings of erudition." Exactly, and so have our own scriptures. Then comes the secret of much of Mr. Tagore's genius and of the charm of his work. "The meaning of the experiences of great hearts can never be exhausted by a one system of logical interpretation. They have to be endlessly explained by the commentaries of individual lives, and they gain an added mystery in each new revelation. To me the verses of the Upanishads and the teachings of Buddha have ever been things of the spirit, and therefore endowed with boundless vital growth."

— *The Manchester Guardian*, Dec. 6, 1913

Pilgrims to A Poet: Indians and Mr. Tagore's New Honour

Bombay, Nov. 29.

The Biblical maxim: "A man is not without honour save in his own country" cannot be applied to Mr. Rabindranath Tagore, the famous Bengali poet, who has just been awarded the Nobel prize for literature. His countrymen in the East are as enthusiastic as his admirers in the West in doing honour to him and congratulating him upon the way in which his work has been recognized.

Mr. Tagore's residence, Santi Niketan, ("the Home of Peace"), at Belepore, has been the Mecca this week of a wonderful pilgrimage of poets and dreamers to pay tribute to the mystic. On Sunday, 600 of his countrymen from Calcutta visited Mr. Tagore and presented him with an address. "Among the passengers," wrote the 'Statesman's' correspondent, "were judges, barristers, doctors, scientists and other men of light and leading."

On arrival the deputation was met by students from the poet's school, dressed in yellow garments. They rode from the station to the Home of Peace — distance of more than a mile — was beautifully decorated with mango and lotus leaves and festoons of flowers. The way was strewn with cowries (shells), coins, garlands of flowers and paddy grain.

At the Santi Niketan, shaded by mango trees, was a high altar with a professional chair. The scene was typically Hindoo, and the blowing of conch shells, the smell of burning incense, the mango groves, the picturesque robes, and the distant temple all added to the poetry of it.

Mr. Tagore, clothed in silk dhooli and chudder, sat on the vedi which was covered with lotus leaves. Mr. Holland, Principal of the C.M.S. College, said that the award of the Nobel prize to the poet had repudiated the lines of Mr. Rudyard Kipling:

"East is East and West is West.

The twain shall never meet."

After the poet had been presented with a magnificent painting of the sun he rose to reply. "As he stood," says the 'Statesman,' "we saw a truly Aryan sage. The neatly brushed flowing hair, the chiseled features, the erect handsome figure and the beautiful, meditative eyes all combined to present a perfect picture of the best type of Aryan philosopher."

Mr. Tagore's voice is sweet and musical. He had never, he said, longed for fame. His claim was to the heart.

— *The Observer,* Dec. 14, 1913

An Indian Thinker: Creative Unity

Indian culture has had characteristic traits of its own from immemorial times. Its aspects at the opening of the twentieth century are attracting renewed attention among observers, free from such prejudices as find their broadest expression in the outworn epithet that calls the East unchanging. No books written in English are more trustworthy guides in this fascinating field of inquiry than the writings of Sir Rabindranath Tagore, whose poetry and whose prose alike throw a light peculiarly their own on the problems raised by the presence of the Western people in the East. His new volume is a collection of ten thoughtful papers, varied in subject, but animated by a common purpose, the dissipation of the misunderstanding that have so often kept East and West apart in apparently hopeless contradictions "The Poet's Religion" as a system of belief which has this advantage over sectarian creeds, that it is "fluid" and it is interesting especially in its comments on Shelly's "Hymn to Intellectual Beauty." The second treats of "The Creative Ideal", explaining the "The Creative Ideal", explaining and in the logic of absolute separateness as rebellion of absolute separateness as rebellion. A paper on the "The Religion of the Forest" touches on nature worship, and says pointed things about Milton as well as about Shakespeare.

Another draws an instructive contrast between the faith of a popular religious sect of Buddha on "The Modern Age" which describes Calcutta as an upstart town with no depth of sentiment in her face and in her manners, not without a river to give her the sacred baptism of beauty," but "surrendered body and soul to her wealthy paramour, the spirit of the ledger, bound in dead leather," and one on "The Spirit of Freedom," which exhorts its writer's fellow-countrymen to ask themselves if the freedom to which they aspire is one of external conditions. Not the least interesting of an Eastern University which will invite students from the West to study the different systems of Indian philosophy, literature, art, and music in their proper environment; and which will have for its larger object to reveal to the whole range of Eastern cultures the Aryan, Semitic, Mongolian and others. The fundamental note that resounds through all the book is best indicated in the closing sentence of the writer's brief introduction — To give perfect expression to the One, the Infinite through the harmony of the many, to the One, the Love, through the sacrifice of self, is the object alike of our individual life and our society."

— *The Scotsman*, Mar. 13, 1922

A Hindu Looks at The World

After reading this book one feels more than ever curious as to how far Sir Rabindranath Tagore speaks for his millions of fellow countrymen. He is a highly-cultured man, well read in the literature of the West as well as that of the East, but his point of view is undoubtedly different in many ways from that of any educated European who has placed his opinions on record. Rabindranath Tagore is acutely conscious of the difference; perhaps somewhat too conscious. At times he undoubtedly exaggerates, or, to put the case more accurately, he accepts as typical of a race the mental attitude of some individual which the leaders of Western public opinion would undoubtedly condemn. There is an instance of this on page 105, in the essay on "East and West" our author, after condemning in strong terms what he calls the "forcible parasitism" practised by Europe on two large continents of the world, quotes a passage from a now forgotten look of African travel. The writers of this cynically advocated forced labour, declaring it to be "the corollary of our occupation of the country." It is, of course, shameful that such proposals should be made; doubly shameful that there should be attempts — as there undoubtedly have been — to put them into effect. But there is another side to the picture, which is ignored in this essay. Slavery has been abolished throughout huge areas where for hundreds of years it was the cause of horrible suffering. To what is its disappearance due? To the coming of those whom Rabindranath Tagore calls "parasites." Even in relatively civilized Egypt the corvec was a native institution. The British suppressed it, Will it be revived now that Egypt is again a sovereign state? If it should be the felaheen at all events will have little cause to rejoice over the "liberation" of their country. It would be very unfair to pass an unfavourable judgement on "Creative Unity" because of that unfortunate passage. Its teaching on the whole is pure and elevated. Rabindranath Tagore is an idealist, and some of his arguments may make the "practical" reader smile. But this little book is full of beautiful, wise, and tender thoughts, often exquisitely expressed. Of very great interest is the account of the author's plans for an Eastern university, which "will invite students from the west to study the different systems of Indian philosophy, literature, art and music in their proper environment, encouraging them to carry on research work in collaboration with the scholars already engaged in this task." He has already formed the nucleus of such a university, and is convinced that it would be one of the best means of promoting mutual understanding between East and West. The Experiment certainly seems a promising one, and its success would make one more hopeful of the solution of that problem of race and colour which seems destined to enter on a highly critical stage long before the end of the present century.

— *The Northern Whig and Belfast Post*, Apr. 8, 1922

Tagore's Challenge

The English writer to whom Tagore, as revealed in his essays, is nearest akin in Mr. Edward Carpenter, but even in his use of the prose medium the essential poetry in him is stronger. Like Carpenter, he is at war with the civilization which has no other base than utility. He realizes that in the West "the ideal of freedom has grown tenuous" because "perpetual anxiety for the protection of gains at any cost" strikes at the love of freedom and justice; and he went back to India "deeply impressed with the truth that real freedom is of the mind and spirit." That true permeates his essays in "Creative Unity" (Macmillan, 7s.6d.). The most fascinating deal with the attitude of the poet towards religion, and nature, and poetry. Here, too, he is at war with utility. In a poem "the subject must be completely merged" — hence the badness of patriotic poems and hymns. An interesting point, but surely difficult to justify, is that the new attitude of Shelley and Wordsworth towards nature-as compared with Shakespeare — is due to "the great mental change in Europe through the influence of the newly discovered philosophy of India." Tagore toughs many subjects in these essays — nationality, women and home, and universities — and is always illuminating. As to East and West, he utters this challenge "The West has not sent out its humanity to meet the man in the East, but only its machine."

— *Birmingham Gazette*, Apr. 17, 1922

Books of The Day: Two Studies: Tagore and Masefield

A. V.

A book bearing the name of Rabindranath Tagore is always sure of a welcome. The circle of his readers widens yearly; his influence spreads like a ripple which washes all shores. But the centre which sends forth that influence remains something of a mystery even to the philosopher's most ardent admirers. We are familiar with his outward appearance — with presentiments of a man with a strange and beautiful face and the eyes of a prophet — but there is a reserve in all he writes which baffles curious investigators into the hidden places of his mind.

"Creative Unity," the volume under notice, consists of a series of essays on "The Poet's Religion," the second, on "the Creative Ideal," and, indeed, the whole contents are flavoured by the philosophy of Keats, at once so hackneyed and so incomprehensible to most of its users, which is expressed in the lines:

Beauty is truth, truth beauty; that is all
Ye know on earth, and all ye need to know.

To Tagore the statement is not incomprehensible; it is akin to his own though; it is an article of his faith. It is a riddle which might have out of the East, instead of the mind of a cockney-born literary aspirant. "Beauty is no phantasy, it has the everlasting meaning of reality. The facts that cause despondence are gloom are mere mist, and when through the mist beauty breaks out in momentary gleam, we realise the Peace is true and not conflict. Love is true and not hatred..."

The philosopher who has made this creed his own can write with calm detachment of the fever of the modern age, its worship of money, its organized selfishness. He urges the need for art in education of his own people, and for idealism in national life. Of the sphere of woman he speaks as is natural to a man of his race; she is allotted an intellectual as well as physical function separate and different from those of her mate. "For life finds its truth and beauty not in any exaggeration of sameness, but in harmony."

Touching the meeting of East and West in his own country, the poet makes a plea for greater reciprocity. "The West has not sent out its humanity to meet the man in the East, but only its machine. You must know that red tape can never be a common human bond, that it is a painful ordeal for human beings to have to receive favour from animated pigeon-holes, and condescension from printer circulars that give notice but never speak."

— *The Yorkshire Observer*, Apr. 25, 1922

Tagore's Essays

Dr. Rabindranath Tagore gives the general title of Creative Unity to a collection of essays on various subjects, the connecting link being the touchstone of all his judgments — his doctrine of the One and the Many. All our attempts to confine this Oriental creed — pantheistic, mystic, whatever one may choose to call it — within the limits of legalistic prose leave us unsatisfied.

We will, therefore, only quote a sentence or two of Tagore himself, leaving them in their native poetic vagueness.

This one in me knows the universe of the many. But, in whatever it knows, it knows the One in different aspects. It knows this room only because this room is One to it, in spite of the seeming contradiction of the endless facts. Contained in the single fact of the room.

...This One in me is creative. Its creations are a pastime, through which it gives expression to an ideal of unity in its endless show of variety. Such are its pictures, poems, music, in which it finds joy only because they reveal the perfect forms of an inherent unity.

We may remark in passing that the implied denial of the conventional aesthetic creed in the least sentence strongly resembles the attitude of Wordsworth (whom Tagore quotes with keen appreciation). He sought ultimately in Nature, not beauty, not unity. Tagore's concern in this volume, however, is not with aesthetics, but with religion, ethics and especially politics.

What really makes the book important (to students of Tagore and of India, at all events) is its revelation, in passages constantly occurring, of Tagore's present attitude towards the West. Briefly, that attitude towards the West. Briefly, that attitude is one of irritation and impatience. In the past this poet has drawn gladly from Western thought and culture, and has interpreted the West to the East as he has interpreted the East to the west. The political events of the last few years, however, seem to have been too much for him. The Western spirit, he fears, with its mechanical and material collectivism, is killing the free impulse of individualism and humanity.

The wriggling tentacles of a cold-blooded utilitarianism, with which the West has grasped all the easily yielding succulent portions of the East, are causing pain and indignation throughout the Eastern countries. The West comes to us, not with the imagination and sympathy that create and unite, but with a shock of passion — passion for power and wealth...I have been fortunate in coming into close tough with individual men and women of the

Western counties, and have felt with them their sorrows and shared their aspirations. I have known that they seek the same God, who is my God — even those who deny Him. I feel certain that, if the great light of the culture be extinct in Europe, our horizon in the East will mourn in darkness. It does not hurt my pride to acknowledge that, in the present age, western humanity has received its mission to be the teacher of the world; that her science, through the mastery of the dark dungeon of matter. For this very reason I have realised all the more strongly, on the other hand, that the dominant collective idea in the Western countries is not creative. It is ready to enslave or kill individuals, to drug a great people with the black mist of stupefaction, and emasculating entire races of men to the utmost degree of helplessness. It is wholly wanting in spiritual power to blend and harmonies; it lacks the sense of the great personality of man.

There is a core of truth in all this, no doubt, but we regret that such a man as Tagore should be irritated into such a general and exaggerated onslaught. Still it is a waring to those among us who ignore the deep fires that burn beneath the philosophic calm of the East. Moreover, Tagore, in another essay, turns with equal candour to his own countrymen and rejects much of their nationalistic aspiration as tainted with the same poison of power, force and materialism. The style of these essays is distinguished and vigorous, the subjects alive and important. We could wish Tagore had revised his allusions to missionaries by the light of his usually unexceptionable good taste.

— *The Christian World*, Apr. 27, 1922

East Meets West

These essays breath a wonderful spirit of understanding and sympathy with the ideals of the Western world. At the same time they do not yield in pride concerning those of the East. Indeed, they speak insistently of the loss to the world through the misunderstanding of the East by the West. There is no doubt that a little give-and-take would be to the advantage of the East and of the unity that lies behind all upward striving this book is most encouraging. The analyses of the forces at work today in the struggles of man to self-expression in government are illuminating, and contain warnings of the evils to which apparent high aims may lead. The paper on "The Nation," wherein crowd psychology is discussed, is a plea for a broader conception of the duties of countries and races to one another. "With the growth of nationalism man has become the greatest menace to man" becomes something of text to the conclusion that "this age of nationalism, of gigantic vanity and selfishness, is only a passing phase in civilization, and those who are marking permanent arrangements for accommodating this temporary mood of history will be unable to fit themselves for the coming age, when the true spirit of freedom will have sway."

Of the position of woman, Mr. Tagore has much to say; but as it is entirely from a masculine point of view, it is necessarily incomplete, though obviously well-intentioned. A great deal of wrong and loss can shelter behind his simple ruling that woman has to be ready to suffer." Is there any human being who escapes suffering? To advise a sex to be content with it would be ludicrous if one did not know the dread realities in all countries and ages against which women have struggled. Can Mr. Tagore not see that one of the most potent factors in creative unity is absolute sincerity and truth? To do her part towards this unity woman must be herself unlimited as to scope of work, untrammelled in the doing of it, and entirely free to choose her own destiny. Mutual toleration and respect make decent minds careful of encroaching upon another's rights, and inculcate a certain self-denial, self-control, and possibly suffering for others' good. Let us strive that it be mutual, and the question of government, law and order will be solved.

— *The Irish Times*, Apr. 28, 1922

Growing Hatred between Hindus &Moslems: Sir R. Tagore's Appeal

Allahabad, Thursday

Throughout the Punjab and the United Provinces communal relations, as the result of the Kohat and Lucknow riots, have become more embittered than for years past. Mr. Gandhi continues his fast, and Mr. Mohamed Ali addresses impassioned appeals for large-hearted toleration and greater forbearance, but Hindus and Mohammedans are deaf to all but their mutual fears. Each community accuses the other of being blameworthy for the riots; each puts forward unveracious accounts of the rioting and the origin thereof, initiated by their utter inability to recognize their own shortcomings or the possibility of any other viewpoint, or the salient fact that the immediate spark which fired the train was less important than inflammable material ready, at the slightest provocation, to burst into conflagration.

Sir Rabindranath Tagore, the famous poet, has addressed wise counsel to his countrymen, but his words are likely to pass unheeded amid the turmoil of communal and political feelings. He says:

I have no faith in fast, but Mr. Gandhi is sincere, as everyone knows. He is trying to bring about Hindu-Moslem unity. That unity cannot be achieved in a day, Hindus and Moslems have been cutting each other's throats for several centuries. I am not blaming either Hindus or Moslems; there is a poison in both communities. The present outbreak of Moslems against Hindus is the reaction consequent on the Khilafat agitation, and I prophesied at the time of the Khilafat agitation that the reaction would soon come, and that when it came it would be severe, Indians have nothing to do with Khiafat, but nobody heeded my warning.

It is noteworthy that even Sir Rabindranath Tagore assumes that the Moslems are the aggressors.

Inflammatory versions of the events at Kohat are embittering Hindu feeling in the Punjab cities. Certain Hindu victims have arrived at Amritsar from Kohat, and their stories of their sufferings at the hands of the Mohammedans have excited the Hindus. At Nagpur feeling is still running high, and the Mohammedans have decided that no music of any kind shall be allowed to pass the mosque, as it indicates disrespect to the house of God. Sixty Hindus and thirty-six Mohammedans have been arrested in connection with the recent riots.

Lucknow remain an armed camp, and troops are patrolling the city, but the Chehlum festival passed off quietly, and the processions were not molested. The Swarajist organ, Indian Daily Telegraph, declares it has no faith in the leaders of the conferences convened at Delbi by telegram, and adds: "So far, the secret of the solution is in the trigger of the British solder's rifle. We have seen no other solution." Yet the journal deliberately shuts its eyes to the obvious moral, and seeks to discredit the British administration, which alone stands between India and anarchy, by declaring: "The Kohat tragedy ought ever to brand the administration under which it has happened as an abject failure," the presumption being that under Swaraj such disturbances would be impossible!

— *The Daily Telegraph*, Dec. 24, 1924

The Library Table Tagore

The short stories of Sir Rabindranath Tagore are curiously reminiscent of the work of the Russian masters; not in style — for even in translation they preserve a fragile Orientalism faintly perfumed: not in method — there is none of that ruthless insight which builds up Dostoevsky's monumental analysis in minute and amazing detail, although a portraiture equally complex is achieved. Neither in style nor method; but in atmosphere. Who has not stopped in his first reading of Tchekov and considered the humour with suspicion? The pathos makes it seem incredible. So it is with Tagore; he has just the same sad smile in his prose. His new book "Broken Ties and other Stories" (Macmillans, 7s. 6d.) contains one tale which gives the volume its title, by far the longest and best; he has mastered the use of allusion, and is convincing where Dostoevsky would fail through over-elaboration; the characters of Uncle Jagamohan and Damini are perfectly drawn. The story, moreover, has the merit of being just the right length. In comparison with "Broken Ties" the others are scarcely worth mentioning, but Russian and more definitely English ironies are well combined in "The Lost Jewls," which introduces a characteristic theory on the influence of modernism in the relations between the sexes.

— *The Yorkshire Post*, Nov. 11, 1925

Indian Romance

Dr. Rabindranath Tagore has an extraordinary insight into the individual life of his fellow countrymen. Amid all the diversities of a vast population, he wanders with close observation and deep sympathy, with the outlook of a poet and of a prophet, with the keenest sense of realism, and yet with a suppressed idealism. Everywhere he is the artist, and through his subject-matter consists of the lives and aspects of his own people, there is behind it all the humanism of the great thinker, who passes beyond the particular, the provincial, the local, and raises his finest impressions into the highest levels of noble aspiration and philosophical suggestiveness.

It is twelve years since Tagore received the award of the Nobel Prize, and his hand loses none of its outstanding artistic skill. His new book, "Broken Ties and Other Stories" (Macmilan, 7s. 6d.), is marked by the old sureness of tough, by the old economy of words, the old joy of psychological truth of representation, and the old deep sense of the spiritual values in the life of

India. His work is wonderful in its revelation of the great human interest in so much of India's life, which but for his presentation would be meaningless or distressingly sordid to the Western mind. He comes to us as an interpreter on the highest plane. The longest of the short stories of this volume (125 pages) is an outstanding psychological study in atheism and in popular mysticism. The other half-dozen very short stories, altogether occupying 103 pages, are of gems of psychological insight and of artistic expression. Tagore's writing is really fine work, and this volume is an excellent specimen.

— *The Birmingham Post*, Nov. 20, 1925

Mr. Tagore's Stories

A. N. M

There are seven stories here, but one of them takes up a good half of the volume. "Broken Ties" is a narrative that might be called simple, and yet there is a notable absence of the explicit. The spiritual history of Satish shows revolt in its most gracious forms. But the narrator says: "I realised that the world into which Satish had been transported had no place for me, his particular friend." You cannot be the friend of an ecstatic; at the most you are a part of humanity. The two young men become devotees of a "master" who "sought to keep Satish and myself content by repeatedly filling for ideal." To the more wordly of the two there is plethora of mystic emotion, and reverence must withstand the assaults of reason. But Satish, a sincere renegade, beginning as a reasonable "atheist," travels through emotion and attains "such simple peacefulness that no one could even guess what he believed or what he did not." He does, on one occasion, claim to be a poet; he declines all bonds of reason and he departs into some kind of formlessness into which one cannot follow him. There is a devoted woman, but she can only attend to his material needs; she is a Mary condemned to the tasks of a Martha in a world remote from human appetites. There is some rally of humanity when the narrator marries the discarded woman.

It is difficult for the average Westerner to appreciate much of this; he dips into something that he cannot fathom. There should be a great future for Indian fiction; in a land of powerful conventions the conventions are being attracted. Mr. Tagore's story suggests rather the search for a philosophical basis than concern with political or social events. He has his ironies: "Sect-mongers rejoice more in capturing adherents than in comprehending truths." The other stories are comparatively slight. They have the charm of a serenity of style even when this is under a burden of emotion. There is something of imaginative relation, something of disenchantment. The novel-reader may feel some lack of the positive, the specific.

— *The Manchester Guardian*, Nov. 20, 1925

New Books

The Stories of Rabindranath Tagore depressed me even more heavily, until I began to fear that I was sickening for something. No; six of the seven stories in "Broken Ties" did not depress me. They are what Westerners call magazine stories; that is to say, they are trivial stuff dependent for their punch on the surprise in the last paragraph. But the title story, occupying half the book, is positively bad. It describes a young man who seeks vaguely metaphysical Truth. He begins by being an extreme rationalist. He proceeds to join a heathen Salvation Army, and make an ass of himself to the clans of cymbals. Eventually he abandons himself to a mysticism of the kind so much admired by Count Hermann Keyserling and such profound thinkers. "If I keep going on in the same direction along which He comes to me, then I shall only be going further and further always from Him. If I proceed in the opposite direction, then only can we meet. He loves form, so He is continually descending towards form, so He is continually descending towards form, we cannot live by form alone, so we must ascend towards His formlessness." So Satish of the flaming eyes goes and sits on a sandbank. And the lady who is in love with him, dies of some pathetic disease, But I spare you the worst passages, those in which Tagore is satirically humorous.

— *The Outlook*, Nov. 28, 1925

The Bookseller's Window

Professor Rothenstein's portrait of the author (it is not reproduced in this volume of the Macmillan series) is the best introduction to a book by Rabindranath Tagore. Rothenstein has caught him, holds him for Western eyes; and to read one of his stories with full appreciation one needs some such assistance. Here he is not to be pinned down; he is a misty figure; he appears and disappears behind the veil of the East. He writes of his own race with the elisions that a man is apt to use when traits strange to others are simple and familiar to him. The Indian spirit is remote from the perception of the ordinary Englishman. Tagore demonstrates, illustrates, in the sensitive language of the poet; but he does not interpret. If you are humbly content to accept the poise and beauty of his writing, and to follow it as far as you may into a region where you are a blind man among the seers, then you will read the stories in "Broken Ties," and re-read them. In the end you will add them to your library, because in them you have sensed something imperishable. And it is there: they are not, neither do they deal with, ephemeral things. Sacrifice, the futility of material wishes, the difficult way of self-deception — these are the weft of their pattern. But the sacrifices of Hindu men and women are not such as fall to our lot; there is a difference between their wordly desires and ours; and their evasions are so subtle that they often bewilder the European reader. Some of the stories are parables; the others are studies of Tagore's people.

— *The Illustrated London News*, Dec. 5, 1925

Tagore's Stories

In his treatment of a story Tagore stands by himself. He sees his character with clear eyes of a poet. He picks a situation which will show forces at work which heighten their gifts whether they be for passion of self-sacrifice or quite endurance — that is to say, he has the essence of drama in him. And he presents his tale with an economy of circumstance which only the artist can achieve with sufficiency and yet without bareness. In this volume prose-poetry is restrained; atmosphere and background are not over-emphasized as they so often are Eastern tales. "Broken Ties," the long story, takes us among the diverse followers of a Master along the track of idealism; the shorter tales are simpler, more concentrated. "The Lost Jewels" and "Emancipation" show a sureness and power which Tagore has nowhere revealed more clearly.

— *Birmingham Gazette*, Dec. 10, 1925

Wisdom of The East: Broken Ties and Other Stories

A. M. A

Tagore's gracious genius leave us, with every fresh volume, more deeply in his debt. Among the many devout poets and teachers of this generation one voice from the East has spoken most clearly and directly to our hearts. India sits at Tagore's feet, but the Western world has listened to him almost as eagerly, and he, for his part, has learned to express his thoughts and ideals as beautifully in English as in his own tongue.

Tagore's thoughts are drawn from deep wells of truth, feeling, and meditation. The long story, "Broken Ties," in this volume is a tragedy of two noble natures, one Damini, a young girl, in love with the other, Satish, a devotee. Damini's love is all humility. It casts no shadow of the world upon

Satish's holiness. Indeed, she accepts in marriage Satish's friend, the good kind youth who tells her story, knowing that she carries in her breast a mortal pain that will make the marriage a brief one. But Tagore must be suffered to explain his own "wise and innocent" creatures. Only he can make their thoughts and actions easily understandable. The mere statement of these things has no value. Six brief stories, one of which, "Giribala," is, we are told, "translated by the author," fill the last hundred pages — rather less than half-of the present volume. Some brief preface to the English versions of Tagore's works would be welcome. Novels and stories now published without dates or translators' names, often seem to belong to the writer's earliest period, when he wrote almost entirely in his own language. All translations by other hands should, I think, be correctly attributed, and the addition of dates to the stories would be equally helpful.

— *Liverpool Post and Mercury*, Dec. 12, 1925

Mr. Rabindranath Tagore

Mr. Rabindranath Tagore's book become obscurer and obscurer, as Alice might have said. The latest "Broken Ties" (Macmillan, 7s. 6d.), has, to a Western mind at least, little more significance than those that preceded it. Possibly to understand Mr. Tagore thoroughly one needs to have an Oriental mind, and that there are a number of Westerners fortunate to possess this is evident from the success that his books have in England. In "Broken Ties" one is forcibly reminded of "If Winter Comes," the same sentiment, if not, the same style. But some of the shorter stories are better. They are all, though chiefly remarkable for an utter absence of point. It may be artistic, but we doubt it, and in any case it is dull.

— *Sheffield Daily Telegraph*, Dec. 18, 1925

后 记

1998 年，在陈思和老师指导下，我开始搜集关于泰戈尔在中国的相关资料，并从 1949 年前的相关资料中择要编了一本书，于 2009 年 5 月以《诗人的精神——泰戈尔在中国》为名，由江西高校出版社出版。因为出版后反应尚好，且谭中、刘建、郁龙余和董友忱等前辈多次以各种方式鼓励，遂于 2015 年整理了《泰戈尔在中国》第二辑，由上海三联书店于 2016 年出版。现在这部，就是第三辑了，书名仍沿袭前书，作为一件工作的自然延续，只是这一辑更侧重收入一些英文报道和文章，并且特意收录了一些英国的报道，作为与中国的对照，表明泰戈尔在中国和在世界上其他国家都受到尊敬，当然也包括误解。

将旧期刊上的文章录入成电子文件并不轻松，幸有我的两位博士生张雅琦和雷雨露，用了一个暑假完成了此项艰苦工作。没有她们的辛苦，也就不会有这本书。在校改过程中，我的硕士生摆雪也参加了部分工作，在此一并表示感谢。

编书是需要工夫的一种功力，也是做研究的基础。泰戈尔进入中国人的视野已经一百多年，编写此书，一是还原一百多年前中国的泰戈尔研究原貌，二是根据这些资料推动中国的泰戈尔研究进一步发展。因为之前缺乏对中国泰戈尔研究历史的了解，导致后来的很多研究似新实旧。希望中国的泰戈尔研究能基于历史，真正的推陈出新，使中国的泰戈尔研究在世界泰戈尔研究领域获得话语权，引领中印人文交流发展。希望本书能提供一点微薄的材料，更希望引出更多的研究成果。希望有一天，中国所有关于泰戈尔的研究成果都能结集成册，这样，即使没有一本书以“中国泰戈尔学”命名，中国的泰戈尔学也已经形成了！

2021 年 12 月 23 日

同济大学